OF LIVERPOOL

Transnational Identities

Governance in Europe
Series Editor: Gary Marks

Transnational Identities

Becoming European in the EU

Edited by
Richard K. Herrmann, Thomas Risse,
and Marilynn B. Brewer

ROWMAN & LITTLEFIELD PUBLISHERS, INC.
Lanham • *Boulder* • *New York* • *Toronto* • *Oxford*

ROWMAN & LITTLEFIELD PUBLISHERS, INC.

Published in the United States of America
by Rowman & Littlefield Publishers, Inc.
A wholly owned subsidiary of The Rowman & Littlefield Publishing Group, Inc.
4501 Forbes Boulevard, Suite 200, Lanham, MD 20706
www.rowmanlittlefield.com

P.O. Box 317, Oxford OX2 9RU, UK

British Library Cataloguing in Publication Information Available

Library of Congress Cataloging-in-Publication Data

Transnational identities : becoming European in the EU / edited by
  Richard K. Herrmann, Thomas Risse, and Marilynn B. Brewer.
     p. cm. — (Governance in Europe)
  Includes bibliographical references and index.
     ISBN 0-7425-3006-X (cloth : alk. paper) — ISBN 0-7425-3007-8
  (pbk. : alk. paper)
  1. European Union.   2. European Union countries—Politics and government.
  3. Group identity—Political aspects—Europe.   4. Nationalism—Europe.
  5. Regionalism—Europe.   I. Herrmann, Richard K., 1952–   II. Risse-Kappen,
  Thomas.   III. Brewer, Marilynn B., 1942–   IV. Series.
  JN30.T7 2004
  306.2′094—dc22
  2003024754

Printed in the United States of America

♾ ™ The paper used in this publication meets the minimum requirements of
American National Standard for Information Sciences—Permanence of Paper
for Printed Library Materials, ANSI/NISO Z39.48-1992.

Contents

Preface

Although an essential part of the twentieth century was the rise of nationalism, socialist and communist objections to nationalism, and the decolonization that reflected nationalism's rise in the Third World, many interpretations of world politics concentrate on the material power of states and not their social and psychological composition. The collapse of the Soviet Union and Yugoslavia drew attention to the importance of identity, as did the prominence of pan-state religious movements in the Middle East and the rise of multiculturalism in America.

It may be widely recognized that mass-based identity with a community makes governance easier, but what leads to these feelings of attachment is not clear. Plenty of leaders have tried to build nations, usually by combining preexisting communities into larger units. Sometimes this has worked, other times it has been seen as imperial and resisted strongly. In an era of globalization and the revolution in technologies that accompanies it, many people fear local identities may erode, as might the collective spirit that leads to individual sacrifice in the name of the common good. Other people hope to transfer the feeling of loyalty to communities to broader groups as a way to reduce conflict among groups and as a way to expand the sense of obligation to help compatriots.

Nowhere has the effort to build pan-nation-state identities been more active than in Europe. The hope of overcoming the sort of nationalism associated with fascist movements and World War II has been the bedrock of European integration. Decades of effort have been devoted to making the European Union, institutionalizing its integrative purpose, and promoting the emergence of a European political identity that could underpin and legitimate its governance. Whether people in Europe are becoming European in the political sense, meaning that they believe Europe is a community that should have its own governance, is the question that motivated this study. The role the institutions of the EU play in this endeavor was also of special interest.

To examine these questions and to gather new evidence we assembled an international team of scholars, drawing on expertise in several disciplines. We pulled together political scientists studying identity politics, social psychologists studying group identity and how groups merge, sociologically inclined scholars expert on reading the discourse of elites and institutions, and ethnographers operating at the individual level of identity and everyday life. The group first met in Columbus, Ohio, at the Mershon Center in December 1999. We agreed on basic terms of parallel research and launched the new data-gathering endeavors. The group compared initial results and draft papers in June 2000 at the Robert Schuman Centre for Advanced Studies at the European University Institute in Florence. Final papers were presented at a workshop entitled "Europeanization: Institutions and the Evolution of Social Identities" in June 2001 at the European University Institute.

Without the support of the Mershon Center at the Ohio State University and the Robert Schuman Centre at the European University Institute this project could not have been undertaken. We owe a special thanks to Richard Ned Lebow, who was at the time the director of the Mershon Center and who initiated the joint institutional endeavor. We also are indebted to the European Commission's Fifth Framework Program for Socio-Economic Research, which generously funded a thematic network on "Europeanization, Collective Identities, and Public Discourses" (IDNET). IDNET provided financial support for the two workshops held in Florence. Special thanks go to Yves Meny, director of the Robert Schuman Centre at the time and now president of the European University Institute, to Angela Liberatore at the European Commission's DG Research, and to Federica Bicchi, Mathias Leonhard Maier, and Sylvie Pascucci for administrative support.

We want to thank Susan McEachern at Rowman & Littlefield. Susan has been a wonderful editor to work with. Despite the range of disciplines and methods represented in this book, she found terrific readers who provided valuable and constructive feedback at a high level of expertise. We thank production editor Alden Perkins and copyeditor Bevin McLaughlin, and we also thank Gary Marks for encouraging us to publish this book in his series at Rowman & Littlefield.

Finally, we want to thank Ann Powers at the Mershon Center, who provided valuable help in organizing the international workshops, and Viki Jones, also at the Mershon Center, who played a key role in the editorial process, keeping track of papers from multiple authors in different word processing systems and formats, getting them all into shape for publication.

1

Identities and Institutions: Becoming European in the EU

Richard Herrmann and Marilynn B. Brewer

WHY STUDY IDENTITY AND INSTITUTIONS?

The international institutions that now comprise an important part of the political landscape in Europe were designed initially in response to the world wars that engulfed the nation-state system in the twentieth century. The normative desire to put an end to war provided a motive for experimentation with international institutions, and over the years several conflict-managing strategies have been employed. Some institutions were designed to provide a forum for pacific settlement, the adjudication of disputes, and when necessary the separation of protagonists, at least in figurative terms and sometimes in physical terms (Claude 1971). Traditional notions of separating combatants and providing third-party mediation and adjudication were seen to be inadequate. They appeared to leave in place and even reinforce the sense of national separateness and division that had proved so destructive in the past. Efforts to move people's thinking and identities beyond the nation-state drove a substantial portion of the postwar effort to build international institutions in Europe (Haas 1964; Mitrany 1966). To an important extent, this effort derived from a basic neofunctionalist strategy.

The neofunctionalist strategy was to promote the development of shared identities and to reduce the exclusionary commitment to nation-states. This was to be done by encouraging cross-state cooperation on a series of functional matters. International institutions that would not simply adjudicate but also coordinate and manage the production of goods and services in fields such as energy production, transportation, communication, and health care were seen as promising starting points for the promotion of co-

1

operation, and, hopefully, over time shared identities (Haas 1964, 6, 49–50). At first, these common identities might extend only to the professional experts who shared technical languages and a commitment to specific functional endeavors (Haas 1964, 48). The neofunctionalist aspiration was, however, that with time these communities of common identity would spill over into broader sectors of society and make mobilization for war based on exclusionary national chauvinistic appeals more difficult.

Although it is not clear whether the neofunctionalist strategy has changed identities (Duchesne and Frognier 1995; Inglehart and Reif 1991), international institutions in Europe have clearly continued to grow and become more powerful. There are several explanations for this development that are not mutually exclusive. For example, West European states may have agreed to the continued institutionalization of Europe because they feared the Soviet Union and participated in the U.S.-led security alliance. They may have agreed to further institutionalization because they felt it would provide economies of scale, commercial efficiencies, and financial benefits. This may have been imagined in terms of competition with the United States and Japan, rather than alliance with Washington. Institutionalization and growing interstate cooperation may have also been driven by desires to secure individual liberties and other normative concerns. Of course, the desire to avoid war by offsetting nationalist identities with superordinate shared European identities was likely also to have been part of the motivational mix.

Regardless of why states agreed to the continued building of interstate institutions in Europe, such institutions have grown, and the European Union (EU) now plays an important role in Europe. In fact, the EU plays a key role in shaping how states define who and what they are. There are other potential institutional frameworks for Europe, but these pale in comparison to the EU in terms of their institutional density or power. In many ways, the EU has become a central constitutive feature of states. It defines them as either member states, states that wish to join, or outsiders that may wish to join or wish that some other institutional alternative were viable. At this point, the most central political and theoretical question is not so much why states agreed to cooperate, but how far the institutions that the states created can go in shaping the identities and perceived self-interests of the original creators (Jervis 1999; Keohane 1993).

Does Identity Matter?

Of course, no one expected common identities to form overnight, nor was this long-range objective the only measuring rod for evaluating the success of institutional strategies. Institutions provide information, enhance confidence, and, by partially filling in the deficits in trust that hinder cooperation, institutions play a valuable coordinating role. This coordinative function provides some buffer against the outbreak of violent conflict, but developing common identity is often seen as an important aspiration as well. Common identity and the idea of community are seen as providing diffuse support that can sustain institutions even when these institutions are not able to provide immediate utilitarian payoffs. Identification with a common community, such as Europe, is also seen as valuable for sustaining mass-based support when institutions at the international level make decisions that promote the European common good but may demand sacrifice from particular national communities.

Political institutions use a mix of devices to govern. They do not rely exclusively on fraternity and the emotional appeal of symbols (Etzioni 1961). They can also employ utilitarian instruments and coercive devices to sustain control. Political institutions can also allow a great deal of habitual behavior to continue and tread lightly into people's lives, thus maintaining public tolerance. It is quite unlikely, however, that the EU will be able to avoid delving deeper into people's lives as globalization and integration continue. The issues on the EU agenda already go far deeper into societal life than traditional geopolitical matters. Institutions of the EU affect not only symbolic matters such as the insignia on the front of a passport or driver's license but also material matters related to economic production, education, and legal rights. Dealing with transnational problems such as crime, disease, public health, and even military security is likely to draw EU institutions even deeper into people's everyday lives. If this happens, the question of common identity is likely to become increasingly important, as is the sense of democracy to which it is related (Schmitter 2000). Given the importance of democracy to the EU's constitutive definition of its members, it seems unlikely that it will be able to rely heavily on coercion or exclusively on utilitarian instruments. If democracy is given its due, then public attitudes and identifications with Europe as a political community will become increasingly important.

There is debate among European leaders regarding what a European government should be. On one hand, Europe might be a nascent nation-state on its way to becoming the United States of Europe. In this image, common identity is seen as especially important, as it was for the legitimation of states in an era of nationalism (Kohn 1944; Shafer 1955 and 1982). On the other hand, the EU might be seen as something quite different than a nation-state, perhaps a security community, as envisioned by Karl Deutsch (1957), or even a looser system of coordinated states (Adler and Barnett 1998). Of course, the degree to which EU institutions become influential and meaningful to people in their everyday lives is likely to affect how much common identity is thought to be needed to legitimate political authority. This will also affect whether a gap in democratic accountability is seen and whether the growth of the EU will provoke serious backlash.

Of course, shared identity alone does not insure political legitimacy. Many Poles, for instance, shared a strong identity with the Polish nation and did not support the Communist Polish state. When communities have a strong feeling of shared identity, political leaders can draw on this as a resource to promote the legitimacy of institutions, but they are not always successful (Cottam and Cottam 2000). However, if within the population there is no sense of community to begin with, then political leaders lack even the possibility of drawing on shared feelings of loyalty and obligation. Given the potential contribution shared identity can make in the support of political institutions, and given the importance changing identities play in the neo-functionalist strategy for sustaining peace, we launch into this investigation of changing identities in Europe. Our aim is not to explain why states chose to construct European institutions, nor do we seek to prove that the institutions that have been created have caused a change in identity. Rather, we begin with a more modest agenda, which is to investigate whether identities are changing and what role international institutions may be playing in this process. Our overarching question, then, is to assess to what extent European identities and identity configurations are changing in light of the emerging institutional structures that define the European Union.

A Multidisciplinary Approach

Identity has become a popular concept in many disciplines, as has the notion of changing identities. At the same time, the notion of identity means quite different things to different people, and even when the concept is commonly defined, measuring it remains extremely difficult. There are several reasons why measuring identity is complicated. People belong to several communities simultaneously, and the salience of these memberships can shift according to issue area, social context, and audience—or, in the interview context, who is asking the question. For instance, a European identity may be more salient to a European when he or she is among Americans or Asians than when he or she is among other Europeans, while the national makeup of other Europeans present can also affect the salience of the European notion. Treating specific policy choices as indicative of feelings of identity can also be problematic because people can oppose or support a policy for various reasons, identification with a group being only one of them.

Because identity is a widely used concept and one that requires innovative methods to measure, we have organized our project in a consciously multidisciplinary fashion. We have included political scientists, social psychologists, ethnographers, historians, and linguists. Our empirical chapters employ a variety of methods for measuring identity, including elite interviewing, analysis of closed-ended questions asked in surveys of the general public, the linguistic analysis of discourse in elite interviews, the examination of responses in controlled experimental contexts, and the analysis of discourse in interviews with ordinary people. We pursued a multidisciplinary and multimethodological approach to the study of identity because we were dissatisfied with the way the concept had been measured in the past and felt that a careful examination of alternative strategies could be a useful contribution to our understanding of identity and change in Europe.

Nearly all of the chapters in our book provide new empirical evidence regarding shifting identities in Europe. They do not, however, always reach the same conclusions. Our authors reach rather different conclusions regarding the depth of European identity, and several raise the issue of whether reports of identity with Europe are simply artifacts of survey methods. Our authors also do not agree entirely over the compatibility of local, national, and European identities and whether broader identities replace and weaken commitments to more local ones. There also is substantial debate regarding what content people ascribe to the community they label "Europe." Our authors, in this regard, discuss whether the divergence in the meaning and attributes attached to the label "Europe" are so great that it would be a mistake to treat individual statements that profess identity with Europe as indicative of a common identity. In the empirical chapters that follow, authors strive not only to present their findings and methods, but to compare their findings to the findings of their colleagues, and to speculate on why they reach different conclusions and what we can learn regarding measurement that might follow from the parallel but methodologically distinct investigations.

Although the scholars in our project come from different disciplinary backgrounds and employ different methods, we did agree on a common understanding of what we mean by "social identity." We also agreed on several other conceptual benchmarks that allow comparison across our studies. In the next section of this chapter we turn to our understanding of "social identity," presenting what we mean by this term, how we deal with the configuration of multiple identities, and how the concept can be dealt with in operational terms, given its inherently subjective nature. In the third part of our chapter we turn to a discussion of the linkages between institutions and identities and how they might affect one another as history develops. Finally, we offer a brief road map for the remainder of the book, explaining how the parallel investigations were conceived of as tackling a common question.

WHAT IS IDENTITY AND HOW IS IT CONFIGURED?

The concept of *social identity* is used broadly to refer to the psychological link between individuals and the social groups or communities to which they belong (Abrams and Hogg 1990, 1999). A frequently cited definition is that provided by Tajfel (1981), who describes social identity as "that part of the individual's self-concept which derives from his knowledge of his membership of a social group (or groups) together with the value and emotional significance attached to that membership" (255). This definition signifies that the concept of social identity incorporates cognitive, evaluative, and affective meaning. Beyond mere recognition of membership in a social group or category, identification implies that the group and its defining characteristics have become integral to the person's self-concept, with associated values, emotions, and extensions of individual self-esteem. Social identity also has behavioral implications, since identification impels attachment, loyalty, and a sense of obligation to the group and group welfare. It is this behavioral component in particular that makes social identification a potential resource for collective action and acceptance of institutions.

Social identities are distinct from other aspects of individual identity and self-concept in that they reflect *shared* representations of a collective self. Social identities are "we" rather than "I" identities (Thoits and Virshup 1997), and as such they depend on collective beliefs that the definition of the group and its membership is shared by all of those in the group, as well as by outsiders.

Within this broad definition, there are at least three distinct aspects of the representation of persons in groups. First, social identity is used in answer to the question "*Who* is us?" In other words, what people belong to the in-group, and, by extension, what defines the boundaries of the group, and who does not belong? For semantic clarity, we call this conceptualization of social identity the *composition* of group identity. Second, social identity often refers to the question of "*What* are we?" That is, what attributes, symbols, and values describe the prototypical member of the group and the defining content of the group more generally? We will label this notion the *content* of group identity. Finally, social identity is used to refer to the relationship between the in-group and out-groups within a structured network of social groups. We will refer to this as *role* identity. Although there has been substantial interest in the impact political institutions have on all three of these conceptions of social identity, both our theoretical conceptions and empirical understanding of any of the relationships are quite limited.

Political Identities

We are interested in particular in social identities that have political consequences—identities that lead people to imagine that a group deserves to enjoy substantial sovereignty, that is, ultimate decision-making authority. The demand for sovereignty and statehood has played a key role in the conception of nationalism. Defining the necessary features of a nation has proved very controversial and often contaminated by contemporary struggles for or against independence. It is easier to define the phenomenon of nationalism. This refers to a movement that has three characteristics (1) people who identify deeply with a community and who (2) believe that community should have a sovereign state and (3) are willing to sacrifice, perhaps risk their lives, for the achievement of that state independence. The linkage of community identity to political sovereignty has allowed scholars to differentiate between all sorts of different communities and roles with which people identify and those that are called national. We are interested in this study in how Europeans connect their community identities to sovereign political decision-making authorities and how they might negotiate the distribution of sovereignty across institutions.

Substantial previous research has identified some of the factors that explain the emergence of shared identities with political characteristics that lead to a demand for a connection between community identity and state sovereignty. For instance, Rupert Emerson (1960) highlights the importance of leaders, the attentiveness of potential followers, the viability of the proposed political entity, and the ease with which the community can be imagined as unique and distinct from other communities. Anderson (1983/1991), Breuilly (1982), and Hobsbawn (1990) emphasize the role leaders play. Huntington (1968) and Snyder (2000) emphasize the importance of mass politics and populist mobilization. Ernest Gellner (1983) has built a theory resting on economic foundations, arguing that groups take advantage of economies of scale and market opportunities. Karl Deutsch (1953) proposes that ease of communication and common language play a large role. Recent constructivist theory (e.g., Eley and Suny 1996) emphasizes the importance of common memories (and their construction), while social psychologists have explored the importance of what Donald Campbell (1958) calls entitativity (that is, the reification of a group into an entity, which Campbell argues follows from perceptions of common fate, proximity, and boundedness).

Although shared identities can form for a number of reasons, political identities can be distinguished by shared beliefs about the origin of the group. People may believe that a group they belong to emerged from pre-existing cultural commonalities, shared sentiments, and shared values. Other people may believe that the group emerged as a product of evolving economic and functional rationality. Still other people may believe that the group identity formed due to the activism of key leaders. Of course, these ideal-typical causal stories are not mutually exclusive, but they may shape beliefs about the content of what is assumed to be shared among the people in the community. Michael Bruter in his chapter later in this book makes an argument for the importance of differentiating between communities that rely on the belief that there is a shared culture and those that believe the origins of the group reside in civic commitments. This, of course, is an old distinction that has played an important role in studies of national identity (Greenfeld 1992; Brubaker 1999). It is possible that beliefs about the origins of the group affect the types of individual attachment people feel to the group—for example, those attachments that are more sentimental and those that are more instrumental (Kelman 1969).

Multiple Identities and Identity Configurations

Because people play different roles in different aspects of their lives, they belong to multiple groups. National, religious, ethnic, professional, gender, familial, and many other criteria may be salient in defining groups that ask for loyalty. Identities are not typically perceived by individuals to be in conflict, and people generally learn to balance their multiple memberships and roles (Stryker 1980). There are at least three different ways that multiple group identities might relate to each other or be configured in a system of multiple loyalties.

First, identities can be *nested,* conceived of as concentric circles or Russian Matruska dolls, one inside the next. In this configuration everyone in a smaller community is also a member of a larger community. For instance, local identities are subsumed in national identities, and national identities subsumed in Europe-wide identities.

Second, identities can be *cross-cutting.* In this configuration, some, but not all, members of one identity group are also members of another identity group. And this other group is composed of members who share identity within that group but also have identities with other groups that are not shared with the same people. Career and professional identities, for instance, cross-cut religious identities. Racial identities can cross-cut local and national identities.

Third, identities can be *separate.* In this configuration the different groups that a person belongs to are distinct from one another, with essentially nonoverlapping memberships. The number of people who share identities across the groups is so small that it does not constitute a potential cross-cutting group. For instance, an individual's work life may create common identities with a completely different set of people than those involved in his or her private life.

Both social psychologists and political scientists have attributed substantial importance to these alternative configurations of multiple identities. Neofunctionalists, as already discussed, hoped that the creation of a superordinate common identity would promote tolerance and foster better relations among national subgroups nested within a common superordinate group. Psychologists have found that cross-cutting identities reduce in-group bias and the stereotyping of out-groups (Crisp and Hewstone 2000; Urban and Miller 1998). Political scientists share this judgment and have debated at length whether democracy is even possible when the distribution of identities produce multiple nested groups rather than broadly cross-cutting groups (Bentley 1955; Lipset 1960; Truman 1951; Lijphart 1977; and Lijphart 1999).

The configuration of social identities is more than the compilation of possible categories people fit into. It has an important subjective component that has at least two dimensions. The first is the subjective identification with the group and not simply the objective sharing of a feature of the category. For instance, the fact that a person is counted by the census in a particular ethnic category does not mean he or she identifies with that ethnic community. Doyle and Sambanis (2000) find that identity wars are strongly associated with failed peace-building endeavors and are particularly tough to resolve. Doyle and Sambanis find no such relationship between ethnic heterogeneity in a society and obstacles to conflict resolution. Evidently, not all ethnic categorizations produce identities relevant to political conflict.

The second dimension of the subjective aspect of the configuration of multiple identities has to do with a person's representation of the overlap in membership of the groups toward which he or she feels loyal—in other words, the complexity of his or her social identity (Roccas and Brewer 2002).

Just as sharing an objective feature of a category does not equate with felt identity, the objective overlap of group membership does not equate with the subjective representation of this overlap in a person's mind. It is possible that a person who belongs to several groups that have cross-cutting members in an objective sense does not recognize this. For instance, a person may be French, Christian, European, and Caucasian. These groups actually are cross-cutting: not all French are Christian and not all Christians are French; not all French are European (at least not in terms of ancestry) and not all Europeans are French; not all French are Caucasians and not all Caucasians are French. In the mind of any particular person, however, these groups might all be nested, with all French being Christian, all Christians being European, and all Europeans being Caucasian. This would be a simple configuration, as distinct from a more complex configuration in which the nonoverlapping and cross-cutting nature of the multiple groups was recognized. Two aspects of social identity complexity are particularly important: (1) the perceived overlap of group characteristics and (2) the perceived overlap of group composition, that is, the perceived extent of shared membership across different groups.

It is our contention that understanding changes in social identity requires not only documenting which groups constitute significant social identities for individuals but also understanding how their multiple identities are configured and related to one another in a dynamic system. The institutions of the EU may be subjectively represented for some individuals as a superordinate group within which national identities are nested, but for others their European identity may subjectively cross-cut their national identity. As we shall see in upcoming chapters, this difference in subjective representation may have a lot to do with whether European and national loyalties are experienced as compatible or in conflict.

HOW ARE INSTITUTIONS AND IDENTITIES CONNECTED?

Interdependence is an unavoidable reality in the modern world. Even states that isolate themselves from the international economy are dependent on the behavior of other states for their security. In a nuclear era, survival depends on the actions of others. Most states also depend heavily on the actions of others for the well-being of their environmental system and recognize globalization as having created interdependent capital markets and production networks that they cannot avoid. It is widely recognized, of course, that interdependence does not necessarily lead to cooperation, much less common identities (Brewer 2000b; Waltz 1999). Interdependencies can be competitive, even zero-sum, and promote cross-group antagonisms and conflict. The exploitation of natural resources is sometimes seen in these terms. Even positive interdependencies in which cooperation can lead to gains for both sides can generate deep anxieties. Being dependent on people you do not trust is an uncomfortable situation. It can lead to conflict along several routes, including preemptive moves to reduce the anxiety by exerting control over the other side or by trying to leave the interdependent relationship. It is possible in situations of positive interdependence to pursue mutual gain, but as every graduate student learns when studying a prisoner's dilemma game, this is not always easy to achieve in practice. In the prisoner's dilemma, two prisoners are interdependent and will benefit from cooperating and not giving evidence against the other, but due to a lack of trust between them they may not achieve this cooperation.

Interdependence can be an important stimulus for the creation of international institutions. Faced with interdependence and substantial uncertainties, states may construct institutions to provide information, verification, and reassurance (Keohane 1989; Keohane and Martin 1995). Institutions can also contribute to more efficient interaction between states and promote a sense of confidence and predictability. Although the incentive to construct institutions may be inherent in interdependent relations, they are not always easy to construct. Some of the uncertainties and fears that promote interest in institutions also complicate and constrain their creation and their operation. Because international institutions are built for different reasons and because they face different obstacles, they differ in terms of organizational structure, decision-making procedures, and authority.

Forms of International Institutions

A great deal has been written about the role international institutions play in managing security dilemmas and in promoting commercial efficiencies between otherwise potentially competing or antagonistic national groups. Peacekeeping, confidence-building, and arms control institutions have received substantial attention. So have trade organizations, monetary institutions, and environmental regimes. Often, this research involves examining the methods these institutions use to provide confidence, information, verification, and adjudication. The trust that participating groups develop in the institution and its effectiveness is understood to be a key issue in understanding its operation and success. Less attention is paid to the effect that experience with the institution has on the images each of the participants might hold of the other participants and of themselves.

Institutions can be successful if they generate trust in themselves. They do not need to produce trust between potential antagonists. Participants can cooperate because they trust the institution, not the other participants. Moreover, successful institutions in this regard can actually work against perceptual change and attitudinal gravitation away from mutual hostility. They can do this by providing a credible explanation for the good behavior of another participant that does not require any adjustment of the negative image of the other participant. People on both sides can attribute compliance and cooperative behavior on the part of others to the institution and not to any good intentions or trustworthiness on the part of the other participants. Using trust in the institution to produce international cooperation may be seen as at best a short-term solution. Whether basic beliefs about the other participants can be changed over time is an open question, as is whether over time the two potential antagonists could come to see each other as part of a common in-group.

A frequent result of the recognition of the limitations in institutional strategies that aim simply to regulate cross-group relations is a call for the construction of international institutions that serve a second purpose, that is, to promote the construction of an overarching common identity among the participating subgroups. The institutional form in this case is a supernational unit, with participating nations as constituent parts.

Although functional international institutions with integrative ambitions seek to create new overarching common identities, they also typically seek to protect the integrity of preexisting national identities (Brubaker 1996, 23–54). This is accomplished often by making membership in the superordinate international institution dependent on membership in a participating nation. In other words, the people serving in the international institution are there by virtue of their membership in one of the participating states and typically as representative of that state. In this way, memberships in the international and national institutions are nested, meaning one is a subunit of the other. Institutional authority in these arrangements is typically distributed across the international and state institutions in a zero-sum fashion. That is, more authority granted to the international institution on a particular issue translates into less authority for independent action by state institutions. This can result in situations in which the international institution becomes very strong vis-à-vis the national units, as was the case in the Soviet Union. It can also result in situations in which the international authority is quite restricted compared to state sovereignty, as in the United Nations, or mixed across different issue areas, as in the European Union.

Because institutions that are nested often imply zero-sum distributions of political authority, corresponding identities are often thought of in zero-sum or trade-off terms as well. States raise questions about dual loyalty, and researchers pose questions that ask whether a person identifies more, or more often, or more intensely, with regional, national, or international communities. This can lead to the impression that identification with the superordinate community is inconsistent with intense identity with the subunit. Existing research has shown that at the individual level this is a false dichotomy, and people who identify strongly with local communities also identify strongly with nations, and with Europe (Martinotti and Stefanizzi 1995). Although it is clear that individuals can manage multiple identities without much psychological difficulty, political institutions seeking authority and jurisdiction often insist on explicit hierarchies among identities that do pose difficult choices.

In summary, the possible relationship between creating institutional structures and creating supernational identities can take several forms. In some cases institutions may serve primarily to reduce conflict and regulate exchange, leaving national identities intact with only a weak sense of common identity. Alternatively, international institutions may promote identity with the superordinate community, erode attachments to previous subgroups, and thus promote integration and cooperation. In yet a different pattern, the identification with the superordinate group can increase in tandem with continued identification with national subgroups. If this dual identity structure works well, national and international identification can be mutually reinforcing. If trust between the groups exists, the increasing integration can lead to positive feedback and growth in a common identity.

On the other hand, for states that have preexisting perceptions of different and incompatible values, increased institutionalization is likely to promote less common identity and higher levels of anxiety and conflict. In short, the route from institutional change to identity change is neither straightforward nor guaranteed. Whether and how European institutions affect political identities in Europe is one of the questions driving the research reported in this volume. To trace that path, it is not sufficient to treat institutions as "input" and social identities as "output." What is needed is additional theory specifying the ways in which institutional arrangements at the societal level may influence and shape identity and community at the psychological level.

Linkages between Evolving Institutions and Changing Identities

Many political institutions make a considerable effort to shape and promote public identification with themselves and the associated community. States, for example, have often tried to promote the notion of a nation, and religious institutions, such as the Catholic Church or the Islamic clergy in Iran, have sought to promote common identification among Catholics and Muslims respectively. The energy institutions put into identity promotion is perhaps indicative of the importance political leaders see in the potential mobilizing and legitimating power of widespread community identification. Of course, that institutions would like to promote common identity does not mean they do. Just as states can fail to make nations, so can international institutions fail to promote feelings of community. When states see the creation of pan-state identity as a threat to their own ability to mobilize citizens on national grounds, the task facing the international institution becomes more difficult.

The question of how far international institutions can go in creating new identities and changing the states and nations that brought them into existence has generated substantial debate in political science (Jervis 1999). This debate can be framed around two alternative causal stories. The first story claims that existing state identities and interests lead states to create institutions. It insists these institutions have limited ability to affect either the factors that brought them into existence or the factors that determine their tenure. The second story claims that institutions become part of the social and power structure that define a state's environment. Over time, consequently, the institution shapes the identity and understanding of self-interest that prevails in the state. Of course, despite the stark contrast that can be drawn between these two stories, there is likely to be a reciprocal process of mutual construction in which states, often based on national identities, create international institutions that, over time, lead to an evolution in identities that affects both the interests of the states and the affiliation felt for the international institution.

Although neofunctionalists anticipated identity change as a consequence of institutional cooperation, just how institutions would have this effect is still not clear. Two models of how institutions can affect identities may provide guidance here. We label these models socialization and persuasion. Each deserves brief elaboration.

Socialization Models

Whereas functional models of identity change assume that the existence of the institutions themselves creates changes in the political *environment* that eventually alter individuals' perceptions of community, interdependence, and trust, socialization models of identity formation and change focus on the role of individual *experience* with the institution and its consequences. According to these models, individuals come to identify with an institution (and the group that it represents) to the extent that the institution is salient in their personal lives. As individuals interact with the institution or its representatives or feel its effects in their daily experience, they are more likely to perceive it as a "real" entity that provides meaning and structure for their own lives. They may even come to believe it is part of the natural order and indispensable. Institutions, and their rules and regulations, also provide for *shared* experiences and shared social norms that enhance group identity and a sense of community. The broader the scope of the institution and the group of people directly affected by it, the more inclusive is the corresponding social identity.

Socialization models allow for different degrees of experience with institutions among people in the same population, with corresponding differences in depth and level of identification with those institutions. From this perspective, institutional socialization can be expected to be most intense for those who are directly involved in the institution and its functioning, as officials (the institutional elite), employees, or liaisons. Such direct involvement in the institution itself should create high levels of identification with the institution and the level of governance that it encompasses. What is particularly interesting at this level is the nature of socialization and identity change among those who are both officials of the European institution at the international level and representatives (and employees) of a component unit at the national level. Individuals in this situation may find it particularly difficult to isolate their national and European identities into separate spheres or domains. So the question becomes one of developing dual identities that are mutually compatible and complementary, or allowing one identity to trump the other when it comes to issues of group loyalty and strategic decision making.

Going beyond those who are directly involved in the institution itself, the socializing influence of an institution is extended to all those who experience its practices in their own lives. Here, the degree of identification should be a function of the breadth and depth of experienced effects. The more aspects of daily life impacted by the institution, the more likely that corresponding social identities will develop around that institution and those who are included in its sphere. Most national movements have begun as elite phenomena. Identification with Europe may also be mostly an elite affair. Highly educated and mobile sectors of national populations may be aware of European-wide institutions, participate in them far more than people in the general public, and adopt stronger identities with Europe than the mass public in their countries. In fact, attitudes and identities among the mass public may move in a direction opposite that of the elite. The elite may be better able to take advantage of the opportunities introduced by wider and deeper institutionalization; ordinary people may see more threat in these developments. These perceptions of threat might also be inflamed by politicians anxious to mobilize public support, playing to public fears that integration means greater economic competition and declining cultural distinctiveness.

Although the scope of influence of an institution can be objectively assessed, the depth and level of impact is more a matter of subjective experience. Beyond perceptions of the purpose, structure and form of international institutions, people can understand their importance in very different ways. Some people may feel that a particular international institution affects critically important issues that directly affect their lives. Other people may value different things and judge the importance of the institution differently, as dealing with minor issues or as relevant to them only sporadically. International institutions that are seen as affecting critically important matters pertaining to controversial topics will have the greatest salience and the greatest potential impact on identity. Institutions that routinize noncontroversial matters, even if these occur on a daily basis, are likely to be experienced as less salient and have less impact in the construction of common identity. The international postal system, for instance, has long been an effective cross-national institution, but has never engaged significant identification or loyalty.

Persuasion Models

A second perspective conceives of institutions as active agents of change. In these models the mutual relationship between institutional development and identity change takes into account the direct role that institutions may play in creating and engaging correspondent social identities among their constituencies. This perspective recognizes that social identity is a potentially valuable resource that can be drawn on to achieve legitimization, engage group loyalties, and energize collective effort. Hence deliberate efforts may be undertaken to build social identification through the creation of symbols of collective identity; propaganda emphasizing common interests and values, or shared history or future destiny; and persuasive campaigns to enhance the perceived legitimacy and importance of the institution itself. Identity-building efforts are aimed at both the "what" and the "who" of social identity—what does the social group stand for, and who is included in the definition of the group or community. Effectiveness is defined as the extent to which members of the group "buy in" to the meaningfulness of the identity and its symbols and extend their perception of shared group membership to all of those included within the group's boundaries.

Within the persuasion model of change, the mechanisms of identity building are parallel to those associated with social influence and attitude change in general, particularly models of mass communication and persuasion (e.g., Roberts and Maccoby 1985). As with any other persuasive effort, the effectiveness of campaigns to convince target group members to accept the meaning and importance of a shared social identity will depend on the strength of the persuasive appeals, the credibility of the perceived source of communications, the effectiveness of the medium of transmission, and the receptivity of the audience. Although most theories of persuasion rest on models of receivers as rational information processors, the role of emotional appeals, threats to self-interest, and social motives are not ignored. When the object of the persuasion effort is a sense of community and shared identity, the extent to which members of the group talk about the messages and their content among themselves may be a particularly important factor. Thus, models of mass communication and interpersonal communication and social influence may need to be combined in order for researchers to study identity change from the persuasion perspective.

New Identities: International, National, or Local?

Although at the popular level nations may be seen as natural categories and identities as primordial givens, most scholars conceive of nations, like other social identities, as human constructions. This does not mean that scholars believe identities are likely to change frequently or rapidly. They generally recognize that many factors anchor identities (Connor 1994). Looking back across history, however, changes in identity are evident. Most contemporary European nations, for instance, evolved from quite distinct subgroups, and in many of these nations regional subidentities still play important political roles. In retrospect it may appear that the formation of the current national communities was inevitable and represents immutable natural forces, but this impression is most likely a product as much of hindsight bias as of understanding of the processes that determine the politically dominant social identities. To see the limits in our understanding of these processes, we need only to look forward in time and consider the substantial debate over what identities will prevail in ten, twenty, or fifty years.

For instance, some observers argue that technical and commercial processes associated with globalization coupled with ambitious and cosmopolitan elites will construct larger community identities that supercede existing cultural divisions (Adler and Barnett 1998; Wendt 1994). Other scholars, who argue that trust derives from common cultural and religious foundations, add that security concerns vis-à-vis other large civilizations will also push in the direction of larger identity groups, such as Europe (Huntington 1996), but insist they will be defined along cultural grounds. On the other hand, still different scholars argue that many of these same factors will push identity in the opposite direction. In these alternative perspectives, the information revolution has empowered smaller groups of people, as has the microchip revolution. Commercial networks are seen as less constrained by national and regional geographic proximity (Kanter 1995). Local communities are thought to be able to interact globally, bypassing state and even interstate institutions (Alger 1990, 1999). In these scenarios, security is often conceived of at the individual level and related to personal living conditions, school systems, health care, and protection from crime. At this level, local institutions are often the most important, and culture, if it is a glue, is understood at the familial and extended clan or pseudo-clan gang level (Kaplan 2000). Rather than international identity building, these scenarios feature "balkanization" as the likely new identity order.

Of course, we cannot investigate the identities of the future. Nor can we determine the singular impact of European institutions on identities in Europe. After all, it is not possible to account for or to control all of the other possible factors that might affect identities. We enter our empirical investigation without the illusion that we will definitively test a causal theory or that we can identify clear trends. Our data will most often represent a snapshot or at best a short time period in the long sweep of history. Nonetheless, we believe that this is a critical time for assessing the nature of identity change processes in Europe and that approaching this topic from an interdisciplinary perspective will contribute to an understanding of the coevolution of international institutions and social identities.

WHAT IS THIS VOLUME ABOUT?

Part I: The Social Psychology of Identity Change

We begin with three chapters written by social psychologists. These explore several theoretical conceptions of how identities change and what mechanisms lead to this outcome. Rather than starting from the neofunctionalist premise so common in political science, they operate at the individual level and examine the social psychological processes of identity change. Glynis Breakwell introduces Identity Process Theory (IPT), arguing that structures of identity are a dynamic product of the interaction of capacities of memory and the person, on one hand, and physical and societal structures, on the other. In this conception change is seen as the modification of a holistic identity structure and not as the addition of a new identity that exists along with old ones. Breakwell argues that the process is regulated by a dynamic process of accommodation-assimilation and evaluation.

Applying Identity Process Theory to the case of Europe, Breakwell questions whether the European category has sufficiently clear category characteristics to serve as a locus of identity attachment. She notes that Europe remains to a large degree an "empty set" for identity purposes, meaning there is little agreed-on understanding of the content of the category in the sense of encompassing the characteristics of the individual national categories that comprise it. In the European case, this process of assigning content to what Europe is can be a very important task because, as mentioned above, there is substantial debate about what the category includes and what attributes people in it share. If the category is largely empty of content and filled up with very different specific attributes by different people, it is not clear what exactly is shared and whether we should conclude that community exists.

Emanuele Castano also addresses the issue of whether Europe as a superordinate category has "reality" as a social identity. He suggests that the ease with which a group can be imagined as an entity enhances identification, and he examines several mechanisms that have been found in social psychological studies to boost identification. Castano looks at four factors in particular that are thought to enhance the ease with a group can be imagined as an entity. These include the clarity of the group's boundaries and the explicit identification of what people in the group share in common. Castano reports on the results of a series of experiments designed to test whether the degree to which participants identify with Europe changes as a consequence of the manipulation of the factors that affect how likely Europe is to be imagined as an entity. Castano finds in these experiments that identity with Europe does increase under conditions that lead participants to see the category in entitative terms. It is still an open question, however, to what extent such perceptions are widespread in the general population and whether perceived entitativity is promoted by EU institutions, policies, and practices.

Amélie Mummendey and Sven Waldzus also explore the process by which identities change; they rely on experimental methods to test a novel and very important theoretical proposition. They accept Breakwell's cautionary note that Europe may be an "empty" category for many people and argue that, therefore, it can be filled up with different content by different people. This process of filling in the content of the prototypical European, Mummendey and Waldzus contend, is a central process in building shared identities. They suggest that it may not proceed as neofunctionalists would hope and that growing identification with the superordinate group called Europe could increase hostility and intolerance toward people from different nation-states who are now becoming members of the superordinate group labeled Europe.

Mummendey and Waldzus suggest that promoting integrated European institutions and European identity could sharpen cross-national animosities rather than mitigate them. This occurs, they argue, when groups define the content of the new superordinate group by projecting their own national in-group characteristics as the defining prototypical content of the new superordinate group. In other words, when people believe the new prototypical European has essentially the characteristics of the people in their national subgroup, their intolerance grows toward people who once were outsiders but are now fellow insiders. The argument is that it is easier to tolerate the differences of outsiders than it is to tolerate the failure of insiders to live up to the prototypic norm. Mummendey and Waldzus find preliminary evidence for their in-group projection theory in experiments conducted in Germany, but they also find that a more complex representation of Europe that emphasizes diversity rather than commonalities can reduce this in-group projection effect.

Following the chapters on how identity might change and the experimental evidence that sustains these conjectures, we turn to empirical studies of European identity. We do this at several levels. Brigid Laffan, a political scientist, and Ruth Wodak, a specialist on linguistic discourse analysis, look first at the elite level, studying people who play professional roles within the EU. It is among this group that we would expect to see the most evidence of European identity and the greatest impact of the EU institutions, especially due to interpersonal socialization. Eugenia Siapera expands the vision to include journalists who cover the EU and serve as a central vehicle bringing knowledge about the EU and images of it to the mass public. In the last part of the book we look at ordinary people and mass attitudes, using both survey data and in-depth interviews and the analysis of natural discourse. Before we discuss the general public, however, we want to say more about how we examine the elite and their connections to EU institutions.

Part II: Identity within the EU Institutions at the Elite Level

Brigid Laffan identities the primary institutions of the EU, noting their structure and decision-making process, and then investigates how identities with local, national, and European communities are managed by the officials of these institutions. It is among these people that neofunctionalists would expect the largest identification with the superordinate institution. In many ways, looking for identity with Europe among this group is an easy test of the notion that identity change is occurring; if there is no identity shift toward Europe here, there is unlikely to be a shift anywhere else.

Because the institutions in the EU are diverse in their organizational form, we can probe for information on whether officials who work in organizational structures that feature supernational nested hierarchical authority develop stronger or weaker identities with Europe and whether the way they configure their local, national, and European identities differs from that of officials working in those institutions of the EU that feature more cross-cutting and issue-specific decision-making structures.

Although all of the chapters in this volume share a common focus on the concept of identity, the methods used to measure it vary widely, reflecting the interdisciplinary nature of the contributions. Laffan in her study of the EU institutions as "identity builders," analyzes the organizational structure of the institutions and conducts case studies of the European Commission, the Council of Europe, the European Court of Justice, and the European Parliament. She reviews both official statements and interview comments made by officials in these institutions to track the ways in which they manage and negotiate between multiple identities. Laffan also discerns how these elites conceive of Europe and identify with that broader community.

Ruth Wodak engages in a parallel study of delegates to the European Parliament, civil servants in the European Commission, and representatives from the Committee of Permanent Representatives. She relies on a series of in-depth interviews and subjects the discourse generated in these interviews to two types of analysis, first a general qualitative content analysis, and second a detailed linguistic analysis. Using these methods Wodak identifies both the set of multiple identities her interview participants manage and the characteristic content they believe constitutes "European." She finds differences in the ways members of the Commission and delegates to the Parliament manage their European and national identities, but some degree of similarity in the characteristics they associate with being European.

Eugenia Siapera uses in-depth interviews and discourse analysis to explore both how local, national, and European identities are managed and how the process of building a common Europe is understood. She reports on twenty interviews with senior journalists who cover the EU in Brussels for the major high-quality outlets in thirteen countries. Siapera conducted these interviews shortly after the Commission resigned in March 1999 and used this event as a vehicle to enter into the mental understandings of what was happening in Europe, what Europe was, and how it related to other community identities. In her analysis of the discourse evident in the interviews, Siapera identifies three major narratives that were prominent in the journalists' accounts of the crisis in the Commission. These narratives highlight the central driving factors to the story of an evolving European political system and feature different relationships between the construction of Europe and the construction of individual nations within Europe. By studying one of the main media through which Europeans experience the EU, Siapera provides a window on how Europe is conceived of and how ideas about the EU might shape how ordinary Europeans think about who they are.

Part III: Investigations of European Identity among Non-elites

In our third section we explore whether identification with Europe is exclusively an elite phenomenon, suggesting that EU institutions may have promoted shared identities among their officials but not among ordinary citizens, and we investigate whether ordinary people experience a painful tradeoff between their feelings for local, national, and European communities or whether they manage their multiple identities in a rather harmonious fashion. Jack Citrin and John Sides report on the identities Europeans acknowledge, and explore the constellation of identities that characterize mass publics in Europe.

Citrin and Sides rely on data from survey questionnaires with mostly closed-ended answer formats. The chapter by Citrin and Sides examines data from the Eurobarometer surveys of a representative sample of Europeans. Citrin and Sides examine trend lines in national and European identity as measured by several questions Eurobarometer has asked consistently over the years. They find that complementary attachments to nation and Europe are increasing over time, although the public identification with Europe is not nearly as intense as identifications with nations.

Both Michael Bruter and Ulrike Meinhof are dissatisfied with the questions that have been used by Eurobarometer to measure identity. They both seek alternative measurement strategies, although the paths they take are very different. Bruter works within the mass-survey format but argues that greater attention needs to be paid to cultural and civic bases of identity. He asks whether the content of what is thought to be shared connects to who is seen as included in the European community. Bruter reports data from a pilot study conducted at three universities; the study was designed to develop a differentiated—and behaviorally relevant—measure of European identity that can be applied to the study of identity change and the relationship between national and European identities.

Meinhof is skeptical of the closed-ended survey format and worries that responses can be misleading when taken out of context and out of the flow of natural conversation. She prefers to rely on lengthy in-depth interviews that are not driven by a series of closed-ended questions. She records her conversations and then subjects the dialogue to linguistic and content analyses. In this fashion, Meinhof taps the mental categories that ordinary people employ. She finds that Europe as a category does not appear in the conversations she conducted and wonders if findings that emphasize European identity are artifacts of the cues delivered in the closed-ended survey questions.

Meinhof is interested in more than method, of course, and conducts her interviews in two pairs of border towns, one pair that straddles East and West Germany, and another pair that straddles Germany and Poland. By concentrating on two pairs of previously separated towns that now could be imagined as part of a new superordinate community (Germany in the first case, Europe in the second), Meinhof explores the process of identity change at the level of ordinary people. She is particularly interested in the images of the Other that define the previous out-group and how in everyday life these stereotypes break down and evolve. She argues that in the absence of a clear definition of the in-group category, social identities may be formed oppositionally—by contrast to the Other. In any case, her analysis captures the language and categories people use everyday in thinking about themselves and Others and uses this as an avenue to the assessment of shifting identities.

Part IV: Comparisons and Lessons

In his concluding chapter to this volume, Thomas Risse highlights the book's findings on the empirical subject of European identity. His chapter focuses on the European identity as the "dependent variable." He pulls together the findings from the various chapters to answer a series of important theoretical and policy questions. These questions include: (1) How do European and other identities of individuals and social groups go together? (2) What do we know about the substance and content of European identity? (3) How can we explain the large gap between elite identification with Europe and the feelings of ordinary citizens, who seem to be more alienated from Europe? (4) Do the institutions of the European Union act as mechanisms of identity change? (5) Are different findings regarding the stability and depth of social identity properly seen as statistical artifacts and best attributed to different methodological strategies, or are they reconcilable in a more complex understanding of European identity? (7) Is a European identity necessary to build a European polity, and, if so, what role should the EU play?

I

The Social Psychology of Identity Change

2

Identity Change in the Context of the Growing Influence of European Union Institutions

Glynis M. Breakwell

An interesting series of issues emerge when one attempts to analyze the ways in which the institutions of the European Union might affect identity development—either at the level of the individual citizen or at the level of categories or groups of people. This chapter is a very preliminary exploration of some of these issues, particularly at the level of the individual citizen. In it, an attempt is made to avoid talking about those parts of identity based on being European but rather to focus on those emanating from being a member of the citizenry of the EU. Some slippage between the two may occur unintentionally; since it is likely to result in confusion, an apology in advance is proffered to the reader. The distinction between identity elements or changes derived from having a sense of being European and those derived from being a citizen of a country that is part of the EU should be maintained in any analysis as far as possible. There is evidence from survey studies across Europe (notably those conducted by the European Commission and entitled the Eurobarometer studies, which track changes over time in public attitudes to topics significant to the EU) that the general public does distinguish between the implications for their sense of self of being European and of being a citizen of an EU state. In some ways, the former is a matter of geographical location and the latter is a matter of political decision. Of course, in reality, it must be said that the drawing of the geographical boundary around "Europe" is also a matter of political process and engenders much debate. However, this tends to be obscured by the general availability of representations of and assumptions about the structure of Europe that have evolved over many generations, against the historical backdrop of international and civil wars. In contrast, the fact that the EU is clearly a political creation with specific boundaries that can be articulated through legal definition has significant implications for the way it impacts on identity—not least because it can do so through the processes that establish and change its formal institutions. Through its institutions (economic, legal, or educational), the EU can require or motivate major swaths of behavioral change, and it would be foolhardy to believe such behavioral changes are isolated from identity changes. Consequently, this chapter examines how certain changes in EU institutional structures (specifically, the adoption of the euro as the common legal tender for most of the member states and the enlargement of the EU as new member states are admitted) may act to change identity.

PRIOR HISTORY OF THE NATIONAL IDENTITY AND THE SPECIFICITY OF EUROPEAN UNION IMPACT

Before looking at the likely effects of specific European Union institutions on the identities of its members, it is worth pausing to acknowledge that these effects will depend on prior identity structures. The existence and action of the EU may influence many aspects of identity. For instance, EU legislation that makes the use of iterative fixed-term employment contracts illegal and that requires temporary employees to be given the same employment rights as permanent employees could transform the occupational identities of millions of erstwhile fixed-term or temporary employees. However, this chapter does not extend to an examination of the potential impact of the EU on all aspects of identity. It focuses in the main on aspects of national identity (i.e., the elements of identity derived from being a member of a particular national category).

Any analysis that seeks to describe and explain the impact of the EU on national identity must be careful to specify the precise nature of that national identity structure. The editors of this volume in their introductory chapter emphasize that when looking at group identity one should distinguish three aspects: the composition (the rules of belonging), the content (the defining attributes of the category), and the role (the relationships that position the category in an intergroup context). Different national identities differ in these three properties. The way in which the presence and activities of the EU affect a specific national identity will in large measure depend on the initial configuration of these three basic properties of the category's identity. The impact of the EU and its institutions on an individual member of any national group will depend on the basic features of the national identity. Thus, the impact of the EU on the British person's identity will not be the same as its influence on the Italian's or the German's. It might be added that among the British, the way it impacts on the English may be expected to be different from the way it affects the Scots or the Welsh. Essentially, the entire history of the evolution of a nation's characteristics and image will determine the ways in which the EU will influence the identity structure and dynamics of that category and of its members. That part of the individual's identity that is derived from national categorizations will differ in stability and meaning according to the longevity and social significance of the national categorization itself. Research from Northern Ireland illustrates this point. Trew and Benson (1996) examined how young adults in Northern Ireland described themselves in terms of national groupings. They found that approximately 30 percent claimed to be Northern Irish, 30 percent Irish, and 16 percent British. Of course, in legal terms all were British, since the technical definition of "British" encompasses the citizens of the United Kingdom (England, Scotland, and Wales) and Northern Ireland. None were actually Irish. The study offers no reason for us to believe that the respondents were ignorant of the legal niceties of their passport status. Self-identification with a particular national category was important for them and was more significant for them than the legal position. The national identity of the citizens of Northern Ireland is not unproblematic. It is a challenged national identity, one that is open to threat, re-representation, and is fundamentally unstable. Such a national identity is a totally different base on which the EU might impact than that of the English. Condor (1996) reports that the national identity of the English is seen as unproblematic—at least in the sense that the English evince little emotional turmoil in claiming to be such and show no sign of believing that there is challenge to their national status. The English seem to take their nationality for granted, and it consequently lacks personal salience. There is a very real empirical question as to whether the national identity that is challenged but salient or the one that is secure and nonsalient will react more to the activities of the EU. It seems, however, reasonable to assume that they will not react in entirely the same way.

Basically, this is to suggest that not all national identifications have the same proclivity or power to assimilate, resist, or redirect the impact of EU institutional developments. While the same underlying processes may be at work (although this is yet to be proven), even so, the substance on which they impact is different and the results they have are different. This chapter mainly focuses on some of these processes as they affect people in the United Kingdom. While it makes some claims for the generalizability of the processes, it makes no claims for the generalizability of their outcomes for the specific content of identities across national categories.

INDIVIDUAL IDENTITY, GROUP IDENTITY, AND IDENTITY PROCESSES

It is difficult to analyze the impact of European Union institutions on identity without acknowledging how important it is to distinguish between the identity of any one individual and the identity of any national category (or group) to which that individual belongs. The EU may influence the individual identity without influencing the group identity. Not all impacts of EU institutions are mediated by changes in the social identity of a group. For instance, Timotijevic and Breakwell (2000) found that refugees fleeing from war-torn former Yugoslavia clearly differentiated between the significance of EU legal structures for them as individuals and for their national group as an entity. The laws concerning immigration had a major impact on their individual identity but not on the identity of their national group.

It is therefore important to use a model of identity dynamics that allows analysis of both the immediate impact of the EU on individual identity and the effects on individual identity through changing category identity. The model of identity used here is that proposed in Identity Process Theory (Breakwell 1986, 1994, 2001a, 2001b). This theory is primarily concerned with explaining how and why identity structures change, especially in the context of social change. The original theory focused on the processes affecting individual identities. It has, however, been elaborated (Lyons 1996) and applied to processes affecting the identities of groups or categories.

Identity Process Theory (IPT) has a number of central propositions, some of which are quite different from those of other social psychological models of identity dynamics. It proposes that the structure of identity is a dynamic social product of the interaction of the capacities for memory, consciousness, and organized construal that are characteristic of the biological organism with the physical and societal structures and influence processes that constitute the social context. The identity resides in psychological processes but is manifested through thought, action, and affect. It can therefore be described at two levels, in terms of its structure and in terms of its processes. IPT claims that people are normally self-aware (that is, they monitor the status of their identity) but that self-awareness levels may differ developmentally and across different cultures. The structure of identity is said to be characterized on two planes: the content dimension and the value dimension. The content dimension consists of the characteristics that define identity: the properties that, taken as a constellation, mark the individual as unique. It encompasses those characteristics previously considered the domain of social identity (group memberships, group roles, social category labels, etc.) and of personal identity (values, attitudes, cognitive style, etc.). *The distinction between social and personal identity is abandoned in this model.* Seen across the biography, social identity is seen to become personal identity: the dichotomy is purely a temporal artifact. IPT does not talk of identities in the plural but of identity in the singular. The individual is deemed to be possessed of one identity that comprises many elements—some of which are derived from category membership. This becomes important when modeling the way new or reconceived category memberships may affect identity—not through the addition of a new identity but through the modification of the holistic identity structure.

IPT goes on to argue that the content dimension is organized. The organization can be characterized in terms of (1) the degree of centrality, (2) the hierarchical arrangements of elements, and (3) the relative salience of components. The organization is not, however, static and is responsive to changes in inputs and demands from the social context. Each element in the content dimension has a specific positive or negative value appended to it; taken together these values constitute the value dimension of identity. The value dimension of identity is constantly subject to revision: the value of each element is open to reappraisal as a consequence of changes in social value systems and modifications in the individual's position in relation to such social value systems.

The structure of identity is regulated by the dynamic processes of *accommodation-assimilation* and *evaluation,* which are deemed to be universal psychological processes. Assimilation and accommodation are components of the same process. Assimilation refers to the absorption of new components into the identity structure; accommodation refers to the adjustment that occurs in the existing structure in order to find a place for new elements. Accommodation-assimilation can be conceptualized as a memory system (equivalent to an information-processing system), subject to biases in retention and recall. These biases are determined by identity principles. The process of evaluation entails the allocation of meaning and value to identity contents, new and old. The two processes interact to determine the changing content and value of identity over time, with changing patterns of assimilation requiring changes in evaluation and vice versa.

The processes of identity are said to be guided in their operation by principles that define desirable states for the structure of identity. The actual end states considered desirable, and consequently the guidance principles, may be temporally and culturally specific (though Vignoles, Chryssochoou, and Breakwell 2000 suggest that distinctiveness, at least, is not), but in Western industrialized cultures the current prime guidance principles are: continuity, distinctiveness, self-efficacy, and self-esteem. These four principles will vary in their relative and absolute salience over time and across situations. Their salience may also vary developmentally.

IPT emphasizes that an identity is created within a particular social context within a specific historical period, and this social context can be schematically represented along two dimensions concerning, in turn, structure and process. Structurally, the social context is comprised of interpersonal networks, group and social-category memberships, and intergroup relationships. The content of identity is assimilated from these structures that generate roles to be adopted and beliefs or values to be accepted. The second dimension consists of social influence processes that conspire to create the multifaceted ideological milieu for identity. Social influence processes (education, rhetoric, propaganda, polemic, persuasion, etc.) establish systems of value and beliefs, reified in social representations, social norms, and social attributions, that specify both the content and value of individual identities. Of course, identity is not totally determined by its social context. There are contradictions and conflicts within the ideological milieu, generated by intergroup power struggles, that permit the individual some freedom of choice in formulating the identity structure. Furthermore, the limitations of the cognitive system itself impose some constraints on identity development. Changes in identity are therefore normally purposive. The person has agency in creating identity. Social changes in the structure or processes of the social context will call forth changes in identity that vary in extent according to: (1) their personal relevance; (2) the immediacy of the person's involvement in them; (3) the amount of change demanded; and (4) how negative the change is deemed to be. Movement of the individual from one position in the social matrix to another will bring pressure to bear for a change in identity, since this is likely to introduce a changed pattern of social influences and restrictions.

IPT argues that a threat to identity occurs when the processes of assimilation-accommodation are unable, for some reason, to comply with the principles of continuity, distinctiveness, self-efficacy, and self-esteem. IPT then goes on to describe how individuals use various strategies to cope with threats to identity (Breakwell 1988). It is not necessary to go into them in this chapter. The essential propositions of IPT for the purposes of this chapter are as follows:

- The categorization as a citizen of a member state of the EU may contribute an element to the global structure of identity, but it is not an identity in its own right.
- The main task is to understand how this element of identity is assimilated-accommodated and evaluated, in the context of a constellation of identity elements that may include other, subnational and national—and even supranational—categorizations. Since the categorization may represent a threat to continuity, distinctiveness, self-efficacy and/or self-esteem, it is also necessary to examine the strategies that individuals deploy to cope with its impact.
- The way the categorization and its implications as an identity element are represented by key agents of social influence will shape the way individuals adopt it as part of their identity.

The individual citizen's identity is the main focus of the approach in this chapter. However, IPT has been used to analyze changes in group identity (Lyons 1996), and it might be argued that any examination of the impact of

EU institutional change on identity should be equally concerned with the EU's capacity to shift the identity of nations. This may be a worthwhile project but it would be enormously difficult, since there is always the problem of achieving a sensible distinction between the stereotype and the identity associated with a national category. In any case, the prime object here is to examine the impact of change in European Union institutions on the identity of the individual citizen.

THE ISSUE OF SUPERORDINATE CATEGORIZATION AND CATEGORY IDENTITY BY DEFAULT

Before examining responses to specific changes in European Union institutional structures, it may be useful to address some of the difficulties to which anyone conducting research in this area must be alert. The first concerns the question of whether the European Union represents a superordinate category for the purposes of identity development. The European Union is often talked about as a superordinate category—as somehow encompassing national categories. In several senses—notably, the geographical and judicial—this is undoubtedly true. In another sense it should be challenged. There is no definition of the EU as a category that is superordinate in the sense of encompassing the characteristics of the individual national categories that might be said geographically and politically to comprise it. No one has suggested that the EU identity is an amalgam of the characteristics associated with the Greeks, the Belgians, the French, the Italians, and so on. It may be superordinate in the geographical or purely logical sense, but it is not inevitably superordinate in the psychological or subjective or stereotyping sense. Essentially, the EU lacks an all-encompassing inclusive identity that it can offer its member citizens. It even lacks a highly specific and unique set of identity characteristics to offer members. In part this may be a product of the relative newness of the EU as an entity. It may be a product of its origin in a union for purely economic advantage. It may be a product of the originators' desire not to threaten national identities by offering too soon a model of an alternative supracategory identification. The reasons for the failure to develop a strong, well-recognized set of identity characteristics up until now are many and are described further a little later in this chapter. Some of the chapters in this book illustrate that the characterization has now begun. However, it is still early in the process.

Surveys that ask whether an individual actively identifies with the EU category membership (i.e., regards it as a meaningful element of identity) yield widely varying results. Even in the UK, where there is still widespread suspicion about the EU and its laws and financial systems, people do, under the right circumstances, claim some aspect of their identity is derived from EU membership. Of course, they may do so when the EU categorization is made more salient by context (e.g., when comparisons are required with other supranational category memberships, or when the role of the EU in moderating intranational conflicts is emphasized). Studies that have allowed people in the UK to freely describe their identity structure virtually never elicit claims for EU membership as a prime self-identification, though being European may be mentioned (Breakwell and Lyons 1996). These findings must be seen against the fact that people generally do not spontaneously use national categorizations as self-definers unless prompted to do so by contextual factors. This emphasizes and echoes the concern expressed in other chapters in this volume that the methods used to audit identity structures are often inadequate.

The relative emptiness of characterization of the EU category (in comparison to national categories) in some respects may be an advantage. If the EU category had a strong set of characteristics it would be more likely to challenge existing identity elements and could be seen to a greater extent to attack the continuity, distinctiveness, self-efficacy, and self-esteem of members. The barriers to assimilating and valuing the EU identity element would then be greater. In some ways, the more it remains an empty identification (i.e., empty of social meanings), the less likely it is to threaten the existing identity structure. The same logic would suggest that as the EU identity element develops, the more it is congruent with or reinforces previous identifications the less it will threaten the existing identity structure. In some member states, it could be said to be starting to do this—particularly in those in which there is no historically strong tradition of nationalism (for instance, Italy) or where nationalism is currently eschewed (for instance, perhaps, Germany). It is likely that these states will have the greatest role in contributing to the development of the character of the EU identity element. By being adopted by them, in turn, the EU will be likely to adopt many of the characteristics most associated with the citizens of those states.

Typically, social categories are defined in terms of various characteristics (though their salience varies according to the type of category considered):

- Norms of behavior of members
- Value systems of members
- Competencies of members
- Rights and responsibilities of members
- Membership entry criteria (both formal and informal)

Identification with a category entails self-definition in terms of category characteristics.

The EU has a major problem in gaining a place as an identity element, since its category characteristics currently are unclear. It has no unambiguous or unchallenged social meaning and has limited symbols. It has a short and unromantic history without what might be called heritage (i.e., the emotion-ridden myths, legends, and personalities used by nations to claim distinctiveness, continuity, efficacy, and esteem). Though doubtless it will develop social meaning, symbols, and heritage with time (and is starting to do so—with, for instance, the corruption of commissioners; iconic associations of momentous decisions with place, for example, Maastricht; and some recognizable personalities).

The EU is both a social category (i.e., comprising its member states and their citizens) and a set of institutions (i.e., a mechanism for government). Currently, in the main, its category identity is:

1. imputed from the actions of its institutions;
2. attributed by other categories in ways that serve their self-interest.

Essentially, the EU is a category that is in many ways defined by other categories with which it is often in conflict. In this it is not unusual. It gains its category identity through oppositional definitions (or polemical social representations; Moscovici 1976; Jodelet 1989; Elejabarietta 1996). This is seen most clearly when nations characterize the meaning and objectives of the EU in order to motivate their nationals to reject EU policy or legislation. Chryssochoou (2000a and 2000b) shows that in samples of French and of Greeks, subgroups choose representations of the EU that serve their specific purposes at the time (those representations consequently vary as the purposes of subgroups change over time). She shows that the representation of the EU could be positive or negative depending on the rhetorical purpose. An example of the use of the representation of the EU as a tool in a dispute comes from the debates in 2003, during the Iraq war. The representation of the role and character of the EU differed significantly across European states depending on their national position concerning the decision to launch the attack on Iraq. In reality, the debate brought into question the likely limits that would be placed on the EU with respect to national defense and international military action.

In fact, Chryssochoou points out that identification with the EU depends on the extent to which it will serve current subgroup objectives. If being a good EU citizen is useful to a subgroup's current objectives, then membership is highlighted. This suggests a much more utilitarian and purposive relationship between the individual and the influence of the EU on identity than might initially be supposed. The identity effects on the individual are apparently directed or modified by the action of the individual and his or her subgroups. While this chapter focuses on the significance of defining people's commonalties terms of what the EU might contribute to identity, it is important to acknowledge that the ways in which that element will be assimilated into the extant identity structure will be idiosyncratic. The element will find a place within an existing complex, organized system of identity elements. It will be customized and personalized in this process. The EU institutions may through their operations cause the evolution of a recognizable EU identity element, but it would be unrealistic to assume that such an element would find a place in the identity structure of any one individual unmodified. People will differ in their awareness of the category characteristics and in the inclination they feel to assimilate them. The process of assimilation and accommodation of the new identity element is purposive.

It is notable that these purposive redefinitional efforts by individuals or groups rarely offer a generic definition of the characteristics of EU members. They mainly focus on the character of the EU as an institution. When people who are members of the EU are discussed, frequently they are careful to draw distinctions between members who are in their own national group and the "rest." They consequently fail to offer easy input for adopting an EU element to individual identity. The diversity of oppositional definitions of the EU as an identity element might rightly result in us questioning whether there is yet any single consensual version. If there is not and individuals are adopting various versions, it makes it necessary to assume that there are multiple EU identity elements.

Nevertheless, because they are a product of oppositional representations, these partial images of the people who make up the EU membership are emotionally highly charged. Regional or local categorizations and national categorizations might be expected to use the EU in quite different ways. Where regional or local categories are striving to gain independence from the nation-state, the representation of the significance and meaning of the EU can be used in the struggle to reduce the psychological power of the national category. There is some evidence to support this in the studies of children aged six to fifteen in England, Scotland, Catalonia, the Basque country, Andalusia, Northern Italy, and Central Italy (Barrett et al. 1999; Lyons et al. 1997). Children from groups that are seeking independence or devolution were more likely to claim that being European was important to them and that it was more important than their national identification, though not more important than their regional identification.

THE IDENTITY OF A CHANGING CATEGORY

One main problem with describing the character of the identity element that might be generated by EU membership is that the EU as a category in itself is changing. New member states have been allowed to join. These have very different traditions, cultures, and economies from the original members. To achieve a coherent, comprehensive, and consistent representation of the EU identity element is consequently virtually impossible—unless it is reduced to something bland or even vacuous. In fact there is a lot of evidence to show that publics across Europe are not able to crystallize the qualities that characterize a EU member (Lyons and Breakwell 1996). This is intriguing given that the mass media could present a globalized representation of the EU identity element if they were provided with the basic content. It seems, however, that the EU as an institution has not sought to erect such an identity for itself and has not actively promulgated identity elements to be assimilated by citizens of its member states. This may be an error, since there is evidence that, when the public image of the EU as an institution or of the qualities associated with being an EU member has greater complexity or depth (irrespective of the accuracy or plausibility of that image), people are happier to claim that they are themselves EU members (Barrett 1996).

The fact that the EU is an "unfinished" category is of vital importance because of its capacity to threaten current identity structures and particularly challenge self-interest. Through the Treaty of Nice, the EU established an instrument that would enable its expansion (i.e., the addition of new member states) to almost double its size. The Irish Republic decided to put the treaty to its electorate for ratification through referendum in June 2001. The majority voted no, but with a very poor turnout. Public opinion polls across EU states reflected similar, though muted, concern about the prospect of enlargement. However, no other country held a referendum at a similar time. In fact it was unlikely that the Irish referendum result would actually seriously deflect the progress of the treaty. Nevertheless, it was symptomatic of the perceived undesirability of expansion at the level of the electorate. The consensus view of the UK mass media reporting this result was that the public fear the way the EU has become distant, unwieldy, and too unaccountable. The opinion polls surrounding the referendum illustrated that a majority of the Irish public had several reasons for rejecting the treaty:

- They feared that the EU would divide into two classes of member states.
- They feared a mass of immigrants from countries lined up to join.
- They feared the creation of a European Rapid Reaction Force (i.e., a joint military unit).
- They feared it would lead to an even less democratic EU process.

Some commentators, perhaps cynically, also suggested that the Irish expected no longer to be a net receiver but to become a net contributor to the EU coffers and that this self-interest drove their vote.

The debate over the expansion of the EU illustrates very clearly how changes in its institutional structures impact on the identity of member state citizens indirectly as well as directly. It is not just the existence of a categorization (available for identification) that influences identity. This is perhaps the most trivial of the effects of the EU on identity. It is the actions of the EU as a powerful political entity that shape and threaten identities. Through its policies the EU has the power to modify economies, reshape armies, remove border controls, and revamp the remit of legislation. It is through these policies that it has its prime impact on the lives of individuals and on the overall structure of their identity (conceptualized in IPT terms).

CAN EU INSTITUTIONS CHANGE THE BASELINE NATIONAL IDENTITY CHARACTERISTICS?

It is consequently not enough to examine the additional identity element that may be offered by the EU as a category. It can be argued that the operation of the EU institutions inevitably will change existing baseline national identity elements. The EU institutions have the power to modify legal, financial, welfare, and other systems. These material changes will have corollary effects on national life (culture, populations, well-being, etc.). In doing so, such material changes may be thought to have the capacity to cause the identity of the national category to be modified. The most obvious example of such an influence might come from the changes in immigration laws that the EU has introduced. Changing migration patterns, over time, may produce a significant restructuring of populations and consequently of their traditions, most notably their religious beliefs.

Fear that they will perforce change "national" identity is an important basis in some places for the rejection of changes made by EU actions and policy. One change that has been studied extensively has been the introduction of the euro as a common currency in the EU. Of course, not all member states had joined the euro at the time this chapter was written. Britain had not done so. It is interesting to examine this rejection by a member state of a major institutional change that the EU introduced. It illustrates precisely how EU institutions can be perceived to challenge national sovereignty and the essential ingredients of national identity.

In 1997, the Labour government decided that the UK would not join the euro until five "crucial tests" were satisfied. These were:

- sustainable convergence between the UK and the euro-zone in terms of exchange rates;
- sufficient flexibility in the UK economy to cope with Economic Monetary Union (EMU) membership;

- an improvement in conditions for investment as a result of joining the European Monetary Union;
- a positive impact on the UK's financial services sector;
- the promotion of sustained employment growth.

The government also stated that the ultimate choice would be made by the UK public via a referendum. This was clearly a major issue for industrialists and politicians within the UK and also for the EU. However, the UK public evinced marked disinterest in the whole question. During 2001, public opinion polls showed that the EU and the euro were not among the top ten concerns influencing voters. Their major concerns were the health services and transport systems. When pushed to give a view on the euro, 70 percent of those sampled said that they did not want to adopt the single currency, but 60 percent said that they expected that in fact the country would adopt it. Interestingly, in 2003, the government again decided to defer a decision on adoption of the euro, claiming that the tests had not been satisfied.

This takes us back to the doubts about the salience of the EU for identity change in the individual person in the UK. There is no doubt that a single currency will impinge on, in the sense of constrain, national sovereignty. Directly, this may have no impact on the individual's identity, since in the majority of cases people will be truly unaware of such implications of adopting the euro. As people said to pollsters, they simply could not understand all of that talk about sovereignty. However, indirectly, through its impacts on job opportunities and prosperity, this institutional change in the EU is likely to have serious implications for identity changes in masses of individuals. In this sense the impact of the EU institutions on identity is highly complex; it works not simply at one remove but through many channels of amplification over a long time period.

Policy makers expect the harmonization of legal, educational, and monetary systems across the EU to improve acceptance of the rate of change and development, acknowledgement of shared responsibility for problems and joint action, communication between member states, mobility of labor and ideas, intergroup relations, and civic responsibility. Harmonization is a form of explicit engineering of societal norms. It cannot be treated as if it would leave national identities untouched. The changes caused by harmonization will be associated with changes in normative assumptions. They may be very subtle, but they are inevitable. The harmonization of institutional structures is unlikely to lead to a harmonization, in any comprehensive sense, of national identities, but it will realign them.

The significance of the timescales for changes in identity should not be underestimated. To return to the role of the EU merely as a possible self-categorization that may contribute directly to identity development, the iterative Eurobarometer surveys in the UK since the early 1980s have shown a progressive gradual shift in knowledge of and attitudes toward first the European Community and then the EU. Partial ignorance has succeeded total ignorance. Cynical suspicion has replaced downright rejection. The timescale for these changes has been twenty-five years. Individual identity changes can be very rapid, but in fact usually they are gradual. The appreciation of societal changes determined by institutional restructuring on the scale of the EU dawns relatively slowly on the lay public. When the personal implications of those changes are manifest only years after the formal institutional changes, and when the origins of the changes remain hidden, the identity implications are diffuse and perhaps unrecognized.

THE INFLUENCE OF INSTITUTIONS AND EMBLEMS

The key arguments that have been presented here are as follows:

- It is inadvisable to conflate the identity implications of being European with the identity implications of being a member of the EU.
- National identities differ in their response to the influences exerted by the EU, such that the salience and the stability of the national identity will limit in significant ways the type and rate of change in identity resulting from EU actions.
- The EU has poor definition as a superordinate category and that, without an agreed-on "portrait" for this identity element derived from EU categorization, there will be great diversity in the ways it is characterized by different people in different countries. While we may find that in a few years many people claim to have a EU identity element, it may have as many visages as there are individuals (or at least subcultures) claiming it. The question then becomes: is it a common identity element? It undoubtedly could be a common self-categorization, but that may simply obscure the variety in the substance of its characterization and impact on identity.
- Through its institutions the EU influences identity at the individual and the category levels significantly, if sometimes indirectly, by changing broader societal contexts and norms. If EU institutions gain increasing power they could be the basis for elaborating a consensual "portrait" of the EU identity element. For instance, the European Court of Justice is acting to create a common legal code that has within it basic assumptions about the rights and roles of citizens.
- The changes produced in individual identity are often a result of complex purposive action by the individual that includes manipulation of the representation of the EU. Such manipulation of the representation

of the EU is particularly possible since the objective definition of the EU is actually changing with the assimilation of new member states and acquisition of new powers.

In seeking to analyze the way the EU and its institutions may affect identity development, it is first necessary to choose a model of identity processes that can be used as an analytical framework. The one adopted here is IPT, primarily because it focuses on how identities change and the significance of intergroup and social representational processes in those changes. Using IPT suggests the need to access data at the individual, group, and societal levels. In pursuing such data, it becomes evident very rapidly that the evidential base for analyzing the effects of the EU on identity is very limited. Calling for more empirical studies is a timeworn way to end a chapter; however, on this occasion it seems more than appropriate. The EU is one of the most important forces for societal change at work in the world today. The research that has been done specifically on its role in changing national identity elements or any others aspect of identity is incredibly small in scale, conducted mostly without adequate funding, and lacking in coordination. It would be useful to have a more comprehensive and coherent empirical examination of the impact of EU action on identity structures.

3

European Identity: A Social-Psychological Perspective

Emanuele Castano

We are uniting people, not forming coalitions of states.

—Jean Monnet

The integration of (Western) European countries initiated after World War II was intended to prevent future conflicts by diminishing old rivalries between European nation-states. This process was mainly led by and for elites, and inspired by a neofunctionalist approach (Haas 1958). Central to the integration process was the idea that the citizens of the EU member states would gradually but inevitably shift their loyalties away from their national government toward the European institutions, which were going to provide greater material benefits.

At least until Maastricht, Eurobarometer data confirm that Europeans have seen the European integration process as a good thing (Eurobarometer, June 1990). However, this has not necessarily translated into an abandoning of national loyalties to embrace a common European identity. The hypothesis of a shift of loyalties might have been too ambitious for institutions that were evolving amid numerous and considerable constraints. A more modest expectation would have been the emergence of some form of attachment to these institutions. In this respect, Eurobarometer data suggest that the European institutions have seen a slow but steady increase in their popular support (Citrin and Sides, this volume). It is not clear, however, how far utilitarian motives may go in boosting loyalty. Even in an era that celebrates consumerist and individualistic values, few would maintain that self-identification at the collective level is the consequence solely of perceived material benefit (cf. Risse, 2001).

It was precisely this need for Europeans to start perceiving themselves as *European* that emerged, however, by the mid-1980s. With the signing of the Single European Act of 1985, which eliminated trade barriers between the countries, leading to the creation of a common market, the European Community (renamed the European Union) became increasingly politicized. The European institutions, while remaining unaccountable to a European popular assembly, began producing a growing number of regulations, and the issue of legitimacy was raised (Cassen 1993; Laffan 1996; Lodge 1979; Niedermayer and Sinnott 1995). Indeed, the whole enterprise seems to be generally regarded as an anonymous, faceless institutional body.

The integration process is thus at an impasse. Improving the legitimacy of the EU would require fostering a sense of belonging among the citizens of the national member states. But this is not guaranteed by economic policies alone, however successful they might be. As Delors poetically reminds us, people do not fall in love with a market.

It thus seems that the issue of identity has come to occupy a central space in the debate around the European integration process. It is on this topic, and more precisely on the development of a European identity, that I focus in this chapter. The perspective that I adopt is social psychological, and I thus consider the European identity as a social identity that can be defined as "that part of the individual's self-concept which derives from his knowledge of his membership of a social group (or groups) together with the value and emotional significance attached to that membership" (Tajfel 1981, 255). As pointed out by Herrmann and Brewer (this volume), this means focusing not merely on the recognition of membership in a social group or category, but also on the fact that the group and its defining characteristics have become integral to the person's self-concept. I will concentrate on the subjective aspects of social identification, defined as "the centrality and evaluative importance of group membership in self-definition" (Turner 1987, 55).

After briefly reviewing factors that may boost such a European self-definition, I propose that the classic criterion of cultural homogeneity be reframed within the broader issue of the *psychological existence* of the community. Following the broadening of perspective on the formation of a sense of community allowed by this analytical exercise, I present the results of a series of experiments carried out in the context of the European identity. These experiments revolve around the idea that a critical factor for identification to emerge is the perceived entitativity of the community, and that this can be achieved in many different ways. Subsequently, I discuss some empirical data relative to the relationship between European, national, and regional identity, and comment on the reasons for the emergence of the correlational patterns between them. The chapter ends with a discussion of the mechanisms through which European identity may become a more important component of self-definition in the future, as well as the reasons why this may be so.

THE BASIS OF A EUROPEAN IDENTITY

Traditionally, a certain degree of homogeneity, real or imagined, has been considered necessary for a sense of community to exist and for that sense to foster a notion of common identity (Anderson 1991; Deutsch 1953; Kelman 1969; Howe 1995) (see figure 3.1a). Although political communities exist that claim to be based on purely civic foundations, in the vast majority of cases, cultural or even ethnic homogeneity is considered the basis of a community. To the extent that these political communities are largely the result of processes of social construction led by elites, one might ask whether European institutions should pursue the same methods of construction in seeking to foster the allegiance they need to legitimize themselves.

Few would venture to respond in the affirmative to this question. Indeed, one of the principles inspiring the European integration process was to mitigate the negative consequences that can follow from nurturing *essentialized* collective identities, with their potential for intergroup conflict and social exclusion.[1] Also, and although there is clearly no agreement with respect to the kind of Europe that is to emerge from this ongoing integra-

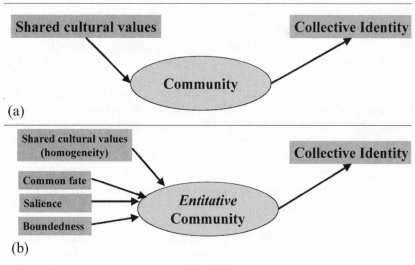

Figure 3.1

tion process, what is augured in the preamble to the Treaty of Rome is a union among the peoples of Europe—not the creation of a European people.

On the one hand, economic integration alone is insufficient to instill a sense of belonging at the European level. On the other hand, there is a strong argument to be made that this sense of belonging cannot be fostered through the formation of a single European cultural identity. Diversity, not homogeneity, is the slogan of European integration.[2]

Consistent with these observations, I contend that cultural homogeneity is not necessary to establish a sense of belonging to a political community. What mediates the impact of cultural homogeneity on the sense of common identity is the extent to which the community acquires a *psychological existence*.

For identification to occur, the new political community needs to establish itself as a possible self-representation at the collective level for its citizens. This is an important distinction. Indeed, if what promotes identification is not cultural homogeneity per se, but the psychological existence of a community, any factor that increases the chances of psychological existence will have an impact on the level of identification.

Is the EU represented as an entity in its citizens' mind? This is not necessarily the case (cf. Breakwell, this volume). To be sure, the EU does not receive the same attention as individual nations in the media.[3] When it does receive attention, it is because of internal disputes between the representatives of its member states, or their inability to reach a common position in the international arena. Such events are more likely to be reported and emphasized, and to draw the attention of the reader/spectator, than news of a successful agreement between European countries or the display of unanimity in an international dispute. The recent case concerning the support of the invasion of Iraq by American and British forces is a case in point. The entitativity of the EU is further undermined in international contexts in which the EU is likely to play a role. In many cases, national governments take direct action circumventing and even contradicting the position of the Union, creating an embarrassing situation in relation not only to other international actors, but to European citizens themselves.

Finally, the lack of clear geographical boundaries also weakens any effort by the EU to be perceived as a real entity. The enlargement of the EU is a key factor in this respect. Looking at Eurobarometer data, Citrin and Sides (this volume) found that a lower percentage of individuals who identified with the "European Union only" were willing to include new members in the EU, as compared to those who identified with both the "European Union and the Nation." This result might appear inconsistent with the spirit of inclusion and diversity that is supposed to characterize European integration. However, it testifies to the importance of a well-bounded image of the in-group, as has been confirmed in experimental research (Castano, Yzerbyt, and Bourguignon 2002; for reviews, Castano 2003b; Yzerbyt, Castano, Leyens, and Paladino, 2000).

In sum, it seems clear that we cannot take for granted that the EU has a psychological existence in its citizens' mind, as seen, for instance, in Meinhof's work (this volume).[4] Is this in any way linked to the supposed weakness of European identification? A first answer to this question may come from research showing that the psychological existence of and identification with the EU are related, and possibly that the former moderates the latter. In the next section, the concept of entitativity is introduced, and research investigating the causal link between the entitativity of a community and identification with it is presented.

The Need for Reification of the EU[5]

In an influential paper, social psychologist Donald Campbell (1958) coined the term "entitativity" to refer to the extent to which a group is perceived as having real existence. Building on Gestalt psychology principles, he speculated that what turns a mere aggregate of individuals into a social group is the perceived entitativity of the ensemble. Four factors are suggested as antecedents of entitativity: common fate, similarity, proximity, and boundedness. The more individuals in the group perceive themselves to share a common fate, to be similar, to be close, and to form a bounded unit, the more they will perceive the group as being a real entity.

A recently renewed interest on the concept of entitativity has proven useful in better understanding and organizing social psychological phenomena such as impression formation, stereotyping, and intergroup relations (for reviews, see Abelson et al. 1998; Brewer and Harasty 1996; Castano 2003b; Hamilton and Sherman 1996; Yzerbyt et al. 2000).

The concept of entitativity is also beneficial to understanding the issue of collective identity formation. Specifically, in acknowledging the mediating role of perceived entitativity in the relationship between (cultural) homogeneity and identification, the possibility that other factors can also influence identification presents itself. As seen above, these factors include: common fate, salience, and boundedness (see figure 3.1b).

My colleagues and I investigated this question in a project that built on Campbell's insights (Castano, Yzerbyt, and Bourguignon, 2003). We hypothesized that increasing the entitativity of the EU would lead to an increase in the extent to which European citizens identify with it. Along the same lines, we expected that decreasing the entitativity of the EU would diminish the level of identification.

We therefore carried out a series of experimental studies in which we manipulated perceptions of common fate and similarity between the members of the EU, as well as the extent to which the EU was at the forefront of individuals' minds and was perceived as a bounded entity. Specifically, each of four studies manipulated one of these dimensions of entitativity. Additionally, we wanted to test the hypothesis that the impact of the manipulation of entitativity would be confined to those individuals holding moderate attitudes toward the EU. This hypothesis, grounded in social psychological research on attitudes (Sherif and Hovland 1961), can be easily understood if we think about Euro-skeptics and Euro-enthusiasts.[6] The former are likely to oppose the European integration process mainly because they believe that Europeans have little in common, and that the differences in language, culture, habits, and so forth are obstacles to integration on the one hand, and something that should be preserved on the other. These individuals are likely to believe that were the EU successful in boosting a sense of European identity, national idiosyncrasies would be overwhelmed.

Euro-enthusiasts are likely to show a very different pattern. Although aware of the diversity that characterizes the EU, these people are more likely to think of European integration as an important enterprise. In short, for the skeptics, the EU does not, and, even more importantly, should not, exist. The enthusiasts feel that the EU does in fact exist, and they are happy that this is the case.

If we go back to the hypothesis that increasing the entitativity of the EU would lead to an increase in identification, it seems reasonable to assume that both of these groups (i.e., Euro-skeptics and Euro-enthusiasts) would not, respectively, increase or decrease their identification with the EU following the presentation of the EU as more or less entitative. Their views of the EU are not easily modified. In contrast, individuals who hold moderate attitudes toward the EU should be more influenced by such a presentation.[7]

In all four studies, attitudes about the EU were measured by means of a list of traits from which participants selected those that best described their feelings when thinking of the EU, and also by means of a single item directly addressing their overall attitude toward the EU (for versus against, on a seven-point scale). A composite attitude score was computed, and participants were categorized into three groups (negative, moderate, positive). As explained above, the categorization into attitude groups was expected to moderate the impact of our manipulations on the dependent variable, that is, identification.

The level of identification with the EU was measured with a six-item identification scale (e.g., "I identify with other European Citizens," "It is important for me to be a citizen of the European Union," "Being a citizen of the European Union is not part of my identity"). Of the four experiments, two included pre- and postmanipulation measures of identification (the identification scale was split into two subscales), while the remaining two included only postmanipulation measures (i.e., the six-item scale was presented at once after the manipulation). Because the participants in all of the studies presented here were Belgian undergraduate students, some comments concerning the generalizability of the findings are necessary.

The generally held view within the social psychological community is that the external validity of research findings depends on the question the research attempts to answer, and on the understanding that an observed pattern may be the result of certain characteristics of the manipulation interacting with certain characteristics of the participant (Sears 1986). It would be a mistake to look at the average level of identification with the EU among undergraduate students and draw conclusions about the magnitude of identification of the European population, even if one collected a representative sample of students across EU member states. When investigating basic psychological processes, however, it seems reasonable to assume similarity between undergraduates and the rest of the population. The specific content of the factors that are manipulated may require adjustment when moving from one population to another, notably because of the different types of knowledge that the populations may have. Nonetheless, conceptual replications of these experiments with nonstudent populations are expected to provide the same pattern of results, and research suggests that they indeed do (Locke 1986). As elucidated by Brewer (2000a) "The quest for external validity is essentially a search for moderators that limit or qualify the cause-effect relationship under investigation" (12). Because of the restricted age range found among undergraduates and because we know that age is negatively correlated with support for the EU, in this context, age is a possible moderator. This, however, should impact the results only in the form of a main effect: older participants in this kind of experiment may have a less positive attitude toward and weaker identification with the EU overall, but the effect of the manipulation should remain the same.[8]

Within the social sciences, the point of equilibrium between causal inference and one's ability to generalize a conclusion varies among disciplines. Social psychologists mostly investigate microprocesses and are interested in making confident conclusions about the direction of causality between the variables under scrutiny. As a social psychologist, I am aware of the limitation of this demarche, but I believe that it is an important and necessary level of analysis.[9] It is with this in mind that my colleagues and I decided to conduct laboratory experiments to test a hypothesis that we believed had some relevance to the understanding of an important, evolving social phenomenon. Below is a summary of the findings emerging from these experiments.

ENTITATIVITY AND IDENTIFICATION: EXPERIMENTAL EVIDENCE

In a first study, participants' attitudes toward and identification with the EU (three of the six items) were measured, and they were presented with a video stressing the common fate of European countries. Identification was then measured again using three different items of the identification scale. The items comprising the two identification subscales were averaged separately to form two scores. The dependent variable was the difference between the pre- and postmanipulation identification score. Results showed that watching the video had a strong impact on the level of identification with the EU, leading moderate individuals in particular to increase their level of identification (Castano, Yzerbyt, and Bourguignon, 2003).

A second study investigated the impact of perceived similarity among the countries comprising the EU. As in the first study, participants' attitudes toward and identification with the EU were measured before they were presented with the experimental manipulation. This consisted of a table showing several characteristics of the political system of the fifteen EU countries. The table, which summarized real characteristics like type of regime (monarchy, parliamentary republic, presidential republic, etc.), was exactly the same for all participants. However, while the high entitativity participants were instructed to concentrate on the similarities between the EU countries, the low entitativity participants were instructed to concentrate on the differences.[10] All participants learned that they would have to write a paragraph expressing their conclusions. It was stressed that the paragraph should be easily understood by an uninformed reader. The task was included to ensure that the participants would process the information in line with the specific instructions. As a result, they should have also constructed an entitative or a nonentitative image of the EU. Finally, identification was measured using the three remaining items of the identification scale. As in the first study, the dependent variable was the difference between the pre- and postmanipulation identification scores.

Again, the results confirmed our expectations, showing a strong impact of the manipulation only among moderate attitude participants (Castano, Yzerbyt, and Bourguignon, 2003). These participants decreased their level of identification in the "difference" condition. Means also showed a pattern consistent with the expected increase in the level of identification in the "similarity" condition among the neutral attitude group—although this decrease did not reach a conventional level of statistical significance.

Two further studies were conducted to test the effect of two additional factors on the level of identification—namely the *salience* of the EU and its *boundedness.* In both experiments (Castano, Yzerbyt, and Bourguignon, 2003), only participants' attitudes toward the EU were measured prior to the manipulation (for practical reasons no premanipulation identification measure was collected; participants responded to the six-item identification scale after the manipulation, and comparisons were made across conditions). In the third study, category salience was manipulated. Participants were asked to participate in a survey allegedly conducted by the Department of Political Science at the University of Montreal, Canada, *or* by the political science department at the participants' own university—of course, the alleged survey was identical in the two conditions. The EU was expected to be more salient in participants' minds in the former than in the latter (control) condition. Indeed, under such conditions, an intergroup context of comparison (Europe vs. Canada) is activated, as opposed to an intragroup context of comparison (cf. Castano and Yzerbyt 1998; Haslam et al. 1995; Turner et al. 1987; Wilder 1984). A measure of identification with the EU was then collected using the complete, six-item identification scale.

Findings supported the hypothesis by showing that in the condition in which the EU was expected to be in the foreground of participants' minds, higher levels of identification with the EU were observed. As with the previous studies, this result was limited to participants holding moderate attitudes toward the EU (results are shown in figure 3.2).

A final study tested whether the extent to which the EU is perceived as a well-bounded entity impacts on identification with it (Castano, Yzerbyt, and Bourguignon, 2003). To manipulate the perceived boundedness of the EU as a geographical entity, in the fourth study we used a straightforward procedure in which we reconfigured its physical borders. In this manipulation, the eastern borders were adjusted, making the manipulation not only credible but timely, given the important debate about the enlargement of the EU taking place when these data were collected (1997).

After their attitudes toward the EU were measured, participants were presented with a brief article, allegedly reprinted from a daily newspaper, in which the issue of enlargement was discussed. The bogus article—which had been written purposely for this experiment—was entitled "The European Union Finds Its Borders" or "The European Union Searches for Its

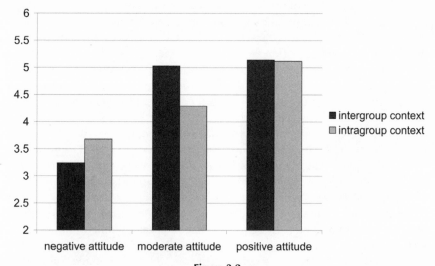

Figure 3.2

Borders" in the high and low entitativity conditions, respectively. The texts either described the eastern borders of the EU as clearly defined or identified a different scenario, in which these borders varied. A map consistent with the description was also presented. As in the third study, identification with the EU was then measured.

As expected, participants in the low entitativity condition displayed lower levels of identification than participants in the high entitativity condition. Again, this was the case exclusively for participants holding moderate attitudes. Interestingly, presenting the EU as having fuzzy borders had a dramatic enough impact to reduce these participants' level of identification to that of participants holding negative attitudes toward the EU (see figure 3.3). Not surprisingly, figures 3.2 and 3.3 also show a linear trend between attitudes and identification: the more positive the attitudes toward the EU, the higher the level of identification with it.

The empirical evidence presented in this section came from a series of experiments, a method that has its advantages and disadvantages. The obvious advantage of experimentation is the degree of control that can be exerted. When all variables but those one is manipulating are kept constant, one can be confident that the effects that emerge are due to the manipulation. The obvious downside to this method is that social reality may not be entirely captured by questionnaires answered in a psychology department laboratory. Confidence in the causal relationship between two variables may come at the cost of the representativeness of the sample available, which may reduce one's ability to generalize the findings, as discussed above.

A radically different approach to experimentation is taken, in this vol-

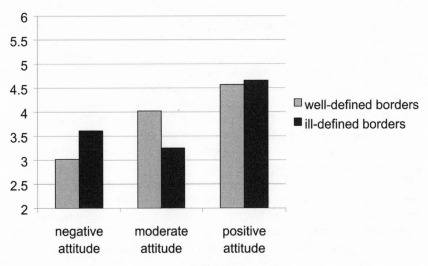

Figure 3.3

ume, by Ulrike Meinhof, who uses in-depth field interviews to explore identity dynamics. In this context, the researcher lacks control over the situation, and her task is to make sense of what is said by the participant. However, the situation is closer to everyday reality, in which in-groups and out-groups are implied in the respondents' comments, and respondents themselves are positioned within these groups sometimes contradictorily. The pros and cons of the two methods suggest that they are equally useful and, indeed, necessary for understanding social reality, and that they should be used in combination.

EUROPEAN IDENTITY AND NATIONAL IDENTITIES: RIVALS?

In the previous section I argued that, for European citizens to feel European, a critical factor is the extent to which the EU is perceived as having a real existence. I reviewed empirical evidence showing that increasing the entitativity of the EU leads to an increase in its citizens' level of identification with it, and that decreasing entitativity has the opposite effect.

By providing insights into the mechanisms that boost or lessen identification with a political community, these findings also raise the issue of "social engineering." This issue is particularly relevant to the construction of a European identity. Indeed, in the same treaty that establishes European citizenship, article F says: "The Union shall respect the national identities of its Member States, whose systems of government are founded on the principles of democracy" (Treaty on European Union, 1992, article F). As has been noted, the rise of a European identity is perceived as a threat to national identity in some member states (cf. Brittan 1996; Delgado-Moreira 1997). Are European identity and national identities in a zero-sum game?

To determine whether the development of European identity occurs at the expense of national identities, one approach would be to observe people's level of identification with the EU and their native countries. If these two competed, high levels of European identity would go hand in hand with low levels of national identity, and vice versa. Interestingly, the data collected among Polish and Dutch citizens by Mlicki and Ellemers (1996) seem to suggest that the two identities do not compete with each other. Indeed, high levels of both European and national identification were observed among Polish participants. Dutch participants, by contrast, showed lower levels of both European and national identification. Although indicative of the link between the two identities, these kinds of data do not allow us to draw strong conclusions. Indeed, the high scores displayed by the Poles (and for that matter the low scores displayed by the Dutch) might be the consequence of a different response style. They do not tell us whether the two levels of identity covary or not.

A second source of information comes from correlational analyses. Chryssochoou (1998) observes a significant, though weak, positive correlation between national and European identity. Another study finds positive correlations between European, national, and regional identities among Andalucians but no correlations between any of these identities among Scottish students (Huici et al. 1997). Cinnirella (1997) observes a negative correlation between the national and the European identity of British participants, but a positive correlation between these two identities in an Italian sample. Finally, using a similar methodology Bruter (this volume) finds the same pattern of correlations.

With the United Kingdom data excepted, it thus seems that European and national identity go hand in hand.[11] In other words, the more people identify with their nation, the more they feel European. Although these correlations tend to be weak, they are noteworthy: they contradict the idea that the two identities are incompatible with one another. Analyses of Eurobarometers (Citrin and Sides, this volume; Duchesne and Frognier 1995; Marks 1999) lead to the same conclusion.

The relationship between European identity and national and regional identities was at the core of empirical work my colleagues and I carried out in Belgium and Italy (Castano, Yzerbyt, and Tousignant 2000). The studies we conducted aimed to complement previous findings using the same identification measure employed by Castano, Yzerbyt, and Bourguignon (2003). These studies expanded on previous work by looking at two additional variables. Firstly, given the link between homogeneity and entitativity, we wanted to verify that identification with the EU actually goes hand in hand with the perception of the homogeneity of the EU. Second, we wanted to investigate whether those individuals who more strongly identified with the EU also attributed more decisional power to the EU than those who identified with it weakly. Participants were therefore asked to attribute decisional power to the EU, their nation, and their region on seven different topics. Finally, by measuring the perception of the homogeneity of, and the allocation of decisional power to, the EU, the nation, and the region, we wanted to provide convergent evidence for the hypothesis that these three levels of identification do not compete with one another.

Our results convey a straightforward message. They replicate previous findings showing that different levels of identification tend to be positively, rather than negatively, associated (see table 3.1). They also show that to strongly identify with one level does not have a negative impact on the perception of meaningfulness of the entities at the other levels, nor on the allocation of power to these entities (see table 3.2) (cf. Citrin and Sides, this volume).

A possible explanation of the positive correlations between identities at different levels of inclusiveness can be found in Inglehart's concept of *cog-*

Table 3.1. Correlations between different levels of identification as a function of participants' nationality.

		Identification	
	European	national	regional
Belgian sample			
European	—		
national	.22*	—	
regional	.10	.37*	—
Italian sample			
European	—		
national	.19*	—	
regional	−.01	.22*	—

* $p < .005$.
Source: Castano et al. 2000.
Note: Data are presented separately for the two national samples.

Table 3.2. Perception of homogeneity of and power allocation to the EU, the nation, and the region as a function of the level of identification with the EU, the nation, and the region.

		Perception of Homogeneity			Power allocation		
		EU	nation	region	EU	nation	region
	Identification						
Belgian Sample	European	.28**	.04	.03	.20**	−.09	−.05
	national	−.13	.23*	.12	.00	.29**	.03
	regional	.11	.10	.51**	.007	.11	.23*
Italian Sample	European	.34**	.17**	−.03	.21*	.08	.05
	national	−.01	.28**	.08	.07	.26**	.02
	regional	−.02	−.06	.37**	−.20**	−.13*	.35**

** $p < .01$; * $p < .05$
Source: Castano et al. 2000.
Note: Data are presented separately for the two national samples.

nitive mobilization (1990). Inglehart suggests that what is at stake is the individual's ability to commit to a remote political community. Although people probably develop a commitment toward a specific community in concrete terms, it is reasonable to assume that once they have established this commitment, they may be ready to commit to other political communities as well (provided that no specific conflict exists between the two; cf. Cinnirella 1997).

However, this interpretation holds that identities should all be positively correlated, whereas our data show that only adjacent identifications are correlated (see also Bruter, this volume). This might reflect the fact that the organization of these identities is hierarchical—a hypothesis that contradicts the idea of a Europe of regions, in which strong regional attachment goes hand in hand with strong Europeanism, thus bypassing the national level. The investigation of cases in which regional identities have a "national" flower, for instance the Flanders and the Basque countries, would contribute very much to our understanding of this intriguing point.

CONCLUSION

In this chapter, I have attempted to add a social psychological perspective to an understanding of the construction of a possible European identity.[12] Specifically, I have argued that for identification with the EU to occur, the EU must be perceived as a real entity. To support this argument I provided empirical evidence stemming from experimental work. This work built on the concept of entitativity, thought of as the extent to which the group, in this case the EU, has psychological existence for individuals. Consistent with theorizing in social psychology (Campbell 1958), the experimental work manipulated four different factors that are considered antecedents of entitativity, and the results conveyed a consistent message: increasing the entitativity of the EU led to an increase of identification with it, and decreasing entitativity led to a decrease in identification (Castano, Yzerbyt, and Bourguignon, 2003). As expected, the impact of the manipulations of entitativity was observed among individuals holding moderate attitudes toward the EU but not among Euro-skeptics or Euro-enthusiasts. The pattern of result thus supports the conjecture that psychological existence and identification are related, and that an increase in the former may indeed lead to an increase in the latter. In light of these experimental results, the hypothesis that the lack of a psychological existence for the EU in the minds of Europeans may be one of the factors responsible for their weak level of identification with it seems even more plausible. What about the future?

With the ongoing changes in the international arena, there is, in my opinion, room for optimism with respect to the possibility of the EU acquiring a psychological existence in Europeans' minds. Indeed, the EU is already behaving as an actor and is recognized as such by other actors (the United States, China, Russia, Japan, etc.). This kind of recognition took place, for the first time, at the level of the United Nations with Resolution 713 on Yugoslavia, in which the European Community was acknowledged as an actor independent from European nation-states (United Nations, Security Council resolution, 1991).

The importance of international contexts in fostering the identity of the EU is not restricted to political ones. As Damro (2001) has recently noted in his analysis of the Boeing–McDonnell Douglas merger case, when the

EU's interests are exercised against a non-EU third party, the EU enjoys a greater opportunity to build an international identity.

Needless to say, changes *within* the EU also impact the perception of it as a real entity. A recent example can be found in the European Court of Justice, which ruled that it was unlawful for EU member states to refuse to refund their citizens for medical treatments received in another state of the EU, unless the states could offer the same or equally effective treatments without undue delay (*Economist,* September 1, 2001). Similarly, Italians working in Britain and France as foreign-language lecturers won support from the governments of these two countries in their fight against Italian universities (and the government) to obtain treatment equal to other Italian lecturers working in Italian universities (*Guardian,* March 7, 2000). The freshly drafted European constitution will certainly contribute to enhancing the psychological existence of the EU, as it has the introduction of the euro (Tousignant and Castano 2001). All of this suggests that, although the process is characterized by a slow pace and high degree of complexity, and is certainly not linear, the EU is an increasingly salient concept. The myriad actions carried out daily by the European institutions are reinforcing its status as an actor in both the extra- and intra-EU panorama. The EU is thus reifying itself, and this will increase the likelihood that its citizens identify with it.[13]

Why Is an Entitative EU More Attractive for Its Citizens?

I have proposed elsewhere that entitative in-groups are likely to be more attractive to their members because of two functions that entitativity serves. I have called these "terrestrial" and "celestial" functions (Castano 2003b). The former refers to the fact that entitative in-groups are perceived as having a capacity for action, as possessing intentionality, and as providing security to their members. As the nation-state provides a progressively less fitting framework for understanding and action in the modern world, it is likely that the "terrestrial" value of the EU will increase.

The "celestial" value of in-group entitativity refers to the satisfaction of symbolic needs, such as the need for a sense of transcendence (Kelman 1969; see also the idea of "correct death" in Berger and Luckmann 1967; Castano, Yzerbyt, and Paladino, in press). For this function to be satisfied, it may not be enough for the group to be perceived as having a real existence *hic et nunc*; its existence may need to be traced back to a very distant past. This is clearly the force of *ethnic* identities and more broadly of national identities (Sindic, Castano, and Reicher 2001). Groups that allow individuals to project themselves beyond their mortal existence in space and time are suited—in fact well suited—to serve as shields against existential concerns (Castano, Yzerbyt, Paladino, and Sacchi 2002).

The terrestrial and celestial functions are, however, strictly intertwined. The early strategies that inspired the European integration processes were allegedly based on a specific form of "terrestrial" value, namely economic benefit. But it soon became clear that people would not participate in such an arid conception of community, and that economic benefits needed to be defined within a system of values. In the last decades, the values that inspire the process of European integration have become increasingly clear. Also, in communication efforts aimed at EU citizens, the European institutions are putting these values forward, rather than focusing exclusively on the material benefits that allegedly follow from membership in the EU. As these values are socially of liberal inspiration, but economically conservative (pro–free market and inspired by a capitalistic model), the EU has become the target of critiques by both nationalist movements and the political left, though for very different reasons.[14] However, it is likely that a shared understanding of a possible European identity will emerge from this debate, thus making the EU a meaningful self-categorization for its citizens. If this occurs, this European identity may serve "celestial" functions, without being grounded in a shared ethno-cultural history (cf. Castano 2003; Castano and Tousignant 1999; Sindic, Castano, and Reicher 2001; Weiler, Haltern, and Mayer 1995).

Promoting Complexity in Identity Representation

The main argument that I put forward in this chapter relates to the perception of the EU as a real entity. Specifically, my contention is that for a sense of European identity to develop, the EU must acquire a psychological existence in the minds of its citizens. This might appear at odds with what is proposed by Mummendey and Waldzus (this volume). Mummendey and Waldzus's rationale is based on the in-group projection model (Mummendey and Wenzel, 1999), according to which, when two or more groups are unified into a common supraordinate category, members of each group tend to project onto this category the in-group prototype. The consequence is that out-groups that are also included in the supraordinate, common categorization are even more likely to be discriminated against, since they do not embody what is perceived to be the normative standard of the supraordinate common categorization.[15] Applying this to the EU, Mummendey and Waldzus predict greater discrimination of, say, Germans toward French, because the former feel somewhat justified to apply what they see as the "European" standard (actually, the projected German prototype) to their French counterparts. In the same way, French would characterize the EU using a French prototype, and thus see their complaints about Germans as equally legitimate. To circumvent this problem, Mummendey and Waldzus suggest, the prototype of the EU should be kept vague. This would prevent members of nation-states from projecting their prototype onto the EU and thus setting a standard that nationals of other member states cannot, by definition, live up to.

Although I certainly agree that the projection of the national onto the supranational identity is problematic, I disagree with the authors' suggestion that the representation of the EU be kept vague. Rather, it seems reasonable to suggest that what is needed to prevent national projection is a clearer, well-defined prototype, rather than a vague one, which would beg to be filled with the in-group prototype. More importantly, a vague supraordinate category may prevent any identification from the outset.

Two further clarifications are needed with respect to a comparison between my claim and that of Mummendey and Waldzus. First, making the EU more entitative fosters identification with the EU (as my colleagues and I have shown), but may have the downside of increasing derogation of other EU national groups (something that one might expect on the basis of Mummendey and Waldzus's model). This might signify that what has been achieved is greater trust among member states in the supraordinate institutions, but not amelioration of the relations between the subgroups. However, I would suggest that the this scenario is less problematic than it might initially appear. In fact, allegiance and closed ranks within the subgroups of a superordinate entity (be they member states of the EU, or Landers of Germany, or national groups in the United Kingdom and Spain) are to be expected in an intergroup context. The challenge for the EU is not so much for the member states agree in all contexts (or that they agree to disagree), but rather for them to be able to close ranks when acting as *Europeans*.

Second, as the studies I have presented clearly demonstrate, entitativity is not another name for homogeneity, and can, in fact, be fostered by factors other than homogeneity. Also, homogeneity does not necessarily follow from entitativity. To say that only an entitative EU will promote identification, and will thus be legitimate, does not imply that Europeans need to be alike. Rather, entitativity may well go hand in hand with internal organization, which presupposes differentiation (cf. Hamilton, Sherman, and Lickel 1998). An entitative EU is a well-integrated one, not necessarily a homogeneous one. In this sense, therefore, my claim is not inconsistent with the other suggestion from Mummendey and Waldzus, that the prototype of the EU should remain *complex* to help avoid national in-group projection.

In concluding this chapter, I have attempted to lay out the rationale for my argument that for Europeans to feel European, the EU needs to acquire a psychological existence in its citizens' minds. I surveyed some of the possibilities and risks of this reification process in the context of an emergence of beliefs in a European essence. I have not said, however, what this reification might be based on. In other words, I have not suggested a set of core values for this European identity. What the European identity is, may be, or should be goes well beyond the scope of this contribution, and has been debated by scholars (e.g., J.H.H. Weiler 1997) and policy makers (e.g., Prodi 2003) whose background and expertise place them in a much better position than mine to speculate. No matter what specific form the European identity will take, however, the presence of multiple *demoi* should not be perceived as a disadvantage, but as a unique opportunity for generating a new blueprint for common living.

NOTES

I would like to thank Marilynn Brewer, Claudio Fogu, Richard Herrmann, Steve Reicher, Nathalie Tousignant, and Vincent Yzerbyt, who contributed to the shaping of the thoughts expressed here. I would also like to thank the participants of the meetings held at the Mershon Center and the European University Institute for their insightful comments on earlier drafts of this chapter, and Mary Hoeveler for editing suggestions.

1. Reflections on the concept of essentialism have recently been imported into social psychology from philosophy and developmental psychology. Rothbart and Taylor (1992) have proposed that people tend to (erroneously) attribute the status of "natural-kind" to social categories, which are, actually, artifacts. Yzerbyt, Rocher, and Schadron (1997) have applied these ideas to the study of stereotyping, and have suggested that the essentialization of social groups—that is, the attribution to them of an "essence" that is considered the underlying cause of surface similarity among group members—is part of a process of meaning making, but is likely to have negative consequences for intergroup relations, since the Other is perceived as possessing certain stable characteristics. The Other is thus *inherently* bad.

2. Note, however, that there have been attempts to appeal to a European "soul." Greek and Latin heritage, Christianity, and the Enlightenment have all been presented as European products, in a kind of repackaging of the raw material that was used to construct the European nation-state (cf. Duroselle 1990; Shore 1996). At the website europa.eu.int, one finds links to "Symbols" and "The History of the European Union." Despite its change in name, the European Union is clearly trying to establish a sense of community. This approach reflects the persuasion model (see Herrmann and Brewer, this volume).

3. Keeping a category constantly salient in people's minds might contribute to reifying it (cf. Billig 1995).

4. It should be noted, however, that conclusions about the extent to which categories are salient in people's minds should be viewed cautiously. Indeed, contextual effects are known to play a very important role. For instance, Rutland and Cinnirella (2000) recently found that European identity among Scottish participants decreased significantly when Germans and English were in the frame of reference. Similarly, the salience of West versus East German and German versus Polish distinctions may account for the lack of salience of the supraordinate, European category in Meinhof's data.

5. By "reification," I mean the perception, by European citizens, of the existence of the European Union as an entity. This concept is not to be confused with that of

"essence," discussed above. For instance, a basketball or soccer team is usually very entitative, but is generally not seen as possessing an underlying essence.

6. In this context, "Euro" does not refer to the currency but rather to the European integration process as a whole.

7. Note that although this somewhat limits our predictions to a part of the population, it is reasonable to assume that this part represents the vast majority of European citizens.

8. The same critique and the same answer can be extended to the generalizing of findings using a single-nationality sample, that is, Belgians.

9. New technologies are likely to help bridge the gap between these two needs, notably by allowing the incorporation of experiments into surveys (Piazza and Sniderman 1998).

10. It is worth noting that this manipulation supports the idea that what is important is not what the reality is, but the way in which people perceive and construct it. The role of politicians and the media in the construction of social categories is thus of critical importance (cf. Reicher and Hopkins 2001).

11. That the UK data does not fit the general pattern comes as no surprise, given the specificity of the UK context. In the UK, the European integration project has always been regarded with skepticism, and has been strongly associated in the media and by politicians, especially conservative ones, with the loss of national identity.

12. Other social psychological analyses of the process of European integration can be found in Breakwell and Lyons (1996) and Hewstone (1986).

13. To the extent that most of these actions are not a deliberate attempt by these institutions to promote the EU, their effects can be understood within the framework of a socialization model (Herrmann and Brewer, this volume).

14. At another level, the philosophy inspiring the EU is also challengeable from a communitarian perspective (cf. Sandel 1998).

15. As a measure of in-group projection, evidence for this model has been found using the difference between in-group and out-group characteristics that are judged as characterizing the supraordinate category. This is, in my opinion, somewhat problematic when used to predict out-group discrimination. In fact, the link between in-group projection and out-group discrimination might be due to the insignificant levels of projection of a disliked out-group's characteristics onto the supraordinate category. This critique finds support in the fact that intergroup attitudes correlate more strongly with out-group typicality than with in-group typicality (Waldzus, personal communication).

4

National Differences
and European Plurality:
Discrimination or Tolerance
between European Countries

Amélie Mummendey and Sven Waldzus

From a social psychological perspective, the currently valid concept of a "Europe of the fatherlands" can be conceptualized as a "subgroups within one group" representation: Europeans can conceive of different groups (nations) as distinct units within the context of a superordinate identity (Europe), which results in a dual identity. The current chapter focuses on the consequences of this dual identity for intergroup relations within Europe. We discuss two different models. Following the Common Ingroup Identification Model, fostering a common European identity is expected to improve the relations between the different European countries and their citizens. In contrast, the Ingroup Projection Model suggests the modified effects of a dual identity on the relations between European subgroups. This model assumes that the prototype of the inclusive category constitutes the norm against which subgroups are compared. The group that is relatively more prototypical for the inclusive self-category will be evaluated more positively. Additionally, members of social groups project their ingroup's attributes onto the inclusive category, and, thus, they tend to perceive their own group's attributes as being relatively prototypical (in-group projection). Consequently, members of different groups disagree on the valid representation of their inclusive category. Following these lines of thinking, the effects of a common identity on attitudes toward out-groups are expected to be moderated by the amount of in-group projection. Strengthening identification as a European might create counterproductive effects; it might fail to improve the relations between citizens of different European countries. The Ingroup Projection Model suggests that more complex and differentiated political efforts and programs will be necessary to create European plurality with mutual acceptance between member groups.

NATIONAL DIFFERENCES AND EUROPEAN PLURALITY: DISCRIMINATION OR TOLERANCE BETWEEN EUROPEAN COUNTRIES

European Identity as Dual Identity

The currently prevailing concept of a "Europe of the fatherlands" signifies a particular relation between groups on the national level on the one hand and their relations to Europe as an all-including superordinate category on the other hand. From a broader social psychological perspective one can say that Europe provides a kind of "dual identity" for its citizens. The individual nationalities within Europe form *subgroups within one group*. Both the subgroup level of nations and the superordinate level of Europe provide several possibilities to identify oneself with the respective social category. There is social identity on the national level, for instance as a *German* or *Italian* European, and there is social identity on the inclusive level, that is as a German or Italian *European*. One characteristic of the European integration process is the explicit expectation—or even desire—that the subgroup level of national identity will remain intact even as the higher-order identity of a European citizen becomes more and more important. Moreover, the structure of "different subgroups within Europe," and together with this structure a "dual identification" on the European level and on a subgroup level, become salient especially when issues of the EU extension to Eastern European countries is discussed. Following this line, in his widely discussed speech in May 2000 at the Humboldt-University of Berlin, Joschka Fischer, the German Minister of Foreign Affairs, started thinking aloud about an institutional distinction between a kernel part of the European Union (a "gravitational center") leading the way to a European federation and a broader set of EU members that are already included but more loosely connected to other EU members. Here again we face the blueprint of subcategories within an inclusive Europe.

In the current chapter, we question the possible—desirable or undesirable—*consequences* of such a dual identification for the relationships between the citizens of different European countries. We approach this question from a broader social psychological perspective, omitting all particular cultural, historical, institutional, or otherwise specific contextual conditions of identity building or change, which are discussed in several other chapters of this volume (e.g., Citrin and Sides; Laffan; Siapera; Wodak). Another particular characteristic of the current chapter is that the theoretical models we will discuss are not theories about Europe in particular but rather general models about intergroup behavior that are not restricted to any particular intergroup context. We talk about intergroup behavior whenever "individuals belonging to one group interact, collectively or individually, with another group or its members *in terms of their group identification*" (Sherif 1966, 12). From a cultural or historical point of view such a level of generalization may seem to be rather unfamiliar, but it is one advantage of social psychology that it examines general psychological principles that can explain part of the dynamics in a very broad range of intergroup situations. The development of Europe, with the rich and complicated relations between the European nations, fits well the overall characteristics of a dynamic intergroup situation, which is described and explained by our social psychological models (cf. Breakwell; Castano, this volume). Thus, models of intergroup relations may be applied to the case of Europe, and, actually, part of the empirical evidence presented here was collected in the European context.

What are the social psychological consequences for the relations between the different European subgroups, if Europe is represented as different "subgroups within one group" and associated with dual identification (i.e., with Europe and with the nation)? The answer is not a simple "good" or "bad." On the one hand, recent theoretical and empirical developments in the social psychology of intergroup relations seem to support a rather optimistic view on the impact of dual identification on intergroup discrimination. On the other hand, based on a new theoretical approach and on recent empirical data, which were gathered during the last years, we are wary of accepting those optimistic conclusions. Intergroup attitudes between citizens of different European countries may suffer from unwanted side effects of an upcoming identification with Europe. In this chapter it will be shown what additional conditions we think are necessary to foster a European identity that increases tolerance rather than discrimination or hostility between different European nationalities or other subgroups of Europeans.

DUAL IDENTITY AND THE COMMON INGROUP IDENTITY MODEL

One theoretical approach that makes a clear prediction for the effects of dual identification is the Common Ingroup Identification Model (Gaertner et al. 1993), which is based on research on in-group favoritism and in particular on Social Identity Theory (Tajfel and Turner 1979; Tajfel and Turner 1986). One important finding of intergroup research is that in intergroup situations people usually favor members of their in-group over members of a distinctive out-group (for reviews see Brewer and Kramer 1985; Brewer and Brown 1998; Messick and Mackie 1989). This intergroup bias often takes the form of in-group enhancement rather than out-group devaluation. Social Identity Theory assumes that members of social groups that are highly identified with their in-group tend to see the in-group in a positive way. Looking for possibilities to improve intergroup relations, Gaertner et al. (1993) tried to make use of that in-group enhancement to reduce intergroup discrimination and conflict. They introduced a common superordinate in-group that includes both in-group and out-group on a higher level. Accordingly, this model may be applied to a conception of Europe that fits the nested design or Russian doll metaphor discussed in the introductory and the concluding chapters of this volume (see Herrmann and Brewer; Risse). Nations are perceived to be subgroups of the superordinate category of Europe. In their Common Ingroup Identity Model Gaertner et al. assume that "if members of different groups are induced to conceive themselves within single groups rather than within completely separate groups, attitudes toward former outgroup members become more positive through processes involving pro-ingroup bias" (Gaertner et al. 1999, 182). Through a process called recategorization, sublevel out-group members become higher-level in-group members and, consequently, are seen more positive. Empirically, Gaertner et al. showed in several studies that the development of a common in-group identity makes in-group members more likely to reduce in-group favoritism on the subordinate intergroup level, to have more positive thoughts and feelings, and to engage in more positive behaviors towards members of out-groups sharing the superordinate identity, i.e., the in-group on the superordinate level (e.g., Gaertner et al. 1990; Gaertner et al. 1989; Gaertner et al. 1994). These results lead us to expect that fostering a common European identity will improve the relations between the different European countries and their citizens.

Following Gaertner et al. (1999), this positive effect of a higher-order identity should hold even if the subgroup identities remain salient. The assumption that subgroup identification does not impede the positive impact of common in-group identification is important because it warrants the applicability of the Common Ingroup Identity Model in contexts like the European integration, in which the sublevel identification is likely to be complemented rather than replaced by a higher-level European identity. For Europe as a common in-group, this model would therefore predict that a dual identification as European and as citizen of a particular home country would improve intergroup relations between members of different European nations.

The empirical evidence for this dual-identification hypothesis of the Common Ingroup Identity Model is, however, rather mixed. There are some studies that support the hypothesis, for instance a study in a multiethnic high school in which interethnic affective reactions were improved by dual identification, that is, by identification with the high school as a common in-group and with the students' own ethnic groups (Gaertner et al. 1994). Data from Eurobarometer also seem to support this hypothesis (see Citrin and Sides, this volume). They show that dual-identified Europeans are more tolerant toward non-Europeans and more likely to accept immigrants and new member states in the EU. There are, however, studies that fail to support the hypothesis (Banker and Gaertner 1998) or that even provide evidence that dual identification has a negative impact on the attitude toward the out-group. In a bank-merger study (Bachman 1993; see Gaertner et al. 1999), for instance, the degree to which the representation of the merged organization mirrored "two groups within one group"—which corresponds to dual identification—was positively correlated with work-related intergroup bias (i.e., in-group favoritism). The degree of the representation as one common in-group without any further salience of subgroup distinctions, in contrast, reduced intergroup bias. A bank merger, one might argue, is a very different process from the integration of nation-states into the European Union. However, the psychological models that are discussed here are developed on a very abstract conceptual level. Counterevidence from a bank merger case can be relevant because it questions the model itself—even if the data are collected in a different context. Altogether, we think that there is not much consistent empirical evidence of positive consequences of dual identification and that reliable predictions about the impact of dual identity in Europe are difficult to make.

Dual Identity and the Ingroup Projection Model

A different approach to the effects of dual identification is provided by the model of in-group projection, which was recently developed by Mummendey and Wenzel (1999). Discussing this model, we refer to Europe insofar as it provides comparison dimensions for European subgroups. Mummendey and Wenzel ask how members of groups deal with the fact that members of an out-group are different from those of the in-group. What are the conditions that determine whether in-group members respond to that difference with tolerance (or even appreciation) or with the devaluation of out-group members?

The Ingroup Projection Model hypothesizes that the differences of out-group members will be negatively evaluated if two conditions are fulfilled: inclusion and in-group projection (figure 4.1).

1. *Inclusion* means that both groups are comparable because they belong to a common higher-inclusive category, which provides relevant dimensions for the comparison between both subgroups.

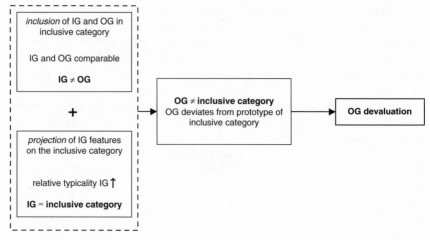

Figure 4.1

2. *In-group projection* means that group members tend to generalize—or project—the features of their in-group to the higher inclusive category. The in-group is taken as *pars pro toto* (as a part that stands for the whole) and is regarded as a standard for judgments on other sub-groups of the inclusive category.

Thus, according to the different relationships between European identity and national identities discussed elsewhere in this volume (Herrmann and Brewer; Risse), the Ingroup Projection Model assumes a combination be-tween a nested design (Russian doll metaphor) and a mixed identity (mar-ble cake metaphor). National identities are related to subgroups of Europe (inclusion); however, European identity itself is partly mixed with national identities (in-group projection).

Important for the understanding of this model is the concept of proto-typicality. A group member (or subgroup) is prototypical for a group (or category) if it is very similar to other group members (or subgroups) and if it is very different from nonmembers of the group. The most prototypical member of a group is the prototype (e.g., the prototype of Europeans is the European who has the most similarities with other Europeans and the most dissimilarities with non-Europeans).

When both conditions—inclusion and in-group projection—are fulfilled, the prototype of the higher inclusive category will be perceived as being more similar to the in-group than to the out-group. Consequently, the out-group not only differs from the in-group on the subgroup level but also de-viates from the higher-order prototype of the common in-group (i.e., the inclusive category). This deviation has consequences for the evaluation of the out-group. As assumed by self-categorization theory (Turner et al. 1987), the lack of prototypicality of the out-group will be correlated with a decrease in attractiveness. The less prototypical the out-group, the more negatively it will be evaluated.

Applying the model to the European context we would assume that Germans who project stereotypical German features onto the European prototype will construct a representation of Europe that is more similar to Germany than to, let's say, Greece. As a consequence, a German displaying high in-group projection will perceive Greeks as deviating from the positively evaluated European prototype, and he or she will evaluate Greeks rather negatively.

What are the consequences of dual identification in that model? First, in-group projection makes it possible to maintain the positive distinctiveness of the in-group compared to other subgroups: The in-group is evaluated positively because it is better than the out-group in terms of prototypicality. Thus, one hypothesis of the Ingroup Projection Model is that those in-group members who are highly identified with the subgroup will show a higher degree of in-group projection. Second, in-group projection provides positive distinctiveness only if the standards and norms of the higher-order category are important and positively evaluated, that is, if the identification with the higher-order category is high. From this, it follows that dual identification will have a rather negative impact on attitudes toward the out-group, because it fosters in-group projection, which will negatively affect out-group evaluation. The Ingroup Projection Model predicts that dual-identified Germans will perceive other European nations as deviating from the European prototype and hence evaluate them more negatively than other Germans will do. The same should hold for citizens of other nations. Dual-identified French citizens should perceive a more "French" European prototype than other French citizens and consequently should show more negative attitudes toward, let's say, Germans, Dutch, or the British.

EMPIRICAL EVIDENCE OF THE INGROUP PROJECTION MODEL

In our studies we found substantial empirical evidence (1) for the negative relationship between in-group projection and out-group evaluation and (2) for an aggravating impact of dual identification on in-group projection (Waldzus et al. 2003; Waldzus, Mummendey, and Rosendahl 2002; Wenzel et al. 2003). We tested the model with several intergroup constellations, for instance with students of different subjects, with East and West Germans within the higher-level category of Germans, with professors of universities versus polytechnic colleges, or, recently, with different types of motorcyclists. Some of our studies, however, were conducted with Germans as an in-group on the subgroup level and Europeans as a higher-order category. We conducted studies with Poles, British, and Italians as out-groups. As these studies nicely illustrate our argumentation concerning possible consequences of dual identification in Europe, we will describe four of them briefly. Three of the studies are reported in more detail in Wenzel et al. (2003; study 1 of the current chapter) and in Waldzus et al. (2003; studies 2 and 3 of the current chapter).

Although these studies varied in their experimental manipulations (which will be discussed later), in each study dual identification, in-group projection, and attitudes toward the out-group were assessed in order to test the hypotheses that dual identification will increase in-group projection, and in-group projection will lead to negative attitude toward the out-group. The method was similar in all studies; a brief description of the operationalizations of the variables should be given here.

Attitudes toward the out-group were measured on Likert-type scales of eight to eleven items. Several items covering four aspects of attitudes toward the out-group were included: sympathy, desirability of contact, positive behavioral intentions, and tolerance—that is, the positive evaluation of differences. Although we assessed these different aspects, all of the items loaded on one dominating factor and were summarized to one attitude scale with sufficient reliability (αs > .80).

Dual identification—which was treated in our analyses as the independent variable—was a synthetic dummy variable that was built from two independent identification scales. Identification with Germany and identification with Europe were measured on separate scales (with a reliability from α = .79 to α = .90). After that, we applied a median split over the identification with Europe ratings and got two subsamples of high and low identifiers. In the next step, within the subsample of high identifiers, we conducted a second median split for the identification with Germans. From that second median split we obtained a subsample of dual identifiers that were highly identified with Germans and highly identified with Europeans. The dual-identified subsample was tested against all other participants.

Last but not least, *the in-group projection* measure should be explained. In-group projection manifests itself in a higher perceived relative prototypicality—for the superordinate category—of the in-group compared to the out-group. Hence we compared both typicalities and took the difference as an indicator of in-group projection. The procedure of the typicality measure varied between the studies. Mostly, ratings on an open-scale method were used. At the beginning, participants had to write down four features that are typical of the in-group as compared to the out-group. After that, they were asked to write down four features that are typical of the out-group as compared to the in-group. Finally, participants had to rate each of these eight features for its *typicality of the inclusive category*. The typicality ratings (typicality for the inclusive category) for the four out-group features were reverse coded. Relative in-group prototypicality was indicated by the mean of the four typicality ratings for the in-group features and the four reversed typicality ratings for the out-group features.

We found evidence for our predictions for Poles, for British, and for Italians as out-groups. Dual identification with Germany and with Europe led to higher in-group projection, and this in-group projection was negatively correlated with attitudes toward Poles, British, or Italians as out-groups (figure 4.2).

The indirect negative effect of dual identification on out-group evaluation was not in every case significant, but there was an overall consistent result: if there is any positive impact of dual identification on the attitude toward the out-group, as it was predicted by the Common Ingroup Identification Model of Gaertner et al. (1999), then it is at least partly suppressed by an indirect negative effect that is mediated by in-group projection. Dual identification can make attitudes toward the out-group more negative if in-group projection takes place.

Our conclusion from these findings is that the positive view on dual identification—which is encouraged by Gaertner et al. (1999)—has to be tempered by a caveat. Moreover, our results provide an explanation of the inconsistent outcomes of the studies conducted by Gaertner and associates on the impact of dual identification. We do think that there is some positive impact of dual identification on out-group evaluation. One part of dual identification is the common in-group identification, as in the case of Gaertner et al. (1994), with the multiethnic high school, and in our case, with Europe. Common in-group identification has—there is no doubt—dominantly positive effects. The picture changes, however, when we have additional high identification on the sublevel, for instance with a particular European nation. In that case, in-group projection comes into play as a "spoilsport" in the intergroup game. In general, the positive impact of recategorization and of raising higher-order identification as a European seems to be moderated by in-group projection, which itself is highest for dual identifiers.

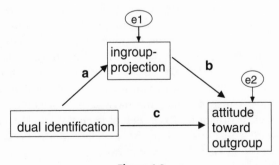

Figure 4.2

OUTLOOK TOWARD TOLERANCE

Given that our results could be generalized not only to other kinds of groups, but also to other European countries, what can be done to prevent intergroup conflict in an upcoming European Union? The situation is not easy to handle. The higher salience of Europe as a relevant self-category necessitates the inclusion of different nations in one inclusive category, and it may lead not only to more interdependence between the different European nations but also to stronger intergroup comparisons. European norms, standards, and values become more binding on the European nations. A subgroup's relative prototypicality in terms of European standards becomes the basis for the acceptance of the treatment of that subgroup in the European context. States like Serbia or Turkey, for instance, are pushed to increase their commitment to human rights, and there was a wide acceptance among the Western European people of the punishment of Serbia for violating "European standards"—even if the success of such punishment can be questioned, of course. Correspondingly, we were able to show that, when Europe was introduced as a positively evaluated category, those participants who perceived Germans to be highly prototypical for Europe also perceived the status superiority of Germans compared to Poles as being legitimate (Weber, Mummendey, and Waldzus 2002). Differences in prototypicality justify differences in status and treatment.

On the one hand, a higher commitment to European standards is for most Europeans a desirable goal of the European integration process. On the other hand, we face the risk of in-group projection if the European identification is raised in combination with in-group identification on the national sublevel. For instance, in a further study we were able to show that the perception of Europe by German participants depended on the out-group with which Germans were compared. Participants who were asked to compare Germans with Italians perceived Germans as well as Europeans to be more orderly, disciplined, and so forth than participants who were asked to compare Germans with the British. In contrast, when Germans were compared with the British, not only Germans, but also Europeans, were rated higher on—from a German perspective—stereotypical non-British attributes, for instance being straightforward and having tasty meals (Waldzus, Mummendey, and Wenzel 2001). The struggle for the best Europe is likely to be biased by an ethnocentric view, with citizens generalizing some characteristics of their own nation as *pars pro toto* to the whole of Europe—not because it makes the most sense but simply because of a basic psychological principle. Examples of such tendencies have been observed already. For instance, when the so-called Mastricht-Criterions were introduced, people in Germany became upset about the supposedly wrong handling of these criteria in other European countries.

What can we do to prevent such an ethnocentric view of Europe? Should we advocate a rather crude assimilation strategy of recategorization within an undifferentiated European supernation? Is it possible to prevent in-group projection only by blurring all the differences between the historically grown and linguistically distinguishable nations that dominate our current self-concept as Europeans?

What seems to be more realistic and more desirable than the disappearance of the national level of identification is the creation of tolerance between different subgroups of Europe, tolerance even in the case of dual identification. Following the Ingroup Projection Model, such a possibility would have to include a reduction of in-group projection. Tolerance between subgroups would require that subgroup members perceive the differences of the other subgroups not as deviations from the prototype of the superordinate category but rather as additional variants of subgroups of that category, which could be just as prototypical as the in-group. As a condition of intergroup tolerance, the *representation of the inclusive self-category* might be important because of its major role in the process of in-group projection. Mummendey and Wenzel (1999) suggest reducing in-group projection by keeping the prototype of the higher-order category *indefinable* or by inducing a *complex* representation of that category. If the prototype of Europe is not definable, in-group attributes cannot easily be claimed to be more prototypic than out-group attributes. Also, an undefined prototype does not provide standards for out-group devaluation. A complex representation of the inclusive category should explicitly include different subgroups as prototypical at the same time. A complex Europe means that differences between nationalities are part of the kernel definition of Europe. With such a representation of Europe it is not easy to maintain an ethnocentric European prototype.

In order to test these hypotheses we manipulated the representation of the inclusive category in studies 2, 3, and 4 of the current chapter (for studies 2 and 3 see Waldzus et al. 2003). In study 2, we manipulated the definability ("vagueness") of the prototype of Europe by giving participants information that reflected either a high or a low level of in-group consensus concerning the prototypical representation of "Europe." Participants were asked to rate Europe on nine attributes. Following these ratings, each participant was shown a graph giving false feedback about the opinions of respondents in similar studies. This false feedback served either to support (i.e., high level of consensus, homogeneous feedback) or question (i.e., low level of consensus, heterogeneous feedback) the possibility of a representation of Europe in terms of a clearly definable prototype. In studies 3 and 4 we manipulated the complexity of the representation of Europe. Participants were told to imagine that they had to describe to another person certain features of Europe. For the complex condition, participants had to define the diversity of Europe, and for the simple condition, participants had to define the unity of Europe. Participants then typed the generated ideas into an open text field. We assumed that defining Europe in terms of its diversity should activate a greater variety of exemplars or subgroups and so prime a more heterogeneous representation of Europe. In both cases, when we manipulated the definability (figure 4.3) and complexity (figure 4.4) of Europe, in-group projection was reduced, and we got an indirect improvement of attitudes toward the out-group by changing the representation of Europe. The result for complexity in study 4, with the British and Italian out-group, was significant only for the Italian out-group, but the pattern is in the same direction for the British out-group.

In a further study already mentioned above (Waldzus et al. 2001) we were able to show that a complex representation of Europe reduced the tendency to generalize typical German attributes to Europe and also had a significant indirect and total positive effect on attitudes toward the British or Italian out-group.

CONCLUSION

Although social psychological theories are rather general, and, when they are translated into interventions, the particular cultural and historical conditions have to be acknowledged in every case, a cautious conclusion might be allowed. If identification with Europe is a desirable political outcome, increasing the entitativity of the European category might be the necessary condition to give the European identity meaning and stability (see Castano, this volume). However, the entitativity of the European category can hardly be based on homogeneity. Keeping national identifications in a united Europe may be the unavoidable condition for a European integration process. Given the empirical evidence of in-group projection, which was found, not entirely but for the most part, in the European context, it is

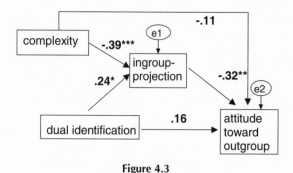

Figure 4.3

Sample 1: outgroup = British

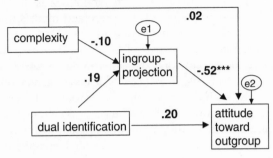

Sample 2: outgroup = Italians; *n* = 35

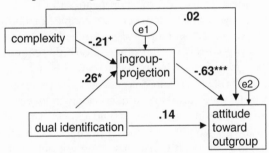

Figure 4.4

not unlikely that we would pay for the merits of such a dual identification (with Europe and with individual nations) with an increase in intra-European conflicts. Ignoring the diversity of Europe would allow crude nationalism to use the—ethnocentrically defined—European identity as a further argument for out-group derogation, with citizens using the standards of their own nation as a norm for other nations. For instance, Germans who dislike Poles because of their deviating from German standards and who don't care about Europe at all today (see Meinhof, this volume) might dislike Poles even more when they develop a European identity, because they generalize German standards to the European norm, which is then also binding on Poles. In order to be successful, dual identification should—on a psychological level—be accompanied by the creation of a concept of Europe that is sufficiently complex to make tolerance between different European nations more likely.

As a final remark we would like to add some conclusions about the political implications of our argumentation. We cannot discuss this issue without pointing out the conceptual level of the presented models. Social psychological theories like the Common Ingroup Identity Model and the Ingroup Projection Model are general theories of intergroup behavior that are tested in several different intergroup contexts, either in the European context or in completely different contexts, like those of a bank merger or professional groups. Accordingly, such theories contribute to our understanding of a variety of intergroup situations; the European case is one of them. However, because of their abstractness, they cannot be applied to any real-life context unless the particular political, historical, and cultural circumstances are taken into account. They are nevertheless useful, for instance, in qualifying underlying assumptions about psychological antecedents and consequences of social identity, which are held by the architects and constructers of the European Union and by many practitioners, journalists, and politicians working in this area. The simple psychological assumption that putting people into the same boat will bring them together, or that establishing a dual identity, which combines identification on the European and on the national level, will reduce intergroup conflicts between the peoples of Europe was questioned in this chapter based on empirical evidence. We have to take into account that in-group projection is the other side of the coin and raises new conflicts. The pervasiveness of in-group projection is not only an issue for "opinion makers" who have to take into account the psychological dynamic of their audience. It is also an issue in negotiations between member states of the European Union, in which we would expect a tendency by many members to take their own national rules, principles, or institutions as a desirable model for the European house. Knowing not only that such conflicts are unavoidable, but also why they are unavoidable, may help us to solve them more efficiently. On the social psychological level a possible solution was suggested in this chapter, in the demonstration that in-group projection can be prevented if the cognitive representation of Europe is complex enough. Given the diversity of its different national cultures and languages, Europe should have a good chance to become established as a complex social entity, to become real without losing its diversity.

NOTE

This chapter is based on an oral presentation on "Europeanization and Multiple Identities," a conference jointly sponsored by the Mershon Center, Ohio State University, and the European University Institute/Robert Schuman Centre for Advanced Studies, Florence, June 9 and 10, 2000. Parts of this paper are based on research that was funded by the Deutsche Forschungsgemeinschaft (Mu551/18).

II

Identity within the
EU Institutions at the Elite Level

5

The European Union and Its Institutions as "Identity Builders"

Brigid Laffan

The European Union has evolved as a densely institutionalised site of governance in contemporary Europe. It has spawned a broader and deeper level of institutionalisation than found in any other system of regional cooperation in the international system. Institution building in the Union is characterised by the creation of new institutions at the EU level, on the one hand, and by strong vertical links to national institutions, on the other. In the literature on integration, there is profound disagreement among scholars on the impact of EU institutions on identities. From the outset, individuals associated with the EU have been part of the construction of new identities in their efforts to get the EU going and to further the process of integration. Thousands of individuals have worked at a microlevel within and through the institutions and at a macrolevel by fostering a new social construction in Europe—the common market, the European Economic Community, the European Community, and now the European Union. The aim of this chapter is to provide an overview of the identity-building capacity of the EU and its institutions and to sketch plausible links between European institutions and identity formation.

The argument in this chapter is that the EU as a macrosocial organisation has had a major impact on the politics of identity in Europe. The EU, having striven for recognition, is now a powerful part of normative and cognitive structures in contemporary Europe. It is deeply embedded in political, social, and economic discourse in Europe. This has been achieved notwithstanding the reified nature of the nation-state as a social construction. Identity building had been fostered by membership, the external projection of an EU identity, the appropriation by the EU of the concept of "Europe," and the cement provided by the founding values and the addition of EU symbols to Europe's forest of symbols. Moreover, it has been achieved by the provision of a benign extranational home for many states in Europe, "a place to belong" (Ahern 2000).

At the microlevel of analysis, individual EU institutions have played a role in identity formation and change. The most significant way in which these institutions foster identity change is through the emergence of new political and functional roles that are "European" in nature. The "logic of appropriateness" in the supranational institutions is to serve the Union as a whole. This chapter draws a distinction between the European Commission as a multiorganisation and the functional organisations, notably, the European Court and the European Central Bank (1999). Members of the latter type of organisation are open to very strong professional identities, as bankers and judges, that intersect with national identity. In the Commission, there are new European roles, but the individuals holding these positions face cross-cutting identity pressures—nationality, profession, bureaucratic unit, and Commission as a whole. In the representative institutions, notably the European Council, the participants face the pressures of double hatting, of representing state preferences while at the same time fashioning collective agreement. The national officials who work in the representations or are active in EU policy making in domestic ministries constitute a significant cadre of officials who operate constantly in a demimonde between the national and the EU. They represent state preferences in Brussels and the EU in the national capitals. The EU has worked on the basis of embedding the national in the European and the European in the national.

The arguments in this chapter are developed in three sections. The first section provides a synopsis of how "identity building" and institutionalisation are conceptualised in the chapter. The second section analyses how the EU as a macrosocial organisation has had an impact on identity formation in Europe. The focus is on the EU as an institution in a sociological sense. The third section explores the role of EU institutions—the Commission, the Council, the European Court of Justice, and the European Parliament—in the creation of new identities. The focus on EU institutions enables us to explore identity change among Europe's elites. There is a significant gap, wider in some countries than in others, between elite and mass attitudes toward the European Union. Engagement in EU institutions appears to enhance a favourable attitude toward integration, or at least the utilitarian benefits are recognised. In 1996, Eurobarometer conducted what it called a *Top Decision-Makers Survey,* which asked the respondents whether their countries' membership in the EU was a "good" or "bad" thing, and whether their country had benefited from membership (Eurobarometer, *Summary Report,* 1996). Among these top decision makers, 94 percent concluded that their country's membership was a "good" thing, and

90 percent felt that their country had benefited from membership. These figures were far higher than recorded among the wider population, and there was far less interstate variation than found in the attitudes of the mass public. This suggests that EU institutions have a socialisation effect.

INSTITUTIONALISATION AND IDENTITY BUILDING

The European Union is a relatively young social construct that is being crafted onto a preexisting reified social construct—the nation-state. It is argued that "states as nation states appear to be almost natural entities beyond the realm of political discourse" (Taylor 1993, 5). The European concept of the nation-state represented a relatively strong congruence between bounded territory, bonded people, and a set of evolving governance functions. The fact that nation-states are presented and perceived as natural entities, in addition to the dominance of nationalism as the source of political legitimisation, poses a considerable challenge to the European Union. It also poses a challenge to scholars seeking to explore the impact of the EU and its institutions on identity formation and identity change in contemporary Europe. Among analysts of integration there is deep-seated conflict about the relationship between integration and statehood and about the nature of the EU as a political and economic order. Does it strengthen, transcend, or transform statehood in contemporary Europe? The underlying premise of this chapter is that the Union transforms traditional statehood, albeit in an incremental and experimental manner, and that a supranational polity is being constructed in Europe. We expect identity building and identity change in the Union to be multifaceted, ambiguous, uneven, and contested, given the embryonic character of the Union and the interaction between nested national identities and cross-cutting European identities. As the tentacles of the Union extend into member state polities, the possibility of a reconfiguration and redefinition of identities in Europe is opened up. Identity in Europe may begin at home, but it no longer ends there.

Institutionalisation is proceeding in the Union through the establishment of formal institutions authorised by a succession of treaties, by informal practices that have grown up around these institutions, and by the creation of strong vertical links with the institutions of the member states. Like identity building, the process of institutionalisation in contemporary Europe is patchy and fragmented. This should not surprise us. The politicisation of integration in the late 1980s, together with the extensive mobilisation of actors in the European arena and the shifting continental geopolitics, ensure that the "stakes" in the integration process have become much higher for the member states and social forces within them. The "stakes" are not just economic but have an important identity and cultural dimension as well.

Attention to the identity dimension of integration enables us to tease out just how embedded a social framework the EU is becoming. The relative newness of the EU and its ambiguous status may lead us to downplay processes of change and identity formation that are occurring in the European system.

Identity building implies the crafting of a degree of commonality and is suggestive of association, sharing, and community. Identity building and identity change are bound up with deep cultural syndromes and are thus not subject to extensive change in the short term. A twofold perspective on EU institutions as "identity builders"—a normative and cognitive perspective—is adopted in this chapter. Too much of the literature on the EU focuses on the impact of the EU on material practice to the neglect of its normative and cognitive dimensions. The dual perspective stems from a conception of "institutions" as "multifaceted systems incorporating symbolic systems—cognitive constructions and normative rules" that shape the social world (Scott 1995, 33). The EU is being constructed not just by regulatory processes, important though these are, but by normative and cognitive systems as well. The dual perspective—normative and cognitive—enables us to tease out the multiple ways in which the EU as a social construction interacts and intersects with changing identity patterns. A normative lens on "identity building" highlights the potential significance of shared values, norms, and new roles in the European Union. A cognitive lens draws our attention to the importance of symbolic representations of the world. From this perspective "symbols—words, signs, and gestures—have their effect by shaping the meanings we attribute to objects and activities. Meanings arise in interaction and are maintained—and transformed—when they are employed to make sense of the ongoing stream of happenings" (Scott 1995, 40). Symbolic systems and shared meanings are brought to life in human interaction. The distinction between the normative and cognitive dimensions of the EU as an organisation is used in this chapter for analytical purposes. We are mindful that cognitive categories or frames of meaning have an important normative dimension.

THE EU AS AN INSTITUTION

The European Union can be characterised as an institution, a polity, operating at a macrosocietal level. It operates within a framework of rules of membership, is bounded territorially, and allocates values. Its reach extends beyond its borders to the wider international system. During the foundational period of the Union's evolution, its development as a framework for interstate relations in Western Europe and as an arena of deep integration was greatly assisted by the east-west divide in Europe and the definition of the eastern half of the continent as "other" (Wallace 1999). As the Union is a relatively young social construction, crafted onto preexisting and deeply embedded social institutions, it is still striving to go beyond its technical/functional character to prove its strength and resilience as a social framework (Scott 1995, 34). Its capacity for "identity building" is important to this quest. The EU has had to strive to be recognized as part of the symbolic structures of contemporary Europe. This section explores four dimensions of the EU as an "identity builder." First, it argues that the existence of the EU and its membership rules have a powerful impact on state identity in Europe. Second, it argues that the Union as an actor in the global system has developed an international identity. Third, the EU is founded on a system of values and beliefs about "civic statehood" that reflect but also shape the values of the participating member states. Fourth, the cognitive dimension of identity building is underlined by the growth of EU-specific symbols in Europe.

Membership Matters

The existence of the Union, from the outset, categorised states into member states and nonmembers, associated states and applicants. The treaties incorporated rules of "inclusion" and "exclusion." Membership in the EU was and continues to be a profound badge of state identity— membership in a club involving a qualitative difference in relations between members and nonmembers. The use of the term "partner" to connote a fellow member state implies involvement in a shared enterprise, a degree of commonality necessary to identity building. At every European Council the heads of state and government pose for what is known in EU jargon as the "family photograph." The use of the terms "family" and "partner" to describe fellow members of the European Council is more than rhetoric. The engagement of Europe's leaders in the European Council is more frequent and intense now than at any time in the past. In addition to their national responsibilities, they carry a collective responsibility for providing political direction to the system as a whole.

The fact the continental model of integration rather than the European Free Trade Area (EFTA) emerged as the dominant European model had profound implications for those states not part of the "original six." All states in Europe, beginning with those in Western Europe but extending to East Central Europe after 1989, had to establish a modus vivendi with the EU in terms either of membership or a special relationship. No state could ignore it. Norway or Switzerland, states that remained outside because their citizens would not endorse membership, have had to negotiate a framework for managing their relations with the Union. The EU exercised a powerful magnetic attraction for countries on its borders. Apart from the human rights activity of the Council of Europe, the attraction of the European Union stems from its successfully appropriating the term "Europe" for itself. The phrases "rejoining Europe" or "returning to Europe" highlight the fact that since the 1950s, the European Union was institutionalised in Western Europe as the dominant framework above the level of the state. Acceptance as a candidate country carried with it a powerful marker of inclusion and identification as "European," however ambiguous that term remains. For Poland membership in the EU implies that it will have a "room in the house" and is no longer a corridor. For Turkey, acceptance of its candidate status at Helsinki in 1999 by the EU affirms Turkey as part of the European order. The state elites in all EU candidate countries affirm their European credentials. In the future, it will matter enormously to peoples in the Balkans, the Ukraine, Moldova, and Russia, for example, where they find themselves in relation to the borders of the Union and the nature of the borders that will evolve from EU policy. From the outset, the EU—through membership and nonmembership, inclusion and exclusion—has exercised a powerful impact on state identity in Europe.

The Quest for a Collective International Identity

The EU has since 1970, through the process called European Political Cooperation (EPC), attempted to project a collective identity in the international system. EPC was transformed into the Common Foreign and Security Policy (CFSP) in the Treaty on European Union, which makes reference to "reinforcing the European identity and its independence in order to promote peace, security and progress in Europe and the world" (Treaty on European Union 1993, preamble). The assertion by the EU of an "international identity" implies that the EU defines this identity and interacts with the international system and other actors in the projection of this identity (Manners and Whitman 1998, 231–249). Traditionally, the Union's self-definition of its identity in the international system was based on the concept of "civilian power," a term coined by Françoise Duchêne. The primary instruments deployed in establishing an international identity were aid and trade. The EU developed a vast array of association agreements with third countries or regional blocks. This is no longer the exclusive identity that the Union aspires to. There is growing consensus that the Union must assert an external identity in the security sphere, and agreement has been reached on the establishment of a rapid-deployment force (sixty thousand soldiers) as part of the European Security and Defence Policy (ESDP). The Union's quest for an international identity interacts with external relationships of significance to the member states, particularly relations with the United States. Divergent historical experiences and traditions of foreign policy make the Union's search for an international identity tortuous.

The Normative Dimension

The construction of the EU and its development as a polity have displayed a strong normative dimension from the outset. The EU has come to represent a model of civic statehood and interstate relations built on shared values. The Union has embedded these values progressively in its treaty-based constitution and in the practice of politics in the Union. The EU has acted as a cultural force in promoting an account of civic statehood in Europe. The Convention on the Future of Europe, meeting in 2002–2003 to draft a constitutional treaty for the Union, is a further step in embedding shared values and civic statehood in Europe's constitutional architecture. It represents a further deepening of the EU system as a normative construct.

The aspiration to a shared "community of values" and to a form of "civic statehood" in Europe informed the creation of the Union. The preamble of the Treaty of Paris (European Coal and Steel Community) promotes a distinct concept of integration based on a desire:

> to substitute for age-old rivalries the merging of their essential interests; to create by establishing an economic community, the basis for a broader and deeper community among peoples divided by bloody conflicts; and to lay the foundations for institutions which will give direction to a destiny henceforward shared. (Treaty of Paris 1951, preamble)

The preamble establishes an aspiration for a "community among peoples" through the merging of essential interests and a "destiny henceforward shared." The language deployed is a language of "community," not intergovernmental co-operation. The manner in which this would be achieved was hinted at by Robert Schuman, the French foreign minister, in the Schuman Declaration of 1950, when he said, "Europe will not be made all at once, or according to a single plan. It will be built through concrete achievements that first create a de facto solidarity" (Schuman Declaration, May 9, 1950). The values of peace and reconciliation underpinned the integration project from the outset. Power and force would be regulated through institutionalised cooperation and a community of values among the participating states. There was a direct link between the identity of the EU as an institution and the taming of state power in Europe.

It was assumed in the original treaties that only democracies would become members of the Union. There was no explicit reference to human rights and fundamental freedoms because of the underlying assumption that membership of the Union was open only to democracies. As the European Court of Justice established a new legal order, it began to incorporate references to human rights in its judgements. In December 1973, the heads of state and government made a declaration on European identity that included a strong reverence for the rule of law, representative democracy, social

justice, and respect for human rights, all of which were said to be "fundamental elements of the European identity" (Copenhagen Summit Declaration, December 14, 1973). The declaration adopted national and universal
values but located them in a European framework and context. These values have a direct impact on membership or inclusion. Greece, Spain, and
Portugal could become candidate states only after the end of authoritarian
government in those states. The countries of East Central Europe were faced
with a high level of conditionality, established in the Copenhagen criteria,
in relation to their membership in the Union.

The values underpinning the Union were given explicit constitutional protection in the Treaty of Amsterdam, the Union's first political treaty. Article F1
established that the "Union is founded on the principles of liberty, democracy, respect for human rights and fundamental freedoms, and the rule of
law, principles which are upheld by the Member States" (Treaty of Amsterdam, Article F (1)). The treaty then goes on to make provision for a sanctions
procedure if there is a "serious and persistent breach by a Member State of
the principles mentioned in Article F (1)." The treaty expression of these values was given political expression in the fissures caused by the inclusion of
Jorg Haider's Freedom Party in the Austrian government in February 2000.
The fourteen other member states, acting through the Portuguese presidency,
imposed limited sanctions on the new Austrian government. Some of the
privileges of club membership were withdrawn. The fourteen were displaying their disquiet at the arrival in power of a party that does not share the
concept of civic statehood that underpins the Union. The EU has been highly
selective to date in drawing on these values in political terms. The 2001 Italian government led by Berlusconi was not subjected to the same treatment.

In addition to the values associated with liberal democracy, the self-
definition of the Union includes strong references to diversity and the protection of difference. Article 6 (3) of the Treaty of Amsterdam states that the
Union "shall respect the national identities of its Member States" (Treaty of
Amsterdam, Article 6 (3)), and the provisions on culture make reference to
"respecting" member states' "national and regional diversity" (Treaty of Amsterdam, Article 151 (1)). The Millennium Declaration of 1999 identifies the
"ties that bind" in the following terms: "The Union's citizens are bound together by common values such as freedom, tolerance, equality, solidarity
and cultural diversity" (Millennium Declaration). The inclusion of respect for
diversity as one of the central values of the Union reflects the fact that in the
EU bonds are defined as much by shared difference as by shared affinities.

The Cognitive Dimension

A cognitive perspective of institutions places emphasis on the emergence
of a "common framework of meaning." The cognitive encompasses the frames

through which meaning is made and the rules that constitute the nature of reality (Scott 1995, 40–45). Social identities allow us to say who we are and what
makes sense to us in different situations. At a macrolevel the emergence and
development of the EU opened up the possibility that new frames of meaning could emerge in Europe and that preexisting national frames could be re-
defined and reconfigured. Or the existence of the Union could lead to a col-
lision between different frames of meaning. Symbols constitute an important
way in which new frames of meaning are constructed. Symbols connect individuals to the social and political order by providing orientations for inter-
preting the world. Symbols may alter individual and collective consciousness
of the world. Political actors engaged in building the Union did not pay particular attention to the symbolic representation of the EU in the early phase of
integration. The construction of the Union proceeded along a utilitarian path,
under the sheltering roof of its founding values. By the early 1970s, the
shadow of the past, the memory of war, was no longer enough. Political actors began to consciously develop the symbolic dimension of the Union. The
resurgence in formal integration and the growing ambition of the project of
integration in market terms led EU institutions to fashion and deploy EU-specific symbols intended to reconfigure the symbolic universe within which individual Europeans and Europe's nation-states interact.

EU symbols are rarely stand-alone symbols. They are not intended to replace national symbols but are additional symbols to connote the embedding
of the national in the European. The symbols used by the EU include the traditional state-building emblems of the past—a flag, common passport cover,
an EU driving licence, and an anthem. The blue flag with its gold stars is
flown from public and private buildings throughout the Union. In many
member states, it is usual for government ministers when addressing a national audience on television to be flanked by the national and the European
flag. It is significant that when Austrians took to the streets of Vienna in February 2000 to protest against the presence in power of the Freedom Party,
many in the crowd carried the EU flag. For those people, the flag represented
the Other with respect to Haider. In addition to political symbols, there are
many other EU symbols, such as the blue flag for clean beaches, car plates,
communal notices, and the EU product tag. Since January 2002 Europeans in
twelve member states have had in their pockets a very powerful material
symbol of membership in the EU, the euro. EU symbols serve to make the
growing salience of the Union visible and to assist Europeans in internalising
the EU as part of their social reality. New symbols, however, may or may not
take root. They may be regarded as relatively benign representations of a
new social construction or unwanted reminders of political and social
change. How individual Europeans interpret and internalise European symbols depends in some measure on the compatibility of national and European symbols and on individuals' attitudes toward the European project.

The argument in this section is that the EU from the outset has been engaged in "identity building" and in fostering identity change. This has manifested itself primarily through the appropriation by the EU of the term "Europe" and the expansion of membership. To be a member state has had a
profound impact on the self-definition of many states in Western Europe,
and more recently the desire for membership has moulded the post-Com-
munist state identities of the countries of East Central Europe. Moreover,
the EU has striven to project an external identity through its interaction with
the wider international system. The evolution of the EU as a polity has been
fostered by a deepening of its normative dimension and the emergence of
EU symbols. It was clear at the outset that a set of values encapsulated in
the term "civic statehood" underpinned the Union, but these were made
much more explicit in the Treaty of Amsterdam. The development of EU-
specific symbols is a feature of the 1980s and 1990s, during which time the
salience of the Union in Europe was heightened.

EU INSTITUTIONS AND IDENTITY BUILDING

We turn from the macroanalysis of the Union as a social construction to
amicroanalysis at the level of EU institutions. In this section, which analyses the identity-building capacity of the Union's formal institutions, the emphasis is on the creation of new EU-specific roles and the impact of these
roles on the identities of individual actors, be they national or European.
From the outset the continental model of integration, in contrast to the
EFTA model, involved the creation of a set of formal institutions—the Commission, the Council of Ministers, the European Council, the European Parliament, and the European Court of Justice—through which collective action could be fostered. As with all institutions, EU institutions reflect a
balance between functional and territorial principles. When analysing the
capacity of EU institutions to act as "identity builders" it is important to distinguish between the "supranational" institutions, one the one hand, and
the "representative" institutions, on the other. The functional principle predominates in the supranational institutions, whereas the territorial principle
predominates in the representative institutions. The *supranational* institutions—the Commission, the European Court of Justice, the Court of Auditors (1993), and the European Central Bank—are formally independent of
the member states, and office holders in these institutions have to pledge
independence from national authorities. This does not mean that nationality is unimportant in the operation of these institutions. Rather the supranational institutions and those who work in them face the challenge of
managing cross-cutting identities—national, European, and functional. The
representative institutions—the Council of Ministers, the European Council

and the European Parliament—represent the member governments and the peoples' of Europe, respectively. Those involved in the representative institutions face the challenge of "double hatting"—acting as representatives of a member government or constituency while at the same time having a responsibility to the Union as a whole.

The identity-building capacity of the formal institutions depends on their place in the institutional landscape, the roles that are associated with the institutions, the proactive identity-building policies that institutions foster, and the attitudes of the individual social agents that occupy those roles. When exploring the identity-building capacity of the Union's institutions, we are faced with a dearth of empirical data, which limits our ability to establish substantial conclusions about this dimension of the EU. Within the constraints of limited data, this section seeks to establish plausible linkages between EU institutions and identity formation by exploring the impact of the EU on roles. Two lines of analysis are pursued. First, the formal supranational roles associated with four EU institutions are analysed. Second, the roles associated with the Union's representative institutions are analysed. Each of the Union's institutions is analysed in turn in an effort to identify the different roles that are associated with them and to establish plausible hypotheses concerning the identity-building capacity of each institution. This is achieved by identifying actors, new or altered roles, and the logic or appropriateness associated with these roles.

The centrality of roles in institutions is underlined by Berger and Luckmann, who argue that "all institutionalised conduct involves roles. Thus roles share in the controlling character of institutionalisation" (Berger and Luckmann 1967). Roles carry with them what March and Olsen have defined as a "logic of appropriateness." According to these authors, "Appropriateness refers to a match of behaviour to a situation" (March and Olsen 1995, 30). Roles imply "a set of expectations (norms and rules) that more or less specify the desired behaviour or the role of the incumbent"; and an "identity is a conception of self organized into rules for matching action to situations" (Egeberg 1999, 45). Roles are exercised by individuals within institutional settings that are characterised by both normative and cognitive systems. Roles may be nested geographically or may cross-cut both functionally and on the basis of territory. Different institutions may evoke different roles and identities. We are mindful that role orientations may not be a good predictor of behaviour, as individuals within organisations often carry multiple roles that may be in conflict.

The Supranational Roles

Treaty provisions established distinctive roles for the so-called supranational institutions—the Commission, the European Court of Justice, the

Court of Auditors, and the European Central Bank. Because of the establishment of the EU there are now European commissioners, European judges, European central bankers, European auditors, and European civil servants. Without the creation of the EU, these roles would not exist. EU officer holders, judges, and central bankers carry a mandate for the Union and pledge that they will "neither seek nor take instruction from the government of a member state." This mandate establishes norms, rules, and role expectations that amount to an "institutional identity." The organising principle of the supranational institutions is functional rather than territorial. The Commission's dual responsibility for policy initiation and as guardian of the treaties requires it to exercise a "European role." Judges in the European Court of Justice, auditors in the Court of Auditors, and bankers in the European Central Bank have EU-wide functional responsibilities dictated by the EU-wide mandate of their organisation. All of these institutions are staffed by officials drawn from the member states and are thus multinational multilingual organisations. Among the supranational institutions a further distinction seems appropriate between the Commission as a multipurpose institution, on the one hand, and single-task institutions such as the courts and the European Central Bank. Judges, lawyers, central bankers, and auditors experience a strong professional formation and share professional values that are likely to engender a more cohesive cognitive structure than is possible in the Commission.

The European Court of Justice and European Community Law

There is general scholarly agreement about the importance of the legal order of the European Community (EC) and the European Court of Justice (ECJ) to the dynamic of European integration. There is less agreement among legal scholars and political scientists about how the legal order was fashioned and the degree of autonomy exercised by the ECJ (Burley and Mattli 1993; Alter 1996; Armstrong 1998; Wincott 1996, 2000). EC law evolved as a significant institution characterised by procedural, substantive, and normative elements. The legal order was fashioned by a range of actors, notably ECJ judges, legal advisors in the Court and Commission, legal practitioners, national judges who referred cases to the ECJ, and the litigants who addressed the ECJ with their concerns. Actors adopted new roles, notably European judges and lawyers, or faced a change in the context of established roles, such as national judges. For EC legal actors the predominant logic of appropriateness is the protection of the emerging legal order and the promotion of legal reasoning. National judges, on the other hand, particularly if they are in the national constitutional courts, have to manage the interface between national legal orders and the emerging EC order.

The following hypotheses related to the capacity of the ECJ and EC law in "identity building" appear plausible.

1. The ECJ and the legal edifice it fostered was constitutive of the EU as a union based on law. Law is central to the self-definition of the Union and is thus central to the framework of meaning that has grown up around the EU.
2. In building the new legal order, the ECJ was assisted by the centrality of law in the conception of the modern liberal democratic state. The "logic of appropriateness" in court deliberations was that of legal reasoning. Politicians who contested the deliberations of the ECJ had to confront the normative weight of the "rule of law" and the underlying value of judicial independence in the member states.
3. Rules such as secrecy, the absence of dissenting judgements, and the impossibility of reappointment shielded individual judges from national pressures and allowed the professional status of judges to predominate.
4. The development of the new legal order was assisted by the emergence of a cadre of lawyers who specialised in EC law in the Commission's legal service, law firms, and academia. Thousands of lawyers in Europe carried a professional identity shaped by EC law. This professional identity also engendered a normative commitment to the development of the EU as a legal order.
5. The most significant tensions created by EC law are experienced by those national judges responsible for mediating between national constitutions and the emerging legal order of the Union.

The tentacles of the EC's legal order extended into national legal systems and affected the rights and obligations of individuals, companies, and state authorities. EC law has become embedded within national legal orders, albeit in a process that was far from smooth.

The Commission

The Commission's powers of policy initiation and guardianship of the treaties oblige the College of Commissioners and all commissioners within their policy domains to exercise a "European role." However, unlike the ECJ or the European Central Bank, the Commission is a multiorganisation performing a number of different tasks in the EU system (Cram 1997, 162). Role orientations in the College of Commissioners are particularly problematic because individual commissioners are far more likely than ECJ judges to face cross-cutting tensions between the national and the European. Commissioners may stay in Brussels for only one term of office and

have usually held political office in domestic government. Individual commissioners do not lose their national identity when they migrate to Brussels. A commissioner continues to have a special concern for the "country
I know best," the kinds of words used at College meetings when a commissioner makes an intervention that refers to his or her home country. It
is well known that commissioners take up national causes particularly in
relation to state aid, fines, and distribution of structural funds and other politically sensitive issues. An extract from an insider's account of Ireland's negotiations in 1993 concerning the share out of structural funds highlights
the potential for role conflict in the Commission. During a long night when
the Irish foreign minister refused to agree to the new structural fund regulations unless there was agreement on Ireland's share, the Irish negotiating
team were joined by Ireland's commissioner for the duration. When the
Irish foreign minister finally agreed an amount, he wanted someone to witness his handshake with Commission President Delors. The Irish commissioner said, "Commissioner Pee Flynn will be proud to be his witness." His
chef de cabinet immediately whispered in his ear, whereupon the commissioner said, "Commissioner Pee Flynn cannot do what he just said he
would. The Commissioner has taken an oath that precludes him from bear-
ing witness on behalf of a member state. Ye had better get yourselves another witness" (Finley 1998, 178).

There are clear limits to the margin of manoeuvre that commissioners
have in relation to their own state. If they wish to be effective and rated in
the College, they have to thread a careful line between their "European
role" and the "country they know best." Commissioners face cross-cutting
identity pressures while at the same time pursuing the European public
good.

We could expect that Commission officials, particularly those following a
lifelong career in the Commission, would adopt a European role with
greater ease. Having been neglected for many years, the impact of the Commission's "European" role on identity is currently the subject of substantial
empirical analysis (Egeberg 1996; Hooghe 1999). Egeberg analysed the impact of nationality on the Commission services and Hooghe addressed the
political orientations of senior Commission officials. The "logic of appropriateness" that operates in the Commission leans toward an articulation of a
"European" public interest rather than the promotion of discreet national interests or preferences. According to Egeberg, "Like the commissioners, the
officials employed by the services are expected to behave like Europeanists,
and avoid favouring their home countries" (Egeberg 1996, 722). The Egeberg study supports the contention that nationality does not have a major
impact on decision making in the Commission. At the unit level "European
considerations, often probably concretised and made operational by the
unit's DG affiliation, are manifest. Being endowed with a set of favourable

organisational and policy-related devices, intentionally or unintentionally shaped, the services seem to have achieved some autonomy for promoting what is defined as common European interests" (Egeberg 1996, 733). A European interest was defined negatively as the absence of national favouritism and the emergence of policy that was not simply the result of a consensus-seeking process with national officials and governments. In almost all units, DG concerns or European concerns were found to be significant (Egeberg 1996, 272). National officials in Council working parties perceive the Commission as independent of particular national interests to a considerable extent; in a study of the perceptions of national officials, 93 percent of respondents felt that the representatives of the Commission were independent of national concerns (Egeberg 1999, 453). Moreover, national officials perceive the Commission as an important actor in the communications networks within the Council (Beyers and Dierickx 1998), and they listen carefully to the proposals and arguments of the Commission (Egeberg 1999, 468). The Commission and its staff are not just agents of the member states but purposeful actors who have forged an institutional identity that is justified on the basis of a "European role" or vocation (Cram 1997).

The conclusion that the Commission fosters an institutional identity does not imply that the Commission is a unitary actor and that Commission officials have a shared mind-set. Hooghe's in-depth research on the political orientations of top-level Commission officials concluded that senior officials vary in terms of on four dimensions—commitment to a supranational or intergovernmental Union, commitment to a technocratic or democratic Union, opinion of the degree of market regulation that should be fostered in the Union, and perspective on the balance between the European public good and national and functional concerns (Hooghe 1999). Her analysis led to the claim that "fifty years after its creation, the Commission still does not have powerful mechanisms for selective recruitment, socialisation or cognitive association that may produce a more unitary 'mindset'" (Hooghe 1999, 365). It would seem implausible that the Commission could amass the resources to produce a unitary "mindset" for a number of reasons. First, it remains a multiorganisation in functional terms, encompassing different policy areas that would be the domain of separate ministries at the national level. There is a strong sectoral dimension to the work of the Commission and extensive intersectoral conflict, such as that between agriculture and environment or internal market and social affairs. Second, the Commission is a multinational and multicultural organisation with staff drawn from very many administrative cultures, characterised by a cleavage between the strongly Weberian administrative traditions of Northern Europe and the clientalist traditions of Southern Europe. Third, member governments continue to exercise considerable influence in the appointment of high-ranking officials and place many national experts in different parts of the Commission.

The following hypotheses appear plausible in charting the identity-building capacity of the Commission.

1. Individual commissioners carry multiple identities, including a representational one for the "country they know best."
2. The identities of Commission officials—as EU functionaries, as nationals of the member states, and as bureaucrats in specific units—are cross cutting rather than nested. Among Commission officials there will be variation in terms of the identities that are assumed, with room for role conflict and role switching.
3. The role of the Commission both as policy initiator and guardian of the treaties engenders an institutional identity that favours consideration of EU-wide concerns rather than national favouritism, but this is highly contingent.
4. Nationality remains important in terms of recruitment, networking, and information channels, but that nationality is embedded in a multinational framework.
5. Sectoral concerns (agriculture, internal market, environment) play an important part in the role identity of Commission officials.

Double Hatting

The Council

The Council apparatus—the European Council, the Council of Ministers, the presidency, Committee of Permanent Representatives (COREPER), and Council working groups—bring national actors out of their national contexts and embed them in a multileveled and multinational process of public policy making. The organising principle of the Council system is predominantly territorial. Those serving the Council machinery carry an explicit mandate to represent the national response to Commission proposals and are responsible for promoting and defending national preferences in the Council negotiating process. However, even the Council system fosters European roles and identity formation. The Council is a complex site of negotiation that is characterised by the following levels/divisions:

- Political (European Council/Council of Ministers)
- Official—high-level committees (COREPER, Political Committee, 130 Committee, Economic and Finance Committee, Special Agricultural Committee), 150–200 working groups
- Organisation—presidency, Troika, Antici and Mertens groups, and Council Secretariat
- Sectoral—20–22 Council formations

The most explicitly European role in the Council apparatus is the presidency, a device that has developed into a powerful component of the Union's institutional landscape. The handbook of the presidency, drafted by the Council Secretariat, clearly states, "The Presidency must, by definition, be neutral and impartial" (Council of Ministers Handbook 1996). The presidency has evolved into an office of the Union and is not to be treated as an opportunity to pursue national interests. The "logic of appropriateness" in relation to the presidency stresses the supranational role of this office (Kerrmans 1996, 229). For the member state whose representative is in the chair, the office reinforces its identity as a member of the European club. The identity dimension of the presidency is particularly important to relatively new member states and to small states. Hayes-Renshaw and Wallace argue that the presidency has an important socialisation effect, because it forces "the relevant member government to pay periodically more attention to EU-wide policy concerns" (1997, 156). Countries holding the presidency may however face tensions between the European and the national. If states attempt to use the chair to promote their own strongly held preferences or interests, they are likely to face criticism from their partners and in the European Parliament. The German presidency in the first half of 1999 was viewed as an "integrationist" presidency, particularly with regard to the management of the Agenda 2000 negotiations. In the lead-up to the German presidency, the German government had signalled its concern about German "net contributions" to the EU budget and its preference for a reduction in them. In the event, the German presidency did not push its national preference in order to get agreement. In contrast, the French presidency in the latter half of 2000 was perceived as far too concerned with its own agenda and protecting French voting power in the Council of Ministers in the closing stages of the negotiations on the Nice Treaty.

Scholars working on the Union's policy processes are divided about the impact of participation in the Council on the socialisation of national actors. It is perhaps necessary to distinguish between the political and the official levels of decision making and, at the official level, between those who are seconded to the permanent representation in Brussels and those who remain in the national capitals. For capital-based officials, the extent of their exposure to EU business is likely to be significant. Hayes-Renshaw and Wallace (1997) in their volume on the Council of Ministers conclude that the Council engenders a collective identity because:

> Decision-makers in the Council, in spite of their national roots, become locked into the collective process, especially in areas of well-established and recurrent negotiation. This does not mean that the participants have transferred loyalties to the EU system, but it does mean that they acknowledge themselves in certain crucial ways as being part of a collective system of decision-making. (Hayes-Renshaw and Wallace 1997, 279)

According to this view, participation in EU negotiations produces a co-hort of officials in each member state, notably those who have worked in the permanent representation and intensively in Council working parties, who are "neither wholly intergovernmental nor wholly supranational in their outlook and approach" (Hayes-Renshaw and Wallace 1997, 235). This cadre of officials act as "boundary managers" between the national and the European. They are an invaluable bureaucratic resource that helps the domestic systems mediate and internalise the European. They operate in that demimonde between the national and the European, promoting national preferences but also committed to "yesable packages" and collective outcomes. Although there is only limited empirical data on these actors, they seem to share certain characteristics. They are at home in a multinational, multicultural environment, are effective negotiators, are highly rated by their peers, and have a deep knowledge of the procedures and norms of the EU.

The representatives of the member states at both the political and official level are taken out of the national and inserted into the collective EU system. Effective involvement in the EU system of public policy making requires them to build up a shared commitment to the collective endeavour. While the primary allegiance remains national, the EU cognoscenti or Brussels insiders straddle the boundaries by learning to double hat. The impact of double hatting is emphasised by Kerrmans, who concludes that

> actor socialisation has also had an important influence on the role perception of the national representatives. They see themselves not merely as representatives of their states in the European Union but also as representatives of the European Union in their member states. Their perception has become one of a double role in which the national representation is still preponderant but in which the importance of the role of "European adviser" in their own capital is increasing. (Kerrmans 1996, 233)

The bridging role between the national and the European is exercised by those involved in the national permanent representation in Brussels. The senior diplomats in the representation act as a conduit of information and advice between the domestic capitals and the decision-making processes of the Union. As participants in the key committees—COREPER 1 and 2—they filter dossiers between the technical working party phase and the political, Council phase. Lewis highlights the "sociality and normative environment within which interests are defined and defended" in COREPER (Lewis 2000, 262). He identifies five performance norms in COREPER: diffuse reciprocity, thick trust, mutual responsiveness, a consensus-reflex, and a culture of compromise (Lewis 2000, 268). All of these norms constitute a thick normative environment within which the "boundary managers" operate. According to Lewis, "There is an identifiable secondary allegiance among the permanent representatives to the collective arena. To their job requirement of 'delivering the goods' at home is added a diffuse responsibility to deliver collectively as well" (Lewis 2000, 274).

Egeberg has empirically analysed the role and identity perceptions of national officials in EU decision making. He distinguishes between the purpose- and function-based Commission structure and the territorial Council structure. The empirical data suggests that there is a distinction between participation in Commission and Council committees. When asked who they feel allegiance to when participating in EU committees, 66 percent of national officials in Commission expert committees, but 93 percent in Council working parties, said they identify with their own government. The proportions identifying with the committees in which they participate were 26 percent and 20 percent, respectively, and with the EU as a whole, 39 percent and 35 percent, respectively. This study concludes that supranational allegiance among national officials is secondary, but that this does not mean that such loyalty is of minor importance. Most officials reported that positions would be modified or altered during the negotiations, which leads Egeberg to conclude that "a considerable portion of collective responsibility for reaching decisions seems to exist" (Egeberg 1999, 467). Trondal utilises the dual perspective of social constructivism and organisational theory to explore the role conceptions of national civil servants in Commission expert groups and Council working parties. He found that national officials attending Commission groups tended to evoke an "independent expert" role more strongly than those attending Council working parties. The latter in turn evoked a "government representative" role more strongly than the former. A supranational agent role was evoked less strongly than either of these roles. However, officials dealing intensively with a particular committee and topic tended to evoke a supranational agent identity (Trondal 2001).

The impact of the Council roles on identity formation varies across levels of the Council hierarchy and in different sectors. The office of presidency appears to have the greatest capacity to build the European identity of member states, albeit for a short period, by giving them responsibility for the operation of the system and ample opportunity to bring the European into the national through European Council meetings in national capitals and other informal councils. Participation in councils at the political level— European Council and Council of Ministers—would tend not to generate a strong European identity, because the political level deals with the most contentious issues in EU negotiations, and all European Council members are answerable to national electorates and national parliaments. The nature of European Council deliberations, particularly on issues such as the distribution of votes in the system of weighted voting, would tend to accentuate interstate bargaining and national preferences. Many councils have, however, developed an esprit de corps. Prime ministers and ministers, as national office holders, are deeply embedded in the national framework, although many have been open to deploying European symbols in national domestic practice. National officials who work within the Council system remain representatives of their member states but develop secondary loyalties to the collective arena. The following hypotheses appear plausible concerning the identity-building capacity of the Council.

1. The presidency as an office has an important impact on identity as a member of the club.
2. National politicians in the European Council and Council of Ministers have a limited capacity for the articulation of a European identity, but this differs across the member states.
3. Officials working within the Council system—permanent representations and working parties—develop a secondary identification with the EU as an arena of governance through intensity of interaction, the development of shared norms, and shared frames of meaning. This is strongest in committees such as COREPER that are cross-sectoral.
4. In all member states there is a cadre of EU cognoscenti or boundary managers with considerable EU experience who are spread throughout the national administrations. They develop a secondary identification with the EU.

The European Parliament

The European Parliament (EP), as its name suggests, endows the Union with one of the universal features of liberal democracy—a parliamentary body. With 626 members drawn from the member states, the EP represents the peoples of the member states. Members of the EP (MEPs) are elected from national constituencies on the basis of electoral and constituency design determined by national law. MEPs are faced with cross-cutting multiple identities—MEP, party affiliation, nationality, region, and functional (EP Committees). They also have an institutional identity fashioned by the decision rules of the Union (consultation, cooperation, and codecision) that force the EP to negotiate with the Council on legislative output. EP institutional actors include not just the MEPs but the officials who work for the EP. Many of these officials have developed a strong affiliation to the EP and a commitment to enhancing its role in the EU. National identity continues to manifest itself in parliamentarians' choices of committee, speaking interventions, and voting. However, since direct elections in 1979 and the growth in the powers of the EP, political parties in the Parliament have developed into a protoparty system, albeit with strong national delegations in all of the main party groupings. MEPs face cross-cutting identity pressures arising from the policy goals of their groups and the EP, on the one hand, and national preferences, on the other (Hix 1999). Empirical analyses of the socialisation effect of membership in the EP have found that the EP exercised a rapid, albeit gentle, socialisation effect on its members in the initial period of membership (Katz and Wessels 1999, 58).

On the face of it, the EP is the institution in the Union's landscape with a mandate to explain and justify the policies and politics of the EU. Direct elections every five years bring its members into direct contact with the mass public and provide an important opportunity for citizenship participation in European politics. Paradoxically, at the same time that the EP has greatly enhanced its role in the legislative system, its connection to those whom it is said to represent has weakened. One of the most striking features of successive waves of European elections is declining participation by voters in these elections from 63 percent in 1979 to 49.2 percent in 1999, a decline of 13.8 percent. These figures hide very significant cross-national variation ranging in 1999 from 90 percent in Belgium, with compulsory voting, to 23 percent in the UK. Possible explanations for low turnout in general and cross-national variation are beyond the scope of this chapter (Blondel, Sinnott, and Svensson 1998). Suffice it to say that MEPs have difficulty in remaining connected to their constituencies.

The following hypotheses appear plausible in relation to the identity-building capacity of the EP.

1. MEPs carry multiple identities, and the main tension they face is between national identity and party affiliation.
2. MEPs vary in their attitudes to the kind of polity they wish to see fostered by integration.
3. Some EP members and officials have supranational identities that have led them to work to enhance the role of the EP vis-à-vis the Council.
4. The capacity of the EP to generate political citizenship among Europe's peoples is limited by low turnout in EP elections and low levels of knowledge about the EP among the European electorate.

CONCLUSION

The focus in this chapter has been on the EU as an institution, macrolevel analysis, and on EU institutions as identity builders, microlevel analysis. Our discussion of the EU as an institution has led to the conclusion that the Union has become a powerful social construction in contemporary Europe and the wider world. It is not an alternative to the nation-state. Rather, Europe's nation-states have become embedded in this framing social construction or have had to accommodate themselves to its presence. The EU has exerted considerable drawing power on its near neighbours. Over time, the Union's normative dimension has been made more explicit, and it is about to be codified in a constitutional treaty. The normative frame is embodied in a set of shared values and a concept of civic statehood. In addition, the Union has developed a set of specific EU-related symbols—the most powerful of which is the euro—that expand Europe's forest of symbols. These are not stand-alone symbols but are usually deployed in conjunction with national symbols. The euro coins, characterised by shared symbols on one side and national symbols on the other, connote the co-existence of European and national symbols.

The microlevel of analysis focusing on EU institutions and the development of new roles in Europe has enabled us to highlight the impact of engagement with EU institutions on national elites. The institutionalisation of the European Union and its evolution as a polity has led to the creation of new supranational roles that carry with them Europe-wide responsibilities. Bankers, judges, commissioners, and European civil servants are part of a European elite formed by the evolution of the Union. More importantly, national officials and politicians whose job it is to promote and protect national preferences are socialised into collective norms through the intensity of negotiations and the search for collective agreement. The European Union is a salient and ever-present social reality for those who make or adjudicate on public policies in Europe. Eurobarometer's *Top Decision-Makers Survey* indicates that Europe's elite cannot envisage governing without the Union at this stage.

The Union does not, however, represent a one-dimensional frame of meaning or an uncontested normative framework for European states or their citizens. It offers multiple frames and many Europes—market Europe, social Europe, human rights Europe, racist Europe, wealthy Europe, poorer Europe—east and west, north and south. Despite its appalling previous history of internal wars and external conquest, which by 1945 had brought it to the point of virtual self-destruction, Western Europe during the past half-century has shown itself to have an extraordinary capacity to remodel relationships between Europe's states and their peoples. It has done so not only through economic interdependence and material practice but also through the reconfiguration of the normative and symbolic context of statehood in Europe. The politicisation of integration and the contested nature of identity building is part of a necessary process by which the EU "is brought to life" and becomes "taken for granted," part of the landscape (Berger and Luckmann 1967, 75).

6

National and Transnational Identities: European and Other Identities Constructed in Interviews with EU Officials

Ruth Wodak

> We have a truth, but this truth is multiform . . . multivisage . . . it has many faces as a truth, which is not the case for Japan and the United States . . . it's a defensive one. We are not Americans and we are not Japanese. . . . Until now it has been like that. We have defined ourselves in comparison with. Slowly we are writing our own definition.
>
> —EC3

> Since every search for identity includes differentiating oneself from what one is not, identity politics is always and necessarily a politics of the creation of difference. . . . What is shocking about these developments, is not the inevitable dialectic of identity/difference that they display but rather the atavistic belief that identities can be maintained and secured only by eliminating difference and otherness. The negotiation of identity/ difference . . . is the political problem facing democracies on a global scale.
>
> —Seyla Benhabib, *Democracy and Difference*

Since its beginnings in the 1950s, the shape of what is now known as the European Union (EU) has been constantly evolving. The original six members have grown to fifteen, the number of official languages to eleven, and the economic, legal, and political ties have expanded and deepened. With former Eastern Bloc countries preparing for membership in the coming decades, the EU's development and expansion continues. At its core, this largely political and economic process also concerns identity. No longer merely the geographical conglomeration of individual and, in the past, frequently belligerent nation-states, the member states of the EU and the web of ties connecting them seem to be evolving toward something beyond the sum of their parts. But what does this something look like? How is the European Union defined? Can we already speak of a European[1] identity or identities? What does it mean to be a member of the EU? How are national, organizational,[2] and individual identities invoked and oriented to in the discourses of EU organizations and those who represent them?

This chapter takes a sociolinguistic and discourse-analytical perspective—one that shares the viewpoint that the EU, its organizations, and its representatives are largely constructed (and construct themselves) discursively—to investigate these sorts of questions on the basis of interviews, conducted in Brussels during a period of intensive fieldwork, with delegates to the European Parliament (EP), civil servants in the European Commission, and representatives from the Committee of Permanent Representatives (COREPER) and its working groups, the secretariat of the Council of Ministers. The analyses presented here form part of a larger multidisciplinary study[3] that examines the communicative processes shaping the discursive decision making on employment policies that takes place in the multinational, multilingual, and multicultural organizations of the EU (see Muntigl, Weiss, and Wodak 2000). After briefly sketching some theoretical assumptions about the concept of identity/difference and providing details about the data, my tools of analysis, and my research questions, I proceed with the analysis, which is divided into two parts. The first (section 3) focuses on and compares the content of the responses of the individuals interviewed and looks for patterns that appear relevant to identity using a taxonomy that my colleagues and I elaborated in our studies on the discursive construction of national identities in Austrian and also in the European Union (Wodak et al. 1999; Weiss 2002; Wodak and Weiss 2003); the second (section 4) takes a more linguistic look at the specific identities established and used in the discourse. The chapter concludes with a discussion of the nature and significance of these identities, and directions for future research.

BACKGROUND

Perspective on Identity

Sociolinguistic studies of relevance to the analysis of individual, national, and transnational identities fall roughly into three groups, those using ethnomethodological/conversation-analytic approaches to charting identity in use, such as Antaki and Widdicombe 1998, Widdicombe 1998, and Zimmerman 1998; studies using a discourse–socio linguistic/discourse-historical approach, in particular Wodak et al. 1999; de Cillia, Reisigl, and Wodak 1999 (which are based largely in the cultural studies work of Stuart Hall, Denis Martin, Seyla Benhabib, and also on the work of Pierre Bourdieu and Paul Ricoeur); and those drawing on concepts such as footing, framing, and positioning, such as Goffman 1981; Tannen and Wallat 1987/1993; and Davies and Harré 1990; or focusing on pronouns or person deictics, such as Wilson 1990; Reisigl and Wodak 2001; and Wortham 1996.

According to the ethnomethodological/conversation-analytic perspective, identity is not something static that people *are* or that they *have* (as is the case in much social science research, in which social categories assigned a priori are often seen as predictive of certain types of behaviour), but as something that they can orient to and use as a resource in the course of interaction. As Widdicombe (1998, 191) puts it, "The important analytic question is not therefore whether someone can be described in a particular way, but to show *that* and *how* this identity is made relevant or ascribed to self or others." In other words, although a person may be potentially classifiable by gender, ethnicity, class or age, or as a doctor, mother, sister and so on, these particular identities are not automatically relevant in every interaction she or he engages in. A person may invoke any number of aspects of identity depending on the contingencies of a particular conversation, or one may be positioned by one's interlocutors in a particular way (e.g., as someone in need of sympathy or help). The main point is rather than using identities as "demographic facts, whose relevance to a stretch of interaction can simply be assumed" (Widdicombe 1998, 194–195), the analyst should "focus on *whether, when* and *how* identities are used. . . . Concern is with the occasioned relevance of identities here and now, and how they are consequential for his particular interaction and the local projects of speakers" (Widdicombe 1998, 195). To sum up, identities are locally occasioned, interactively constructed, and are resources "*used* in talk" (Antaki and Widdicombe 1998, 1).

With respect to the individuals interviewed for this study, it is important to note that while I introduce them above as delegates to the European Parliament, civil servants in the European Commission, and representatives from COREPER and the working groups that serve the Council of Ministers, these labels represent exogenous identities, that is, identities that these individuals can be interpreted as "wearing" by virtue of their positions within particular institutions of the EU. In light of the theoretical introduction here, it is important to stress that these classifications may or may not end up being relevant for these individuals in their discursive behaviour in an interview situation, even if the interviewer has selected them specifically because of the expertise associated with their professional titles. Moreover, the borderlines between bureaucrats, diplomats, and politicians are be-coming blurred; politicians more and more have to act bureaucratically, and bureaucrats have the power of politicians (Weiss and Wodak 2000; Wodak and Vetter 1999). Thus, for example, in one interview a member of the European Parliament (MEP) may speak with any range of identities (or "voices," in the sense of Bakhtin 1981): as an MEP speaking as he/she might to a journalist, as one woman to another, as a Finn or Spaniard or Belgian, as a member of a particular committee or political group, and so on. Precisely which identity(ies) is (are) relevant at a given moment will de-pend on any number factors obtaining for the particular discourse in which the interlocutors are engaged.

Zimmerman (1998, 90ff.) makes a useful distinction among three types of identities found in talk: discourse (e.g., speaker, listener, narrator), situated (e.g., shopkeeper, customer), and transportable (e.g., African American, Eu-ropean, female). In this chapter, I am particularly interested in transportable identities, those that

> travel with individuals across situations and are potentially relevant in and for any situation and in and for any spate of interaction. They are latent identities that "tag along" with individuals as they move through their daily routines. . . . They are identities that are usually visible, i.e. assignable or claimable on the basis of physical or culturally based insignia which furnish the intersub-jective basis for categorization. . . . It is important to distinguish between the registering of visible indicators of identity and oriented-to identity which per-tains to the capacity in which an individual should act in a particular situation. Thus, a participant may be aware of the fact that a co-interactant is classifiable as a young person or a male without orienting to those identities as being rel-evant to the instant interaction. (Zimmerman 1998, 90–91)

In a sense, then, I am interested in the degree to which these potential, transportable identities—that is, parliamentarian, Commission official, Greek, female—are actually *oriented to* in the interview data.

Among the transportable identities we could imagine as potentially relevant for the individuals interviewed is that of nationality, or even *supra*-nationality, a particular "Europeanness." In a recent study on Austria national identity, Wodak et al. 1999 offer a discursively based definition of nation as well as a viable framework for its study. In this research, Wodak et al. draw on Ander-son's (1988) characterization of nations as "imagined communities," noting that

> If a nation is an imagined community and at the same time a mental construct, an imaginary complex of ideas containing at least the defining elements of col-lective unity and equality; of boundaries and autonomy, then this image is real to the extent that one is convinced of it, one believes in it and identifies with it emotionally. The question of how this imaginary community reaches the minds of those who are convinced of it is easy to answer: it is constructed and

conveyed in discourse, predominantly in narratives of national cultural. National identity is thus the product of discourse. (44–45)

With respect to examining discursive data for instantiations of or orientations to national identity, we use the discourse-historical approach, which emphasizes three dimensions of analysis: contents, strategies, and means and forms of realisation (see Wodak 2001c and details in the appendix). It is especially the *contents* aspect of this approach that is relevant for the first part of the analysis in section 3. As in the present chapter, my colleagues and I have analysed (among numerous other types of data) topic-oriented qualitative interviews, arguing that "these interviews can . . . throw light on how patterns of national identification and identity find expression in individuals" and "can illustrate the subjective dimension of the contents and figures of argumentation; the construction of Austrian identity conceived on a more 'macro' level" (Wodak et al. 1999, 88). While the focus of this chapter is clearly not Austrian identity, we believe that our insights are relevant to studying the discursive construction of other identities, both national and supranational (see Wodak 2003, in which the similarities and differences between the construction of national and transnational identities are elaborated).

Data

The data for this analysis consist of twenty-eight interviews with fourteen members of the European Parliament, all members of the Committee on Employment and Social Affairs; ten Commission officials, among them eight from DGV (one of twenty-four directorates-general, DGV being the administrative service responsible for employment policy), one from DGXV (financial institutions/company law), and the commissioner in charge of employment and social issues; and four Austrian delegates to the Council of Ministers, one to COREPER II (ambassador level, permanent representative), one to COREPER I (deputy level), and one a member of the Council's working group responsible for employment and social affairs issues.

It is important to note that I make no claims to having representative samples of individuals from the EP, European Commission, and Council. All persons participating in the study were self-selected to the extent that they responded to our written and/or telephone requests for an interview. Moreover, of the MEPs who participated, ten were from three, largely left-oriented, political groups: the European Socialists, the European United Left, and the Greens. Only four MEPs came from what would be considered more conservative groups (e.g., European People's Party). In addition to the fact that we were able to interview only four individuals from the Council, all of those interviewed are Austrian, and thus we can make no comparison with members from other countries. Finally, with regard to language, only those interviews conducted in English or German are analysed here, these languages being either the first or second languages of both the interviewers and most of the interviewees. All interviews were audiotaped and later transcribed. In sum, then, we are working with a body of data that is suitable for in-depth qualitative, but not statistical, analysis. Quantitative analysis is limited to categorizing and enumerating the content of answers to questions in section 3 and is intended to demonstrate patterns suggestive for the interviewees in this study only.

The interviews focused on four general topic areas, meaning that although certain topic-related questions were generally included in all interviews (e.g., "What do you feel are the reasons for the rise in unemployment in recent years?"), interviews were structured loosely enough so that interviewees had considerable freedom in developing the topics and steering the conversation as they wished. The main topic groups in the interview protocol, each with several subcategories of possible questions, comprised (1) unemployment, including reasons for, possible solutions to, and perspectives on current employment-related policy making, especially the Luxembourg Employment Summit; (2) the role of the EU organization in which the interviewee works, including relationships with other EU bodies, the interviewee's own role within the organization, and his or her "access points," or contact with "ordinary" EU citizens; (3) day-to-day working life, including multicultural issues and the development of documents such as reports and opinions; and (4) the interviewee's personal history, for instance, career development and definition of "being European." Through the specific methodology applied, it was possible to gather information about the perspectives, ideologies, and opinions of the interviewees. Moreover, and even more importantly, the discursive realisation of all these answers displays the identity constructions in many singular linguistic units, such as in the use of pronouns, in the narrative constructions, and in the use of argumentation patterns (see Reisigl and Wodak 2001, chapter 2, for the detailed linguistic taxonomy).

In the analyses that follow, interviewees are referred to by an organizational code and number—for instance, MEP (Member of the European Parliament) 4, EC (European Commission) 6, and CM (Council of Ministers) 3—to provide anonymity.

Methods of Analysis

The interviews were analysed using what is basically a triangulated approach, as is consistent with the Vienna School. Triangulation (Cicourel 1974) implies "that discursive phenomena are approached from a variety of methodological and theoretical perspectives taken from various disciplines." This study employs triangulation to the extent that it bases its findings on the results of two different types of analysis. First, it employs a general qualitative content analysis, as is common in the social sciences; second, it uses a more detailed linguistic analysis. Both phases focus on participant responses to the questions most explicitly connected to identity (e.g., "How would you describe the role of the European Parliament in employment policy making and how do you see yourself in the same context?" and "Do you consider yourself to be European and, if so, what are the characteristics of being European?").

Part 1 of the analysis (section 3) essentially involves the "contents" aspect of the discourse-historical approach (the discourse topics) and what Kvale (1996, 192) has described as "meaning condensation" and "meaning categorization" (Kvale 1996, 192), in other words, the compression of statements by interviewees into succinct paraphrases, which can then be organized into categories. After this process has been applied to each interview, responses are compared for similarities and differences in patterns, and these patterns are then examined in light of their significance as potential indicators of identity. Especially the explicit question "Do you consider yourself to be European?" is of interest here with respect to what it may reveal about both national and supranational identities. Grounded on Pierre Bourdieu's notion of "habitus" we believe that

> national identity is a complex of common or similar beliefs or opinions internalised in the course of socialization . . . as well as certain out-groups distinguished from the national "we-group", and of common or similar emotional attitudes and dispositions with regard to these aspects and out-groups, as well as common or similar behavioural dispositions, including inclusive, solidarity-oriented and exclusive, distinguishing dispositions. (Wodak et al. 1999, 55)

While the scope of this chapter precludes tackling the more psychological issues of "internalization" and "socialization," the point that is relevant is "similar beliefs or opinions." In other words, in the contents portion of my analysis, I will assume that similarity of responses to certain question types *may* be indexical of orientation to a similar type of identity or identities. At the same time, I will look for the discursive creation of "out-groups." For instance, is a particular "we" group consistently characterized with reference to what or whom it is *not* (see Reisigl and Wodak 2001 and appendix)? Here, work by ethnomethodological conversation analysts is relevant too, for example, McKinlay and Dunnett 1998 and Widdicombe 1998: "Similarity in opinion can be used to claim solidarity and achieve group status" and difference of opinion the contrary (Widdicombe 1998,195–96). Thus, similar responses to particular questions are potential indicators of group affiliation or identification; but—of course—we are aware that even the same person may have multiple contradictions and "ideological dilemmas" in his or her statements (see Billig 1995).

Part 2 of my analysis (section 4) examines the same body of data, but uses different, more explicitly linguistic tools (1) to see whether patterns determined in the first phase of analysis are supported when considered from another perspective, and/or (2) to uncover new patterns. Essentially, in the second phase of the analysis I am looking for when and how certain identities are achieved and oriented to. I would like to focus on certain strategies of constructing sameness and difference (see Wodak and Weiss 2001).

In the data analyzed here, narratives (or personal examples and anecdotes that may or may not follow the "canonical" narrative form, i.e., consisting of abstract, orientation, complicating actions, evaluation, and coda, as described by Labov 1972, Labov and Waletzky 1967) are particularly fruitful sites for footing changes that are related to transportable identities. As noted by Schiffrin (e.g., 1996, 1997), Linde (1993), Mumby (1993), Ochs (1997), and others, narrative is, among other things, "a tool for instantiating social and personal identities" (Ochs 1997, 202). Schiffrin argues that

> narratives can provide . . . a SOCIOLINGUISTIC SELF-PORTRAIT: a linguistic lens through which to discover people's on views of themselves (as situated within both an ongoing interaction and a larger social structure) and their experiences. Since the situations that speakers create through narratives—the transformations of experience enabled by the story world—are also open to evaluation in the interactional world, these self-portraits can create an interactional arena in which the speaker's view of self and world can be reinforced or challenged. (Schiffrin 1997, 42; emphasis in original)

What Schiffrin highlights in particular is the dynamic aspect of identity construction in interaction, especially in narratives. Most relevant for the analysis here, however, is simply that narratives can reveal footings that in turn reveal orientations to particular constructions of self. I will demonstrate this with examples in section 4.

In addition to narratives, focused attention on participant deictics, or pronominal reference, has been successfully used to unlock the dynamics of a particular interaction (see Ehlich 1991; Maas 1984; Wodak et al. 1999; Reisigl and Wodak 2000). John Wilson found that the "broad range of personal pronominal choices were indicative of how the individual politician viewed the world, and how that politician manipulated the meaning of pronouns in order to present a specific ideological perspective" (1990, 56). Moreover, certain rhetorical and argumentational strategies are of interest (Reisigl and Wodak 2001; see appendix).

ANALYSIS OF DISCOURSE TOPICS

In this section, I examine the subjective responses of MEPs, Commission officials, and COREPER/Council representatives interviewed for this study to questions referring to whether the interviewee views her/himself as European and, if so, what the characteristics of "being European" are.

The question in focus here is "Do you consider yourself to be European and, if so, what are the characteristics of being European?" which requests rather direct labelling of self-identity. Since the question involves two components, the self-labelling and the listing of specific qualities, my presentation here is also handled in two parts. And because response patterns appear to correspond with the interviewees' respective EU organizational affiliation, my discussion looks at MEPs, Commission officials, and Council representatives, respectively.

MEPs

In table 6.1, we see that most MEPs among those who were asked/responded to the first part of the question, "Do you consider yourself to be European?" responded explicitly with "I am European" (one MEP simply stated "yes"), and five of these further added their self-identification with the country they represent in the Parliament, for instance, "I am European and I am Dutch." At the same time, other characteristics are relevant, for example coming from a particular region, supranational or national, such as Scandinavia or Hessen, or labeling oneself as from a particular city, such as Berlin. Four MEPs mentioned explicitly that "being European" involved more than simply the EU, but entailed being a "world citizen" or "cosmopolitan" as well. Interestingly, all four MEPs who added this to their self-definition are affiliated with the Green Party.[4] One MEP defines herself in several "layers" of these characteristics:

First I feel like I come from Västerbotten in the North of Sweden. I feel like a Västerbotten. I don't live there, but I feel like that. I feel like a Swede. I feel like a Scandinavian. I feel like a European and I feel like a world citizen. (MEP10)

Commission Officials

Concerning organizational identity, the responses of Commission officials suggest somewhat more homogeneity than those of the MEPs (see table 6.2):

Specifically, all except one Commission official made an explicit statement to the effect of "Yes I feel European" or responded with an unequivocal "Sure!" or "Yes." Here, too, about half of the interviewees added that they also identified themselves in terms of their home country/nationality; in other words, a standard response was along the lines of "Yes, I am European, but I am also French."

I think the Commission officials tend to be European, who have a vision of trying to get the best of each component of the EU. At the same time, I'm

Table 6.1. Self-definitions of members of the European Parliament (MEPs)

	European	Region in Europe, e.g., Scandinavia	Country/ nationality	Region in country, e.g., Bavaria	City, town	World citizen; not just EU	Not in terms of citizenship	Definition variable in relation to others
MEP1	X		X		X			
MEP2	X	X	X					
MEP3	(X)[a]				X			
MEP4	X					X		
MEP5	X			X				
MEP6	X							
MEP7	X	X	X			X		
MEP8	N/A							
MEP9	X		X					
MEP10	X	X	X		X	X		
MEP11	N/A							
MEP12	N/A							
MEP13				X			X	
MEP14	(X)[b]		(X)		(X)	X		X
	9/13 (10)/13	3/13 (4)/13	5/13	2/13	3/13	4/13	1/13	1/13

[a] MEP stated that she is and is not European, depending on how one looks at it.
[b] Characteristics for this MEP hold only in contrast to other countries, for instance, feeling European when in the United States.
N/A = These respondents gave characteristics of what "European" means, but did not explicitly state that they felt European.

Table 6.2. European Commission officials' self-definition

	European	Region in Europe, e.g., Scandinavia	Country/ nationality	Region in country, e.g., Bavaria	City, town	World citizen; not just EU	Not in terms of citizenship	Definition variable in relation to others
EC1	X							
EC2	X							
EC3	(X)[a]		(X)					
EC4	X		X					
EC5	X		X					
EC6	X		X		X			
EC7	X		X					X
EC8	X							X
EC9	X							X
EC10	X							
	9/10 (10)/10		4/10		1/10			9/10

[a] This respondent noted that he felt no more European than before coming to the Commission and that he had never felt particularly bound to his home country.

always a Finn. My philosophy is that you cannot really be a European if you don't have your roots anywhere. (EC5)

Some also indicated feeling European when they are abroad, that is, in contrast to some other nation:

You feel European when you're in the middle of New York. That's when I feel European. (EC8)

No other characteristics appear particularly salient. Unlike the parliamentarians, none of the Commission respondents made a point of explicitly describing themselves as reaching beyond Europe, as "world citizens," and generally they did not speak in terms of regional or more local affiliations.

According to these data, then, it seems that the EC officials we interviewed are slightly more oriented to the idea of a European identity, one that is clearly compatible with maintaining one's national roots. The MEPs here expressed "Europeanness" as well, but tended to emphasize more regional and local identities as well as specifically national ones. One might speculate that these tendencies reflect on the one hand another of the roles commonly associated with the Commission, and on the other hand the nature of the EP electoral system. First, as I noted earlier, the Commission is sometimes viewed as "the conscience of the Community," which, among other things, emphasizes the role of the Commission as a "multinational organization which does not seek to represent any one particular governmental position within the Union" (Cini 1996, 16), but aims to find what is good for the Union as a whole, as a supranational entity. In the words of one EC official:

I'm a Swede and I'm a European because I'm working on the European level and that means that I'm not here to represent Sweden. I'm here to see to all— the interest of ALL countries. (EC4)

In other words, much of what the Commission does is somehow connected with promoting what is European rather than the interests of particular member states.

In contrast, the broader palette of identities mentioned by MEPs in this context could reflect the nature of the parliamentary electoral system, which is not yet unitary across the EU. While some countries abide by a system of constituency representation (e.g., the UK), others have more proportional systems in which the entire country serves as the representative's electoral area (see Corbett, Jacobs, and Schackleton 1995, 13–29). As such, MEPs may in their self-definitions tend to orient to the factors that are relevant to their particular electoral situation, thereby variably emphasizing national, regional, or other such identities.

Council of Ministers Representatives

As was the case in assessing the responses of Council delegates above, here, too, we have difficulty making any clear generalizations because of the limited data. One of the four, like many of the MEPs and Commission officials above, mentions feeling both European and Austrian. Another identifies herself as Austrian, and a fourth merely signals "yes" in response to the question "Are you European?" without elaborating further. Finally, two of them emphasize their scepticism with regard to the present existence of a united "Europe(an Union)," citing the relative strength of *Nationalstaat*:

> Ich glaube, es ist etwas was sich wandelt. . . . Es wird immer mehr, irgendwann werden wir wahrscheinlich alle mal Europäer sein und werden . . . aber für mich ist Europa keine geschlossene Veranstaltung. Und je länger ich im COREPER und im Rat sitze, unsomehr denke ich "Jessus, nein, das kann nie was werden!" . . . In Brüssel werden mit einer Brutalität nationale Interessen vertreten, das mit Europa, oder einem europäischen Gefühl nix zu tun hat. (CM2)
>
> I think it is something that is changing. . . . It is increasing steadily, someday we will probably all be and become Europeans . . . but for me, Europe isn't something that's finished. And the longer I'm in COREPER and the Council, the more I think, "Jesus, no, this can never amount to anything!" . . . In Brussels national interests are represented with a brutality that has nothing to do with Europe or with a European feeling. (my trans.)

This particular description also supports the perception expressed by Commission officials and MEPs that the member states composing the Council sometimes impede developments in the direction of a more united Europe, namely, by brutally representing national, as opposed to supranational, interests.

We can compare the features of what constitutes "European" by examining table 6.3. The characteristics here represent those most frequently mentioned by all interviewees, grouped according to their EU organizational affiliation.

While no definitive comparison among groups can be made, it appears that MEPs and EC officials, while overlapping in the mention of several characteristics, may stress certain features differently. Note, for example, that six of ten—more than half of the Commission officials—stress the "added value" of the member states being united in the European Union. In the words of one official (EC8), it is necessary to "capture Europe's diversity in an economic way," that "Europe's strength is its diversity." In other words, this economic characteristic underscores the legitimacy of the EU. Working together under "one roof," member states can prosper more than if they were to act independently.

Table 6.3.   Characteristics of "European"

	MEP	EC	CM	Total
Way of thinking; exchanging ideas; being concerned with own and others' problems	4/13	1/10	0/4	5/27
Different but shared cultures, traditions, history, languages	5/13	3/10	2/4	9/27
Way of dealing with social, environmental problems; social model; not U.S., Japan	4/13	4/10	1/4	9/27
Part of geographic map, more than EU	4/13	2/10	0/4	6/27
Globally competitive, especially against U.S. and Japan	2/13	3/10	0/4	5/27
Whole is bigger than its parts: being under one roof; added value of EU; strength in diversity	3/13	6/10	1/4	10/27
Vision, direction for the future	4/13	1/10	2/4	7/27
Model for peace	1/13	1/10	1/4	3/27

MEP = Member of European Parliament
EC = European Commission officials
CM = Council of Ministers representatives

Among MEPs no one cluster of characteristics is particularly prominent—instead, several attributes receive similar mention—except, perhaps, for an emphasis on the fact that member states share a certain cultural, historical, and linguistic richness that binds them together, despite differences in specifics.

When we combine the responses of all three groups, however, we see that certain characteristics of "European" are somewhat more prominent than others: (1) differences notwithstanding, generally shared cultural, historical, and linguistic traditions; (2) the "added value" of a united Europe; (3) the European social model, one that is emphatically *not* the same as those in the United States or in many Asian countries; and (4) Europe as a direction for the future. If we look at these attributes more closely, we could argue that they resemble the "matrix of discourses" that Wodak et al. (1999, 57–60) see as capturing the themes relevant to the discursive construction of a nation: the linguistic construction of the *homo Austriacus,* a common culture, a common political present and future, a national body, and the "narration and confabulation of a common political past." Among the characteristics of "European" highlighted by the interviewees, we see repeated reference to a common culture and past (i.e., shared cultural, historical, linguistic traditions; similar social models) and a common present and future (i.e., the European social model; the "added value" of being united; a direction for the future). Moreover, if identity is to some extent "based on the formation of sameness and difference," we see this in the frequent referral to Europe, especially in terms of its social model(s), as *not* the United States or Asia (most prominently, Japan).

LINGUISTIC ANALYSIS OF INTERVIEW SEQUENCES

Let us now take a somewhat more detailed look at these different types of identity construction, beginning with an excerpt from one of the interviews with an EC official. To begin, I focus on the pronouns "I" and "we"; the alternations between them that are of particular interest. The sections most relevant for the discussion have been italicised in the example.[5]

Example 1

1   IF: Are you satisfied with the direction that employment policy mak-
    ing has
2   taken?
3   EC: Yes, yes. *Because I—the thing we identified* there
4   and if you go back—
5   Mr. Flynn has a stageaire trainee working for him
6   and he asked, he has asked her to do a kind of history of the last five
    years of
7   employment
8   and that's why some of it is fresh in my mind
9   because she came to see me two days ago
10 and suddenly started asking me to remember all these things back in
    '93.
11 But one of the things—
12 I actually looked again at the framework,
13 the document on a framework for a community, European commu-
    nity initiative
14 *which we produced in '93,*
15 *I, and what we said then is exactly what we have now achieved*
16 which was a process.
17 *Ah, we always identified that*
18 *what the European Union or the European level could best bring to this
    discussion* was
19 not specific interventions in the sense of transeuropean networks
20 which would create loads of jobs
21 or telling people, y'know, how to change their tax systems or whatever.
22 What *we* could bring was a process
23 whereby people accepted to enter into an intuitive debate about what
    works and

24   what doesn't work in terms of employment policy
25   and to do that at the European level
26   and to accept that they would,
27   they would put their policies on the table, explain them, and have
      them opened to
28   some comparative criticism
29   *where we would say, well sorry, we're not convinced that that's such a
      good*
30   *idea . . .*
31   and that is effectively what *we* have got from the Amsterdam Treaty.

In this excerpt, the interviewer has asked a question that was intended
as a request for EC6's personal opinion. Rather than answering strictly from
his own point of view, EC6 appears to make a switch to the voice of the
Commission. In other words, he orients his identity to being essentially one
and the same with that of the Commission. Note how he begins his response with "Yes, yes," which seems like a straightforward response to the
question ("Are you satisfied with . . ." "Yes, [I am satisfied]"). As he begins
to expand his response with an explanation in line 2 he makes a shift from
"I" to "we," the "we" representing the Commission's perspective: "Because
I—the thing *we* identified there and if you go back—." A similar switch occurs again in lines 14 and 15. Here EC6 is talking about having reviewed a
1993 Commission document and begins from the "I" perspective, when
again he switches to "we": "*I*—and what *we* said then is exactly what *we*
have now achieved." From this point on, EC6's own position in the text remains melded with that of the Commission itself.

A further point of interest in the same example is the way the terms "European Union," "European level," and "we," referring to the Commission,
appear to be used as equivalents. Specifically, one can see this beginning
in lines 16 and 17: "*We* always identified that what *the European Union or
the European level could best bring* to this discussion." From a first reading
of this utterance, one need not conclude that "we" is used in the same
sense as "European Union" or "European level." However, the utterance
that follows in line 21 substitutes "we" for "European Union" or "European
level": "What *we could bring* was a process."

The claim that "we" (the Commission), "European Union," and "European
level" are used as equivalents is strengthened when we consider example 2,
in which the same speaker, EC6, is describing the role of the Commission.
Specifically, in lines 20 to 28 below, he defines the Commission in terms of
the "process" that was referred to in line 21 above. Above, it is "we," "European Union," "European level" that become synonymous in their positions as
"bringers" of a process. Here we see that role is specifically ascribed to the
European Commission and somewhat more elaborately defined.

Example 2

1   I think the Commission has two main roads.
2   I mean the first is that in those policies where we actually have a clear
3   lead—economic and monetary union, the single market, the structural funds,
4   common agricultural policy—that in those policies that we insure as the treaty
5   now obliges us to do
6   that we fully take into account the employment impact
7   that we think through the employment consequences . . .
8   that you thought through
9   that you have the arguments to explain that if you are proposing
10 Telecom's liberalisation
11 and that in the short term there may be job losses
12 that you are well able to explain
13 that we believe those losses are worth having because in due course there
14 will be employment gains . . .
15 The second role is in terms of employment, in terms of impacting on the
16 member states employment policies
17 which we don't wish to subsume more
18 or over which we have no aspiration to have a European harmonisation
19 or that this is decided at the European level
20 But there the role is one of catalyst and of if you like
21 of leading the debate
22 and of pushing the member states
23 sometimes dragging them into a process of mutual dialogue, comparative
24 analysis, and common guidelines. . . .
25 And that's the role of the Commission to bring them into that process
26 to orchestrate that process
27 to animate it
28 to provide it with analysis, with document

"Bringing the process," then, involves the European Commission's being a catalyst, leading the debate, pushing (or dragging) the member states into the process, orchestrating, and animating. In all of this, terms such as "we," "European Union," "European level," and "Commission" appear relatively interchangeably. Moreover, the speaker continues to identify with the Commission, as exhibited in lines 1–2, in which he switches from describing the Commission as a third party ("I think the Commission has two main roads") to including himself in the group constituting "Commission" ("I mean the first is that in those policies where *we* actually have a clear lead").

Other EC officials reveal similar linguistic patterns, as in this excerpt, in which EC5 responds to the interviewer's question about the results of the Luxembourg Employment Summit:

Example 3

1   IM: . . . the so-called Jobs Summit in Luxembourg, ah,
2   what do you think about the results.
3   Are you satisfied with the results,
4   what is your general opinion on—this
5   EC5: *My general opinion is* that *we* are—
6   *we* are quite pleased with the results.
7   Of course, *we: the Commission.* Had ah: somewhat higher ambition than
8   the Council resolution and conclusions actually show but—
9   so in technical terms *we*—would have perhaps wished to go a little bit
10 further. But ah: politically *I think* this was more than *we* had hoped for,
11 because there was a commitment by the member states now to initiate the
12 process
13 where they bind themselves to some quite operational targets.
14 And they also bind themselves to a ah: country surveillance process.
15 In other words ah: reporting regular reporting analysis by the Commission—
16 examination by the Council
17 and then new guidelines next autumn.
18 So the Commission in that sense now has much more weight in the
19 employment field than before, and
20 but that's of course not so important.
21 More important is that the employment issue now is equally relevant as
22 the EMU and the macroeconomic issues,
23 ah *I think* the next big program in the European Union after the EMU
24 and the convergence will be a convergence in the employment field.
25 So *we* initiated in that process here
26 and that's why *we* are very pleased.

In this example, it is again notable that the interviewee's opinion is wed to the voice of a collective, the Commission. In line 5 he begins with "my general opinion is" but quickly switches his orientation to "we": "we are quite pleased." In line 6, he makes clear that this "we" is in fact the Commission. Although this speaker uses "I think" twice, in lines 10 and 22, potentially signalling a personal opinion separate from that of the collective, the overall voice oriented to in this excerpt is "we, the Commission." This is emphasized as he closes his response with "So *we* initiated the process here and that's why *we* are very pleased."

One last example in this section highlights the fluid lines between individuals working in and identifying with the European Commission (as in examples 1 and 3) as well as the link between the European Commission and European Union (highlighted by example 2). This excerpt was preceded by the interviewer asking his interlocutor to compare his experience in an EU organization with having worked in other multinational organizations, like the Organization for Economic Cooperation and Development (OECD).

Example 4

1 *the European Union* is by fa:r ah the most efficient
2 and ah the closest to the governments.
3 the closest to the member states.
4 cause here *we* don´t make only analysis.
5 or *we* don´t make only standards
6 *we* make policy here.
7 and ah actually
8 *the—Union* is is a or *Commission* is an exTENsion of the—national
9 policy making.
10 It's it's not—it doesn´t—
11 it is not indePENdent from the national ah States ah policies.
12 and I find this useful.
13 ah because *we* are constantly controlled by the Member States.
14 but it is positive to be controlled.
15 when *we* are controlled
16 you can also see that *we* are believed—
17 considered to be relevant for them.
18 otherwise they would not care. you see.—
19 there are big differences.

As in the previous examples, by using "we" and listing the activities that are seen as Commission responsibilities (analysis, making standards), the speaker signals his belonging to the Commission. Here, though, the "we" that signals himself and the Commission in lines 4–6 takes the place of "European Union" in line 1. In line 8 he makes a slight refinement, in that he begins to say "Union," but immediately shifts to "Commission." What all of this suggests is that those working in the Commission may indeed identify closely not only with the organization they work for, but with the idea of the European Union as a whole. In other words, following Wilson (1990), in the talk of EC officials we find consistencies in the use of pronouns and their referents that suggest similarities in the officials' discursive construction of the world. Recall that in the "Commission Officials" section, above, we observed that with respect to self-descriptions in response to the question "Do you consider yourself to be European?" Commission officials appeared to orient to "Europeanness" somewhat more than the MEPs interviewed. Now, through these patterns we have additional linguistic evidence pointing toward the Commission to some extent fulfilling its role as "European conscience" (Cini 1996) in the discursive behaviour of its civil servants.

In contrast to the European Commission officials, who tended to speak of themselves in terms of "we," referring to the Commission, and equated this with the European Union or European level, the MEPs oriented to numerous identities, both professional and personal. Among the professional identity types frequently oriented to by MEPs are those of (specific) EP political group member, EP committee member, *rapporteur*, national party member, and representative from a particular member state; very often, however, relatively more personal aspects of identity emerged as well, from social worker, family man or woman, or grandmother to more abstract presentations of personal or moral positions, such as tolerant, active, diplomatic, or pragmatic. Many of these presentations of self manifest themselves in brief personal anecdotes or longer narratives.

As discussed above, narratives are particularly revealing indices of identity because they offer a sort of "window" onto how individuals evaluate their past experience and position themselves in their world. Example 5 is a narrative in which MEP2 talks about her first experience as a *rapporteur*.

Example 5

```
1    when I—entered the parliament—              Orientation (lines 1-3)
2    on my first report it was about Leonardo
3    I don't know if you know:
4    ((smiles)) well—I said "I'm going to speak to the commissioner"
5    and—I—/ I knew—he only speaks very bad French
6    and my äh my French was very bad as well.
7    so I said "I want to have interpretation"
8    So—I went to the commissioner     Complicating Actions (lines 4-14)
9    with a very good int / int / interpreter
10   and I / I / I / I talked more than an hour with him.
11   because we talked the same about it
12   and at the end he said—
13   "well: I have here the advice of my: civil servants but I—agree with you:
14   and this and this and this all goes through.—"
15   so you have to be:—äh:—
```

16 I don't know h / how do we call it in English in / I
17 in the Netherlands we say (bruta:l)
18 so you have to: ((laughs)) be polite   *Evaluation (lines 16–20)*
19 but you have to—you: / you mustn't be /
20 you mustn't <u>sit</u> behind your—/ your <u>desk</u>.—
21 because that doesn't help. ((laughs))
22 but then then you have the worse system
23 that I tried several times   *Coda (22–31)*
24 then you have the Council.—
25 a:nd—it's very difficult äh:
26 to negotiate with the Council is my:—/ äh is my experience:
27 it's possible to do:—
28 bu:t——now they have their own strategy:
29 and their own—reasons:
30 äh: and they don't like the power of the parliament
31 so: the: / the / that's—/ that's the most difficult part

In this example, which has been marked for basic narrative structure according to the model designed by Labov (1972) and Labov and Waletzky
(1967), we see that the MEP's story is objectively about having a successful
meeting with a commissioner while acting as *rapporteur* on a report about
Leonardo.[6] In lines 4–6, the complicating actions, she says she went to the
commissioner with an interpreter, and because she and the commissioner
had the same understanding of the issues involved ("because we talked the
same about it"), he was willing to support her, despite contrary advice by
his "civil servants" on the matters involved. The main point of the story, or
evaluation, from MEP2's perspective, is to show that as an MEP, to get
things done, you must be active and assertive, "not sit behind your desk."
While MEP2 might have felt hindered by her (and the Commissioner's) limited language skills in French, she found help through an interpreter and
argued her points before the commissioner—with success. Thus, in this
narrative, MEP2 positions herself as an MEP who is proactive and who will
do what it takes, including arguing directly with commissioners, to see that
her voice is heard. She also orients to being a *rapporteur* (line 2), which
carries some responsibility in a committee, and to being from the Netherlands (line 17), although this last identity is evoked only to characterize her
style of work (*"brutal,"* in Dutch, or "assertive").

At the same time that she presents herself as a proactive MEP who has
served as *rapporteur* on more than one occasion, she paints a picture of
both the Commission and the Council in a way that is consistent with what
many other MEPs and EC officials in these data observe about the respective organizations (see Wodak 2001a for an analysis of gender issues in
these interviews). Here we see a benevolent commissioner who is willing

to listen to an individual MEP and to make decisions according to reason and his own conviction, even if that means occasionally going against the advice of his Directive Generale or perhaps cabinet ("Well, I have here the advice of my civil servants but I agree with you, and this and this and this all goes through"). In the coda of the story we see that MEP2 compares the accessibility and cooperativeness of the commissioner to the difficulty and uncooperativeness of the Council ("[I]t's very difficult to negotiate with the Council. . . . [T]hey have their own strategy and their own reasons"). Thus, MEP2's narrative also constructs a world in which the Parliament and Commission can work together as partners, whereas the Parliament and Council remain at odds.

In the following example, taken from the part of the interview with MEP10 that focused on the reasons for unemployment, we see how national and party identities may be oriented to as a context for understanding a particular interpretation of a political, economic, and social issue, in this case unemployment.

Example 6

```
1    it/it's quite simple.—why we have this——high—unemployment rate no
2    and it's because we are changing soti/society
3    I mean we had a—highly in/industrial society and now we are changing
4    so.—so: äh—this is completely new for us
5    and -/and then we are trying—to amend that
6    and to try to——äh: help that up
7    with—/with—kind of old——/old structures: and—old—answers.—
8    äh: and—we don't want to face that we really have to—
9    adjust a lot of—thinking
10   I mean that/that's—/what it is about.—and—/and—
11   we have to—reconsider—
12   äh what is full employment and what is
13   what is äh:——/to have a äh/äh—a work for salary:—
14   and a lot of that so/sort of things.—
15   because I don't think that—we will ever—
16   ever have what called—
17   usually *in Sweden* /fo full employment ((laughs))/
18   and—/and—/and my solution to that and/and
19   *the Green group* is of course that
20   for the first you have to see:—
21   *we* have a/had a—/äh have another—äh äh another äh:—approach
22   and another—view: of—full employment.—
23   just to say that——okay.—this is—nineteen ninety.——seven
24   and h—/we had so many f/people in—/unemployed.
```

25 so the first thing we should do:—is of course to reduce:—the working
26 time.—
27 because—äh forty hours:
28 a week *as we are working in Sweden* now
29 it was not—äh institution of god.—
30 it/it was—decided of with /us ((laughs))/
31 the/the time when we—/when we needed a lot of people to work
32 so—re—/reduction of working time of course
33 and also—to change the attitudes in society against
34 the people that have work and don't have work
35   . . .
36 and äh:—/and then also of course we have to——support and
37 /and say that flexibility in that sense
38 you could work the hour that you like
39 and you could have a half-time j:ob and so on
40 and have a small company in size
41 so all these taxations
42 and all—the regulations
43 has to be:—sh—/changed
44 and altered also.—to make this possible
45 äh:—and of course—the taxation or the/the:—
46 you don't say taxation you say—äh:—
47 the tax on labour—/on labour.——
48 it's it's quite high
49 I s:uppose it's—äh:—all the same in the European Union
50 but *in Sweden*—äh which I /know most of course ((laughs))/
51 in the northwest
52 there äh—/there we have—really high
53 percentage of tax on—labour.—
54 and that should be s:witched and changed
55 of course so you put it on—*as I'm a Green*—
56 *äh MEP*—on energy:
57 and non resourceable—
58 äh: äh:m—ninedren/non
59 renewable resources and energy and so on
60 so—this: should be switched of course

In this example, MEP10 orients to both her nationality (Swedish) and her political affiliation (Green). Although it is not clear why she points out her nationality in lines 17 and 27, in lines 19 to 26, where she has included herself as belonging to the Green Group, she appears to use this identity as a resource (in the sense of Antaki and Widdicombe 1998) or context (Zimmerman 1998) for understanding the measures she advocates for addressing

unemployment: reinterpreting the traditional understanding of "full employment" and reducing the standard number of hours worked per week. In line
50 she again orients to her national identity, even to a more local identity, as
a type of frame for her claims about high labour taxes. She is from northwest
Sweden, where labour taxes are quite high, so she can speak as an authority on this issue. Finally, in this excerpt, she resumes her orientation to her
political affiliation. She favours a switch in taxation from labour to energy and
nonrenewable resources, a position fully consistent with her identity as an
MEP from the European Greens. Thus, in this example, we see how national
and political identities can be invoked as a resource or context for understanding a particular perspective or presenting a frame of expertise.

At this juncture, it is worth observing that among all the MEPs interviewed, it tended to be Swedes and Finns, as well as MEPs from either the
European Greens or United European Left (many of whose members are
from Green parties in their home countries), who mentioned their nationality and/or party affiliation at several points throughout an interview. In
other words, while almost all MEPs made reference to their party affiliation
or nationality in the course of the interview (long before the "Do you consider yourself to be European?" question), the Swedes and Finns, and/or
Greens, appeared to draw on this resource more than others. The one EC
official who invoked his national identity before being asked the "European" question also belonged to the Scandinavian group (a Finn). Although
the analysis of more data (with more representative distribution of nationalities and political affiliations) would be necessary to confirm these tendencies, one might conjecture that Swedes and Finns, who have a long history of political association (e.g., in the Nordic Council and European Free
Trade Association), and who were two of the three countries to last join the
EU in 1995, may tend to identify more strongly with each other as Scandinavians and less so as "Europeans" in the strictly EU sense.[7] This is illustrated in an anecdote told by one EC official (not a Scandinavian):

Example 7

```
1    I was at a conference in Stockholm recently and I said
2    Someone was asking me, a Scanda/
3    It had to be a Scandinaviena because
4    And I said I lived in Brussels
5    And they said, "Well you know, well are you Irish or something"
6    And I said, "Well, I'm also a European"
7    And they looked at me and said,
8    "That doesn't mean anything.
9    What does that mean?
10   I mean, you're a European commission official, that's why"
```

11 I'm European you know, I live on the continent
12 and you all live—
13 not the continent as distinct from the British Isles
14 but I mean continent, the territory of Europe
15 and that for me has meaning
16 I mean it has influenced my history, thinking, and economics
17 and will continue to do so
18 I mean this girl was absolutely shocked
19 "You are the first person who ever said that to me," she said.
20 I never never thought of it that way.
21 She said, "I know many people—"
22 It was, I know now
23 She was from Finland
24 And she said, "I don't think anyone in Finland will think of themselves as
25 European."
26 So that's very interesting.

This kind of observation is also relayed by the Scandinavians themselves. Almost all Swedes and Finns interviewed made comments regarding a Scandinavian way of thinking or noted the fact that (especially in Sweden) only a very slim majority of popular votes led to joining the EU, as in this excerpt:

Example 8

1   I know that *we* are a very stubborn country.
2   Most of the people ah: are now: ah well.
3   A ha./ mo/ most of the people—
4   At least when was it 51.4 percent or something like that
5   Voted in the referendum for entering the European Union
6   But today *we*—almost never meet anyone who did—
7   I don't know what they did
8   Yeah because everybody said—do/ they said, "No: I voted no:" and
9   Ye said, "Well I really do I re—I really do regret" ((laughs))
10 Aha:.—so it (happened) ((laughs)) okay:
11 So I mean it's make/ it doesn't make the whole ah—/
12 The whole billing—easier. (MEP3)

This anecdote reports a reluctance on the part of many Swedes to associate themselves with the EU, which corresponds to the fact that it was largely Scandinavian MEPs (who were also Greens) who qualified their self-definitions of "being European" as *not* being restricted to membership in the EU.

CONCLUSION

This chapter is concerned with looking at interviews with individuals from the main EU organizations to see what kinds of identities—specifically those that can be seen as "transportable" (Zimmerman 1998) to some degree—they orient to and use in their talk. In the first portion of the analysis, I examine the content the interviewees' responses to one group of questions connected to questions of identity. One pattern involves the relative cohesiveness of responses by the Commission officials in comparison to the responses of the MEPs interviewed. Recall that they not only described the role of the Commission with considerable consistency, but also responded to questions on the subject of unemployment, including assessments of the Luxembourg Summit, in strikingly similar ways. If, like McKinlay and Dunnett (1998) and Widdicombe (1998), we assume that similarities of this sort may be used to mark group status of some sort, then it appears that these EC officials, especially those working in the DGs, orient fairly strongly to their "Commission,"—that is, specifically organizational—identities.

The second and third patterns emerging from the content analysis concern the interviewees' definitions of being European. On the one hand, it was noted that the Commission officials interviewed assessed themselves as feeling "European" somewhat more than the others interviewed and did so with less reference to other potential categories. In other words, while almost all of the EC officials interviewed qualified their being "European" with an assertion of being a particular nationality, other potential markers of identity (e.g., region) did not come into play. In some ways, their responses point to what may be perceived as—at least partly—an identity for the European Union: not just one or the other, not just national or supranational, but building on and benefiting from the best of both worlds. At the same time, it was suggested that the relative consistency and clarity of the officials' expressions of "being European" reflect the Commission role (among others) of acting as a sort of "European conscience" (Cini 1996).

On the other hand, and this is the third important pattern emerging from the content analysis, there were similarities in the types of definitions of "European" given by all of those interviewed, whether MEPs, Commission officials, or Council officials. Specifically, we cannot ignore characterizations that EU member states are tied historically and culturally, that there is an added value to being part of the Union, that the EU is a direction for the future, and that part of what distinguishes Europe from other political/geographical entities is its social character. This last characteristic, that Europe is known for its social models and that it is essential that this be retained in the future, is one that also occurs repeatedly in reference to questions concerning employment issues. Even more specifically, this "social

Europe" is one that contrasts itself almost exclusively with the United States and Japan. In essence this bundle of characteristics resembles what Wodak et al. (1999, 55) observe about national identity: it is "a complex of common or similar beliefs or opinions . . . as well as certain out-groups distinguished from the national 'we' group." In other words, although here we are talking about a particular *supra*national identity, those interviewed appear to share a core of beliefs concerning what Europe is, and this core involves a shared past, present, and future. At the same time, we find that "out-groups" are created: Europe is different from the United States and Asian countries such as Japan.

The linguistic portion of the analysis reveals patterns of reference by Commission officials that complement the content analysis, namely, that in these data individuals working in the Commission—as opposed to those in the European Parliament—appear to orient more consistently to the transportable identity of being part of the Commission as an organization ("we," the "Commission"), as well as that of being relatively "European." In fact, often organizational identity seems to provide the foundation or context for the way in which other identities are oriented to (or not). Thus we see that the articulation of a supranational—European—identity (rather than a specifically national or other identity) was couched in terms of organizational role: "I'm European because I'm working on the European level. . . . I'm here to see to all—the interest of ALL countries."

We also see that while the MEPs in these data certainly also oriented to collective identities such as being part of the EP, there was more variety in their "identity-making," both with regard to the groups they affiliated with (e.g., EP, Green Party, Swedish) and the way they created individualized identities for themselves (active, atypical). Specifically national identities were regularly oriented to by MEPs, often as a way of framing a particular point of view or interpretation of a certain issue, and as such are a prime example of Antaki and Widdicombe's (1998) claim that identities can be used as resources in talk. In contrast, except in response to the question explicitly asking them whether they considered themselves to be European, the EC officials interviewed rarely, if ever, oriented to their national identities, indirectly underscoring both their organizational and European identities. Finally, throughout our data, including in narratives, individuals interviewed created worlds in which Europe is developed as an economic entity with a social conscience and in contrast to both the United States and Japan.

Although I have already suggested that the type of identities oriented to by the EC officials dovetails nicely with the Commission's being described as carrying the "European conscience" (Cini 1996), that is, as promoting specifically European interests, I have still not made explicit why we might find the degree of variation in identities oriented to by MEPs. In some ways, this multiplicity of orientations appears to be functional for the way in which the EP operates. Corbett, Jacobs, and Schackleton (1995, especially 44–63) nicely describe the pressures under which MEPs work, and the directions in which they can be torn: Although many EC officials undoubtedly also travel extensively, for the most part they are based in Brussels. MEPs deal with extreme time and location pressures tied to the EP's four-week cycle of activities (e.g., meetings and sessions in Brussels, one-week plenary sessions in Strasbourg, regular travel to the home country, visits to other countries as part of being members of inter parliamentary delegations, etc.). At the same time, MEPs are involved with their political groups (both in the Parliament and possibly at home), sit on several committees, are called on to speak as experts at conferences and other public events, and act as hosts to visiting groups from their own or other countries. In short, there is no simple description for the "job" of being an MEP. Corbett, Jacobs, and Schackleton (1995, 63) suggest that in order to cope, an MEP must ultimately make choices and prioritise:

> The priorities of individual members are very different, as are their profiles within the European Parliament. Some become known as men or women of the House, and are constantly present in the plenary. Others are more effective within committee, or in their Group or their national party delegation, others concentrate more on their national or regional political image. Some members remain generalists, whereas others become specialists, and are always allocated reports or opinions within a particular policy area. Some even develop functional rather than policy specialities. . . . Some only pay short visits to Brussels or Strasbourg, whereas others are always present, and have even bought accommodation there.

Depending on how individual MEPs organize their priorities, we may find very different kinds of identities relevant for MEPs across the board, and for an individual MEP. Thus the variability that we find in the interviews with MEPs as to the types of "we" and "I" identities they orient to seems functional, reflecting in large part the peculiarities of the European Parliament itself.

In closing, a caveat is order. It would be easy to draw false conclusions about the nature of the organizations involved in this chapter, especially the European Commission and the European Parliament, and the individuals who work for them. The Commission, for example, is by no means a "monolithic unit" (Cini 1996, 130), a fact that anthropological work (e.g., Abélès, Bellier, and McDonald 1993; Abélès and Bellier 1996) more than substantiates. Therefore, the analyses presented here are not intended to be interpreted as *the* way EC officials or the Commission or the European Parliament or MEPs *are*. In addition to being inaccurate, such a conclusion vitiates the premise underlying this chapter, namely that those identities are dynamic in talk, and that potential, transportable identities may or may not be invoked in a given interaction. Instead, this chapter intends to provide a plausible interpretation for some of the similarities and differences in *orientations to* and *constructions* of identities by the individuals in these EU organizations who participated in the interview component of our study, including their understandings of "Europeanness," if, indeed, they felt it could be defined.

APPENDIX: THE DISCOURSE-HISTORICAL APPROACH

In investigating historical, organizational, and political topics and texts, the discourse-historical approach attempts to integrate much available knowledge about the historical sources and the background of the social and political fields in which discursive "events" are embedded. Further, it analyses the historical dimension of discursive actions by exploring the ways in which particular genres of discourse are subject to diachronic change (Wodak et al. 1990; Wodak et al. 1994; Wodak 1996; Reisigl and Wodak 2000, 2001; Wodak 2001a, 2001b; Wodak and Meyer 2001). Finally, and most important, this context knowledge is not only viewed as "information": at this point we integrate social theories to explain the so-called context.

One methodical way for critical discourse analysts to minimize the risk of critical bias and to avoid simply politicising, instead of accurately analysing, is to follow the principle of triangulation: one of the most salient distinguishing features of the discourse-historical approach is its endeavour to work interdisciplinarily, multimethodically, and on the basis of a variety of different empirical data, including background information. Depending on the respective object of investigation, it attempts to transcend the pure linguistic dimension and to include more or less systematically the historical, political, sociological, and/or psychological dimensions in the analysis, theory, and interpretation of a specific discursive occasion.

The linguistic analysis of texts used here follows the discourse-historical approach most recently elaborated in a book by Martin Reisigl and myself (2001). We employ the following categories, focusing foremost on the construction of "us" and "them," thus on the construction of political identities as a basic theme of political discourse; this is usually done by positive self-presentation and negative other-presentation. In our methodology, we rely on Functional Systemic Linguistics (Halliday 1978) and on an elaboration of Theo van Leeuwen's Actors Analysis (1996); and most importantly on argumentation theory, mainly on Manfred Kienpointner's work on Classical Rhetoric (1992).

In analysing the texts, we pose the following basic questions, which correspond to argumentative and other strategies:

1. How are persons named and referred to linguistically?
2. What traits, characteristics, qualities, and features are attributed to them?
3. By means of what arguments and argumentation schemes do specific persons or social groups try to justify and legitimise the inclusion or exclusion of others?
4. From what perspective or point of view are these namings, attributions, and arguments expressed?
5. Are the respective utterances articulated overtly, are they even intensified, or are they mitigated?

According to the questions above, we are especially interested in five types of discursive strategies, which are all involved in the positive self- and negative Other-presentation. By "strategy" we generally mean a more or less accurate and more or less intentional plan of practices (including discursive practices) adopted to achieve a particular social, political, psychological, or linguistic aim. We locate the discursive strategies—that is to say, systematic ways of using language—at different levels of linguistic organization and complexity:

First, there are *referential strategies* or *nomination strategies* by which one constructs and represents social actors, for example, in-groups and out-groups. This is done in a number of ways, such as membership categorization devices, including tropical reference by biological, naturalizing, and depersonalising metaphors and metonymies, as well as by synecdoches in the form of a part standing for the whole (*pars pro toto*) or a whole standing for the part (*totum pro parte*).

Second, once constructed or identified, the social actors as individuals, group members, or groups are linguistically provided with predications. *Predicational strategies* may, for example, be realized as stereotypical, evaluative attributions of negative and positive traits in the linguistic form of implicit or explicit predicates. These strategies aim either at labelling social actors more or less positively or negatively, deprecatorily or appreciatively. They cannot neatly be separated from the nomination strategies.

Third, there are *argumentation strategies* and a fund of *topoi* through which positive and negative attributions are justified—through which, for example, it is suggested that the social and political inclusion or exclusion, the discrimination or preferential treatment, of the respective persons or groups of persons is justified.

Fourth, discourse analysts may focus on the *perspectivation, framing,* or *discourse representation,* by means of which speakers express their involvement in discourse and position their point of view in the reporting, description, narration, or quotation of events or utterances.

Fifth, there are *intensifying strategies* on the one hand and *mitigation*

Positive self-presentation
and Negative Other-
presentation
　　　　　　┌─ Reference
　　　　　　├─ Predication
　　　　　　├─ Perspectivation and involvement
　　　　　　├─ Intensification or mitigation
　　　　　　└─ Argumentation

Figure 6.1:　Strategies of self- and Other-presentation

strategies on the other. Both of them help to qualify and modify the epistemic status of a proposition by intensifying or mitigating the illocutionary force of political utterances. These strategies can be an important aspect of the presentation inasmuch as they operate on it by sharpening it or toning it down.

Figure 6.1 sums up the overview of selected strategic aspects of self- and Other-presentation.

NOTES

1. I use "Europe(an)" (unless noted otherwise) in the sense of "Europe consisting of the EU." As pointed out by several members of the European Parliament who were interviewed for this chapter, what is geographically "Europe" extends considerably beyond the EU's current borders. Nevertheless, since the focus of this chapter is European identity building in the European Union, I use "Europe(an)" in the more restrictive sense.

2. In this chapter, as in other works (e.g., Straehle et al.1999) written at the Research Center "Discourse, Politics, Identity" (see note 3 for a description of the center), a distinction is made between "organisation" and "institution" that follows Rehberg (1994, 56). While "institution" is defined as the "social regulations" (rules) in which the principles of a specific social order are expressed, organizations are the social and structural formations that embody institutions. Thus, in this chapter I refer to the European Parliament, the Council of Ministers, and the European Commission as EU organizations rather than institutions.

3. The Discourses of Unemployment in Organizations of the European Union is one of the projects undertaken at the Research Center "Discourse, Politics, Identity" at the University of Vienna (Austria) with the support of the Wittgenstein Prize for Elite Researchers (1996) awarded to Ruth Wodak. Research center projects build on numerous previous studies on organizational discourse and identity under the direction of Ruth Wodak at the Department of Applied Linguistics at the University of Vienna. (see Muntigl, Weiss, and Wodak 2000). This chapter is based on a preliminary analysis and pilot-study by Carolyn Straehle during her stay at the Research Center in 1997–1998. I am very grateful to her for further discussions and comments. Carolyn Straehle also conducted most of the interviews in Brussels, together with Gilbert Weiss.

4. A similar observation is made in a study by Nick and Pelinka (1993). Their research suggests that members of the Green Party tend to be more world oriented than representatives of other political groups.

5. The transcription conventions are as follows.

- A colon indicates an extension of the sound it follows. Longer extensions are shown by more colons.
- A dash stands for an abrupt cutoff.
- Emphasized syllables, words, or phrases are underlined.
- When words are in single parentheses, it means that the speech was very difficult to understand and could not be transcribed with complete certainty.
- Empty parentheses mean that something was heard that could not be understood.
- Double parentheses contain descriptions of non- and paralinguistic utterances by the speakers and noises, such as telephone rings or the clink of glasses.

Comments that characterize the talk are contained in double parentheses above the speech they concern. The left double parentheses show the beginning and the right the end of the section they describe. When descriptions pertain to several lines of the transcript, the comment is repeated and/or the continuation of the description is indicated by arrows (>>).

6. Leonardo is one of three EU youth- and education-related programs—Socrates, Leonardo, and Youth for Europe—established in 1995. It provides financial support for professional development and job training.

7. Individuals interviewed from Austria, the third of most recent states to join the EU, did not seem to mention their nationality as often or in as explicit ways as the Swedes and Finns.

7

EU Correspondents in Brussels: Between Europe and the Nation-State

Eugenia Siapera

The role and power of the media in the construction of the nation-state has been well documented in a series of influential books, such as, among others, Benedict Anderson's (1983/1991) *Imagined Communities*, while a parallel scholarship, evolving around Jürgen Habermas's (1962/1989) seminal *Structural Transformation of the Public Sphere*, has sought to theorise the role of the media in the construction of political communities and the legitimation of political power. The two arguments regarding the media refer, first, to their privileged position in building the nation through unifying experiences of space, time, and language (Anderson 1983/1991); second, the media are viewed as instrumental in providing a space in which the citizenry can discuss and exchange opinions on public matters, leading to the formation of an informed public opinion (Habermas 1962/1989). Given the importance and centrality allocated to the media and/in the nation, it does not come as a surprise that discussions of further European integration and Europeanization have privileged the role of the European media (e.g., Schlesinger 1992, 1999; Grimm 1995).[1] In terms of Europe,[2] thus, the media can be seen as crucial both for the formation of a European identity, analogous to national identity, and for the forging of a European political public, attuned to and oriented toward discussion and the exchange of opinion on subjects of common concern.

This double significance of the media for Europe points to the importance of the role played by media actors, journalists themselves, operating in the space between Europe and the nation-state. This community of journalists, working as EU correspondents in Brussels, is the focus of the current chapter. The Brussels press corps occupies a unique position, writing for a national public while reporting on Europe and living in an international environment. Members of the press corps have to continuously negotiate between the pull of the national and that of Europe, while they also need to balance their own political beliefs on the project of Europe with their professional ethics as journalists. A case study focusing on this community can therefore provide important insights on the processes of negotiation of different identities, and the potential political outcomes this negotiation may have. These insights carry an added significance given the mediating role of these journalists, who stand between Europe and their national publics. Based on a set of interviews with elite journalists of this corps,[3] the current chapter seeks to outline the processes of negotiation of different meanings of Europe and the nation, and their outcome for European politics. The context in which these are discussed is formed by the events that preceded and followed the resignation of Jacques Santer's European Commission in 1999, after a series of allegations of mismanagement of funds, nepotism, and bribery. The analysis reveals the circulation of three different understandings of the relationship between Europe and the nation, leading to three different outcomes for reporting on Europe and its politics. These understandings can be linked to the substantive contents of three different identities associated with Europe: a nationalist one, precluding Europe; a Europeanist one, precluding the nation; and a post-Europeanist one, which builds on and expands the national.

This chapter will proceed, first, with a discussion of theories of identity, which will set the theoretical context for the empirical analysis; second, with a discussion of the media and their role in European politics, which will provide the substantive focus of the empirical analysis; third, with the empirical analysis itself, which discusses the different understandings of the relationship between Europe and the nation alongside the ways in which they are mobilised to account for, and justify, the role of the media in the demise of the European Commission. Finally, the concluding section discusses the implications of the empirical findings for European identity and politics.

THEORIZING IDENTITY

The current theoretical position on identity is based on the work of Jonathan Potter and Margaret Wetherell (1987; Wetherell and Potter 1992; Potter 1996; Wetherell 1998) on discourse and the construction of identities. Dissatisfied with what they view as the "lingering perceptualism"[4] (Wetherell and Potter 1992, 47) of social cognitive approaches, such as Social Identity Theory (Tajfel 1981; Tajfel and Turner 1986) and Self-

Categorisation Theory (Turner 1985; Turner et al. 1987), Wetherell and Potter, in their discursive approach to identity, focus instead on the constitutive role of language and discourse in the construction of identity. In other words, for Wetherell and Potter, the issue is to uncover the ways in which categorisations and groupings come into being through an active clustering and linking of certain terms, attributes, and characteristics; the main contribution of this approach is described as an analysis of these constructions "around groupings such as race, culture and nation" (Wetherell and Potter 1992, 72). The emphasis placed on meaning is what makes this approach of particular relevance for the current chapter. Given that the central questions here revolve around the negotiation of European, national, and professional identities, an approach that allows for a bottom-up exploration of the meanings attributed to these identities is of more help than one that takes such meanings for granted and the boundaries between the categories of Europe and the nation as given.

The discursive approach to the construction of identity privileges the domain of language over other cognitive processes, such as perception, and views it as central to social life and the building of personal and social identities. Thus, Wetherell and Potter (1992) view identities as constructed in talk and as representing the "sedimentation of past discursive practices" (78), which, in turn, are based on the interpretative resources circulating in a given culture, and to which people may have differential access. People, argue Wetherell and Potter, actively construct their identities while involved in conversation or other forms of talk/discursive practices, and they do so in a manner that is functional: they mobilise identities and identity talk in order to explain, justify, or dispute and question the world around them. The continuity of identity can be accounted for in terms of the involvement of past discursive practices, while the variety of interpretative resources found in any given culture can account for differences in the social identities of people belonging to the same culture. In this manner, this approach does not refute the role played by other social practices, which may, for instance, determine access to certain interpretative resources, but rather seeks to emphasise the contribution of discourse and meaning in the construction of identities, subjectivities, and the social world. By focusing on the active and constitutive role of discourse and talk, this approach, finally, can account for the observed flexibility and variation in mobilising identities; thus, identities are viewed as being under continuous construction, since people are continuously involved in talk and conversation, and are thus better understood as fluid resources than as static possessions of individuals.

Adopting such a perspective on identity has several implications. First, it prioritises people's talk; second, it views this talk as constitutive of identities; and third, it acknowledges the functional dimension of this identity talk as mobilised in order to accomplish certain ends. In this sense, the tasks of this chapter include, first, the identification of the range of European and national identity constructions encountered in journalists' talk; and second, the examination of the ends to which these identity constructions are mobilised. Finally, the previous two tasks can lead to a discussion of their implications for European politics more generally. The question of how to empirically or methodologically approach such identity talk is discussed in a later section. For now, an elaboration of the current substantive focus, the Brussels press corps, will further outline the significance of this case study and the importance of identity constructions circulating among Brussels journalists.

THE EUROPEAN MASS MEDIA AND THE BRUSSELS PRESS CORPS

The dual importance of the media in constructing the nation-state (Anderson 1983/1991) and in providing a political space for the citizenry (Habermas 1962/1989) has been noted in the introduction. To these points it can be added, following the above theoretical discussion, that the media can contribute to the construction of identities, in, at least, the sense that they can disseminate certain understandings or interpretative resources on which people can subsequently draw (Liebes and Curran 1998; Morley and Robins 1995; Morley 2000). All three point to the significance of studying media output, as this can reveal the range of understandings of "Europeanness" or identity constructions regarding Europe, as well as the extent to which the European media can be seen as providing a European public sphere. Indeed, the relevant literature on European media output has provided intriguing, albeit inconclusive, evidence for both. This section discusses this literature, arguing that focusing on the practitioners of European journalism in Brussels will provide a better and deeper understanding of the media output, or representations of Europe and its news.

The literature on the coverage of Europe and/or European issues in the media has been both national and comparative in its focus. Examining topics as diverse as the launch of the euro (de Vreese, Peters, and Semetko 2001), the 1996 European Football Championships (Maguire, Poulton and Possamai 1999), the European elections (Kevin 2001), and more generally EU issues (van de Steeg 2002), this literature has shown both differences and similarities in the coverage of issues in the news media of different countries. Specifically, a study on the launch of the euro (de Vreese, Peters, and Semetko 2001) found that German, Dutch, and Danish television overwhelmingly framed the launch in terms of its economic consequences, despite the generally different journalistic cultures found in these countries. Similarities are also reported by van de Steeg (2002), whose analysis of German, Dutch, Italian, and British news media led her to conclude that we may be witnessing the birth of a European public sphere, conceived in terms of a thematic convergence. Yet the picture changes dramatically if the focus is on subjects such as the BSE/CJD crisis (Brookes 1999) and the EURO 96, referring respectively to bovine spongiform encephalopathy/ Creutzfeldt-Jakob disease—the so-called mad cow disease—and the European Football Championship of 1996. Here conflict predominates, and national, and often nationalistic, frames are extensively used. For instance, Maguire, Poulton, and Possamai (1999) found that in covering EURO 96, the British press used metaphors of war and nostalgia, and was openly hostile to Germany, while the German press coverage centred on current political and sporting issues, albeit with an antagonism equal to that of the British. These findings led Maguire, Poulton, and Possamai to argue that this media coverage "acted as a 'drag' to further European integration" (1999, 85). The hostility of the British press to "all things European" is indeed notorious, and has been extensively discussed by Anderson and Weymouth (1999), who argue that this overwhelmingly negative coverage of European issues is due to a mapping of the European onto domestic politics, and that this intertwining has rendered European issues highly contentious and politicised.

These findings are intriguing: most authors recognise differences in national journalistic cultures as leading to differences in reporting, but how are we to account for the similarities observed? On the other hand, if we observe similarities in media coverage, can we then conclude that national differences have given way to a European way of reporting? If so, how is this European way understood? These are crucial and difficult questions to which no conclusive answers have yet been found. Contributing toward addressing these questions, this chapter argues that understanding how the Brussels press corps deals with the dilemmas of European, national, and professional identities may provide important insights on the ways in which it reports on Europe. Focusing on the negotiation between these identities may provide the means by which we can subsequently understand similarities and differences in reporting that go beyond national and cultural specificities. But the Brussels press corps is also significant for two other reasons: it mediates between European institutions and the European public; and it constitutes Europe's "first public."

More specifically, despite recent attempts to directly reach the European public through a satellite channel broadcasting the daily press briefings,[5] the voice of the EU and its institutions is transmitted predominantly through print media. Few TV channels have permanent correspondents in Brussels, preferring the lower cost associated with sending a crew when need arises. At the same time, most European "quality" daily and weekly periodicals have resident correspondents who report on the EU and often write comment and analyses as well. Moreover, for some newspapers—such as, for

instance, *Frankfurter Algemeine Zeitung, Le Monde,* and the *Guardian*—
there are two or more correspondents covering the increasing amount of
news coming from Brussels. Taking the above into account, it is evident
that the EU institutions cannot address the European public without the
help of the media, and the print media more particularly—they cannot, in
other words, circumscribe the media and directly reach the public.[6] For
most European citizens, then, the voice of the EU is the one they encounter
in the press.[7]

In this sense, the media and their operators in Brussels become the "first
public" of the Union. Jean Quatremer, the Brussels correspondent of
Libération, argues that the Brussels press corps forms the first public opinion about events, which it subsequently disseminates:

> The Commission is obliged to go through us. This means that we are both the
> mediators and also the public opinion. It cannot but go through us. Romano
> Prodi [. . .] is obliged to give an interview to *Libération, Le Monde, Le Figaro*
> [. . .] and if we don't wish to give him a platform, then we don't. It is an ex-
> traordinary situation that the mediators are at the same time the public opin-
> ion. Hence the importance of the Press Room. If ever the Commission loses
> the press, if the press becomes hostile, that's it, they are finished. (interview,
> October 1999)[8]

In other words, the Commission and other European institutions address
the press corps in its capacity as a European public, and in this sense the
opinion of the press corps is, for all intents and purposes, the first European public opinion. The Brussels press corps can be seen as the first European public to discuss, debate, argue, and write on European politics.

The literature on the coverage of European-related matters has given rise
to an intriguing set of questions that cannot be addressed by examining only
the media output. To understand this output it is necessary to look at its pro-
ducers and the processes of negotiation between conflicting demands that
have characterized the production of the news on Europe. This is not to say
that media output is only or primarily determined by these factors. Indeed,
there is ample evidence in the literature showing the role played by technical factors, such as scheduling, timing, space, and so on (e.g., Gans 1980), as
well as by other sociocultural, professional, and even ideological factors
(Schlesinger 1987; Tuchman 1978; Tunstall 1971). But there is an increasing
number of voices calling for an examination of the involvement of identity
narratives and processes in the construction of news (e.g., Jacobs 1996;
Liebes and Curran 1998; Wolfsfeld 1997). In this respect, focusing on the negotiation of European and national identities—as a contributory, and not a
definitive, determinant—will provide a deeper understanding of what is involved in the construction of the news output of Europe. At the same time,
considering the Brussels press corps as a public in its own right implies that

the way EU correspondents negotiate their identities can further contribute toward understanding how the general public discuss, question, reconcile, and, in the end, construct their national and European identities.

NEGOTIATING IDENTITIES: THE BRUSSELS PRESS CORPS AND REPORTING ON EUROPE

This section will present and discuss the empirical findings of this chapter. The problematic outlined earlier concerns the constructedness of identity, its functional deployment in explaining and justifying events in the social world, and the contribution of identity processes in the reporting on Europe. Following this problematic, the discussion of the empirical material includes, first, an identification of the different constructions of Europe and the nation, and, second, the ways in which they are mobilised in accounting for a single event: the resignation of the European Commission on March 16, 1999. Preceding the discussion of the empirical material is a section on how the data were collected and subsequently analysed.

Issues of Method and Analysis

The empirical material analysed here consists of the transcript of a series of twenty-two in-depth interviews with senior Brussels correspondents conducted by the author. While the requirement of anonymity precludes the publishing of specific details on the interviewees, some information can nevertheless be provided. All interviewees were experienced and senior journalists, working for some of the top newspapers in Europe. Altogether, the journalists interviewed represented thirteen different countries, comprising twelve EU member states—the ones not represented were Austria, Belgium, and Portugal; among the interviewees was a journalist working for a Hong Kong English-language publication. The majority of the interviewees were male—of the twenty-two journalists interviewed only six were women. The choice and number of journalists to be interviewed was determined by the objective of covering as wide a range of understandings on Europe, the nation, and journalism as possible.[9] Indeed, these interviews were considered as covering such a range, since the same themes were starting to be repeated.

The interview itself was not structured, as it was important that journalists speak about what they felt was more central or important in their work and their jobs. The interviews lasted from one to two hours, and while the themes broached varied from journalist to journalist, the interviewer ensured that certain subjects were discussed with all the interviewees. These included: (1) the subject of journalism; (2) the interviewee's relationship with colleagues; (3) the interviewee's relationship with sources; (4) the subject of politics and European politics; (5) news stories and the news on the EU; and (6) the readers, or the public. The language of the interviews was English, with two exceptions: an interview conducted in French and one in Greek.

Repertoires

The interviews were subsequently fully transcribed, yielding a text of around three hundred pages. In analysing this text, the technique used here is based on Potter and Wetherell's (1987; Wetherell and Potter 1988, 1992) notion of interpretative repertoires. An interpretative repertoire is "a culturally familiar and habitual line of argument comprised of recognizable themes, common places, and tropes" (Wetherell 1998, 400). To identify such repertoires, therefore, the analyst must look at the metaphors, images, or descriptions and figures of speech employed by speakers. Thus, although the focus is on language and its use, the analysis is not strictly speaking a linguistic one, but rather an analysis of the ways in which accounts and explanations are organised through specific lines of argument. The methodological translation of these premises in the current context includes the identification of all the images, arguments, metaphors, and figures of speech around Europe, the nation, and journalism, and their subsequent classification as interpretative repertoires, that is, as "belonging" together in the same scheme, and as being deployed for the same or similar purposes. Wetherell and Potter consider these repertoires as actively involved in constructing identities; in other words, a repertoire on Europe and the nation signals the ongoing construction of an identity relating to Europe and the nation.

Narratives

The emphasis on function found in the discursive approach adopted here implies that these repertoires are functionally deployed, or, in other words, that they are used in order to provide specific explanations for events and actions. To get at this function, the analysis focuses on a specific event, the resignation of Jacques Santer's European Commission. The resignation of the Commission in March 1999, and the events that led to it, constituted a very topical event at the time of the author's fieldwork in the spring, summer, and autumn of 1999. Thus, the journalists interviewed allocated a lot of time and importance to it, particularly since some of them were directly involved in investigating and publishing articles openly critical of the Commission. The events that led to the resignation, as well as the role of the Brussels press corps in this, are under dispute by journalists, who provide different stories, explanations, and justifications for these events and the press's involvement.[10] The current analysis thus includes a narrative analysis of the events surrounding the resignation. This narrative analysis draws on Brockmeier and Harré (1997), for whom the great variety of narrative forms are all linked together by sharing certain characteristics, including a set of characters and a plot that evolves over time. The element of time implies an ending to the story, which can then be linked to a moral outcome or an intended closure over the possible meanings of the story (cf. Ricoeur 1981; Barthes 1977). The analysis of narratives on the resignation of the European Commission is based on the identification of the characters, the plot, and the moral of the story told.

Links: Negotiating Identity

These two types of analysis—the interpretative repertoires on Europe and the nation and the narratives on the resignation—are brought together through the repertoires of journalism deployed by journalists. Thus, when the same understanding or repertoire of journalism was found in both a narrative and a Europe/nation repertoire, these were bound together as part of the same scheme. This linking of the two analyses enables the identification of the functional components of these repertories, while at the same time allowing a glimpse into the negotiation of different identities. The dilemmas posed by the push and pull of different identities, including European, national, and professional ones, are resolved through the deployment of specific repertoires, or understandings of the contents of different identities, which enable a consistent story to be told and an at least temporary closure to be achieved. From this point of view, in understanding and subsequently dealing with a case such as the resignation of the Commission, journalists mobilise their understandings of what is the nation and Europe, as well as their understandings of what is their journalistic role in Europe. In other words, in "managing" the resignation, they employ their European, national, and professional identities.

The discussion of the empirical analysis first presents the repertoires on Europe and the nation, and subsequently links them to the narratives through the repertoires of European journalism. This format was chosen in order to enable the reader to observe the deployment of the repertoires in the narratives of the resignation. Interview excerpts, selected because of their ability to illustrate the different positions created, support the discussion of all repertoires and the narratives.

REPERTOIRE I: OVERCOMING THE NATION AND CREATING EUROPE

This repertoire constructs the nation and national identity as a problem vis-à-vis Europe. The existence of the nation is here viewed negatively, as an obstacle in the way of European integration, a problem that needs to be resolved in order to build Europe. This discourse posits a dilemmatic relationship between Europe and the nation, an either/or existence, whereby the survival of one depends on the extinction of the other. In the context of this discourse, journalists speak of the nation in negative terms, as something that has to be overcome, or, in some cases, something that is already a thing of the past, with its passing opening up the way to integration.

> [W]e are thinking as if we are still in the times [of the old nation-state, which has been overpassed by the circumstances in a lot of things, in a lot of functions, so the media should try to, not yet in the short term, but in the medium long term, to establish a real sense of a real delegation, I mean a significant even numerically significant delegation here in Brussels. [I-1, Spanish journalist][11]

> [T]he negative thing is of course that we are faced by very different priorities in our readership in fifteen different countries. This is very apparent if you see a briefing, because the press concerns are not the same, because we are looking for national stories, or European stories from a national point of view, but then it is also [.] but I have the impression that something is moving, it's really the beginning of the beginning. [I-2, Italian journalist]

> I think also there is a problem with nationalities, and I think and hope that the next Commission would address that. The spokesman of every commissioner should be of a different nationality, because there's too much, there's definitely a feeding of the national press of that commissioner, in a way that gives them privileged access, and that's, that's pretty [.] I think it should change. [I-3, Irish journalist]

In all the above, the nation is spoken of as a thing of the past, a negative thing, and a problem. While for the above speakers this translates into somewhat different things, the common line here is that the nation is "in the way of things," and that this needs to change. Thus, the first extract holds that the media should try to follow the political developments as a supranational delegation; in the second quote, national interests and national priorities are viewed in negative terms; the third extract includes a proposal of how to actively change this focus on national interests and preoccupations. In these terms, nationality is constructed as a problem—not necessarily a problem in its own right, but a problem if a tighter union is to be achieved. According to this repertoire, therefore, achieving a united, fully integrated Europe will mean resolving these "problems" posed by the nation. In addressing this issue, it is necessary for Europe to seek or construct consensus: "Europeanness," in this repertoire, means having a single voice, or one common European public opinion.

> [T]his is the largest press corps in the world in Brussels, one of the biggest collective international projects ever undertaken [.] and an effective press ser-

vice, press operation is going to take as long as it takes to evolve the whole
system I think, and it may [.] it probably will be very, very difficult until there's
a clear, until sort of national cultures and national ways of doing things have
been much more replaced by an accepted and common European way of doing things, and until you do that you'll have problems. [I-4, British journalist]

[F]or democracy to work and for a Union, a Union that has a statal nature
to work it takes a public opinion, one public opinion, Europe doesn't have it,
Europe is just starting to [. . .] Europe has as many public opinions as it has
countries, maybe more, look at the differences of approach to the war [in
Kosovo], the British, the Germans, the Italians, the Greeks, the French, they
are almost un-understandable, so can you imagine Europe going to war on its
own with ten public opinions behind it? [. . .] [T]he result of our daily war if
it is done properly in the end is to create a more European homogenous public opinion for, I mean vis-à-vis Europe, it is not a good in itself, but I think
it's key to European integration. [I-2, Italian journalist]

What is evident in the above is the link between the nation as problem
and the construction of a European union based on a common public opinion. In the first quote, the journalist holds that communicative effectiveness
for the European Union depends on overcoming or "replacing" national
with European "ways of doing things." This view is shared by the second
journalist, who, moreover, seems to be making a dual argument: first, an argument involving the importance of, and, in the end, the necessity of, a
common European public opinion for the construction of a European union;
and second, an argument aimed at establishing the importance of the Brussels press in this construction. The position advocated in this repertoire
seems to be the following: nationality is in itself a problem, or otherwise it
creates problems that need to be addressed if the goal is a united Europe;
a united Europe can materialise only if there is a single European public
opinion. Europe is here constructed in opposition to the nation, and that is
why the latter has to be overcome or replaced; in the same vein, the construction of Europe is seen as possible only if it takes a form that will replace the nation. Integration is possible, and the way forward is through replacing the nation, and through the construction of a single public opinion.

The position that this discourse creates for journalism is an active one, in
which European journalism is essential for the construction of a European
public opinion, and through this, of a united Europe. The construction of
a definition of journalism that entails participation in politics on an equal
footing, and the establishment and justification of a position of engagement
with, and involvement in, politics, appear to be linked to the current discourse. In other words, the solution to the problematic existence of the nation is to be found in active attempts to overcome it, in participation in European politics, which will eventually lead to the creation of the
essential—according to this discourse—European public opinion. The

justification of direct journalistic participation in European politics links this discourse to a narrative of the crisis of the Commission that constructs the Commission as an incompetent and corrupt institution, and the press as a hero.

NARRATIVE I: THE CORRUPT COMMISSION

Dramatis Personae

1. The press/journalists feature as the protagonists/heroes.
2. The Commission is cast as the villain.
3. The European Parliament is cast as the enemy of the Commission, and the national governments as moving opportunistically.

Plot

The plot revolves around a series of acts by the Commission viewed by journalists as scandals or evidence of corruption. Motivated by a will to find out the truth, to unveil corruption and wrongdoings, journalists began investigating issues regarding the Commission finances, the humanitarian aid that the Commission was managing, and the appointment of persons in high positions; they started to openly criticise the Commission and to demand change. These investigations and criticisms were not appreciated by the Commission, which not only attempted to cover up any signs of irregularity, but was also involved in threatening and slandering journalists, and otherwise putting them under pressure. While the situation led to a deadlock between the press and the Commission, other players moved in: the European Parliament, operating from the perspective of its own interests, demanded that the Commission clarify the situation. In the meantime, the national governments were letting matters run their course, although they moved in a behind-the-scenes manner to protect the Commission. Officially, they did not get involved until after the resignation, keeping their distance from a Commission associated with corruption, offering support for changes toward more transparency in European politics. Thus, journalists here are seen as acting alone, or having only one another for support in attempting to clean up a "dirty" situation, while politicians are examined from a rather cynical point of view, behaving in an opportunistic and even amoral manner. In this respect, the resignation of the Commission was a direct result of the investigations and actions undertaken by the Brussels press, which has since (re)gained its status and authority.

[T]his was the case last year when there was [.] we reported about fraud you could see very well with a few very good exceptions like the Libération and

Nouvelle Observateur but most of them immediately gave way to political pressure, they gave way to political pressure, they were under political pressure, they couldn't write these things, it was nearly impossible, and a Commissioner like Mme Cresson could tell stories like that one of our colleagues is a neo-Nazi, for which she had no proof, but which she repeated many times, she was telling stories of conspiracy, of German conspiracy and so on [. . .] there is too much political pressure, of course in Germany there is political pressure as well [. . .] people don't want to be cheated, they don't want corruption or fraud neither in Germany, nor in Italy nor Spain, I mean people don't want this anymore, and what we have seen in Brussels is last bunch of this old corrupted, not corrupted, but the last bunch of politicians who tried to cover fraud and corruption, whereas people in Italy don't want to have it anymore, we don't want these people to take our money away [. . .] so we have to check this, we have to check how this bunch of politicians were taking our money and were spending our money on their friends or for personal networks. [. . .] I mean we are going to fight it in every level. [. . .] I mean it's incredible, it was a real power play that took place for a whole year, I've never seen anything like this, I've spent six years in the Soviet Union, I was threatened by the KGB, they told me that they would kill me if I kept going on like this, that I would have a nice car accident, so I was under a lot of pressure, but I didn't expect such a lot of pressure here in Brussels, I didn't expect it, it was a very dirty, very dirty game. [I-5, German journalist]

The journalist here tells a story in which he is personally involved: his narrative comes from the point of view of a committed investigative journalist, who in the process of investigating the Commission was personally slandered and pressured, and was made aware of other pressures on some of his colleagues. He is, in this sense, the prototypical lone hero who perseveres despite all the risks involved because of the moral certainty that he seems to carry. The choice of words, expressions such as "dirty game" and the reference to the KGB at the end of the quote paint a bleak portrait of the politicians involved. Overall the picture presented here is one in which the Commission appears in a very negative light, in the role of being involved in scandals, or at the very least in a cover-up operation that entailed putting considerable pressure on journalists. Yet, the heroic journalists of this story persevered and ended up asserting their power as the fourth estate in the context of Brussels.

Moral

The events as described/constructed above led to changes in the "moral characters" of everybody involved. The old Commission had to resign, thereby paying for its lack of political responsibility; the spokesman's service learned that they have to be more open and less secretive; the European Parliament flexed its muscles and learned the limits of its powers; the national governments cut their losses by quickly accepting the resignation; and last but not least, the press changed from being complacent, and almost reverential toward the Commission, to actively reaffirming its role as the "fourth estate," an independent power, teaching everyone involved that it is a power to be reckoned with. The lesson then is political accountability, and the press acted both as the teacher and as the means of accomplishing it, thereby asserting its power.

> [T]he fact that the press played a role in triggering, if you want, the crisis made us realise [. . .] that in this process of trying to fill the democratic gap, the democratic deficit in Europe, journalists are a power, close to the other institutions, and they are seen as a power by the policy makers, much more than we realised till a few years ago. [I-2, Italian journalist]

The arguments involved here include, first, the recounting of a story in which journalists construct a politically active position for themselves, which they justify by casting politicians in the role of the villain. Having constructed and justified such a position, they further seem to direct their efforts toward justifying their role in the construction of a European public opinion, which is seen as necessarily involving the replacement of the nation-state, and its old-style, corrupt politics. In other words, the view of the nation as problem seems to entail a positioning of journalism as actively involved in efforts to overcome such a problem, by constructing a united European public opinion. In these terms, the narrative of the heroic journalist, besides the positing of an engaged journalism, further involves the positioning of politicians, and the Commission in particular, as villains, at the very least incompetent and at the most corrupt. The heroic press of this narrative is active in improving European politics, thereby actively constructing a consensual public opinion.

> For the moment there is no European public opinion in a general sense. But this will change. We have seen it in the case of the fraud. For the first time during this affair there was a true European public opinion. [. . .] Here [in Brussels] there is a European morality, and this was the end of the Commission, and it took them a long time to realise this, it took them a long time to believe this. For the first time there was an expression of a transnational public opinion. Because, to begin with, I have seen it clearly in the behaviour of my own editors, they were not driven by the political ethos that we have in France, in Italy, in Greece—the political morality of the south. [. . .] There are fifteen national public opinions and perhaps the emergence of something else [. . .] every culture was agreeing at least since November, the whole world was of the opinion that the Commission had to go. [. . .] There was a convergence and this convergence could not have happened ten years ago, for instance, because each [newspaper] would have continued with their own national line. This here was not the case, the whole Europe has heard of the fraud in the Commission. [I-6, French journalist]

Indeed, the above provides a very appropriate example of the articulation of nationality as problem, and Europeanness as requiring a unified public opinion within the context of the crisis. The argument here is that initially there was no European public opinion; however, the crisis changed everything. The fraud, associated with certain nationalities and their problem of corruption, through the way in which it was reported led to the creation of a public opinion united across Europe that the Commission should resign. According to this account, the convergence in public opinion followed the stance of a press active in pursuing the case, a press that exposed the scandal to the eyes of Europe as a whole. The divergent nation-state "morality" is to be replaced by a commonly accepted European one. If scandals of nepotism and corruption are associated with the nation, then these problems have to be overcome along with the nation in the construction of a new Europe, based on transparency and political accountability, and in which the press is active in pursuing social harmony.

This repertoire on Europe and the nation, along with the repertoire of an active, investigative European journalism that will lead to a unified public opinion, has its resonance in the literature. Schlesinger (1999) argues that a European public sphere should have as its minimal requirement the establishment and dissemination of a European news agenda, whose recipient, the European public, must think itself as "transcending the level of the member nation-states" (277); he goes on to argue that since this agenda would be "domesticated" according to each distinctive national culture, it needs to be replaced by "an orientation toward a *common* 'European' frame of reference" (277, italics in the original). Not by accident, therefore, in the same article Schlesinger, writing just before the resignation, diagnosed the Commission crisis as due to its lack of accountability (268). Grimm (1995) assumes a similar position on Europeanness, arguing that the creation of a European public requires a nation-transcending communicative context. Both authors employ an understanding of Europe and the nation very close to the one above, since they posit a commonality of public opinion as central to the European project, while seeing the nation and its distinctiveness as obstacles in the way of further integration that have to be "transcended."

Within this repertoire, therefore, the nation and Europe are constructed as pulling in different directions, and they can be reconciled only if the former is left behind; for the journalists quoted above, the way in which they reach this reconciliation is through abandoning "old," national style journalism in favour of a common European investigative journalism, committed to the principles of transparency and accountability, with a view toward the construction of a common European public opinion. These views are, almost inevitably, openly contested in the second repertoire and associated narrative.

REPERTOIRE II: EUROPE AND THE NATION:
IRRECONCILABLE DIFFERENCES

This discourse constructs a version of Europe and the European project as impossible and/or highly problematic. The nation is constructed as based on difference, a difference that is seen as not only vital for the survival of the nation, but also essential to the nation in an almost primordial way. The existence of a nation is not something that can be easily discarded or sacrificed for the construction of Europe; rather, essential difference adheres to each nation and will remain there despite attempts to overcome it. In these terms, building a common Europe is neither feasible nor advisable. The active attempts to build a unified public opinion linked to the previous discourse and associated narrative have become here the passive inevitability of the failure of the project of European unification. The emphasis here is on differences, belongingness, interests, permanence and deep-seated disagreement:

> I mean this is fifteen countries working together, that it is it, and it's countries with national interests, national outlooks and this will stay for years, if ever it changes, which I doubt. [. . .] I will insist on the fact that trying to cover Europe is for the time being, unfortunately, still a national thing, not in the foreseeable future will we cover Europe as a whole, it will always be the importance of this directive for this country, or the implications of this case for our country, and this will stay on. [. . .] [T]he Germans [. . .] are obsessed with the parliament and democracy, just as the Northern Europeans are obsessed with transparency and glasnost, as the Spanish are obsessed with tomatoes and fish, and the Greeks are obsessed with tobacco subsidies and state aid, every single country has their own priorities, their own agendas. [. . .] OK it was important [to write "European" stories] when they started, or at the end of the year new intergovernmental conference on the institutions, real European matters, voting rights, number of Commissioners, totally European in itself, you would agree, but voting rights means the influence of your country, and will each country, which includes your country, always have a Commissioner or not? So, the big European idea, if you look carefully has many national implications, nobody is willing to give up a Commissioner, not for the sake of Europe, and not for the sake of anything. [I-7, French journalist]

The position of Europeanness as irreconcilable with the nation is very clear in the above excerpt. The journalist here holds that there is no "Europe," and no possibility for it either; different countries have different priorities, and this national interest is what dictates their behaviour. National agendas are seeping through, thereby undermining even the most "European" decisions of all. The European project is constructed here as futile and impossible because of the nature of the nation. The picture emerging is predominantly one of difference. Nationality is seen as essential and inherent difference, and as such a change is impossible, and, also, undesirable, because of the destructive implications it will have for the nation.

I believe that the national interest divisions are bigger, also the culture, the cultural heritage, that is true—the Brits are much more Euro-sceptic, I'd say genetically [said with humour], because they learn it, eh, and you know when in a country there is a strong national identity, people are less European minded. Greece for example, Greeks were always, you understand very well that this Orthodox solidarity plays a bigger role in the journalists, than the, the NATO and European solidarity. I think that's quite normal, I'm sure it will not be good if all these characteristics disappear because they are part of our identity. [I-8, French journalist]

[T]he Greek Commissioner does not even have a press officer, the Portuguese, and I don't know who else, the Spanish, and the Spanish also had to accept it, because Prodi also did this, the cabinets will have a, let's say, multinational dimension, they will not have administrators from the same nationality as the Commissioner [. . .] and we have now reached a point where the French have a press officer for their Commissioner, and another one for the Directorate General, they have two press officers and the Greek one has no one, and this has led to a very confused situation. [I-9, Greek journalist][12]

[A]nd they altered the geographical constitution of the spokesman's service, there's not even a Spaniard there. [I-1, Spanish journalist]

The position of nationality as difference is clearly illustrated in the above quotes. The issue of national divisions, of the British Euro-scepticism and the Greek "orthodox solidarity" form part of the picture, and their disappearance is not seen as "good." In these terms, it should not come as a surprise that any attempt to build up an international institution is resisted on the basis of national lines. In the last two quotes, the appointment of press officers whose nationality is different from that of the Commissioner is seen in very negative terms. In an argumentative move similar to that of the previous repertoire, the nation and Europe are positioned antithetically, with the existence of one precluding the development of the other. In this repertoire, however, the central argument is the converse: the nation is either too important and precious to destroy, making the European project undesirable, or else, it is far too deeply rooted to be able to change, making the European project impossible. There is, nevertheless, a common aspect in these two repertoires, namely, the basic assumption of an incompatibility between the nation and the project of European integration. Despite, however, this common assumption, the two are moving in completely different directions both for Europe and European journalism.

In constructing the nation as difference, this second discourse appears to create a particular type of European journalism, primarily concerned with observation and reporting from a perspective that comes naturally: a national interest journalism. If participation in the political process is central to the previous discourse and narrative, the current preoccupation is with distance, noninvolvement, and detached observation. Journalism here is not about participating in, but about reporting on, politics. Since nationality and nationhood are natural, essential, and even primordial, there is no space for European journalism to act; the only position left for journalism is to observe the goings-on in European politics. There is, apparently, a circularity involved here that further supports the link between nonparticipatory journalism and nationality as difference or uniqueness: if the press does not participate in European politics then nationality and the nation-state will inevitably prevail; at the same time, if nationality is inherent difference or precious uniqueness, then press involvement is either of no use or inappropriate/undesirable. This is exactly the position justified in the second narrative, which constructs the crisis as inevitable.

THE NARRATIVE OF THE POWER STRUGGLE

Dramatis Personae

1. The press/journalists are cast as the chroniclers of an event that unfolds.
2. The Commission is cast as the "loser."
3. The European Parliament and the national governments are cast as power hungry, getting involved in the crisis of their own political purposes.

Plot

The events recounted here start with the existence of a tension, and perhaps even antipathy, between the Commission and the European Parliament. These two became involved in a kind of power struggle, with the Parliament wanting more power over the Commission, and the Commission wanting to preserve its power. The Parliament is viewed negatively insofar as its own interests and quest for more power motivate its actions. National governments are also involved in a negative way, implicated because of their reluctance to support the Commission. Finally, the Commission has to resign, thereby losing the battle. At the same time, the events of corruption, scandal, and cover-up that featured so prominently in the previous narrative are here consistently played down. In all of this the press is seen as a detached observer of the goings-on, while the part of the press that was involved more actively in the crisis is criticised. Rather than a story of the triumph of truth, honesty, and investigative reporting, this narrative is a chronicling of a series of mistakes and weaknesses on behalf of everyone involved, with the resignation being the result of a power game between the different institutions.

> [T]here is no ideology in this, just facts. [. . .] There were the affairs themselves, which were in my opinion a very small thing, and then there are other things, the wish of the Parliament to take power against the Commission, [. . .] and as for the French Commissioner Edith Cresson, while in France, in Greece, in Italy, in Belgium, it's quite normal to, to, well not to take ten people but to take one-two-three people who are close to you, people that you trust. [. . .] I believe the Parliament also overreacted, but the Parliament is normal, the Parliament doesn't have the capacity to take power over the Commission with, eh, by political or economical debate, because the Parliament is very difficult to manoeuvre, and this Parliament is not very good, the people are badly elected, especially in France, with the list of the political parties [. . .] and the Parliament used these affairs, in, in, it chose it because it was a good opportunity and it was more, well the French state played an important role in this too, but it was mostly the journalists that, and why the journalists, because, I believe the press is, is more, the big press, and especially the TV is more on the right side, and in these affairs, the right lost the previous election, and the journalists that were most involved were the journalists of the countries in which the conservatives lost the election, the power, became curiously more Euro-sceptical, Kohl's party which is a typical pro-European party is going, I believe, is more and more oriented, you see, to the Bavarian wing of the party, the social union from Munich. [I-8, French journalist]

In the above excerpt, the events described have actually very little to do with the heroic stance depicted in the previous repertoire. The situation described here is one in which the affairs for which the Commission was accused were either unimportant, or what one "normally" would expect. By portraying the affairs themselves as not warranting the type of reaction they got, the journalist moves on to examine the actions of the other players: thus, the Parliament is put in the position of seeking more power, while the national governments are also implicated in consolidating their position of power vis-à-vis the European institutions. The involved press is seen as partisan, but in an inappropriate way. Far from serving their public, the journalists involved in the Commission crisis are constructed in this quote as right wing, and their reporting is explained as the result of their playing an oppositional role in national politics. In short, this journalist is depicting a situation in which all players are at fault, with the Commission being essentially a victim of all these other forces joining against it.

Moral

Given the dubious motives of everyone involved in this crisis, with the exception of the Commission, whose achievements in terms of the Agenda 2000, the euro, and so forth are highlighted here, the eventual resignation means that the political battle was won by the not-so-morally-superior play-ers: the Parliament and the national governments. In this sense, this is a story with no clear and unambiguous ending: being good is not enough, and the Commission learned this the hard way; conversely, the Parliament here appears as the "winner" of the power struggle, having earned its power over the Commission, which from now on is seen as subservient, or at least accountable to the Parliament, while the national governments re-assert their primacy over the European institutions. The overall lesson here appears to be a cynical one of politics as the survival of the fittest—the "fittest" here being the Parliament and the national governments. The press, in these terms, should learn to keep their distance and independence from those in power; otherwise they are liable to be used by them. A further, and perhaps more pertinent, lesson here involves the inevitable failure of the European Commission, the most "European" of all the EU institutions[13]: although not really guilty of the offences, the Commission had to pay be-cause the national governments and the European Parliament (itself con-sisting of members elected by their national electorates) prevail over the Commission's "flimsier," nonnational, "European" interests.

> I mean the Parliament is a continuous power struggle, they are arrogant, they used their budget to get influence, but this was such a big game, they knew they could only do it if they would win. [I-10, Danish journalist]

> I mean in all the countries [. . .] they have this love-hate relationship with the Commission, you know, on the one hand they support what they are doing, and yet, and yet they also love to be able to, to be able to attack it, be-cause it just doesn't do [.] it's somebody else to blame, you know, the gov-ernments blame the Commission instead of, you know, blame it all on the Commission [. . .] I'm not actually sure whether it was Santer's fault really [. . .] Santer's fault that the Commission failed. [I-4, British journalist]

The above excerpts reiterate in a way all that was wrong in the case of the Commission crisis: first, the European Parliament and the national gov-ernments were actively involved in undermining the Commission; at the same time, the Commission was unable to manage the affair in terms of the type of message it was to present, and unsure as to how to deal with the accusations made against it. Thus, in the first excerpt, the point made is that the Parliament was just waiting for such an opportunity to jump against the Commission; the second quote talks about the attacks of national govern-ments on the Commission as contributing to the crisis. Overall, the point of the story is that power struggles are typical, and perhaps even inevitable, in European politics, and they reflect deeper, national-based divisions.

This narrative, particularly in its depiction of the crisis as a power strug-gle, provides further evidence of the impossibility of the European project and the inadvisability of journalistic involvement. The crisis here is not the result of old-style national corruption, brought forth and exposed by a heroic press, which thereby contributes to the overcoming of the problem of the nation-state and leads to a new Europe; rather, the crisis is further proof of the inevitable failure of an ill-advised move to change the imma-nent nature of nationality, while any participation on behalf of the press is in breach of journalistic requirements for impartiality and objectivity. The narrative seems to be holding that the crisis in the European Commission was an inevitable consequence of attempts to change the inherent nature of nationality as difference, and all the press could do was to report on the fail-ure of such attempts. The repertoire on which this narrative is based can be linked to primordial positions on national identity, positing a deep link among all those comprising a nation, who share the same essential and deep-seated characteristics. Prevalent in the era of nation building in Eu-rope, this position is currently theoretically discredited (e.g., Gellner 1983; Hobsbawm 1990), while several wars in Europe have brought the political ideology of nationalism[14] into disrepute (see, for instance, Ignatieff 1993). Nevertheless, theorists such as Anthony Smith (1995) insist on the persist-ence of both nations and nationalism, arguing that nationalism still provides the "sole vision and rationale of political solidarity today" and is likely to continue to do so for a long time to come. Smith's argument is premised on the history not only of nations, but of ethnicities, and ethnic-based alliances; according to Smith, a European project that seeks to transcend these, seek-ing solidarity elsewhere, is operating against history, and is thus bound to fail. National perspectives and interest-based interpretations and justifica-tions of events will inevitably prevail in Europe; the crisis of the Commis-sion was inevitable, not because of any actual fraud, but because of the fun-damental antithesis and antagonism between Europe and the nation.

In negotiating the two identities of Europe and the nation, journalists in this repertoire have opted for the latter, justifying a European journalism that reports on European issues from a detached, national interest per-spective. The basic assumption of the incompatibility of the nation with the European project, and the polarisation between the two journalistic posi-tions of participation and detachment are actively disputed in the third and last repertoire on the nation and associated narrative of the crisis.

REPERTOIRE III: NATION AS A RESOURCE FOR EUROPE

This repertoire constructs the nation as a resource and the European proj-ect as something dynamic. Rather than constructing nationhood as prob-lematic for the European project, or as immanent difference, precluding the development of a united Europe, this repertoire considers the nation as an entity that has the potential to evolve. Similarly, Europe is constructed as a project in evolution, with a future that is a matter of political debate rather than predetermined by nonpolitical factors. The nation and Europe, according to this repertoire, can coexist; nations can learn from one another, see what other nations have to offer, improve, and evolve. Overt political references are also central to this repertoire.

> I really think that we can learn from the Germans from that point of view, because they are one of the few real democracies, also from the Greeks. [. . .] The Italian press understood after the German press that all the process that fed to the resignation of the Commission was about legitimacy and democracy, because in the end for all the Europeanism of the Italian public opinion, we didn't understand this simple truth that Europe is [. . .] a democratic power, so a power that can be held accountable, it's exactly the same process we, as Italians, we are definitely late, because our public opinion, and our leaders looked and still look at Europe as a way to save Italy, it's not a matter of being sure that we are the shareholders of a common enterprise, but rather something else, instead it is now a matter of understanding that we are soldiers, otherwise [. . .] we would not grow as a democracy. [I-2, Italian journalist]

The main premise to be found in the above excerpt is that nationality is something that can be enriched, something that can change through contact with other nationalities; the journalist refers to the outcome of the crisis as a lesson in democracy, which his nation (Italy) can learn from Germany. Another issue involved here is the apparent view that Europe has also changed, that the European project has grown or evolved. If, thus, nationality can offer and accept new understandings, in the process changing its "character," then the European project also has to be in constant evolution, at least insofar as it consists of such dynamic nations.

In these terms, Europe is talked about as a common enterprise whose future outlook has not been decided yet, but will be the outcome of negotiation among different aspects and elements. In this respect, a single public opinion is not posited as a necessary criterion for the "survival" of the EU, but rather, the whole process is seen more in political terms, thereby allowing for divergence of opinions, for disagreement rather than harmony. The existence of diverse interests and problems is acknowledged, but not seen as critical for Europe's continuous existence.

> [T]he European Union is, has a huge array of issues to deal with, and it deals with conflicting interests very openly, in NATO it's all kept under wraps until they reach an agreement. [I-11, German journalist]

> I think it [the resignation of the Commission] was extremely positive, painful; democracy is never, never painless, the people who think that Europe is about harmony are probably the least democratic of us all. [I-2, Italian journalist]

> They [other journalists] believe in a project that is the European project. For me, I am a European, but if I have to write an article that exposes Europe, then

so be it, because my only concern is to do journalism, I am a professional, not a militant, not someone who is prepared to hide the truth so that Europe can continue with its construction. [. . .] The articles written then [during the Delors Commission] were: "It's fantastic, Europe is advancing rapidly, the internal market, the single currency, it's great, the future will be rosy." This is a very Marxist-Leninist vision of history. And it has finished. [I-6, French journalist]

The first extract points to the existence of diversity within the EU and the fact that it is not repressed, but dealt with in an open and transparent manner. Similarly, the second extract acknowledges the conflict involved in the resignation of the Commission but holds that this points to growth and (positive) change. The final quote refers to conceptions of Europe that, for the speaker, belong to the past. The fragility of Europe is no longer an issue; the issues concerning Europe now are political and as such open to debate and contestation. This quote is also telling of the position of journalism within this version of events: here journalism is cut off from its local, national preoccupations and is linked to something bigger. This journalist views himself as a professional, by which he apparently means that his position is not a "militant" one, but nor is it a passive one: what we have here is the construction of a third position for journalism, a position that seems to be one of detached involvement. It is this journalistic stance that is linked to the third story of the resignation, a story that performs an anatomy, as it were, of the events and players involved in the crisis.

THE NARRATIVE OF THE ANATOMY OF THE CRISIS

Dramatis Personae

1. The press/journalist features as the analyst.
2. The Commission suffers from political weakness.
3. The Parliament is striving for emancipation.
4. The national governments are cast as the political "parents" of both the Commission and the Parliament.

Plot

Using the analogy of psychoanalysis, the press can be put in the position of the analyst/therapist, with the politicians involved, that is, the Commission, Parliament, and national governments, as the "problem owners." The instances of corruption, nepotism, and general mismanagement are considered to be the symptoms, but not the cause, of the problem: the interpretation or insight provided by the press/analyst is that there is a lack of democracy, transparency, and accountability, which leads to the problematic behaviour exhibited through the above-mentioned symptoms, and through the eventual resignation of the Commission. Resolving the prob-lem of the Commission's lack of democracy and democratic legitimacy will enable both the Commission and the parliament to stand on a par with na-tional governments. It is this insight and understanding that is offered by the press/analyst in his or her interpretation or analysis of the crisis, and the suggested treatment is democratic reform.

> When the Commission resigned, even before, when the Parliament voted a censure motion against the Commission, when at that moment editorials were written, very few people understood what was happening, many people said from a, you know, federalist perspective, an integration perspective that it was against Europe, very few people understood that it was part of a greater legit-imacy, a democracy, and so the role of the Parliament [was upgraded]. [. . .] So the journalist who understood that at the time, for me was the best. [. . .] I think the reason why the Commission resigned was not about whether it did or not a good job, I don't think it did a good job, but then many governments haven't resigned even though they did much worse jobs, so why did it resign? Because it didn't have legitimacy, and there is a point of integration, which means in more clear terms that there is so much power in Brussels that of course there is a backlash if there is no legitimacy, and an institution that is powerful but not legitimate is, if you want, besieged by the press every single day, it's much more vulnerable, much more serious allegations. [.] Elected gov-ernments would not have resigned if they were facing much more serious al-legations, because they would have the Parliament behind them in a much truer way if you want, no? So this is the reason, that the Commission is not demo-cratic enough to, it's not legitimate and democratic enough to keep the place and this is why they resigned, I mean it's not a matter of the money, if you look at how governments spend money, then I think that all the governments should go, but they don't, because they are more solid. [I-2 Italian journalist]

The above quote is in many ways indicative of all the issues involved here: first, it points to the role of the journalist as an analytical one, a role with the object of understanding; then, the issue of scandal and misman-agement is seen as epiphenomenal to a deeper issue, that of lack of legit-imacy. It is this lack that made the Commission vulnerable and that even-tually made its position untenable. In these terms, the points involved in this story include the position of the journalist as an analyst, and the asso-ciated view that journalism should go beyond the apparent symptoms to the causes of the symptoms, which were, in this case, the scandals and eventual resignation, and the lack of democratic legitimacy, respectively.

Moral

This story and the analysis it contains provide a particular insight into the events. The story does not "unearth" scandals, nor is it concerned with the eternal fight for power, but it searches into the deeper causes of events, thereby underlining the lack of a wide democratic basis for the Commission as the main reason for its demise. In line with the analogy of psychoanalysis, the whole point of the analysis is "therapy," or in the current terms, to redress this issue of the lack of democratic legitimacy through acknowledging its centrality for European institutions and politics. The outcome of this story thus has been to foreground democratic legitimacy through delving into the crisis and attempting to understand what has caused or precipitated it, and how to remedy the situation.

This narrative appears to construct the nation as something dynamic, an entity that changes and grows as it comes into contact with other nations; in this vein, Europe is something that changes constantly on the basis of the exchange of ideas between nations, but also on the basis of conflict and disagreement. The reverse formulation of this is that because Europe is in a dynamic state, the nations that constitute it can evolve or learn and change. This constant exchange between nations and also between nations and Europe makes the job of the Brussels correspondent a highly political job; crises and events in Europe are reported not from a national interest point of view, nor from a "harmonious Europeanization" point of view, but rather from a political stance, a point of view of the "struggle" over the (political) future of Europe. Overall, this view of the nation and Europe does not deny the possibility for a united Europe, nor does it posit the conditions under which this is possible, but rather holds that both the nation and Europe are locked together in a common future, in a mutually interdependent relation, whereby there are more possibilities than impossibilities. The issue here is that the construction of Europe is more a matter for political debate than for a debate along national lines. This prioritisation of politics over national and/or ethnic affiliations is at the heart of Habermas's construct of constitutional patriotism. For Habermas (1994), "the political culture must serve as the common denominator for a constitutional patriotism which simultaneously sharpens an awareness of the multiplicity and integrity of the different forms of life" (27). National affinities need not be replaced, nor do they necessarily posit problems for further integration, provided that this is understood as a political project. If Europe is understood in political terms, then the crisis and resignation are political matters and should be addressed as such; the crisis events do not reveal old-style national habits, nor are they the result of institutions locked in a constant power struggle. Rather, they reflect a dynamism and a movement toward change associated with a political project that is growing.

The negotiation between the national and the European has here taken the form of a reconciliation based on making the former a resource for the latter. In so doing, a space opens up for keeping them both, for imagining a different relationship between them, which allows for disagreements without reverting either to national primordialism or to a movement toward national annihilation. The position created and justified for European journalism is therefore one in which it can pursue in-depth reporting on, and analyses of, European matters, without the need to "manufacture consent," as it were, or the narrow-mindedness of filtering everything through a national-interest perspective.

CONCLUSION

The tasks of this chapter include the identification of the interpretative repertoires on Europe, the nation, and journalism encountered among the Brussels press corps. These repertoires are considered functional, in that they are mobilised in order to explain events and justify actions. The functionality of these repertoires is examined through looking at the crisis and eventual resignation of the European Commission. The functional way of mobilising these repertoires reveals, in turn, what can be seen as the outcome of the negotiation between Europe, the nation, and journalism, representing three different identities, political, "ethnic" in a wider sense, and professional.

The following table summarises the empirical findings.

Table 7.1. Summary of Presentation of Crisis Narratives, Nationality, and Europeanness

	Repertoire I	*Repertoire II*	*Repertoire III*
Construction of nationality	Problem/obstacle	Essential difference	Resource
Construction of Europe	In search of a single voice	Impossible/ undesirable	A political project evolution
Justification for crisis	Corruption	Power struggle	Lack of democratic basis
Position for journalist	Heroic/ investigative	Chronicler/ reporter	Therapist/analyst
Moral	Political accountability	Survival of the fittest	Increase of democratic legitimacy
Journalist definition	Investigative journalism	Journalism as chronicling/ reportage	In-depth, analytical journalistm
Negotiation outcome	Replace the nation with a common Europeanness— a "Europeanist" outcome	Retain the nation— a "nationalist" outcome	Accommodate both— a "postnational" and "post-Europeanist" outcome

Encountering the above repertoires among some of the elite members of the Brussels press corps is, as already noted, doubly significant, because they mediate between Europe and its publics, and because they, in themselves, constitute a European public. In the first case, the current findings are significant because they provide an insight into how European journalists report on Europe. In the earlier discussion on the media and Europe, we saw that studies of the representation of Europe and its topics are inconclusive, reporting both national differences in reporting and overall similarities. The current findings suggest that this may be, at least partly, due to the mobilisation of different understandings of Europe and the nation, as well as of the role and function of European journalism. This can explain why, for instance, within France there were important differences in the reporting of the crisis: *Le Monde*, *Le Figaro*, and *Libération* all carried different stories. *Le Monde*, overall, was supportive of the Commission; *Le Figaro* was rather detached, publishing interviews with Edith Cresson; while *Libération* was openly critical.[15] The explanation of national cultures, usually evoked by authors, cannot be valid here, since we are within a single national culture. Similarly, of the British press, only the *Guardian* was actively pursuing the scandal allegations, while in the German press, it was mainly the German magazine *Focus* that mobilised extensively against the Commission. Journalistic culture seems an equally unsatisfactory explanation, since other newspapers, equivalent in terms of their journalism, were not carrying the allegations. Looking at the repertoires, we see that the way in which the negotiation between Europe, the nation, and journalism is resolved leads to specific journalistic positions vis-à-vis Europe. The involvement of identity positions cannot be ignored as a contributory factor to the reporting of Europe, alongside other considerations already documented in the literature, and alluded to earlier in this chapter.

Thus, although the controversial and inconclusive literature on media effects (McQuail 1994) prohibits any claims for direct media effects, it can be reasonably argued that reporting along the lines of the above repertoires and narratives, and associated journalistic stances, contributes to the circulation of meanings of Europe, on which the publics of Europe will draw in constructing their own understandings. This argument is further strengthened by Eurobarometer findings showing the dependency of European publics on their national media for information on Europe.[16] But the Brussels press corps also constitutes a public in its own right, the "first" European public, and as such, the ways in which they negotiate different identities provide an important insight that can be examined alongside findings from other publics. EU correspondents, thus, in understanding and subsequently reporting on Europe, seem to mobilise three different repertoires of the nation and Europe, which carry very different implications for the politics of Europe. The first imagines a Europe based on commonality and a uniformity of opinion, the second refuses to imagine Europe as a project, while the third imagines a political Europe. The easy conclusion here would be to support the last, since it leaves more space for Europe than the former two. Yet, on a closer look, all three understandings need to be simultaneously present in order for Europe to actually work as a political project, that is, as a project that allows for disagreement and dissent, and a project with a future that is yet to be constructed. Similarly, there can be no argument in favour of discarding any of the different identity repertoires we encountered among this public, since, following Habermas (1994), both the multiplicity and the integrity of different forms of life are vital. This becomes even more crucial if we consider the mediating role of this public of journalists. The most important conclusion we can draw here is that the contemporaneous existence of different identities vis-à-vis Europe and the nation, as well as the different outcomes these may have, constitute a singular guarantee for the continuous imaging of Europe and the multiple forms it can take.

NOTES

1. Schlesinger (1993) critically discusses the European Commission's attempts to forge a European cultural identity through a cultural and audiovisual policy that protects and supports European media production over American/global media products because of its assumptions of an intrinsic Europeanness and overall protectionist stance. Of importance here is also that the European Commission assumes that European media play a pivotal role in matters concerning Europeanness.

2. The term is here used to convey the project of European unification as well as the geographical and political entity.

3. These interviews formed part of the author's doctoral dissertation (Siapera 2002a), which examined journalism and European politics under the light of normative, social, and political theories of the relationship between the media and politics.

4. This criticism refers to the way in which social categories are seen as perceptual givens within most social cognitive approaches, which thereby tend to essentialise categories. Social Identity Theory and Self-Categorisation Theory, according to Wetherell and Potter (1992), while accepting the social constructedness of categories and groups, still place the onus for categorisation on the perception of differences and similarities between groups. The discursive approach, on the other hand, prioritises the process of (discursive) construction of boundaries between groupings as worthy of study.

5. Such an attempt, incidentally, is very strongly resisted by parts of the Brussels press corps.

6. This is true with the exception of EU-instigated information campaigns, which, however, tend to go through the national governments. For an interesting analysis of the Commission's information policy on the euro see Mak (2002).

7. Evidence supporting this argument can also be found in the Eurobarometer surveys (e.g., 2000), which show that the European public overwhelmingly depends on its (national) media for news and information on European matters.

8. The interview was conducted in French; the above translation is the author's.

9. Potter and Wetherell (1987) refer to this criterion as the main determinant for sampling in discourse analysis.

10. For a detailed description of the events and the role played by specific journalists in the crisis leading to the resignation, see Meyer (2000). Meyer argues that the involvement of the Brussels press corps in this affair signals a turning point for European journalism, moving toward an investigative style of reporting. For an analysis of the resignation from the perspective of Habermasian political theory see Siapera (2002b), who argues that the circulation of competing interpretations of the resignation is linked to different normative ideals of journalism, which may be construed as leading to a vibrant European public sphere.

11. Some notes on the quoted material: everything in italics is a direct quotation taken from the interviews—no alterations were made in the style, vocabulary, grammar, and so on used by the speakers; all the material in brackets [ ] is the author's comment, included for clarification; [. . .] means omitted material; while [.] indicates a pause. The words in bold comprise the key terms for the interpretation of each quote.

12. Note here the direct disagreement with the Irish journalist quoted in the previous repertoire [I-3], who, interviewed before Romano Prodi took over, proposed precisely this policy of disentangling the press officers' nationalities from those of the Commissioners they serve.

13. For instance, Christiansen (1996, 78) describes the Commission as the "motor of the integration process."

14. Gellner defines nationalism as entailing the principle that nation and state should always coincide (1983, 6).

15. These observations are based on the notes of the author, made at the time, and are rather suggestive and not meant to represent any in-depth content analysis. For a more detailed description (but again, not content analysis) of the particular newspapers and media involved in the reporting of the scandals, see Meyer (2000).

16. For instance, Eurobarometer 57 (2002), reports a 65 percent reliance on television, and 44 percent on newspapers (EU fifteen averages). See http://europa. eu.int/comm/public_opinion/archives/eb/eb57/eb57_en.pdf.

III

European Identity among Non-elites

8

More than Nationals: How Identity Choice Matters in the New Europe

Jack Citrin and John Sides

Europe now has a draft constitution, a common currency, a flag, and an anthem. It is widening, taking in new members from the east, as well as deepening, as the European Commission and European Court of Justice issue new rulings overriding national laws in domains as varied as pay equity and weights and measures. Clearly, Europe has slouched toward statehood. But is this quasi-state populated by a European quasi-nation, a set of people with a shared sense of identity that distinguishes them in their own minds from non-Europeans? If so, what is the content of this identity, how does it relate to inherited national identities, and what are its implications for the future development of European institutions and policies?

The idea of a united Europe flexing its muscles to limit American economic and diplomatic power has long held widespread support among elite groups (Wallace and Wallace 2000). Even in 1991 and 1992, when substantial popular opposition to the Maastricht Treaty arose and a sense of crisis loomed, a survey found that more than 90 percent of elites in every country favored moving further toward political union (Reif, personal communication). How far ordinary people are prepared to follow is another matter. Several years ago, Karl Kaiser, a German scholar of international affairs, claimed that "there has been a qualitative jump in the sense of a European identity. What you are seeing are the first signs of shared beliefs, rights and responsibilities of young Europeans" (*New York Times*, January 14, 2000, A3). At the same time, however, there is much talk of a "democratic deficit" in the development of a united Europe, implying widespread public reservations about, if not resistance to, further political integration.

THE ROLE OF ELITES AND INSTITUTIONS

The founders of the "European movement" after World War II regarded a common European identity as an antidote to the antagonisms fostered by ethnocentric national loyalties, and hoped that European institutions would promote a broader sense of community that would facilitate further integration in governance. However, given the linguistic, religious, and ethnic heterogeneity within Europe, the cultural basis of a sense of common identity is elusive. In fact, some observers (Schimitter 2000, 28) question whether individuals in a Euro-polity need to feel themselves "conationals" in order to act like "cocitizens." They propose a "civic" Europeanism based on what Habermas (1994) calls "constitutional patriotism," an attachment that arises through participation in shared institutions based on liberal political principles. Among the dominant elite groups in Europe, a consensual political sensibility does seem to prevail (Haas, Roever, and Schmidt 2002). In positive terms, this shared outlook encompasses a commitment to settling international disputes by peaceful means, policy making through multilateral institutions, giving aid to poorer countries, protecting the rights of ethnic minorities, and maintaining a generous welfare state. In negative terms, Europe contrasts its identity with that of the United States, the exemplar of the crude rough-and-tumble in both domestic and international affairs, which serves as the disdained "other" in drawing psychological and political boundaries (Judt 2003). One implication of this conception of European identities is that national loyalties and interests are subordinated to collective norms and policies.

If authority is the exclusive right to make rules, then the European Union has substantially eroded the sovereignty of its constituent nation-states. For example, the takeover of the American company Seagrams by the French company Vivendi had to pass muster with merger regulations administered by the European Commission and the European Court of Justice. More generally, the doctrine of "direct effect" established the principle that European Community law can confer rights on individuals even without supplementary actions by national institutions. When individuals then invoked their rights as Europeans against states, the European Court of Justice declared that Community law was supreme, and states grudgingly went along. In one case, Tanja Greil earned the right for females to serve in combat units in the German army (*New York Times*, January 14, 2000, A3). In another, one with more far-reaching consequences for the emotional lives of ordinary citizens, the Bosman ruling overturned limits on the number of foreign players on soccer teams. This created free agency for soccer players in Europe. Four years later, Chelsea, the darlings of London's West End, had an Italian manager and fielded a team without a single English player. And recently, David Beckham, the iconic captain of the British national soccer team, was sold by Manchester United to Spain's Real Madrid. With soccer losing its national identity and war no longer an option, what task is left for patriotic gore?

The recent divisions within the EU over whether to support military action in Iraq show that states as represented by national governments have not been wholly displaced. Indeed, Moravcsik (1998) argues that the trajectory of European integration records the pursuit of national interest through a process of intergovernmental bargaining among actors keenly sensitive to domestic sentiments. However, as Wallace and Wallace (2000) detail in a comprehensive and balanced survey, the European Union's institutions and agencies, although nominally the property of the member states, penetrate deeply into national affairs. Wallace and Wallace argue that domestic political actors increasingly find it worthwhile to leapfrog national agencies and interact with European Union policy makers to devise programs and approve budgets.

As Laffan points out in her chapter in this volume, engagement in European institutions has the capacity for building supranational identities among the political and interest group leaders who participate in the policy-making process. These elite actors frequently form bonds and develop patterns of interaction that reframe the way in which they address national problems. Put differently, the national representatives in Brussels have multiple identities and recognize the need to balance national and European goals. This chapter focuses on whether ordinary citizens mimic this attitude and have developed a psychological attachment to Europe that constrains national loyalties and provides an impetus for a federal European "meganation" (see Citrin and Sides 2003 for a complementary analysis).

THE ROLE OF PUBLIC OPINION

What role has public opinion played in the process of European integration? Collective government in Europe implies a shared commitment to the common enterprise, some sense of common values and goals. But shared by whom? As noted, European integration has been an elite-driven process, pushed along by experts and officials rather than by popular movements. Some scholars (Haas 1958) explicitly state that the similarity of elite values and expectations across nations, developed through a process of learning by doing, is all that has mattered. Yet others (Hoffman 1966; Wallace 1999) dissent and argue that a "we-feeling" among the population at large must take hold if the nation-state is finally to die; in their view, a sense of shared identity among ordinary citizens is critical to Europe's future development as a political union.

Empirical research on public attitudes toward the European Union generally has characterized the public's outlook as a "permissive consensus" that supports elite initiatives favoring more integration without actively demanding such steps (Reif 1993; Lindberg and Sheingold 1970). In this view, integration inches rather than leaps forward because of the recognized strength of national identities. At the same time, it is difficult to roll back the authority of European institutions because the anti-European elites who might mobilize opposition are weak (Risse 2002). Permissiveness has its limits, however, and these are reached when proposals for more supranational power impose serious costs or challenge cherished national values. More generally, public opinion matters because it places constraints on the measures elites can safely contemplate.

This chapter reviews survey data to explore how far the idea of a common European identity has penetrated mass opinion. Clearly, in any complex society people belong to many groups and communities. When one's country belongs to the European Union, a person has dual citizenship—European and national. In this context, it is important to explore whether people regard loyalty to their country and the emerging European polity as competing or complementary. In other words, do people identify as nationals *or* Europeans, or as nationals *and* Europeans? And if they identify as both, what is the relative strength of these two attachments, and in what contexts does one identity rather than the other have priority? Has the growing strength of European institutions been accompanied by more public willingness to cede national sovereignty in important policy-making domains? Or do people fear that a stronger Europe threatens their nation's unique traits? For people who do see themselves as Europeans, what political beliefs and values accompany that self-representation? Finally, how do European and national identities shape attitudes toward "outsiders"—in this case, cultural minorities within a specific member nation?

In addressing these issues we are guided by concepts drawn from social identity theory in psychology (Ashmore, Jussim, and Wilder 2001). In particular, we assume that European and national identities are not an either-or affair. Instead we accept the widespread presence of multiple identities and consider the factors that explain differences in how they are prioritized. To briefly preview the results, our analysis of Eurobarometer data finds that attachment to the nation remains strong in all European countries. Nevertheless, attachment to Europe grew throughout the 1990s. Even as people came to question the instrumental benefits of belonging to the European Union, expressing a similarly strong attachment to Europe and nation became the modal response in all member states. Incorporating a European component into one's political self-concept increased support for supranational authority in many policy domains. At the same time, the continuing power of nationality is reflected in the reluctance to cede authority in areas, such as education, that are closely related to the transmission of a distinctive cultural identity. Finally, an exclusive attachment to the nation does make one less tolerant of cultural minorities. A self-concept that accommodates plural identities seems to reduce ethnocentrism.

CONCEPTIONS OF "WE" AND "THEY" IN EUROPE

European and national identities are *social* identities. They refer to a dimension of the individual's self-concept shared with some but not all other people (Herrmann and Brewer, this volume). A social identity originates in the act of self-categorization as a group member; the individuals answer the "Who am I?" question by naming a subset of people "I am like." So a social identity entails drawing boundaries. One is the same as those inside what the American historian David Hollinger (1995) calls the "Circle of We." A social identity therefore simultaneously integrates people and divides them. Identifying *as*, however, is not the same as identifying *with*. One can say "I am a European" and feel quite neutral toward other Europeans. As Tajfel famously stated (1982), social identities vary in their value and significance to the individual, which has implications for how the individual treats insiders and outsiders. Finally, a social identity rests on shared beliefs about the criteria for inclusion and exclusion. In other words, a stable definition of the putative European Circle of We entails agreement about the attributes of the prototypical member of the group, traits that function as unifying factors. So when the boundaries of a given community are redrawn, the normative content of its identity similarly may need redefinition, a process that often is highly contested.

Social identity theory posits that a strong collective identity fosters feelings of mutual obligation among group members. Yet because people generally belong to several groups at once, how they reconcile their multiple identities becomes critical. In this regard, the distinction between "us" and "them," the contrast between "self" and "other" that is fundamental to identity politics, is a shifting one. In some contexts, nationality is the dividing line, in others region, in others class. So the important question is not the fact of multiple identities, but how they are ordered. In the present case, do national identities dominate attachment to Europe, and to what extent? Indeed, are these identifications competing or complementary, in the sense that one can feel European while simultaneously expressing pride in and belonging to the nation?

THE NATURE OF EUROPEAN AND NATIONAL IDENTIFICATION

Public support for the European Union as an institution has waxed and waned over time. In figure 8.1, we present a temporal portrait based on

Jack Citrin and John Sides

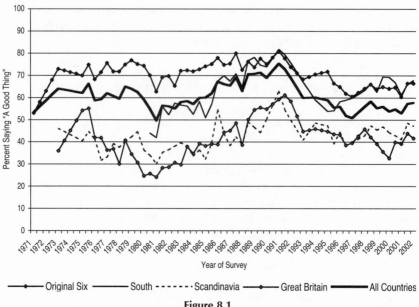

Figure 8.1

Eurobarometer data, focusing on the percentage of Europeans who believe that membership in the European Union is a "good thing."[1] We construct trends for the Eurobarometer sample as a whole, as well as for the original six member countries, southern Europe, Scandinavia, and Great Britain.[2] In general, support for the EU increased through the 1980s but declined sharply after 1990. The proportion of the entire Eurobarometer sample saying that membership was a good thing dropped from 75 percent to 50 percent in only seven years. There is also variation across the constituent countries: the original six and the countries of southern Europe tend to be more supportive than Great Britain or Scandinavia.

How does this trend compare with actual identification with Europe? One Eurobarometer question that has been included for the last decade asks respondents to prioritize their identities as Europeans and as nationals: "In the near future, will you see yourself as (nationality) only, (nationality) and then European, European and then (nationality), or European only?" We will refer to this indicator as "identification." Figure 8.2 presents the proportion of Eurobarometer respondents giving each of the four response options from 1992 to 2002. A first finding is that the majority of the sample claims a European identity of some sort, that is, less than half of respondents say that that they think of themselves only in terms of their nationality. However, the proportion of people who put their European identity first is quite low: less than 10 percent of the sample says "Europe and then

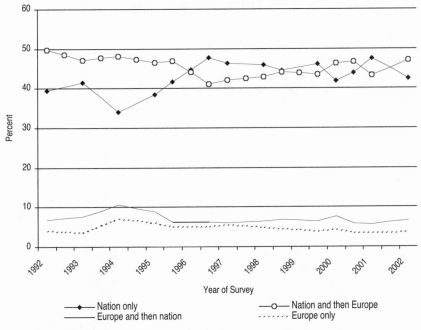

Figure 8.2

nation" or "Europe only." Moreover, in the early 1990s there was an increase of about 10 percentage points in the proportion saying "nation only," though in general the distribution of responses has been steady since 1996. But perhaps most notable is that a majority of respondents does identify with Europe, even during a period when support for the European Union dwindled.

Naturally, the trends in figure 8.2 elide variation across EU member countries. In table 8.1, we present the distribution of European and national identification in each country in a 2002 Eurobarometer survey (EB 57.2). The range of responses is quite large. In Italy, only 20 percent of the sample declares an exclusive attachment to country. But in the United Kingdom, 62 percent claims such an attachment. Unsurprisingly, the country-level differences in identification roughly parallel those in support for the EU in figure 8.1. Citizens of the original member countries and the countries of southern Europe are more likely than those of either the United Kingdom or the Scandinavian countries to identify as Europeans. It is notable, however, that in every country, including the original six, only a small percentage of the sample prioritizes Europe over nation.

While the question of priorities is a significant one, it is also important to investigate the strength of multiple identities without forcing people to

Table 8.1. European and National Identification, by Country (2002)

	N	Europe only	Europe then nation	Nation then Europe	Nation only
Belgium	985	5%	10%	51%	33%
Denmark	993	1	5	55	38
Germany	2,008	5	9	44	42
Greece	1,000	2	4	46	48
Spain	978	5	4	62	29
France	1,011	5	9	52	34
Ireland	970	3	5	44	48
Italy	1,032	6	10	65	20
Luxembourg	437	4	11	49	37
Netherlands	974	2	7	49	42
Portugal	1,040	5	5	47	43
United Kingdom	1,255	4	4	30	62
Austria	967	2	11	41	46
Sweden	991	1	5	40	54
Finland	1,005	1	3	40	55
Total	**15,646**	**4**	**7**	**47**	**43**

Source: Eurobarometer 57.2.

choose among them. To do so, we take advantage of a series of Euro-barometer questions that asks respondents to characterize their degree of "attachment" to their town, region, country, and Europe on a four-point scale (very, fairly, not very, or not at all attached). These questions have been asked periodically since 1991 and thus provide another interesting time series. Table 8.2 presents the percentage of respondents who say they are "somewhat" or "very" attached to Europe and the same percentage who are attached to the nation. We present these figures for each country and for four points in time from 1991 until 2000.

Overall, attachment to country is quite high. Large majorities in every nation say they are somewhat or very attached, and this changes little over time. By contrast, while attachment to Europe is less strong, it has increased substantially over this period. For example, the proportion of Dutch respondents expressing attachment increased from 30 percent in 1991 to 56 percent in 2000. In Sweden, there was an even larger increase, from 46 percent to 77 percent. There was even a small increase in the traditionally Euro-skeptical United Kingdom. This trend is all the more striking given that it occurred during a period when support for the European Union as a whole was declining, at least as measured by the indicator in figure 8.1. Europe-as-nation became more potent even as Europe-as-state became less popular.

How well do attachment to Europe and attachment to country go together? That is, to what extent are these identifications psychologically

Table 8.2. **Trends in attachment to Europe and nation (1991–2000; percent somewhat or very attached)**

	1991	1995	1999	2000	Change ('91/'95–'00)
Attachment to Europe					
Belgium	50%	46%	64%	65%	15%
Denmark	61	41	72	68	7
Germany	48	41	60	60	12
Greece	55	47	42	44	-12
Spain	57	40	71	72	16
France	55	51	55	60	4
Ireland	36	44	55	55	18
Italy	67	56	68	70	3
Luxembourg	59	62	81	80	21
Netherlands	30	28	51	56	26
Portugal	44	47	63	65	21
United Kingdom	35	31	39	42	7
Austria		53	65	67	14
Sweden		46	73	77	31
Finland		43	67	67	24
Total	**49**	**44**	**59**	**62**	**13**
Attachment to Country					
Belgium	75	84	77	81	6
Denmark	98	97	97	96	-2
Germany	88	87	87	86	-2
Greece	97	97	97	95	-2
Spain	90	91	90	92	1
France	91	91	89	90	-2
Ireland	96	97	96	95	-1
Italy	90	91	91	91	0
Luxembourg	93	92	88	94	1
Netherlands	81	79	87	81	0
Portugal	95	97	95	95	0
United Kingdom	89	88	92	90	1
Austria		95	92	91	-4
Sweden		97	90	94	-3
Finland		96	96	94	-1
Total	**90**	**92**	**90**	**91**	**0**

Source: Eurobarometers 36, 43.1bis, 51, and 54.1.

compatible? And how has this changed over time? To get at these questions, we combined the measures of attachment to Europe and nation in a single indicator, simply subtracting one from the other. We then collapsed this indicator for the sake of presentation, categorizing respondents as more attached to Europe than nation, more attached to nation than Europe, or equally attached to both. Table 8.3 presents the distribution of responses, comparing the two endpoints of the time series, 1991 and 2000. One finding parallels responses to the identification question discussed above: very few respondents (less than 5 percent) are more attached to Europe than to their nation. A second finding is perhaps more unexpected: a growing number of respondents express *equal* attachment to both Europe and nation. As a result, there is a decreasing number who say that they are more attached to their nation than Europe. Though there remains considerable variation among countries in terms of the level of attachment—for instance, in 2000, 68 percent of the Irish were more attached to Ireland than Europe, whereas only 35 percent of Belgians were more attached to Belgium than Europe—the trend toward dual and equivalent attachment is evident in nearly every country. While the nation retains primacy in most people's minds, the growing sense of Europeanness implies that more people are integrating a sense of belonging to two overlapping polities.

One 2000 Eurobarometer survey (EB 54.1) affords an opportunity to compare various measures of solidarity with Europe and with nation. This survey included the identification and attachment items, as well as two questions asking respondents about the extent of their pride in their national and European identities.[3] Though we do not discuss these measures in detail here, it is worth nothing that while respondents were typically more proud to be their nationality than to be European, the proportion

Table 8.3.   Trend in dual attachment to Europe and Nation, by country

	Closer to Europe			Equally close			Closer to nation		
	1991	2000	Change	1991	2000	Change	1991	2000	Change
Belgium	12%	8%	-4%	38%	57%	19%	50%	35%	-15%
Denmark	2	2	0	21	41	20	77	57	-20
Germany	5	4	-1	28	53	25	67	43	-24
Greece	1	1	0	20	21	1	78	78	-1
Spain	6	4	-1	33	52	20	62	44	-18
France	4	5	0	34	46	12	61	49	-12
Ireland	0	1	1	17	31	14	82	68	-15
Italy	7	5	-2	39	49	11	54	45	-9
Luxembourg	3	4	1	33	57	24	64	39	-25
Netherlands	5	8	4	25	46	20	70	46	-24
Portugal	1	3	2	15	41	26	85	57	-28
United Kingdom	4	3	-1	18	30	12	78	67	-11
Austria		3			50			47	
Sweden		5			49			46	
Finland		3			40			57	
Norway	4			27			69		
TOTAL	**4**	**4**	**0**	**26**	**44**	**18**	**69**	**52**	**-17**

Source: Eurobarometers 36 and 54.1.

proud to be European was generally higher than the proportion who said they were attached to Europe. In the entire sample, 71 percent said they were somewhat or very proud to be European, versus 62 percent who said they were somewhat or very attached to Europe. This is further evidence that Europe has become a viable and positive identity.

Table 8.4 presents a cross-tabulation of the identification item with the attachment and pride items. Several interesting relationships emerge. Predictably, those respondents who identify first with Europe or exclusively with Europe are less likely to say they are attached to their country or proud to be their nationality. Seventy percent of those who define their identity as "Europe only" express attachment to country, as compared to 92 percent of those who say "nation only." But it is striking that even among those who prioritize Europe, attachment to and pride in country are still quite high. A second finding of note is that national attachment and pride are as high among those who say "nation and then Europe" as among those who say "nation only." Maintaining a supplementary European identity does not erode one's feelings toward country. Another finding is that increased attachment to or pride in Europe depends only on identifying with Europe in some respect, regardless of how one prioritizes European and national identities. There are only small differences across the "Europe only," "Europe then nation," and "nation then Europe" categories. Only among those who say "nation only" does attachment to Europe and pride in Europe drop—and, to be sure, they do so precipitously. Still, however, even among those whose identity is ostensibly exclusively national, roughly half of respondents still express attachment to Europe (47 percent) or pride in Europe (59 percent).

Unsurprisingly, there are also strong correlations between the attachment and pride items. The strongest correlations are between those indicators with the same focal point—for instance, the correlation between pride in country and attachment to country is .47, and that between pride in Europe and attachment to Europe is .54. But most striking is that the correlations

Table 8.4. The relationship between identification and attachment and pride (percentage)

	N	Somewhat or very attached to Country	Europe	Somewhat or very proud to be Nationality	European
Europe only	550	70%	75%	68%	76%
Europe then nation	925	80	77	73	80
Nation then Europe	7277	93	74	91	82
Nation only	6818	92	47	90	59

Source: Eurobarometer 54.1 (2000).

among all four of these measures are of significant magnitude and positive. This is to say, pride in one's nation is associated with pride in Europe ($r = .38$), and likewise for attachment to nation and Europe ($r = .33$). Thus, these two identities appear complementary rather than competing. Europe and country are not inexorably opposed in the minds of most Europeans.[4]

A final question about the nature of European identification concerns variation across individuals. The political impact of public opinion depends not just on the aggregate distribution of preferences but on the skills, resources, and participatory orientation of those sharing a given opinion. In the present context, are those inclined to define themselves as Europeans more knowledgeable, educated, and wealthy? Are they younger, suggesting that the future augurs weakening nationalist sentiments? And does political ideology play a role, since the nation is traditionally a more potent symbol for the political right, while the internationalist ideal of a united Europe tends to attract the left (see Niedermayer and Sinnott 1995b; Inglehart 1990)? Table 8.5 presents the bivariate relationships between identification, attachment, and pride and a set of demographic and political variables that includes education, age, income, gender, and ideology. For the sake of presentation, we focus on the percent of respondents saying "nation only," the percent equally attached to nation and Europe, and the percent equally proud to be their nationality and European.

The level of formal education is positively related to a European identity, however measured. The proportion of respondents saying they identify with the "nation only" declines from 54 percent among those in the lowest education category (those with less than fifteen years of education) to 35 percent among those with twenty or more years of education (and still further, to 28 percent, among those still in school). Similarly, the percentage of respondents equally attached to their nation and Europe increases from 38 percent to 51 percent, and the percentage of respondents equally proud to be their nationality and European from 50 percent to 61 percent as one moves from the least to the best-educated category of respondents. Younger respondents are also more likely to orient themselves toward Europe in some fashion. For example, those aged fifteen to twenty-four are the least likely to say "nation only" and the most likely to express an equal attachment or level of pride. Income's effect on identification mirrors that of education, though its effects on attachment and pride are minimal. There are only small differences between men and women on all of these measures. Finally, there is some evidence that those on the ideological left have a more pro-Europe orientation than those on the right—though these ideological differences are not large and most likely vary across countries depending on their respective domestic politics. On the whole, then, these results underscore the potential for the growth of a stronger and more pervasive European identity, since a pro-Europe outlook is particularly

Table 8.5. The correlates of European identity

	Identification (percent saying "nation only")	*Attachment* (percent equally attached to nation and Europe)	*Pride* (percent equally proud to be nationality and European)
Education			
Up to 15 years	54%	38%	50%
16–19 years	47	44	54
20 or more years	35	48	57
Still studying	28	51	61
Age			
15–24	35	48	59
25–34	41	47	57
35–44	41	44	57
45–54	42	43	55
55–64	48	42	50
65 and above	56	39	49
Income			
Low	50	45	55
Medium low	48	42	53
Medium high	44	44	54
High	35	45	57
Gender			
Male	41	44	53
Female	46	44	56
Ideology			
Left	39	48	35
Center	43	53	40
Right	46	57	45
Don't know	49	52	38

Source: Eurobarometer 54.1 (2000).

strong among those most attentive to politics and since cohort replacement will diminish the ranks of the most nationalistic segment of the population.[5]

THE CONSEQUENCES OF EUROPEAN AND NATIONAL IDENTIFICATION: SUPPORT FOR THE EU

Though we have thus far sought to distinguish certain trends in a diffuse sense of identification with Europe from support for the European Union as an institution, it would be surprising if these bore no relationship to one another. While models of support for the EU typically build in many indicators of how EU membership bears on the respondent's economic situation (see Gabel 1998), there is much less evidence that social identities play a role. Though our analysis is not a comprehensive one—and, indeed, one would want to disentangle what could easily be a reciprocal relationship between European identity and support for the EU—it does highlight the nature and magnitude of the bivariate relationship.

In table 8.6, we present several indicators of support for the EU: whether the respondent considers EU membership a "good thing" (see figure 8.1), whether the respondent believes that EU membership has benefited his or her country, the mean "desired speed" of building Europe, and the average number of EU institutions that the respondent said he or she trusted.[6] Each of these indicators manifests a relationship with European identity, however measured. One notable pattern across all three indicators of identity is that the effect of identity is not linear. It does not necessarily matter whether one prioritizes Europe over the nation or vice versa, provided one expresses some sense of identification with Europe. The largest differences in support for the EU are between those who feel some sense of European

Table 8.6. European identity and support for the EU

	Percent saying EU membership is a good thing	Percent saying EU membership has benefited country	Desired speed of building Europe (1=standstill; 7=fast)	Number of EU institutions trusted (0–9)
Identification				
Europe only	76%	80%	5.3	4.5
Europe then nation	76	79	5.2	4.6
Nation then Europe	70	75	5.0	4.5
Nation only	38	48	4.2	2.7
Attachment				
Closer to Europe	74	74	5.1	4.3
Equally close	65	70	4.9	4.2
Closer to nation	50	58	4.5	3.3
Pride				
Prouder to be European	71	70	5.1	4.0
Equally proud to be European and nationality	65	71	4.9	4.3
Prouder to be nationality	46	55	4.4	3.2

Source: Eurobarometer 54.1 (2000).

identity and those who define themselves solely in terms of their nationality. For example, the percentage saying that EU membership is a good thing ranges from 70 to 76 percent among those who identify exclusively, primarily, or secondarily with Europe, compared to 38 percent among those who identify with the nation only. There is nearly as large a gap when respondents are queried about whether their nation has benefited from EU membership (75–80 percent versus 48 percent). Those who identify with the "nation only" are also more likely to advocate a slower speed for building Europe and to trust a smaller number of EU institutions.

Similar relationships are evident when attachment and pride are employed as the measures of collective self-definition. Those who say they are more attached to Europe or more proud to be European are not much different than those who are equally attached to or proud of their nation and Europe. Support for the EU drops only among those who are more attached to their country than to Europe, or more proud to be their nationality than European. For example, whereas those who say that EU membership is a good thing constitute 71 percent of those prouder to be European and 65 percent of those equally proud to be European and their nationality, they constitute only 46 percent of those who are more proud to be their nationality. These results demonstrate that creating support for a stronger European state does not require a European identity that dominates national identity. It is sufficient if a European identity is established alongside one's national identity.

Another way to measure support for the European Union is to ask about the role that the European Union should play in certain policy domains. In some respects, this is a tougher test of support because it suggests specific ways in which nation-states might have to delegate power to or at least share power with EU institutions. We examine in particular three of the most salient policy domains: currency and the economy, foreign policy and defense, and education and culture. Table 8.7 presents three different sets of questions relevant to these domains. The first simply asks respondents whether they agree or disagree with having common EU policies in each domain. The second set asks respondents whether decision making in a certain domain "should be made by the (nationality) government, or made jointly with the European Union." The third asks respondents whether they have certain fears about "the building of Europe." We present the total percentage of respondents who agree with each statement as well as the percentage broken down by the level of identification with Europe. Identification here is measured by a trichotomized index combining the measures of identity priority, attachment, and pride discussed previously.[7]

A majority of respondents agrees with each of the first four statements in table 8.7: that there should be a common currency, a common foreign policy, a common defense and security policy, and a policy of teaching

Table 8.7.   Effect of identification on building Europe: economics, defense, and culture (percent agreeing)

	Overall	By level of identification with Europe		
		Low	Medium	High
There has to be a European Monetary Union with one single currency, the euro.	55%	36%	58%	72%
The member states of the European Union should have one common foreign policy toward countries outside of the European Union.	64	51	68	74
The European Union should have a common defense and security policy.	70	57	73	81
Children should be taught at school about the way European Union institutions work.	85	79	88	90
EU should share decision making: currency	55	37	58	72
EU should share decision making: fighting unemployment	48	37	51	58
EU should share decision making: defense	41	28	42	56
EU should share decision making: foreign policy	66	54	70	77
EU should share decision making: education	29	20	29	39
EU should share decision making: cultural policy	32	24	33	39
EU should share decision making: immigration policy	41	29	41	54
Fear: the end of national currency	57	70	56	43
Fear: transfer of jobs to countries with lower production costs	62	67	63	57
Fear: our language being used less and less	44	50	43	36
Fear: the loss of our national identity and culture	48	59	48	36

Source: Eurobarometer 54.1 (2000).

children about the EU. However, support for the euro is lower (55 percent) than support for the other policies. Moreover, there is less widespread agreement on this issue. Just over one-third of those with low identification support a common currency, as compared with 72 percent of those who strongly identify with Europe. By contrast, even among those who have little identification with Europe, slim majorities still support, at least in the abstract, a common foreign policy and common defense policy (51 percent and 57 percent, respectively), and a large majority (79 percent) supports teaching children about the EU. The salience of the currency debate may have in some sense "primed" underlying national and European identities, making them particularly strong predictors of preferences in this domain.

When asked about the allocation of decision-making power in specific domains, identity choice is consistently related to willingness to share authority between European and national institutions. It is interesting, though, that there is a greater overall willingness to share decision making in currency matters (55 percent) than in fighting unemployment (48 percent), defense (41 percent), education (29 percent), cultural policy (32 percent), or immigration policy (41 percent). These last three policy domains go to the heart of a nation's distinctiveness, which may explain why sharing authority with the EU is less acceptable. It is striking that even among those who strongly identify with Europe, support for joint decision making in education and cultural policy is low (only 39 percent). Clearly these domains constitute touchy subjects, ones that most Europeans want to keep solely under national purview.

When people are asked what they fear about the creation of a stronger European Union, a somewhat different pattern of results emerges, with economic anxieties seemingly more prevalent than worries about the loss of national culture. Whereas 57 percent of the sample fears the end of the national currency and 62 percent fears the loss of jobs, only 44 percent fears the loss of language and 48 percent the loss of national identity or culture. While there is greater opposition to delegating questions of culture to the EU, it is clear that concerns about the EU's economic effects are more predominant. Again, the effects of feelings about the nation and Europe are most evident in regard to currency—70 percent of those who only weakly identify with Europe fear the loss of the franc, the lira, and so on, as compared to 43 percent of those who strongly identify with Europe—though similar, albeit smaller, differences emerge when people are asked about language and culture.

These data suggest that while European encroachments on national sovereignty have been substantial, public opinion can still act as a constraint. There is particular opposition to an overweening EU role in such things as education and cultural policy. There is still only tenuous support for the euro, even though it is a fait accompli. Moreover, it is clear that support for the EU and EU decision making depends substantially on identity choice.[8] Both EU proponents and opponents can find support for their beliefs in the mass public; the future direction of EU policy may depend on who is most successful in mobilizing ostensible Europeans to their cause.

THE CONSEQUENCES OF EUROPEAN AND NATIONAL
IDENTIFICATION: ATTITUDES TOWARD MINORITIES

Among elites, tolerance for internal minorities has emerged as one criterion of European identity. Indeed, demonstrated commitment to this principle is one test would-be members of the European Union must pass—see, for example, various concerns among EU member countries about Turkey's treatment of its Kurdish population. These issues engage attitudes toward the boundaries of identity and community, so it is reasonable to hypothesize that people with a highly circumscribed sense of group identity will be more suspicious and hostile to outsiders than will those with multiple and heterogeneous loyalties. In other words, people identifying exclusively with the nation should have more negative feelings toward people of different backgrounds than do those expressing a more cosmopolitan sense of European identity.

We draw on a different 2000 Eurobarometer survey (EB 53.0) to investigate this issue. Unfortunately, this survey includes only one measure of European and national identity, the "identification" measure we used previously that asks respondents whether they see themselves as part of their nation only, their nation and then Europe, and so on. For the purposes of this analysis, we dichotomize this indicator into a "nation only" category and a category that includes some level of identification with Europe, whether secondary, primary, or exclusive (which we will refer to, in shorthand, as "Europe").

One question about minorities is simply whether they are too numerous: "Again, speaking generally about people from minority groups in terms of race, religion or culture, do you think there are not many, a lot but not too many, or too many of them living in (our country)?" In table 8.8, we present the proportion of respondents who said that there were "too many," broken down by country and by this dichotomized indicator of identification with Europe and nation.

A first finding of note is that opposition to minorities varies significantly across countries. More than half of Belgians and Greeks (56 percent and 58 percent, respectively) said minorities were too numerous. However, only 24 percent of Spaniards and 17 percent of Finns expressed this view. We leave aside an explanation for this country-level variation, which would undoubtedly hinge on objective demography as well as the presence of a salient antiminority politics, to focus on the individual-level effects of identity. As table 8.8 demonstrates, the nature of identity choice has a substantial effect on attitudes toward minorities in every country. Those who identify solely with the nation are much more likely to express hostility toward minorities. In the entire sample, 51 percent do so, as compared with 30 percent of those who have a European identity of some kind. The gap

Table 8.8. European identification and attitudes toward minority numbers (percent saying "too many" minority groups members live in country)

	Identify with Europe	*Identify with nation only*	*Total*
All Countries	**30%**	**51%**	**39%**
Belgium	46	73	56
Denmark	23	48	35
Germany	34	63	47
Greece	46	68	58
Spain	21	33	24
France	34	67	43
Ireland	22	46	34
Italy	38	64	44
Luxembourg	22	44	29
Netherlands	36	55	43
Portugal	31	43	36
United Kingdom	27	50	41
Austria	26	40	33
Sweden	16	37	28
Finland	9	24	17

Source: Eurobarometer 53.0 (2000).

between these two groups is quite large in some countries: 27 points in Belgium, 29 points in Greece, 33 points in France, and 26 points in Italy, for example. Clearly those with an identity that is inclusive of Europe are more tolerant of different and potentially marginalized races, religions, and other groups within individual nations.

To probe more deeply into public opinion toward minorities, we also draw on an extensive battery of questions that asks respondents whether they agree or disagree with certain statements about the effects of minorities, the situation of minorities, and policies toward minorities. Some items refer to deleterious consequences ("In schools where there are too many children from these minority groups, the quality of education suffers") and others to beneficial consequences ("Where schools make the necessary efforts, the education of all children can be enriched by the presence of children from minority groups"). Several statements get at how minority groups should be treated—that is, with additional attention from the government, or even with preferential treatment from the government. In table 8.9, we present the percent agreeing with these various statements, broken down by the binary indicator of identity.

Though the absolute level of agreement with these statements varies considerably, the effects of identity choice are robust and consistent. In nearly every case, those who identify only with the nation are more likely to agree with statements unfavorable to minorities, and less likely to agree with

Table 8.9. European identification and attitudes toward minorities (percent agreeing with statement)

	Europe	Nation only
Statements unfavorable to minorities		
In schools where there are too many children from these minority groups, the quality of education suffers.	50%	57%
People from these minority groups abuse the system of social benefits.	46	59
The religious practices of people from these minority groups threaten our way of life.	21	33
The presence of people from these minority groups is a cause of insecurity.	40	49
People from these minority groups are given preferential treatment by the authorities.	26	38
When hiring personnel, employers should only take account of qualifications, regardless of the person's race, religion or culture.	84	73
The presence of people from these minority groups increases unemployment in (COUNTRY).	45	58
Statements favorable to minorities		
People from these minority groups get poorer housing, largely because of discrimination.	47	38
Without people from these minority groups, (COUNTRY) would do less well in international sport.	35	26
The authorities should make efforts to improve the situation of people from these minority groups.	67	51
People from these minority groups are enriching the cultural life of (COUNTRY).	60	40
People from these minority groups pay more into our social security system than they claim.	17	14
Where schools make the necessary efforts, the education of all children can be enriched by the presence of children from minority groups.	68	49
People from these minority groups do the jobs that others do not want to do.	65	53
People from these minority groups keep entire sections of (COUNTRY)'s economy going.	34	23
People from these minority groups are being discriminated against in the job market.	62	49
Discrimination in the job market on grounds of a person's race, religion, or culture should be outlawed.	79	66

Source: Eurobarometer 53.0 (2000).

statements favorable to minorities. For example, whereas 60 percent of those who identify at least in part with Europe agree that that "People from these minority cultures are enriching the culture life of" their country, only 40 percent of those who identify solely with the nation agree. Similarly, more of those who say "nation only" believe that "[t]he presence of people from these minority groups increases unemployment" (58 percent versus 45 percent).

To confirm the empirical power of identity choice, we first combined these indicators into two scales—one of favorability toward minorities and one of unfavorability—and then regressed each scale on the dichotomous measure of identity and a host of control variables.[9] These variables included: age, education, gender, income, and ideology, as well as whether the respondent felt a part of a minority, whether the respondent's parents or grandparents were born outside of the country, overall life satisfaction, a measure of economic insecurity, the urbanity of the respondent's town, and a set of dummy variables for country. In figure 8.3, we present a graphic illustration of the results of these equations, including only those variables with the most notable and statistically significant effects. Each bar

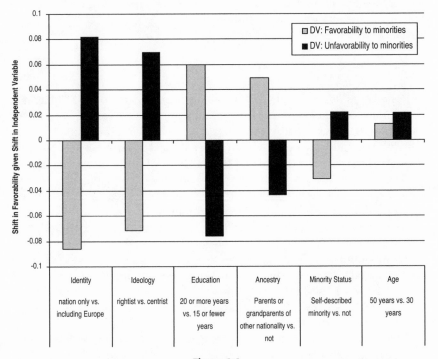

Figure 8.3

represents the shift in favorability (gray bars) or unfavorability (black bars) associated with the stated change in the independent variable. The dependent variables range from 0 to 1.

A number of variables have a commonsensical effect. Minority status is associated with greater favorability toward minorities (and, conversely, lesser unfavorability). Similarly, those whose parents or grandparents were born outside of the country are more favorable toward minorities. Education and a liberal ideology also predispose respondents to be more favorable. What is striking is that the substantive magnitude of the effect of identity is the *largest* of any of these variables. Identifying with nation only is associated with about a .08 shift in unfavorability and a -.08 shift in favorability. This shift is larger than that associated with shifts from the ideological center to the extreme right, from less than fifteen years of education to more than twenty years, and from age thirty to age fifty years. It exceeds the effects of self-identified minority status or ancestry. As Gaertner et al. (1999) found in another context, a superordinate group identity can mitigate ethnocentrism and prejudice even when one retains a strong sense of loyalty to an ethnic (or national) subgroup. The critical step appears to be adopting a sense of identity that is not exclusively national. Even if national identity retains emotional primacy, a sense of belonging to Europe softens feelings of antagonism toward minorities.[10]

CONCLUSION

In Benedict Anderson's (1983/1991) famous phrase, a nation is an imagined community, a group of strangers with a vicarious sense of kinship. Ernest Gellner (1983) insists that what makes a nation different from other groups with a shared identity is the search for political autonomy, a state of their own. A nation's identity refers to a particular set of ideas about what makes the community distinctive, and history shows that these criteria have been varied, malleable, and contested. There is no single factor that is a necessary or sufficient condition for the development of a nation. Whatever its content, however, Anthony Smith (1991, 143) writes that "national identity is perhaps the most fundamental and inclusive" of all collective identities in the modern era, a claim that poses a significant hurdle for building a European identity that can supercede national identity. If a European identity means that an Englishman feels equally at home in London and Warsaw and an Italian equally at home in Rome and Frankfurt, its gestation period is bound to be long (Byatt 2002).

What can be the basis of a constructed European identity? Although most European nation-states have more than one ethnic community within their borders, they still define themselves in terms of a common culture. This common culture almost always reveals the influence of ethnicity and its common myths and symbols, so that even within a plural society, there tends to be a dominant or core group—the English in Britain (and America), the northern French, the Castilians, and so on. In this respect, there is no core group or culture for Europe in its entirety. Neither language nor religion is an adequate marker for inclusion. Nor are there obvious geographical barriers that demarcate the limits or the center of a European "homeland." Brussels evokes quite different emotions from Jerusalem and Mecca.

In this context, scholars such as Habermas (1994), J.H.H. Weiler (1997), and Shaw (1997) recognize that a constructed European identity would have to be "civic" rather than "ethnic." They therefore advocate a "constitutional patriotism" that ironically resembles the dominant conception of national identity in the United States, where there is a largely successful formula for creating one out of many, *unum* out of *pluribus*. Europe's "civic religion" would encompass a demonstrated commitment to democracy, a tolerance for minorities, and a spirit of transnational cooperation. In addition, the European ethos would include support for a welfare state that tempers neoliberal market policies. These political ideas are believed to distinguish Europe from the less-democratic societies on its fringes and from the United States, which is less committed to multilateralism and to welfarist notions of social justice.

At the level of individuals, a European identity would simply mean allegiance to the political values and principles listed above and to derivative policies such as opposition to the death penalty and support for multilateral institutions. There would be a Europe-wide acceptance of a rights-based conception of citizenship founded on EU law rather than national tradition. J.H.H. Weiler (1997) asserts that this ideological conception of Europeanism can coexist with a set of loyalties to particularistic national, ethnic, or cultural entities, but there are important caveats. First, even at the elite level, the meaning of Europe and European values may vary from one country to the next. As Risse (2002) points out, the British consider continental political and legal traditions alien; Europe is the Other—them, not us. By contrast, the French readily may claim a European identity because they imagine its culture and institutions as a replica of their own (Byatt 2002). And for Germans, the primary meaning of a European identity is a denial of their nation's recent history (Risse 2002). In other words, what it means to be a European is a variable, not a constant. And even if civic conceptions of identity are advertised throughout the Union, whether they have a thick enough emotional gruel to overcome the entrenched conceptions of nationality based on more vivid and accessible cultural markers is questionable.

Byatt (2002) writes that the only thing the varied Europeans she interviewed agreed on was that when they were in America, they knew they were European. This hearkens back to the definition of a social identity in negative terms: "I am what I am not." Sometimes this oppositional version of self-definition is antagonistic, as expressed in hostility toward immigrants and foreigners. Recent talk (Judt 2003) focuses on the way in which Americans constitute the out-group that demarcates a separate European identity, performing the very function that allows Canadians to feel different.

The data available to us via the Eurobarometer unfortunately provide no information about subjective conceptions of European identity—about what people think it means to be a European. Bruter's chapter in this volume probes this question, and future research on the topic is essential. What is striking, however, is that even viewed as a diffuse symbol with potentially different associations across nations and individuals, Europe evokes increasingly positive responses with significant political implications. We have shown that identity choice, especially a plural identity that encompasses Europe as well as the nation, matters for beliefs about sharing power and for the treatment of minorities. This is particularly significant because the groups in the mass public who supplement their national identity with attachment to Europe are likely to grow in the future.

NOTES

1. The exact question wording is: "Generally speaking, do you think that (our country's) membership in the European Union is a good thing, a bad thing, or neither good nor bad?"

2. The country groups presented in these graphs are as follows: "Original Six"— France, Belgium, the Netherlands, West Germany, Italy, and Luxemburg; "South"— Greece (since 1980), Spain (since 1985), and Portugal (since 1985); "Scandinavia"— Denmark, Norway (1990–1996), Sweden (since 1994), and Finland (since 1993); "Britain"—Great Britain; and "All Countries"—all of the above plus Northern Ireland (since 1975), East Germany (since 1990), and Austria (since 1994).

3. The exact question wording is: "Would you say that you are very proud, fairly proud, not very proud, or not at all proud to be (nationality)?" and then "Would you say that you are very proud, fairly proud, not very proud, or not at all proud to be European?"

4. This may not be a recent development. Reif (1993) finds that in the years before Maastricht more people viewed the European Union as protecting rather than threatening their national identity.

5. A multivariate analysis of identification, attachment, and pride that includes these demographic and political indicators, as well as a set of dummy variables for the countries, generates results very similar to the bivariate relationships in table 8.5.

6. The wording of the "benefits" question is: "Taking everything into consideration, would you say that (our country) has on balance benefited or not from being a member of the European Union?" The question about the desired speed of

building Europe follows a question about how fast the respondent believes Europe is being built: "In your opinion, what is the current speed of building Europe? [The respondent is shown a card on which 1 indicates "standing still" and 7 "as fast as possible."] Choose the one which best corresponds with your opinion of the current speed of building Europe. *And which corresponds to the speed you would like?*" (italics added). Finally, the list of EU institutions that the respondent could either trust or not trust (response categories were dichotomous) included: the European Parliament, the European Commission, the Council of Ministers, the Court of Justice, the European Ombudsman, the European Central Bank, the European Court of Auditors, the Committee of the Regions of the European Union, and the Social and Economic Committee of the European Union.

7. The reliability of this index is reasonably high (α = .65). It was trichotomized by dividing the sample into terciles.

8. Though we do not pursue a more extensive model here, it is worth noting that the relationship between the identification index employed in table 8.7 and these various indicators of support for the EU is quite robust, even when controlling for various demographic and political factors.

9. The reliability of the favorability scale is α = .72, and that of the unfavorability scale is α = .65.

10. Other indicators of feelings toward minorities that we do not examine here show a similar relationship. When respondents were asked whether they found other nationalities, races, and religions "disturbing," those who identified solely with their nation were more likely to say yes (though the absolute magnitude of affirmative responses was low—less than 25 percent even among those who said "nation only"). Similarly, those who said "nation only" are less willing to accept immigrants into the country, whether those immigrants come from Muslim countries, Eastern Europe, or countries with internal conflict.

9

Civic and Cultural Components of a European Identity: A Pilot Model of Measurement of Citizens' Levels of European Identity

Michael Bruter

WHAT IS IT ALL ABOUT?

In *Du Contrat Social*, Rousseau (1762) explains that through a social contract, citizens choose to give to their political community its legitimacy and its right to determine what is the *General Will*. After the original "explicit" contract, the social contract that links citizens to their state implicitly remains legitimate because citizens choose to *identify* themselves with their community.

Without identity, it seems that there can be no true, durable, legitimacy attached to a political entity, no conscious acceptance of the power of the state and of its monopolistic right to use legitimate coercion (Weber 1946).

Every time a new political community is created, therefore, the legitimacy of the contract that links it to its citizens and gives it its fundamental institutional acceptability requires the creation of a new mass political identity.

It remains difficult, however, to understand what exactly citizens mean when they claim that, indeed, they "identify" with a given political community. Do the identity reactions of citizens refer to a homogeneous and unified conceptual content? Do they all have different political "communities" in mind? Can we find unified patterns of identification, components of political identities to which citizens refer implicitly? As Peter Burgess says,[1] when directly expressed, identity remains "prisoner of language," that is, a prisoner of the highly idiographic conceptions human beings can have of what "their identity" means.

The goal of this chapter is, therefore, to propose an operationalisable theory of political identities based on political science literature. This conceptual framework distinguishes between two "objective" components of political identities in general and of a European identity in particular— "civic" and "cultural" components, which are implied by the spontaneous (general) identity claims of citizens. The conceptual framework is then transformed into an operational measurement theory, whose relevance is tested using a pilot study conducted in Britain, France, and the Netherlands.

WHY DO WE NEED A CONCEPTUAL AND EMPIRICAL MEASUREMENT MODEL FOR EUROPEAN IDENTITY? THE STATE OF CURRENT PROBLEMS

Currently, the main direct measures of European identity available to political scientists come from twice-yearly Eurobarometer surveys. Over the years, the questions asked by Eurobarometer on European identity have changed. The questions are also asked on a fairly irregular basis. They have notably included such phrasings as: "In the near future, do you see yourself as: [nationality only; nationality and European; European and nationality; European only]?"[2] and sometimes also direct measure respondents' attachment to Europe and other political communities.

Many political scientists agree that the variables available through Eurobarometer are unsatisfactory on many grounds. The first type of question mentioned is particularly difficult to make sense of. First, it posits an arbitrary tension between European and national identities which contradicts most contemporary political science findings (Licata 2000; Bruter 2004). Second, it is ambiguous whether the phrasing measures a preference or a factual prediction ("probably, in the near future, I will be . . . ") with no normative or identitarian attachment. Third, it assumes an uncertain scale: would all respondents perceive some clear hierarchical difference between feeling European and French and feeling French and European? The second question is a little bit more straightforward, but does not resolve the problem of the "language prison" formulated by Burgess. This empirically implies that the answers of different respondents might not be directly comparable, as they might not refer to the same fundamental definitions and conceptions.

The only way to solve this problem is to provide a series of concrete indicators, grounded in a specific conceptual framework. Those indicators, or subcomponents, of political identities would allow us to get comparable measures of citizen's identities and of the different aspects of those identities.

The following model is based on the definition of two broad components of political identities: civic and cultural. They are relevant for all political communities, but particularly for communities in which the "state," or "institutional system," identification—which is primarily measured by the civic component—and the "cultural community" (whatever it may include: common values, language, religion, ethnicity, history, myths, etc.), attachment to which is primarily measured by the cultural component—do not match geographically.

This is obviously the case in Europe: institutionally, civic identity will probably refer to the European Union, while culture and shared heritage will probably refer to Europe as a whole (it is unlikely that, however it may be defined, a European culture would be expected to embrace Germany and France but not Switzerland or Monaco). This could also be the case in such countries as the United Kingdom, Belgium, or India, in which human communities of reference might be smaller than the institutional state.

The civic/cultural distinction, however, opens up new possibilities for sorting out major theoretical paradoxes in the study of European identity and its various components.

CIVIC AND CULTURAL COMPONENTS OF A EUROPEAN IDENTITY: SORTING OUT SOME THEORETICAL DEBATES

Even in the context of this volume, some seemingly contradictory findings might ultimately be due to the heterogeneity of feelings of political identity. The extent to which European identity has emerged (Meinhof on the one hand, Citrin and Sides on the other), the positive or negative correlation between European and sub-European identities (Mummendey and Waldzus on the one hand, Bruter on the other) might be found to be different depending on the very conception of identity we retain. Similarly, the complexity of political identities as not just simple forms of social identity (Breakwell) may be illustrated by the two dimensions. Cultural identity has a social connotation that "civic" identity probably does not have (cultural identity referring to the perception that one feels closer to the members of the groups than to those outside the group, civic identity referring primarily to a set of relevant institutional contexts that define the individual's values and perceptions of freedom, rights, and obligations as an individual). The distinction between the civic and cultural components of political identities might help us sort out these contradictions and more.

DEFINING THE CIVIC AND CULTURAL COMPONENTS
OF POLITICAL IDENTITIES

Following the distinction between social and personal identities and the idea that political identities have a little bit of both, it becomes necessary to distinguish between two conceptually different components of the political identities of individuals. Conceptually, political identities have been the subject of heavy theoretical and ideological quarrels between political scientists. Defining the fundamental basis of political identities implies the formulation of assumptions regarding what constitutes and unites a nation or a political group.

Three main perspectives have been used since the eighteenth century to characterise the foundations of the legitimacy of political communities. The first, derived from the French Enlightenment and the 1789 French Revolution, links the legitimacy of political communities to the very existence of political institutions that are implicitly accepted by society through a social contract (Rousseau 1762). The second, developed by German political thinkers such as Fichte (1845) and Herder (1913), links the legitimacy of political communities to a corresponding "nation," defined by a common culture (and principally, for Fichte and Herder, a common language). Finally, the third conception, formalised by Renan in 1870, modernises the original universalistic theory of the French Revolution and associates the legitimacy of state institutions with the existence of a "common desire to live together" of its citizens. At the aggregate level, dealing with the top-down "reality" of citizenship, Leca (1992) and Deloye (1997) find that citizenship is generally based on a mixture of these ideal-typical perspectives of national rationales. It is also clear, however, that specific countries have emphasised more the various aspects of national definitions and their consequences. The French revolutionary perspective led to a clear universalism of the revolution, intended, in the early 1790s, to extend to the rest of Europe, and led to the development of theories of a cross-national interest to the "citizens of Revolutionary Europe" (Bernstein and Milza 1994). At the same time, the German culturalist conception led Fichte to propose maps of the German nation that "democratically" included almost half of Europe, from Austria to Belgium, from Sweden to Ukraine, and from Poland to Switzerland through Hungary, Alsace, and the Italian Veneto (Fichte 1845). Needless to say, many of the "Germans" concerned did not share the German identity claimed by Fichte for them.

From these three theories, we can derive two interpretations of the notion of the identification of individual citizens with existing political communities. The first, a culturalist perspective, would analyse political identities as the sense of belonging an individual citizen feels in a particular group. This can be defined by a certain culture, social similarities, ethics, or even ethnicity. The second, a civic perspective, would interpret political identities as the identification of citizens with a political structure, the state, which can be summarised as the set of institutions, rights, and rules that preside over the political life of a community. To some extent, in order to relate our conceptual discussion with two of the main notions used in political science, the first perspective links political identities to the idea of a nation, and the second to the idea of a state.

Rather than assuming that political identities are one or the other, we make the contention that the two components of political identities are parallel in citizens' minds and should simply be differentiated conceptually and empirically whenever possible.

One of the reasons why this has not traditionally been the case is that differentiating empirically between the cultural and civic components of most political identities is impossible, because in many cases, the dominant state and nation of reference are superimposed. Even in cases of countries in which regionalist and separatist tendencies are strong (see the studies of Lipset and Rokkan 1967; or Seiler 1998 on that question), differentiating between cultural and civic identities might be possible only for peripheral, minoritarian groups. For example, in Britain, many Scots think of themselves as having a dual Scottish/British identity. For most Englishmen, however, Englishness and Britishness are considered as implicitly or explicitly similar.

Europe, however, presents a completely different pattern. Indeed, while conceiving of Europe as a cultural identity would imply a reference to Europe as a civilisation that stretches from the Atlantic to the Ural, conceiving of Europe as a civic identity would imply a reference to the European Union, which covers less than half of the continent. In these particular circumstances, the political entity referred to in the hypothesis of a European civic identity does not match the cultural entity as yet. This makes tests for the differences between the two types of identities and their relative strengths—even tests for the "centre"—much easier to perform than in any other existing case, and more interesting when it comes to the study of the political significance of further enlargements of the European Union for local as well as Western European public opinions.

THE CHALLENGE OF MEASURING A EUROPEAN IDENTITY: THE RESEARCH DESIGN

Following this conceptual clarification, we still face significant challenges regarding the definition and measurement of a "European identity." The conceptual framework and theoretical model defined above was used as the basis of the design of a questionnaire used in the context of a pilot experimental study conducted on 212 respondents in France, Britain, and the Netherlands. The respondents were partly students and partly nonstudents, coming from three very different countries of the European Union. This makes the sample varied, but in no way representative, hence the difficulty in drawing too-general conclusions from the univariate behaviour of the items.

This pilot primarily aims at finding good, valid, direct measures of the general, civic, and cultural elements of a European identity, as defined above, and assessing the relevance of this distinction. We will now explain how and why we set out to measure these three components.

The European General Identity

In spite of what we said about the problems in assessing answers to direct general questions on European identity, we did include some of them in the questionnaires. Two important elements must indeed be mentioned here. First, all direct measures in the analysis of political behaviour would be equally weak from the point of view of the role of respondents' interpretation of the variables targeted. When one tries to measure the degree of satisfaction with democracy of a respondent, does one not depend on the respondent's reading of the scale and variable? Yet, we find the results useful to the extent that not only the variance of the absolute concept but also the perceptions of a concept and a scale are relevant to those who study human behaviour in the social sciences. Second, if language-dependent measures can be confirmed by "objective" measures of identity with which they covary, it will seem reasonable to use both. This is the objective of the measurement strategy that will be detailed here and a solution to one of the main problems with measuring a European identity. Moreover, this will help us to understand better what most respondents mean when they say that they "feel European" and, more precisely, to understand whether they identify primarily with the European Union as a relevant institutional context defining them as citizens, or to Europe as a general cultural community or "civilisation" to which they identify "socially."

The questions used to measure a European "general" identity are, therefore, meant to be as direct and general as possible. The two questions chosen are reproduced below from the British questionnaire:

Question 1: In general, would you say that you consider yourself a citizen of Europe? (Please, choose ONE ONLY)
  1. Yes, very much.
  2. Yes, to some extent.
  3. I don't know.
  4. Not really.
  5. Not at all.

Question 6: On a scale of one to seven, one meaning that you do not identify with Europe at all, and seven meaning that you identify very strongly with Europe, would you say that you . . . ? (Please, circle ONE NUMBER ONLY)

The second of the two questions is followed by controls for other levels of governance (country, region, town/village).

The European Civic Identity

These measures of citizens' general European identity only make sense, however, to the extent that they are accompanied by two more specific sets of questions measuring European civic and cultural identity, the correlation of which with general identity measures will be carefully analysed.

As explained earlier, the civic identity of citizens has to do with their identification with the European Union as a relevant institutional framework in their life, which defines some of their rights, obligations, and liberties. For this reason, the items chosen to measure civic identity have, in large measure, to do with citizens' identification with the statelike symbols of the European Union (flag, anthem, passport, etc.), and in part with the recognition of the political and institutional relevance of the European Union as a source of definition of their personal citizenship.

The six measures used in our survey to assess citizens' levels of civic identity are outlined below.

Question 2: Since 1985, citizens from all the countries of the European Union have had a common "European" passport on which both the name of their country and "European Union" is written. Do you think that this is a good thing? (Please, choose ONE ONLY)
  1. Yes, a very good thing.
  2. Yes, a rather good thing.
  3. It doesn't matter at all.
  4. No, a rather bad thing.
  5. No, a very bad thing.

Question 4: What would best describe your reaction if you saw someone burning a European flag? (Please, choose ONE ONLY)
  1. I would be shocked and hurt.
  2. I would be shocked but not hurt.
  3. I would not mind.
  4. I would be happy.

[control:] Question 5: What would best describe your reaction if you saw someone burning the Union Jack? (Please, choose ONE ONLY)
  1. I would be shocked and hurt.
  2. I would be shocked but not hurt.
  3. I would not mind.
  4. I would be happy.

Question 11: A group of athletes from all the countries of the European Union have proposed that at the Sydney Olympics, whenever an athlete/team from the European Union wins a gold medal, the "Ode to Joy," the European anthem, should be played after, and in addition to, their national anthem. Do you think that this would be a good idea? (Please, choose ONE ONLY)

1. Yes, a very good idea.
2. Yes, a rather good idea.
3. Neither a good idea nor a bad idea.
4. No, a rather bad idea.
5. No, a very bad idea.

Question 12: When the heads of state/government of a European Union country (such as Queen Elizabeth II, Tony Blair, the French President or the German Chancellor) make a speech on TV, both the national flag and the European one appear behind them. Do you think that this is a good thing? (Please, choose ONE ONLY)

1. Yes, a very good thing.
2. Yes, a rather good thing.
3. Neither a good thing nor a bad thing / It doesn't matter at all.
4. No, a rather bad thing.
5. No, a very bad thing.

Question 13: Does being a "Citizen of the European Union" mean anything for you? (Please, choose ONE ONLY)

1. Yes, it means a lot.
2. Yes, it means something.
3. No, it does not mean anything.

Question 14: If you answered yes to question 13, would you say that, among other things, it means . . . ? (Please, choose AS MANY AS APPLY) [civic items only included here]

2. The right to vote in the European Parliament elections.
3. Common institutions.
5. A common European flag, European anthem, European passport.
6. The right to travel to another EU country without passing through customs.
7. The right to travel to another EU country without having to show your passport/ID.

As can be seen, the six items try to capture different components of the citizens' levels of civic European identity.

The European Cultural Identity

Finally, the last component targeted in this survey has to do with the cultural component of a European identity. By that, we mean literally the perception by citizens that they feel closer to fellow Europeans than to non-Europeans. As explained earlier, this is not assumed to come into conflict with sub-European cultural identities (feeling closer to fellow Swedes than to fellow Europeans, or feeling closer to fellow Parisians than to fellow Europeans), but simply in contradiction to considering the European dimension irrelevant to one's broader cultural identity. Similarly, we do not want to assume anything about the contents and perceived logic of this relative closeness. This is explored in a series of focus group discussions in a related project (Bruter 2001). Therefore, we do not presume that cultural identity is based on a perceived common ethnicity, religion, values, or anything else. It could be attributed by respondents to any of this or, indeed, to nothing at all.

Thus, our four measures are limited to assessing the perceived relative closeness of respondents to Europeans and non-Europeans, or the perception that there is such a thing as a shared European heritage in the broadest (and therefore least clearly defined) sense conceivable. The four variables used in the survey are reproduced below:

Question 3: Here is a list of some of the games that will be featured at the next Women's Volley-Ball World Championship in June. Could you say which team you would rather won each of these games? (Please choose ONE team for each of the four games)
A—Ghana vs Denmark
  1. Ghana
  2. Denmark
B—Italy vs USA
  1. Italy
  2. USA
C—Spain vs China
  1. Spain
  2. China
D—Saudi Arabia vs Republic of Ireland
  1. Saudi Arabia
  2. Republic of Ireland

Question 10: Some say that in spite of their numerous differences, Europeans share a "common heritage" that makes them slightly closer to one another than they are to, say, Japanese or Chilean people. Do you . . . ? (Please, choose ONE ONLY)
  1. Strongly disagree with this view.
  2. Somewhat disagree with this view.
  3. Neither agree nor disagree with this view / I don't know.
  4. Somewhat agree with this view.
  5. Strongly agree with this view.

Question 14: If you answered yes to question 13 [see previous section], would you say that, among other things, it means . . . ? (Please, choose AS MANY AS APPLY)
  1. A shared European heritage.
  2. A common European history.

3. Some common ideals.
4. To be a member of the "European family".

Question 15: Would you say that you feel closer to fellow Europeans than, say, to Chinese, Russian, or American people? (Please, choose ONE ONLY)
   1. Yes, strongly.
   2. Yes, to some extent.
   3. I don't know.
   4. No, not really.
   5. No, not at all.

The first of the four questions, using fake sports situations, is obviously the most problematic of all the measures. It is based on the assumption that if citizens feel closer to fellow Europeans than to non-European they will unconsciously be prone to choose the European team against a variety of non-European challengers in games in which they do not have real specific preferences (international women's volleyball is not the most widely followed sport in the world). This assumption can be checked by simple correlation with other variables in the index.

The general definition of the variables targeted and the operationalised items used to measure them is summarised in table 9.1 and can be checked against the questions outlined above.

Table 9.1 represents the basic pattern of what should be measured as part of the general, civic, and cultural European identities of citizens. This pattern and the "quality" of the indicators proposed now have to be empirically confirmed.

CONFIRMING THE RELEVANCE OF THE MEASUREMENT STRATEGY

General Patterns of Univariate Distribution

It has been suggested that one of the reasons why political identities should be assessed in opposition to each other is that asking people about their identity outside of a constraining context would just lead to a high skewedness of the answers (i.e., everyone "probably" feels somehow European, everyone "probably" feels closer to fellow Europeans than to Africans or Chinese, etc). With the caveat that once again our sample is, while varied, not representative, our results tend to show the contrary. For eleven of the twelve items considered, the answers are normally distributed with a mean close to the medium possible answer. This is true for the sample of 212 on the whole, for each country subsample, and for the student and nonstudent subsamples. The only exception has to do with the "games" measure of cultural identity, which shows a very high skewedness

Table 9.1.   Conceptual definition and operationalisation of European identity variables

Variable	General identity	Civic identity	Cultural identity
Conceptual summary	Do respondents naturally think of themselves as Europeans?	Do respondents identify with the European Union as a political institution?	Do respondents identify with Europe as a cultural community?
Targeted elements	• Do I feel European? • How strongly do I identify with Europe?	• Does it mean anything for me to be a "citizen" of the European super-State? • Do I identify with the symbols of European political integration? • Do I identify with the civic aspects of European integration?	• Do I identify with Europe as a shared heritage? • Do I think of Europe as a concentric identity level, finding Europeans less close than fellow nationals but closer to me than non-Europeans?

toward high-identity levels. For this reason, the item cannot correlate highly with the other items in the scale and will be dropped later in the analysis. It should be noted, however, that this overwhelming predominance of European "choice" in fake sports situations suggests a certain underlying European identity in the sample considered.

The next stage of the analysis consists in showing that the conceptual and empirical division of identity into a civic and cultural component is proved relevant by the data.

DEMONSTRATING THE RELEVANCE
OF THE CIVIC/CULTURAL DISTINCTION

The relevance of the civic/cultural distinction is best demonstrated by providing a quick factor analysis of the whole sample. In spite of the poor loading of one of the cultural identity items (the games variable), the factor analysis "correctly" results in a two-factor solution. The results of the factor analysis are reported in table 9.2. Although it is mostly consistent with the theoretical expectations of our measurement strategy, it sees the fourth cultural item and the two general identity items load, albeit not strongly—on the predominantly civic factor. Apart from this marginal anomaly, the way the items load on the two factors created by the analysis is extremely satisfactory and confirms that the conceptual distinction between civic and cultural identities, at

Table 9.2. Exploratory factor analysis of the ten civic and cultural identity items

Commonalities (extraction)		
civic 1	0.50	
civic 2	0.27	
civic 3	0.63	
civic 4	0.61	
civic 5	0.68	
civic 6	0.64	
cultural 1	0.77	
cultural 2	0.38	
cultural 3	0.56	
cultural 4	0.51	
Eigenvalue and % variance explained		
Factor 1	4.42	44.2%
Factor 2	2.13	21.3%
Factor 3	0.94	9.4%
Factor loadings matrix (factors 1 and 2)		
civic 1	0.70	0.07
civic 2	0.50	0.14
civic 3	0.70	0.25
civic 4	0.75	0.22
civic 5	0.82	0.09
civic 6	0.80	-0.05
cultural 1	0.56	0.39
cultural 2	-0.02	0.88
cultural 3	0.35	0.66
cultural 4	0.31	0.64

Notes:
Extraction method: principal axis.
Rotation method: varimax.
Factors kept when eigenvalue greater than one.

least in the European context, is at once (1) confirmed empirically and (2) well captured by the items chosen. The null hypothesis (that there are no such things as distinct civic and cultural European identities) can clearly be rejected based on this exploratory factor analysis.

To proceed to the measurement of the two variables, and in order to improve the cleanliness of the measures, separate factor analyses are run for cultural and civic identities (general identity, being measured by only two items, cannot lead to factor analysis) with, respectively, four and six items entered in the analyses. Moreover, we simultaneously run a global analysis of the whole sample and separate analyses for each country in order to get more refined loading structures. The factor scores are used as dependent variables in the final analysis of the experimental results. In all cases, reliability, measured by the Cronbach's alpha coefficient, reaches acceptable to good levels: 0.60 for cultural identity, 0.65 for general identity (with only two items), and 0.81 for civic identity.

The results of the factor analysis are presented in table 9.3. They show that in the three countries, the factor analyses of both the civic identity variables and the cultural identity variables all result in one-factor solutions. It is therefore operationally viable to measure separately but consistently the levels of civic and cultural European identities of respondents, using a vast array of measurement items.

SOME PRELIMINARY FINDINGS ON RESPONDENTS' LEVELS OF EUROPEAN IDENTITY

When it comes to comparing the global levels of civic and cultural identities of the respondents, we create 0–1 indices for each variable. Again the first cultural item is excluded from the index. The 0–1 limits of the index represent the theoretical range of civic and European identities. All items are weighted equally in the construction. Consistently with what we said of the univariate distributions of the individual items, the overall distributions are slightly skewed toward high levels of identity (table 9.4). It is also clear that overall levels of identification with Europe are highest for the Bordeaux sample and lowest for the Amsterdam one. The Hull sample is slightly skewed toward high levels of identity overall, but particularly so in terms of cultural identity. The results can be simplified by comparing the proportion of respondents who fall below and above the theoretical means of the variables (that is, the score a respondent would have gotten if he chose the indifferent or "don't know" answer to all identity questions; see table 9.5). The results, then, show a clearly positive balance of respondents in terms of both cultural and civic identities globally and in each location. In other words, the overall distribution of the sample is clearly skewed toward high levels, and the medians for both civic and cultural identities are definitely in the "positive" half of the theoretical identity spectra. Civic identity appears to be globally higher than cultural identity if the game variable is excluded from the index. Again, the exception lies in the British sample, in which cultural identity is dominant regardless of the procedure of index construction that is chosen.

In terms of comparing levels of civic and cultural identities of citizens, when the two indexed variables are put on a comparable scale, the sample is split almost evenly between respondents having a predominantly civic and a predominantly cultural identity (table 9.6). Overall, in the total sample, 55.1 percent of the respondents had a higher level of civic identity, only 44.4 percent a higher level of cultural identity, and 0.5 percent exactly the same level for the two.

Table 9.3. Factor analyses of civic and cultural identities in Hull (UK), Bordeaux (France), and Amsterdam (Netherlands)

(a) Factor analysis for civic identity

		Whole		UK		France		Netherlands
Communalities (extraction)								
Civic ID 1		**0.43**		0.55		0.41		0.28
Civic ID 2		**0.21**		0.35		0.20		0.18
Civic ID 3		**0.56**		0.70		0.40		0.46
Civic ID 4		**0.58**		0.57		0.54		0.53
Civic ID 5		**0.55**		0.64		0.48		0.25
Civic ID 6		**0.48**		0.58		0.48		0.22
Eigenvalue and % variance explained								
Factor 1	3.32	<u>55.4%</u>	3.80	<u>63.3%</u>	3.06	<u>50.9%</u>	3.37	<u>59.0%</u>
Factor 2	0.83	**13.8%**	0.68	11.2%	0.98	16.5%	0.96	16.7%
Factor 3	0.71	**11.9%**	0.60	10.0%	0.59	9.8%	0.62	10.3%
Factor matrix								
Civic ID 1		**0.66**		**0.74**		**0.64**		**0.53**
Civic ID 2		**0.46**		**0.59**		**0.44**		**0.38**
Civic ID 3		**0.75**		**0.84**		**0.63**		**0.68**
Civic ID 4		**0.76**		**0.75**		**0.73**		**0.73**
Civic ID 5		**0.74**		**0.80**		**0.69**		**0.50**
Civic ID 6		**0.70**		**0.76**		**0.69**		**0.47**

(b) Factor analysis for cultural identity

		Whole		UK		France		Netherlands
Commonalties (extraction)								
Cult. ID 1		0.13		0.05		0.07		0.21
Cult. ID 2		0.27		0.37		0.34		0.19
Cult. ID 3		0.55		0.65		0.60		0.38
Cult. ID 4		0.34		0.51		0.13		0.30
Eigenvalue and % variance explained								
Factor 1	1.92	<u>47.8%</u>	2.06	<u>51.5%</u>	1.75	<u>43.7%</u>	1.79	<u>44.7%</u>
Factor 2	0.91	**22.8%**	0.97	24.5%	0.98	24.6%	0.96	24.2%
Factor 3	0.64	**16.1%**	0.54	13.6%	0.78	19.5%	0.64	16.01%
Factor matrix								
Cult. ID 1		**0.37**		0.20		0.26		0.46
Cult. ID 2		**0.52**		0.61		0.58		0.43
Cult. ID 3		**0.74**		0.81		0.78		0.61
Cult. ID 4		**0.58**		0.71		0.37		0.55

Notes:
Extraction method: principal axis.
No rotation (all analyses lead to one-factor solutions).
Factors are kept when their eigenvalue is greater than 1.

Table 9.4. Mean levels of civic and cultural identities

	Whole	France	UK	Netherlands
Civic identity	**0.60 (0.22)**	0.70 (0.19)	0.54 (0.23)	0.47 (0.17)
Cultural identity	**0.56 (0.23)**	0.67 (0.19)	0.55 (0.24)	0.45 (0.22)

N = 210 (Bordeaux 97, Amsterdam 60, Hull 55).
Notes:
Entries are mean score and standard deviation for civic and cultural identities. Variables are scored on a 0–1 scale.
Cultural identity excludes game variable.

Table 9.5. Break-out of the sample in terms of positive and negative identifiers

	Whole	UK	France	Netherlands
Civic ID				
Positive	**69.6**	85.6	62.0	50.0
Negative	30.4	14.4	38.0	50.0
Cultural ID*				
Positive	**68.1**	82.5	82.5	46.7
Negative	31.9	17.5	34.0	53.3

Notes:
Entries are percentages of the total sample.
"Negative" represents the proportion of respondents with an index score of 0.5 or lower. "Positive" represents all respondents with a score greater than 0.5.
0.5 is the index score that a respondent would obtain if he chose the "indifferent" option whenever possible and the "don't know" option in all remaining cases.

Table 9.6. Comparison of the levels of civic and cultural identities of respondents

	Whole	France	UK	Netherlands
Predominantly civic identity	55.1	60.8	53.3	46.0
Equal	**0.5**	0	0.5	0
Predominantly cultural identity	**44.4**	38.1	46.1	54.0

Note: All items have been converted on 0–1 scales. The means of the converted scores for all civic and all cultural items have then been calculated. Respondents identified as "predominantly civic" are those whose civic index score is higher than their cultural index score.

Another interesting element lies in the cross-country comparison of the overall levels of civic and cultural identities of respondents. Indeed, while civic identity is clearly predominant in France and in the Netherlands, cultural identity tends to be more salient in the United Kingdom sample. In spite of the impossibility of generalising results from nonrepresentative samples of respondents, it seems logical to hypothesise that such a difference might come from the self-exclusion of the United Kingdom from some of the main civic components of European integration, such as the European Monetary Union (EMU) and the Schengen agreements on citizen mobility. This hypothesis may be tested using a truly representative sample.

This said, it should be remembered that the correlation between the factor score variables for civic and cultural identities are still highly correlated, with a Pierson r of 0.57. This is high enough to confirm that the two variables are largely explained by the same factors and evolve together, but not so high that we should consider them as one single dimension. We may want to remember that, usually, survey analysis shows much higher levels of correlation between such variables as party identification and ideology, which no political scientist would think of collapsing (the correlation is usually 0.6 to 0.7 in the analysis of American National Elections Surveys).

To conclude this first section, we can therefore derive from the data that:

- We can clearly differentiate empirically two components of European identity corresponding to our conceptual distinction between: (1) a civic component that makes people identify with the European Union as a significant "superstate" identity and (2) a cultural component that makes people identify with Europe in general as an area of shared civilisation and heritage.
- The two dimensions are highly correlated (0.57) but distinct, and each can be measured by an internally consistent and reliable set of variables.
- When people answer nonspecific questions about their European identity in general, it is of their civic identity that they think primarily.
- It is also respondents' civic identity that is most developed, except in the case of the British sample, in which Europe means "technically less" (no EMU, no Schengen agreement) in terms of actual superstate political integration.
- Overall, and in spite of a perfect balance of the stimulus applied, a clear majority of the students interviewed have a rather high level of civic and cultural European identities. This finding must be taken cautiously, as students can be expected to feel "more" European than the general population, due to various social and demographic reasons. This would nevertheless be difficult to evaluate using traditional Eurobarometer questions.

EUROPEAN AND SUB-EUROPEAN IDENTITIES: CONFLICT OR COMPLEMENT?

We have said that the conceptual framework used here did not prejudice the possible opposition, independence, or positive correlation between European and sub-European identities, unlike the traditional questions sometimes used by Eurobarometer.

The second question we intend to answer using the insight of the experimental survey is, therefore, whether people who identify more with Europe tend to identify less with sub-European political levels or if, on the
contrary, different political identifications are positively correlated.

This is made possible using a series of four similar questions asking respondents to self-position themselves on a scale measuring their level of
identity with Europe, their nation, region, and town, city or village. The exact questions and scales can be found in the appendix.

Two competing hypotheses can be formulated on the emergence of a
European identity. The first states that people with weaker national and
subnational identities would be more likely to identify with Europe. This is
because Europe represents, in traditional Euro-sceptic discourse, an anti-
identitarian structure that tends toward globalisation and the negation of
national peculiarities and homogenisation. The second hypothesis states
that, far from being contradictory, identities are complementary and that
stronger national and regional identifiers should also be stronger European
identifiers, since Europe represents a "positive" identity grounded in the
perception of a common civilisation. Here, it is hypothesised that the latter
hypothesis is correct and that, indeed, there is no contradiction between
political identities but, on the contrary, a positive correlation between the
various territorially defined political identities of citizens.

The arbitration between these two theories, which cannot be tested empirically when attention is paid only to the "hierarchy" of identities of respondents (the only variables targeted by most identity questions in Eurobarometer surveys),[3] is easily provided by simple correlation tables
between the four identity variables measured by the questionnaire. These
are presented in table 9.7.

Even though we have to be careful in this analysis because of a possible
upward bias due to a construction artefact,[4] it seems quite clear from table
9.7 that identity levels are, indeed, positively correlated.

It is also clear that positive correlations are strongest between closest territorial levels, that is, between European and national identities (0.17, sig-

Table 9.7. Correlation between European, national, regional, and local identities

	European identity	National identity	Regional identity	Local identity
European identity	1.00			
National identity	0.17*	1.00		
Regional identity	0.13	0.17*	1.00	
Local identity	0.07	0.10	0.58**	1.00

$N = 212$.
*sig. < 0.05, **sig. < 0.01.

nificant at 0.014), national and regional identities (0.17, significant at 0.012), and mostly regional and local identities (0.58, significant at 0.000).

In absolute terms, while the sample was shown to be quite strongly identifying with Europe, it is made of quite strong identifiers to all four levels of identification on the whole. This is illustrated by table 9.8, which reports average identification scores for each territorial level for the whole sample and subsamples in each location. The theoretical range of the scale is from 1 to 7 with a theoretical mean of 4. It is clear that respondents score higher in general for every single level of identification in every single location, with local identity of the French being the only exception.

Additionally, the cross-country comparison of average identity scores tends to confirm the positive correlation between identities to closest levels of government at the aggregate level. Indeed, the highest average level of European identity (4.94) is reached by the French sample, which also has the highest level of national identity (5.86), while the lowest average level of European identification (4.33) is that of the Dutch sample, which also has the lowest level of national identification (5.20).

Incidentally, it should be noted that France has the lowest average levels of regional and local identifications but the highest levels of European and national ones, which tends to dismiss the idea of a strong construction artefact (see note 4).

Dealing with identity hierarchy, table 9.9 shows the breakout of the global and national samples by "rank" of European identity out of the four levels of identification proposed. Here again, global conclusions are hard to draw, but it should still be noted that overall, respondents ranking Europe as their first identity represent the most numerous category. It should be noted, however, that this fact is due mostly to the student subsample in the survey, which feels expectedly "more European" than the nonstudent sample.

Table 9.8.   Average levels of European, national, regional, and local identity in each location

	Whole	*UK*	*France*	*Netherlands*
European identity	**4.65**	4.46	4.94	4.33
	(1.44)	(1.53)	(1.27)	(1.57)
National identity	**5.55**	5.38	5.86	5.20
	(1.53)	(1.56)	(1.25)	(1.72)
Regional identity	**4.94**	5.20	4.00	4.15
	(1.27)	(1.72)	(1.86)	(1.85)
Local identity	**4.33**	4.92	3.86	4.82
	(1.57)	(1.69)	(1.89)	(1.87)

Notes:
Entries are mean and standard deviation for each category.
Theoretical range is 1–7.

Table 9.9.   Rank of European identity out of four possible levels of identification

Rank of European identity (out of 4)	Whole	UK	France	Netherlands
1st	29.0	24.0	34.0	25.0
2nd	27.5	22.0	35.1	20.0
3rd	19.8	18.0	15.5	28.3
4th	23.7	36.0	15.5	26.7

Notes:
Entries are percentages of total sample/country subsample. Each column adds up to 100 except for round-
ing error.
The rank of European identity can be held alone or *ex aequo* with any other level of identification.

Finally, a last very interesting finding is the extremely high level of correlation between the gross score of European identity of respondents and
the rank of European identity out of four levels of political identity. For the
whole sample, this correlation is −0.57, with a significance level of 0.000.
The negative sign is of course perfectly logical (the lower the rank number,
the "higher" the rank—for example, first = 1), but mostly, the very high
level of correlation means that either variable can be quite safely used as a
proxy for the other. This is an important finding from the perspective of using data from mass surveys such as Eurobarometer to further study the
emergence of a European identity. This also allows us to argue again quite
strongly against the idea of a high artificial bias in the construction of our
identity variable. Indeed, were the levels of identity of respondents highly
dependent on each respondent's perception of the identity scale, the gross
level of European identity and its rank as compared to sub-European identities would obviously be totally uncorrelated.

Overall, the second section of the analysis allows us to draw a certain
number of conclusions, enlightening our knowledge of European identity
at the individual level. We now know the following:

- Respondents with high levels of subnational identities—particularly of
  national identity—are more likely to identify with Europe than respondents who have overall weaker levels of political identification. This
  contradicts traditional Euro-sceptic discourse on the anti-identitary basis
  of European integration.
- There is great variance in the way citizens "rank" their European identity as compared to sub-European identities.
- The gross level and rank of European identity, as compared to those
  of sub-European identities, are highly correlated, meaning that "relative" levels of European identity can be partly inferred from "absolute"
  levels of European identity and vice versa.

The third part of our analysis consists of a study of the distinction between European identity and support for European integration.

EMPIRICALLY ILLUSTRATING THE INDEPENDENCE OF EUROPEAN IDENTITY FROM SUPPORT FOR EUROPEAN INTEGRATION

As explained earlier, aside from its mere theoretical interest, the question of the development of a mass European identity is important in that one would hypothesise that it is necessary for the support for and legitimacy of further political development of European integration. It is therefore useful to test the existence of a link between European identity and European integration, but, also (and therefore), of an empirical distinction between the two variables—a distinction that part of the literature refuses (see for example Inglehart 1997; Duchesne and Frognier 1995).

In the test of the experimental design, as a precaution, support for European integration is used as a control variable in the multivariate test of the model proposed. From a theoretical point of view, however, political science literature has clearly shown that values and identities precede and constrain attitudes, such as support for a political project, in causal models, and not the contrary (Hurwitz and Peffley 1987; Jacoby 1991). Indeed, the main goal of this section is just to support the fact that, not only conceptually, but also empirically, European identity and support for European integration should be considered as two separate variables, which can and should be captured distinctly in survey analysis.

First of all, even though questions on support for European integration and questions on European identity were, respectively, part of the pretreatment and posttreatment questionnaires, it is important to evaluate their levels of correlation. These correlations are reported in table 9.10.

While support for European integration is obviously—and expectedly—correlated with all three sorts of European identity, the moderate levels of correlation (from 0.21 to 0.36) clearly show that they should be considered as distinct variables. Of course, correlations would have been higher without an experimental treatment taking place between the administration of the two questionnaires, but it is unlikely that they would have reached high enough levels to prompt a collapse of the variables.

Table 9.10. Correlation between support for European integration and general, civic, and cultural dimensions of European identity

	Support for integration	*General identity*	*Civic identity*	*Cultural identity*
Support for integration	1.00			
General identity	0.36**	1.00		
Civic identity	0.26**	0.68**	1.00	
Cultural identity	0.21**	0.48**	0.58**	1.00

$N = 210$.
**sig. 0.01.
Note: General identity is the mean of the two indicators (see appendix); support for European integration, civic identity, and cultural identity are factor scores.

The fact that the highest level of correlation with support for European integration is reached by the general identity variable is probably due to similarities in question framing. Indeed, asking respondents whether they "feel" European might partly tap into their attitudes toward Europe as well as into their identity *stricto sensu*. In other words, the respondents might have a clear conscience with regard to the "political" sense of the plainly subjective question, which might not always be true in the case of the "objective" measures used to construct the civic and cultural identity variables. At the same time, the higher correlation with the civic component of European identity than with its cultural one is explained by common sense. Cultural identity has no direct political implication and applies to "Europe" in general, not to the European Union.

The next important step of the analysis is to determine whether European identity and support for European integration regress on the same major social and demographic variables. The results of this comparison might be useful in a context of possible instrumentalisation, or to test structural equation models that would include both European identity and support for European integration as endogenous variables.

Support for European integration, European civic identity, and European cultural identity are therefore regressed on an identical set of social, demographic, political and cultural variables. These include indicators of age, sex, media readership, ideological preference, satisfaction with democracy, European experience (life in another country, travel to other countries, knowledge of other languages, family origins), size of the place of origin, and country dummy variables. The comparative results of the regression models are presented in table 9.11. The first important conclusion that can be drawn from these regression equations is that none explains a significant part of the variance in the dependent variables considered. This variance goes from virtually none ($R^2 = 0.07$) in the cultural identity model to very little ($R^2 = 0.12$) in the support for European integration model. This might be partly explained by the fact that the variance in the variables considered is limited because of the sample. The range of age is obviously very small; the ideological distribution, as is traditionally the case with students, is skewed toward the left; the size of locality lacks variance in the Netherlands, where a majority of the sample came from the Amsterdam agglomeration; and we do not have any good measure of social and economic status to include in the models.

It is also interesting, however, to compare the independent variables that have the greatest explanatory power in the three models.

It is clear that aside from a common core (the positive relationship between polyglots and all three dependent variables), each dependent variable responds to different predictors. Globally, the cultural variables that measure the European "experience" of respondents are the most consis-

Table 9.11.   Regression models of support for European integration, civic identity, and cultural identity on traditional social, demographic, political, and cultural variables

Variable	Support for integration	Civic identity	Cultural identity
Ideology of media read	0.13*	—	—
Lived in European country	0.12*	0.13*	—
Travelled to European country	0.13*	—	—
Foreign languages	0.15*	0.22**	0.16*
Satisfied w/ democracy	0.12*	—	—
Netherlands	−0.17*	—	—
Left/right	—	—	0.17**
R^2	0.12	0.09	0.07

$N = 212$.
*sig. < 0.10; **sig. < 0.05.
Notes:
Values are β coefficients.
The only variables entered are those with a significance coefficient lower than 0.10.
Originally, 14 independent variables were entered in each model.

tently influential. Speaking foreign languages and living in another European country make respondents more likely to feel European and more likely to support European integration. Travelling abroad regularly makes them—logically—more likely to perceive the concrete significance of a "People's Europe" whose citizens can travel without border control (within the Schengen area), and therefore increases their civic identity. Only having some family origins in another European country has no significant effect on any of the three dependent variables considered, probably because of a general lack of variance (only 17.9 percent of the sample have a family member originating from another European country).

Unsurprisingly enough, support for European integration is the most "political" of all four dependent variables, and is significantly dependent on such variables as satisfaction with national democracy and the ideological tendency of the newspapers read by the respondents. It is also the only one of the three models for which the Dutch sample has a significantly lower mean score than the other two samples, with the Dutch dummy having a β coefficient of −0.17.

It is more surprising, however, to note that cultural identity is the only one of the three models in which the self-placement of respondents on a left-right scale has a significant—and quite strong—effect. Moreover, the positive sign of the relation means that right-wing respondents are the most likely to have a high level of cultural European identity. This can be explained *a contrario* by the fact that three of the questions on European cultural identity implied a direct or indirect comparison of proximity between the rest of Europe and the rest of the world. In other words, these questions forced respondents to arbitrate between global cosmopolitanism and a European identity defined by a common—and therefore somewhat exclusive—civilisation. Common sense might naturally lead us to expect left-wingers to be on average more cosmopolitan and right-wingers more likely to oppose a consistent European, Judeo-Christian, Western civilisation to the rest of the world.

This third element of our analysis of the conceptual and empirical nature of European identity enables us to draw the following conclusions.

- European identity, in both its civic and cultural dimensions, is conceptually and empirically distinct from support for European integration, even though the two are obviously correlated.
- Support for European integration and civic and cultural European identities do not show the same statistical relationships with traditional social, demographic, political, and cultural independent variables. All three are influenced by the level of European experience of respondents.
- The moderate but significant correlation between support for European integration and European identity variables suggests that even though they are distinct, the theory suggesting that identities and beliefs determine political attitudes can probably be verified here using structural equation models.

CONCLUSION

In this chapter, we have shown that political identities in general and a European identity in particular could be conceptually divided into two specific components, called civic and cultural, which are implied in citizens' general identity claims.

We have shown that the difference between these two components was empirically sustained by a basic factor analysis, and that European identity in general is conceptually and empirically different from support for European integration in spite of the assumptions made by part of the existing political science literature. We have also shown that general, civic, and cultural aspects of a European identity could be captured by a set of eleven direct questions (reported in the appendix) in mass surveys.

In addition, we have shown that when respondents are asked whether they feel European or not in general, it is, before anything else, of their European civic identity that they think. This is possibly due to the political salience of the question of European integration, but also, maybe, to the relative abstraction, in citizens' minds, of a common European heritage, as opposed to the obvious influence of European integration in citizens' everyday lives.

Other insights from our empirical analysis suggest that European and infra-European identities are not contradictory, that the predominance of civic and cultural components probably varies in a comparative perspective, and that European identity is relatively little correlated to traditional social and demographic indicators.

Further studies will need to include European identity or any of its components not only as dependent variables, to explain how they form and evolve, but also as independent variables, to determine whether some effect might have been wrongly attributed to neighbouring concepts such as support for European integration. The dichotomisation applied here to the context of a European identity could also be applied to other major political identities, either strong or weakening.

APPENDIX: QUESTIONNAIRE ON EUROPEAN IDENTITY

Question 1: In general, would you say that you consider yourself a citizen of Europe? (Please, choose ONE ONLY)
1. Yes, very much.
2. Yes, to some extent.
3. I don't know.
4. Not really.
5. Not at all.

Question 2: Since 1985, citizens from all the countries of the European Union have had a common "European" passport on which both the name of their country and "European Union" is written. Do you think that this is a good thing? (Please, choose ONE ONLY)
1. Yes, a very good thing.
2. Yes, a rather good thing.
3. It doesn't matter at all.
4. No, a rather bad thing.
5. No, a very bad thing.

Question 3: Here is a list of some of the games that will be featured at the next Women's Volley-Ball World Championship in June. Could you say which team you would rather won each of these games? (Please choose ONE team for each of the four games)
A—Ghana vs Denmark
    1. Ghana
    2. Denmark
B—Italy vs USA
    1. Italy

   2. USA
C—Spain vs China
   1. Spain
   2. China
D—Saudi Arabia vs Republic of Ireland
   1. Saudi Arabia
   2. Republic of Ireland

Question 4: What would best describe your reaction if you saw someone burning a European flag? (Please, choose ONE ONLY)
   1. I would be shocked and hurt.
   2. I would be shocked but not hurt.
   3. I would not mind.
   4. I would be happy.

Question 5: What would best describe your reaction if you saw someone burning the Union Jack? (Please, choose ONE ONLY)
   1. I would be shocked and hurt.
   2. I would be shocked but not hurt.
   3. I would not mind.
   4. I would be happy.

Question 6: On a scale of one to seven, one meaning that you do not identify with Europe at all, and seven meaning that you identify very strongly with Europe, would you say that you . . . ? (Please, circle ONE NUMBER ONLY)
   1 (Do not identify with Europe at all)
   2
   3
   4
   5
   6
   7 (Identify very strongly with Europe)

Question 7: Applying the same scale as in question 6 to Britain, would you say that you . . . ? (Please, circle ONE NUMBER ONLY)
   1 (Do not identify with Britain at all)
   2
   3
   4
   5
   6
   7 (Identify very strongly with Britain)

Question 8: Still applying the same scale as in question 6 to your region, would you say that you . . . ? (Please, circle ONE NUMBER ONLY)
1 (Do not identify with your region at all)
2
3
4
5
6
7 (Identify very strongly with your region)

Question 9: Still applying the same scale as in question 6 to your city / town / village, would you say that you . . . ? (Please, circle ONE NUMBER ONLY)
1 (Do not identify with your city / town / village at all)
2
3
4
5
6
7 (Identify very strongly with your city / town / village)

Question 10: Some say that in spite of their numerous differences, Europeans share a "common heritage" that makes them slightly closer to one another than they are to, say, Japanese or Chilean people. Do you . . . ? (Please, choose ONE ONLY)
1. Strongly disagree with this view.
2. Somewhat disagree with this view.
3. Neither agree nor disagree with this view / I don't know.
4. Somewhat agree with this view.
5. Strongly agree with this view.

Question 11: A group of athletes from all the countries of the European Union have proposed that at the Sydney Olympics, whenever an athlete/team from the European Union wins a gold medal, the "Ode to Joy," the European anthem, should be played after, and in addition to, their national anthem. Do you think that this would be a good idea? (Please, choose ONE ONLY)
1. Yes, a very good idea.
2. Yes, a rather good idea.
3. Neither a good idea nor a bad idea.
4. No, a rather bad idea.
5. No, a very bad idea.

Question 12: When the heads of state/government of a European Union
country (such as Queen Elizabeth II, Tony Blair, the French President or
the German Chancellor) make a speech on TV, both the national flag and
the European one appear behind them. Do you think that this is a good
thing? (Please, choose ONE ONLY)
  1. Yes, a very good thing.
  2. Yes, a rather good thing.
  3. Neither a good thing nor a bad thing / It doesn't matter at all.
  4. No, a rather bad thing.
  5. No, a very bad thing.

Question 13: Does being a "Citizen of the European Union" mean anything
for you? (Please, choose ONE ONLY)
  1. Yes, it means a lot.
  2. Yes, it means something.
  3. No, it does not mean anything.

Question 14: If you answered yes to question 13, would you say that,
among other things, it means . . . ? (Please, choose AS MANY AS APPLY)
  1. A shared European heritage.
  2. The right to vote in the European Parliament elections.
  3. Common institutions.
  4. A common European history.
  5. A common European flag, European anthem, European passport.
  6. The right to travel to another EU country without passing through cus-
     toms.
  7. The right to travel to another EU country without having to show your
     passport/ID.
  8. Some common ideals.
  9. To be a member of the "European family."

Question 15: Would you say that you feel closer to fellow Europeans than,
say, to Chinese, Russian, or American people? (Please, choose ONE ONLY)
  1. Yes, strongly.
  2. Yes, to some extent.
  3. I don't know.
  4. No, not really.
  5. No, not at all.

NOTES

  This research would not have been possible without grants awarded by the Re-
itmeyer Fund, the University of Amsterdam, and the ESRC (ref. R000 223 463). The
author would like to thank Mark Franklin, Ulrike Meinhof, Cees van der Eijk, and

the editors of the volume for their very useful comments, as well as Claire for her precious help. Finally, this chapter is dedicated to Sarah.

1. Peter Burgess, ID-Net Meeting, European University Institute, Florence, June 9–10, 2000.

2. For example, Eurobarometer 54, 2001.

3. Eurobarometer traditionally asks respondents whether they feel [British] only; [British] and European; or European only. This implies a conflict between the possible identities of respondents.

4. The respondents are asked to position themselves on a one-to-seven scale on which only the two extremes are labelled, as "do not identify at all" and "identify very strongly." Their answers might therefore be slightly influenced by each respondent's perception of the meaning of the scale, that is, what a three or a five means, and whether a respondent "goes for the extremes" easily or not. This would create artificial internal consistency between the four answers of a given respondent. This problem, although limited in terms of quantitative effect, is quite usual whenever arbitrary scales are used, for example to ask experts to evaluate the ideological profiles of political parties or when respondents are asked to position their own preference and those of the main parties to test spatial hypotheses. Because "absolute levels" are not interesting then, one can avoid bias by dividing all answers by the mean of the values chosen by a given respondent. This solution, however, would make it totally impossible here to test the hypothesis of positive correlation between identity levels, since it would precisely kill the variance in terms of overall identity levels between "strong" and "weak" identifiers, implicitly assuming that this difference is a pure scale artefact. Further tests will help us argue against that criticism.

10

Europe Viewed from Below: Agents, Victims, and the Threat of the Other

Ulrike Hanna Meinhof

In the spring and early summer of 2003, the vision of Europe "viewed from above," through its politicians and the media, has two very different faces.

On the one hand, the imminent enlargement of the European Union with its Eastern ascendant nations finally promises to lay to rest the terrible legacies left by the Second World War. Polish, Czech, Hungarian, and Slovenian entries to the European Union—including their future access to the Schengen open-border agreements and potential membership in the single currency—will complete a process of East-West reconciliation which began with the fall of the Iron Curtain in 1989 and German unification in 1990. From the Baltic to the Adriatic Sea, one of the most traumatic and most guarded borderlines of the twentieth century will transform into a mere transition point between European Union partners with free mobility for EU citizens.

On the other hand, Europe at present is still smarting under one of the biggest divisions of its recent history, sparked by the war against Iraq, which saw the United Kingdom as a staunch partner of the United States' hawkish attitude and behaviour, with some of the other Eastern ascendant nations to the EU, most prominently the new NATO member Poland, in support of the trans-Atlantic axis. In sharp opposition, most EU countries, but foremost Germany and France, continued with their support for the UN's further request for weapons inspections. The U.S. presidential elite insultingly described the division in Europe as between the old (Western) and the new (Eastern) Europe. Even if one wants to dismiss such remarks as propagandist rhetoric, it was undeniably the case that European governments had failed to respond with one voice to an international crisis, though—as before—attempts at patching over such divisions are in process.

Our work on identity construction on the borders between the European Union and its (south) Eastern ascendant nations does not deal with the forging of European unity or identity at this highest political level, nor with the divisions or agreements between its statesmen. European identity, if defined through a political, economic, and (with some notable exceptions) a monetary union, is a reality that continues with its own momentum, even where it remains controversial among the population at large, and in spite of some— often absurdly—hostile media.[1] But how do these large-scale processes interact with the perceptions, feelings, and attitudes of European people about one another? Are the administrative top-down moves toward greater unity among EU nations matched by a growing together of the people, especially of those who live on the borders along which some of the most momentous changes have recently taken effect or are about to take effect?

Our research, backed by a research grant from the Economic and Social Research Council and a subsequent substantial three-year grant from the European Commission's fifth framework programme, focused on precisely that: the feelings and attitudes of Europeans who live on either side of this border from the Baltic to the Adriatic Sea, including the former and now dissolved East-West German border. This border not only represents one of the major fault lines of historical hurt and trauma; it also coincides with a deep socioeconomic rift between the relatively richer and relatively poorer nations of Europe. (For a detailed analysis of this see Meinhof 2003, especially the chapters by Meinhof, Holly et al., and Wastl-Walter et al., which thematise this asymmetry and its effects). Both of these aspects, the historical and the socioeconomic, have profound influences on the experiences of ordinary people living there, and on their attitudes about the people on the other side. Hence our interest was whether and in which ways major public events and sociopolitical processes and upheavals appear in ordinary people's everyday life narratives, and how they interact with people's identity construction and confirmation. Is there a European identity growing "from below" along this faultline, which unites the people on either side, and if this is not the case, what are the potential hurdles that affect these processes in everyday life practices? Do people on these formerly traumatic and still today economically unequal borders envisage the possibility of a shared identity with their neighbours on the other side? These are the key questions that my chapter addresses.

Four areas of particular significance for the discussion of national and European identity were revealed by our fieldwork and discourse analysis of the interview data; they are addressed in subsequent sections in this chapter:

The first of these areas is a fluid but nonconsistent construction of multiple identities. These were composed, with varying content, from different sociopolitical layers—local, regional, national, and transnational. Importantly, they included incompatible and contradictory identifications within the same individual's narratives.

Second, there was a strong difference in the form that in-group and out-group constructions took, depending on the occurrence and intensity of personal lived experience as against mediated opinion.

Third, we found a remarkable similarity in content and form of narrative among those individuals who constructed their own identities by negative dissociation from the people living on the other side of their respective rivers. While these out-group strategies were similar, the same individuals retained a very mixed form of in-group identifications.

Finally, we found an almost total absence of either positive or negative European identity markers in the spontaneous narratives of our interviewees. Unless specifically thematised in the interviews, European reference points did not feature in the everyday life narratives of our informants. When prompted by direct questioning, our informants used "Europe" and the "European Union" ambivalently in different contexts, and—as with the out-grouping strategies at the level of the region or the nation—produced the strongest positive in-group identifications in opposition to other unwanted outsiders. By analysing in detail selected extracts from our ethnographic interview data, this chapter draws out some of the methodological and analytical implications for our understanding of regional, national, and transnational identity construction in conflictual settings, and for identity research in general. I also hope to show that our findings are, on the one hand, complementary to those obtained by mass surveys (Bruter; Citrin and Sides, this volume) and by social psychology experiments (Castano, this volume), in that they provide an alternative conceptualisation for processes of identity construction (but see Siapera; Wodak, this volume). On the other hand, our findings may provide some explanation for the differences in results obtained by social scientists researching the interrelations between different layers of identity (Inglehart and Reif 1991; Inglehart 1997; Duchesne and Frognier 1995; Martinotti and Stefanizzi 1995; Mlicki and Ellemers 1996; Castano, this volume; and Risse, this volume).

The chapter falls into two parts, with several subsections in each.

The first part, "Researching Cultural Identity(ies)," addresses the theoretical and methodological underpinnings of our research, foregrounding the ways in which our discourse-based model of identity construction and our indirect methods of questioning lead us to some different, though in some cases complementary, conclusions to those of other writers in this volume. It also addresses some of the implications and problems that the "absence of Europe" as self-identification in our data has for research on European identity.

The second part, "Out-grouping the Other," demonstrates in detail the ways in which our informants used out-grouping strategies for constructing their identities. Since European self-identification did not occur in the spontaneous narratives, I show the working of these strategies by focusing on attitudes toward other European and same-nation neighbours. Such attitudes form the basis of the feelings toward the "Others" that a united Europe would embrace, and point toward the many problems that need to be overcome if a genuine sense of togetherness is to be felt among the citizens of Europe.

RESEARCHING CULTURAL IDENTITY(IES)

Models of Identity

In the final volume of his trilogy on the Information Age, entitled *The End of the Millennium*, Manuel Castells describes the project of European unification as "one of the most important trends defining our new world" (Castells 1998, 310ff.). At the same time he points out that there is an ambiguity concerning what this Europe will look like and who will be involved in it, making unification a process rather than something clearly defined and fixed. Castells sees in this an opportunity rather than a failing: "European unification grew in the past half-century from the convergence of alternative visions and conflicting interests between nation-states, and between economic and social actors" (Castells 1998, 310ff.). For the time being however, he notes the absence of clearly identifiable building blocks for a homogenising European identity that a shared religion, ethnicity, language, or other such means might provide: "The very notion of Europe as based on a common identity is highly questionable" (Castells 1998, 310ff.).

Rather than looking for one all-subsuming European identity, we can imagine models of multiple identities in which European identity features as one among other possible formations. This then raises the question of how these different layers of identity interrelate. In the many different disciplines within the social sciences in which collective identities are being investigated, several competing models implicitly or explicitly underpin theories and methodologies of research: the introductory chapter to this volume by Herrmann and Brewer refers to some of these, as do the chapters by Bruter and Castano, and the concluding chapter by Risse, which sets out a whole array of different conceptual models. I would like to elaborate on only two models, taken from the very opposite ends of the scale of mutual inclusiveness or exclusiveness.

The first we could think of as the "Russian doll model" (see also Herrmann and Brewer, this volume; Risse, this volume; Meinhof 2001a, 112ff.).

Here the different identifications, from the most local to the most global, are seen as complementary, mapped as ever-widening concentric circles: a person living in Hirschberg an der Saale may think of herself as a Thuringian, a German, and a European, just as the little black and red dolls fit into one another from the smallest to the biggest. As an antagonistic alternative, we could imagine multiple identities as conflictual, and potentially destructive of one another; because of their hostile and violent implications. We could visualise this model through the image of a volcano or an earthquake. In this view, national identity may be threatened by a more transnational formation—such as a European one (a threat from above); or it may be threatened by a more regional subnational formation—as Welsh or Basque separatists would wish, or the Northern Italian political party Lega Nord (a threat from below). Finally, some collective identities may simply be linguistically and conceptually incompatible because of the connotations that the label itself carries: an "East German" or "West German" self-identification, for example, may already presuppose a "nonunited" Germany" identity. (For a different and more elaborated set of models, see Risse in this volume.)

In their introductory chapter to this volume, Herrmann and Brewer differentiate between individual and institutional levels. In line with research conducted by Martinotti and Stefanizzi (1995), Herrmann and Brewer suggest that "people who identify strongly with local communities also identify strongly with nations, and with Europe." At the individual level people are capable of negotiating multiple identities without coming up against too many hurdles. At the institutional level, by contrast, political authority may—or, indeed, must—impose more explicit hierarchies, which would render loyalties to different or disempowered layers conflictual (Herrmann and Brewer, this volume).

My own research, exemplified by the analysis of my informants' narratives, adds a further layer of complications to these already complex interconnections. If we investigate how individual ordinary people construct their identities in their everyday discourses we find, indeed, that a focus on institutional, cultural, or personal matters affects people's identification with, or distancing from, a town, a region, a nation, or a group of nations. In that sense my findings complement those obtained by Castano in experimental settings, in which he highlights the "salience" of the European Union as a key factor for his informants' levels of identification with the European Union (Castano, this volume). Where our data differ is in the lack of constancy of key identity markers and their ways of interrelating with one another within the same informant's discourse. This undoubtedly points to the different methodological possibilities of experimental and nonexperimental designs, and could suggest interesting comparative research for the future. In our interviews we did not preconstruct saliency using direct questions; we preconstructed saliency very loosely by the use of photography (see below), and briefly at the end of the interview, but allowed positive and negative identity markers to emerge spontaneously through the narrative context. These did not correlate in any easily predictable manner, but depended on the self-selected local context created by the narrative itself. This shows that there is a variation and a fluidity in what spaces of identity actually mean for the individual. The same linguistic labels—"Europe," "Germany," "the Poles"—hide not only a variety of meanings between one individual and the next, but we find variation even within the same individual's accounts. Depending on these narrative contexts, different meanings come to the fore that affect the ways in which certain positive (Who are we?) and negative (Who are the Others?) identities get constructed, prioritised, labelled, and relabelled. Hence not only do we find multiple combinations of strongly felt identifications between sets of different layers, but we also find contradictory positions within and between each layer. Importantly (and perhaps alarmingly for researchers on European identity) we also find lacunas—especially as regards the significance of a European identity (see Meinhof and Galasinski 2002; and "If There Is a European Identity, What Does It Mean?" below).

Constructing Identities through Discourse

One significant explanation for the coexistence of these contradictory positions may, of course, arise both from the focus of our research on the *discursive* construction of identity, and from the related methodology of our data collection, analysis, and interpretation of what constitutes identity and identity markers. We do assume that people construct their identities rather than "hold" or "possess" them, and that a key agent for these constructions is language. In assuming this, we belong to a larger community of scholars within linguistics, cultural studies, and critical social psychology[2] who see the connection between social reality and language as mutually interdependent: the language we use not only reflects the values and beliefs of our social environment, it actively confirms and constructs them. In our view (see also Wodak, this volume), an analysis of people's way of speaking gives access to these constructions and the processes that challenge or confirm them in particular contexts.

Furthermore, people's experiential narratives involve them in a range of different processes, ranging from the most unconscious and even repressed emotional memory, to the most analytical, consciously held opinion. Between the telling of a story and the evaluation of what it means, people often "deconstruct" their own consciously held beliefs, especially as regards their own self-identification and the assignment of in-groups and out-groups. This may happen on the content level, but—and this is where discourse analysis, with its finely tuned methods, comes to the fore—it may also happen on the level of linguistic form.

A body of writing including and following the seminal works by Bakhtin and Volosinov (Bakhtin 1981; Volosinov 1927/1976, 1928/1973) underpins such observations theoretically and analytically by describing language itself as a hybrid, multivoiced, and polyphonic system. When people narrate their experiences, their accounts contain many different voices that are not entirely controllable by the speaker's more consciously held attitudes. Narratives of everyday life often dramatise tensions between differently loaded experiences by thematising them in anecdotes, but such experiences, when constructed through the complex medium of speech, often contain contradictions. Moreover, what is being expressed at the anecdotal level also often differs from the evaluation or ascription of meaning at the more analytical level (see also Meinhof 1997). In the recounting of certain key events and encounters, individuals construct identifications and disidentifications that range across various levels: from the most concrete and personal (the one nasty "Wessi" girl in the school, the good Pole who saves the food or the blanket for the child), to the experience of collectivities (the Poles who steal our cars), to the most abstract and/or institutional (the Pole—our war enemy). Identification with a collective, however small or large, will thus always involve more than just opinions and beliefs about social groups to which one feels one does or does not belong; it will engage positive and negative emotions about experiences with these groups, which in the telling of longer narratives are not so easily monitored. It is thus not surprising if in longer narratives we are more likely to encounter inconsistencies between these different layers of in-grouping and out-grouping. In content, form, and evaluative framing these narratives do not compose cohesive wholes that could easily be fitted into any one of the identification models discussed in the beginning of this section. Their analysis thus helps us to understand the processes of identity construction in the more complex setting of everyday life experience, in all its contradictoriness.

If it is the case, as our data suggest, that people's identity narratives comprise wide-ranging, mutually interdependent, and accumulative constructions, but also discrepant ones, then this must have wider implications for all identity research in that the very categories of identity become problematical both at the conceptual and the methodological level. The increasing sophistication of identity research in social psychology takes account not only of multilayering but also of context dependency (see for example Triandafyllidou 1998; Hopkins and Murdoch 1999; Castano, this volume). Mass survey questionnaires also continue to further refine their methods of enquiry by allowing more sophisticated combinations of layerings of identity than does the Eurobarometer (see Bruter, this volume).

What our emphasis on longer, experiential, everyday life narratives can contribute to this complex area is a better understanding of the fluidity of identity construction at the discursive level. My chapter thus underlines the need for more interdisciplinary and complementary research across the social sciences, to which this volume offers a further contribution.

Research Design and the Use of Photography as a Trigger

Briefly then, the focus of my own work and that of my colleagues[3] is on families of three generations whose members have experienced major socioeconomic upheavals during their lifetime—new borders, dissolution of borders, changes of ideology and political and economic systems, expulsion and resettlement—with every conceivable aspect of their public worlds affected. Within each of these communities we selected a minimum of five and up to ten families in which three (sometimes four) generations were still alive and had spent their entire lives in the target communities. Where the move to the target community was only possible after the redrawing of the national borders (such as in the post-1945 Polish border communities of Gubin and Zgorzelec), we selected families in which the oldest generations had moved into the community at the earliest possible moment. Within each family, we interviewed independently at least one member from each generation. Husbands and wives, and brothers and sisters, were occasionally interviewed together, but we avoided the mixing of generations, since we were particularly interested in potentially different selections of narrative themes within the same family, and any similarity of themes within the same generations. Because of the extension of the project from a smaller scale to a large comparative study, the German-German and the German-Polish border had twice the number of families (between ten and fifteen families for each border region) in two cycles of fieldwork. As pointed out before, the communities in which our informants live are located on state borders along the current axis that divides European Union states and open-border "Schengen" territory from former Warsaw Pact states that are seeking early admission to the European Union, but we included the former border of East Germany, whose people became de facto members of the European Union in 1990 as a result of German unification. We hoped that the close vicinity of the border and the geographical closeness of people from formerly hostile and now friendly nations would give us some understanding of the respective roles—positive or negative—that people from neighbouring communities with complex and conflictual past relations play for the identity construction of our informants. We also wanted to see whether in the East-West German case a differentiation into distinct groups would have become superseded by an "all-German" discourse after a decade of unification.

Finally, we were interested in understanding the extent to which Europe or the European Union had any salience in ordinary people's sense of identity: does Europe and/or the European Union enter people's experiential everyday life narratives of past and present?

Our emphasis on the discourses of identity—or, in other words, on the microphenomena of linguistic form and content—had further implications for our research design, since we needed to be careful to avoid circularity by introducing through our questions some of the markers of identity we were subsequently using for analysing our informants' narratives. As much as possible we wanted our informants to be able to self-select the themes and topics of their conversations with us, so that we could use their selections as evidence for salient or absent experiences. Furthermore, since we wanted to subject our interview data to detailed analysis of linguistic form, the avoidance of prior introduction of labels by the researchers—such as, for example, certain "loaded" terms ("GDR" or "East Germany"; "EU" or "Europe")—was a significant factor in planning the methodology. Instead of using questions as initial triggers, we used highly charged and immediately identifiable photographs from the three phases of the communities' existence (prewar, postwar, post-1989/90).

Although the images themselves directed peoples' attention to particular spatio-temporal markers of their communities' existence and to often emotive moments in their history, we found, firstly, that there was wide disparity in the uptake of the same photos among different informants, not simply and obviously according to generation, but also within each generation. Second, images did not constrain our informants' narratives beyond the initial trigger, but people moved freely in and out of the spatiotemporal and emotional frame suggested by the image. Third, we also found that some pictures through which we had intended to trigger a particular theme did not produce that effect. The latter was particularly noticeable in relation to the theme of Europe, which could only be addressed by a more direct line of questioning. We shall return later to what was to us a most surprising absence in the uptake of the European theme.

To give just one set of examples of the images we used, the three pictures below all feature the river Neisse and its eastern and western bank. Figure 10.1 is a prewar photograph (phase 1) with its central focus on a river island and the theatre of Guben, connected by a bridge to the eastern shore. Figure 10.2 shows the same island in the Neisse, but now the river forms the border between Germany and Poland, and former Guben on its eastern shore has become the Polish town Gubin. This second picture was taken in 1998 and thus relates to phase 3 of our communities' existence.

These two phases are immediately placeable in space and time by local German people of the oldest generation, since the theatre, together with most other buildings in the centre of—then—Guben, did not survive the

Figure 10.1

Figure 10.2

heavy fighting of the last phase of the war and subsequent demolitions. By its close resemblance to the later picture, it ought to be recognisable by people of all ages on both sides, though there were some blank responses among some younger Germans and some of the Polish people from several generations. We cannot here discuss the implications of the lack of recognition of or refusal to recognise German/Polish triggers (but see Galasinski and Meinhof 2002). Figure 10.2 is placeable as postwar and was recognised as such by everyone. The clues are the absent theatre and, in the left corner of the picture, the old café Reichenbach turned into the German customs office. Everyone also recognised the picture as post 1990, and hence signalling a phase of new German-Polish relations, since there is once more a bridge to the island built with the financial support of the newly unified Federal German Republic. In response to the first picture, people selected from a whole range of topics such as memories of past pleasure (e.g., stories of the plays attended in the theatre, or how one could or could not afford going into the café Reichenbach); stories of crossing the river at great danger during the escape from the incoming Poles and Russians; and statements by some of the young people to the effect that they didn't want to hear these old stories anymore.

In response to the second picture there were stories of the border; how one could or could not go across to the other side during the 1980s, whether one does or does not wish to go across now. But in all instances the initial picture frame opened out into much wider themes and narratives that are not visually represented in the image, moving out or back and forth geographically, or moving across different times: focusing on the home community, sometimes on the community on the other side, often on both. These themes and narratives included dramatic escape stories; stories of losing one's home; descriptions of the current state of Gubin (nothing there anymore) and Guben (no centre, boring city), prompting sadness, disgust, and fear.

Figure 10.3 again shows the river but foregrounds a huge placard announcing the fact that the European Union together with the German national and the Brandenburgian Federal State governments have invested in a new joint wastewater plant erected on Polish territory and serving both towns.

This picture invariably led only to a discussion of the wastewater plant itself—usually in very negative terms by both Poles and Germans—and never led to any mention of the EU. Other pictures that foregrounded buildings with the European flag, or the stars, or any other reference to the support given by the EU to these regions, were similarly bypassed. Europe or the EU simply did not feature in the narratives, neither in reaction to our intended triggers, nor as a spontaneous narrative arising from different contexts. Only when we specifically asked a question about how people felt

Figure 10.3

about Europe (Do you feel European? About which identity(ies) do you feel strongly?) or how they felt about particular EU-supported projects, such as those featured in the pamphlet "Modellprojekt Eurocity Guben-Gubin," did we solicit any reactions about Europe. (For further details, including a reproduction of some of the pictures used, see Meinhof and Galasinski 2000; also Meinhof and Galasinski 2002; and Armbruster, Meinhof, and Rollo 2003.) In short, some triggers aroused long narratives about the time/place shown, others provided no more than the original stimulus for moving on. Some triggers were "resignified" into something else, others were completely ignored. The method thus proved to be an excellent instrument for combining ethnographic interviews with discourse analytical procedures.

OUT-GROUPING "THE OTHER"

In the second part of this chapter, I present some of the results we obtained through the interviewing techniques described above. These fall into four sections:

In the first, entitled "Challenging Experiences," I concentrate on one informant only (from the oldest generation) in order to demonstrate the complexity and contradictoriness of labelling Others as "friends" and "enemies" within the same narrative, but under different narrative constraints.

In the second, entitled "Constructing the Negative Other," I concentrate on the negative labelling of Others by comparing the ways in which young people employ distancing strategies against perceived out-groups that render the assignment of "national identity" labels problematical.

In the third section, entitled "Out-group and In-group Strategies," I briefly compare the nature of these out-group strategies with those employed for constructing one's own group.

In section 4, and in summary, I discuss how these strategies relate to the construction of a transnational European identity.

To focus the discussion I draw on data from one particular set of case studies, based on our work in three German communities, all located on rivers that are, or used to be, national borders: Guben on the western bank of the river Neisse, which since 1945 has formed the eastern border of Germany with Poland, and opposite its former eastern half, now renamed as Polish Gubin; and Tiefengrün and Hirschberg on opposite sides of the river Saale, which in this location divided Germany for more than forty years into two separate states. The data represented here were recorded in 1999 and 2000, that is, a decade after German unification and the collapse of the Soviet Union (see also Meinhof and Galasinski 2000, 2002; Galasinski and Meinhof 2002; Meinhof 2002; Armbruster and Meinhof 2002; Armbruster, Meinhof and Rollo, 2003; Meinhof, 2003). The particular interest of this focus on German communities within the larger European project lies in the fact that we have here an opportunity to study (a) an existing border community between Germany and Poland, and with this an example of an area where eastward expansion of the European Union will soon take place; and (b) a former highly conflictual border between the two Germanies, which had ceased to exist for ten and more years at the time of our fieldwork, with both sides reunited as one nation and a united member of the European Union. Hence the dissolution of one border and the subsequent reunification of its border communities provides us with an interesting contrast to and comparison with the impending dissolution of the inner European Union border in our German/Polish border communities.

Challenging Experiences

In this section I exemplify how detailed discourse analysis of people's key narratives allows us insights into the linguistic processes of in-grouping and out-grouping whereby multiple and even contradictory collocations can be constructed by the same individual. This is significant in that it demonstrates paradigmatically what we found to be the case in all our texts, namely that processes of inclusion and exclusion that are fundamental to our identifications with others are shifting, multiple, and context bound. It thus underscores the need for more subtle and multidisciplinary instruments in identity research, since questionnaires and even structured interviews by definition create particular discursive environments that foreground a very limited and self-monitored context. What people say that they do or say, what they think they do or say, and what they actually do in practice cannot be assumed to be identical if our discursive behaviour over a longer stretch of talk already points to major incongruities and differences. These differences have been well demonstrated by sociolinguists and social psychologists and have led to intriguingly inventive research designs (see, for example, Potter and Wetherell 1987). With our elicitation methods of longer, more open narratives and our attention to linguistic form we can begin to understand some of these complexities.

The extract below comes from an elderly woman's account of her war experiences. She relates her displacement from her home (located in what is today the Polish town of Gubin), and her subsequent attempt to come to terms with that loss, the new border, and her new Polish neighbours. Her narrative typically shows how lived experience can challenge and interfere with essentialising categories, in this case that of the bad Other, "the Pole." The different evaluative frames that her own memory narrative imposes are echoed by consistent grammatical manoeuvres (highlighted in the text; for further examples of such interconnection see Meinhof 2001b).

Interviewee: Mrs. Schwalbe (MS)[4]

Location: Guben

> [I]ch hatte für den Kleinen von der, wo ich das erste Mal von der Flucht zurückwar, die Frau die gab mir die Wirtsfrau noch ein bisschen Grieß und ein bisschen Milch und so was alles, dass ich für den Kleinen was hatte und Zucker, und das wollten mir die Polen auch noch wegnehmen. Und **der eine Pole** kuckte dann aber rein in den Wagen, da tat er den andern wegschirmen, dass ich das behalten konnte

[A]nd I had a bit of semolina and milk and things like that for the little one, I had been given that by the landlady when I had come back from the flight the first time, and sugar, too, and **the Poles** even wanted to take that away from me. And one of the Poles peered into the pram, but he did not let the other one near, so that I could keep it.

MS: Da hat man gar nicht drüber nachgedacht, ob da der Russe oder ob der Pole dahintergesteckt hat, da konnte man eigentlich gar kein richtiges Bild machen. Denn ich weiss noch, wie wir denn noch drüben waren, dass der Pole—man kann es nicht denken, ich würde auch heute noch nicht ganz dran glauben, ich denke, dass da der Russe dahinter gesteckt hat, denn viele Polen drüben—ich bin denn mit meiner Nachbarin mal, war mal drüben zu Hause Nachbarn, und . . . drüben gewesen, da hatten die Eltern auch n Haus und wies denn war frei war, dass wir rüberkonnten mal n' paar Tage so, da sind wir da in das Haus, meint sie, komm meint sie, ich geh mal kucken, wie unser Haus aussieht, und da bemerkten das die Leute und winkten uns rein, und das war ein Lehrer, ein polnischer, und die gaben uns auch da zu trinken, machte gleich heißen Tee und alles, und denn sagt er: "Also uns gehts nicht besser wie Ihnen." Nu weiss ich nicht mehr, von welcher Ecke Polen die waren, meint er: "Wir mussten auch alles zurücklassen und mussten raus. Und uns wurde gesagt: Ihr habt eure Grundstücke bezahlt gekriegt. Und wir müssen auch bezahlen. Uns haben die hier reingesetzt, und wir müssen auch bezahlen." Und da haben wir gesagt: "Was, wir, wir haben bezahlt gekriegt? Von wem denn? Wir haben nicht mal können ein zweites Hemde zum wech-seln mitnehmen, wir hatten gar nischt als wie unsere Kinder und raus." Da staunte der bloß.
UM: Da gibts Propaganda auf jeder Seite.
MS: Deswegen war ich immer der Ansicht, es steckte der Russe dahinter, denn die ganzen, die man da gesprochen hat, das ist alles von einer Ecke von Polen, wo sie rausmussten, was der Russe wieder haben wollte. Und mein Sohn, wenn der mal hier ist von Berlin, der fährt viel hier auf das eine Dorf hier oben, Weilditz [?] heißt das, und da ist ein Reiterhof, hat ein Pole einen Reiterhof, und da bin ich mal mitgewesen, da haben wir auch gesprochen, und der sagte dasselbe: Wir mussten raus, genauso wie ihr, sind wir vertrieben worden. . . .
Die Grenzen, dass man nun darüber n' Hass hat, ja, vielleicht, mehr auf'n Russen als wie auf'n Polen, aber wir ändern ja nischt damit, man muss sich ja abfinden. Trotzdem ich ja immer im Innern noch gehofft, immer noch gehofft, nützt nischt. Und mein einziger Wunsch war auch immer nochmal ein kleines Eigentum haben.

MS: One didn't think about the fact whether there was the Russian or the Pole behind it, one didn't have a clear picture of it. Because I remember, when we were still over there, that the Pole—one can't believe it and even nowadays I wouldn't really believe in it, I think that the Russian was behind it, because many Poles over there—I went over there with my neighbour, we had been neighbours at home over there and the parents had a house and when it was open and we were able to go across for a few days, we went into the house, she said, come on, she said, I'll have a look at our house, and the people noticed and called us in, and it was a teacher, a Polish one, and they offered us something to drink and made hot tea straightaway and all, and then he said: "We aren't in a better situation than you." Now I don't remember from which corner of Poland they had come, but he said: "We had to leave everything behind and get out. And we were told: you had received money for your land. And we have to pay, too. They put us in here, and we have to pay, too." And then we said: "What, do you mean, we got paid? Who should have paid us? We didn't even have time to take a second shirt for changing, we had nothing but our children and out." And he was very surprised.

UM: There is propaganda on each side.

MS: That's why I always thought that the Russian was behind it, because all the people one talked to are from one corner of Poland, where they had to leave [the land] the Russian claimed back. And my son, whenever he comes here from Berlin, he goes to the village up here, W., and there are stables, a Pole owns a riding centre, and I went with him once and we talked and he said the same: "We had to get out just like you, we were driven out. . . ."

MS: That one feels hatred because of the borders, maybe, and more toward the Russian than the Pole, but we don't change anything by doing so, one has to come to terms with it. Although I kept on hoping and hoping, it was to no avail. And my only wish had been to have a little property again.

ANALYSIS

These two extracts from my interview with Mrs. Schwalbe exemplify the clash between more abstract and more concrete experiences: her encounter with Poles shows them in their role as enemies and as helpers, as occupiers of her beloved former home city and as friendly neighbours within the same narrative. The tension between these positions not only features in the story telling itself, it goes into the very fabric of the grammatical structure of her narrative, highlighting the discursive strategies that she employs in order to manage the contradiction. Her discourse thus exemplifies her attempt to create a cohesive narrative and a logical evaluation of what her experience means across the different planes of her memories as well as her attitudes. In extract 1 she differentiates between "die Polen"—the collective group of enemies who are threatening to take away the bits of food she had just been given, and "der eine Pole"—one individual Polish soldier who comes to her rescue. This differentiation between the collectivity and the individual is even more noticeable in extract 2. Here she shifts between the abstract essentialisation of "der Pole" and "der Russe" (as highlighted in the text); the collective, "viele Polen drüben"; and the individuals "ein Lehrer," "ein polnischer," or "ein Pole," a friend of her son's who owns a riding school. Individual Poles in both extracts appear as helpful, friendly people, and in extract 2 share experiences of loss. With them she can "coconstruct" a shared sense of homelessness (see also Galasinski and Meinhof 2002). This experience of and with individual Poles makes it hard for her to keep up an essentialising negative other "der Pole." Her only incomplete utterance in an otherwise highly articulate continuous narrative occurs at the very point when she is caught in the dilemma between these three levels of the Polish Other: the essentialised, the collective, and the individual. At that point she displaces all negative feelings and blame to "the Russian." This allows her to continue her sympathetic narrative of encountering Polish neighbours.

Constructing the Negative Other

In the next section, I show how lack of engagement makes it much easier for the individual to discursively construct cohesive in-groups and out-groups. This can take the form of either positive or negative stereotyping, and for reasons that will become obvious in the discussion, it is the latter rather than the former on which I concentrate. In-depth qualitative data are notoriously difficult to generalise, since samples are relatively restricted in quantity and less easily arranged according to demographic or other sociological parameters. When patterns do emerge, they need to be treated with care and sensitivity and in full awareness of the limitations that restricted samples may engender. In the case study presented here, I exemplify some of the ways in which negative stereotyping plays a powerful role in the self-identification of the groups in question by restricting my sample to the narratives elicited from the youngest generation of the families we interviewed in only two of the communities. This has a double justification: One, we found more similarities between members of the same generation across communities than between members of different generations within families within the same community (see also Hipfl, Bister, and Strohmaier, 2003). Two, in focusing on the youngest generation of people in (a) western Germany on the former border to the East and (b) eastern Germany on the border to Poland, we were talking to people who had none of the grievous experiences of their parents and grandparents, which structured their adult lives. I present the extracts from interviews with members of the youngest generation in Guben and Tiefengrün in thematically arranged pairs. In both cases the extracts illustrate what young people said about their neighbours on the eastern bank of the rivers dividing their communities. But whereas in the first instance of each paired extract, the neighbours are those from another nation-state—the Poles—in the second instance they are fellow Germans, albeit from former East Germany. Given the age of our young informants at the time of our interviews—(they were between sixteen and eighteen years old)—it is significant to note that German unification took place when they were between the ages of six and eight.

They had thus been children at the moment when the major momentous changes had taken place, and had grown up in a period of relaxation of tension between East and West, opening or disappearing borders, and at a transnational and transregional level had encountered nothing but official goodwill regarding intracommunal relations. I show in the section to follow that in spite of all this we found the most deeply disturbing patterns of out-grouping compared to the other generations, especially among those youngest members in our families who lived in the relatively more privileged parts of our border communities. This has to be of grave significance for the growing together of Europe on these former conflictual borders. Time alone will clearly not further closer unity if the negative feelings of young Europeans about one another continue to work against any shared identification.

I arrange the extracts thematically by reoccurring topics that are very typical for the processes of negative stereotyping that we have encountered right across our data. These are as follows: fear, in the form of (a) anxiety and generalised fear (of spaces/groups associated with the other side) and (b) specific fears (theft, etc.); and dislike, in the form of (a) disapproval and dislike of the behaviour and appearance of people and (b) disgust at the appearance of a town and environment. For each heading I select one typical example from each community that allows me to foreground the similarity in these negative constructions, irrespective of the difference in sociopolitical setting and identity labelling.

Fear

In the first set I use extracts by two young women, the first from Guben and the second from Tiefengrün.

Anxiety and Generalised Fear

Extract 1 (salient features are highlighted in the text)
Interviewees: Young female, Daniela Amsel (DA), interviewed with her brother Sven Amsel (SA)
Location: Guben

> DA: Nee. Das is denk ich mal, durch den schlechten Ruf irgendwie, weil die Polen— Ich mein, wenn man rübergeht, dann *erschreckt man sich*, denk ich mal. Ich mein als Westdeutscher der erschrickt sich denn doch vielleicht, wenn er da mal rübergeht, wie das da aussieht. Also is vielleicht noch n bißchen krasser als in der DDR, wie se immersagen. Also so genau weiß ich das auch nicht aber— Wie das da aussieht manchmal, da kommt man dann rüber und dann *erschrickt man ja und dadurch wird das vielleicht auch so'n bißchen* Abschreckung sein, dass die da so verarmt leben. Da streunern denn die Hunde da rum und das is irgendwie *abschreckend*

DA: No. Let's say that is through the bad reputation somehow, because the Poles—I mean when one goes over there, *one gets scared,* I think. I mean as a West German he gets a bit scared when he goes over there, what it looks like over there. Well, it's perhaps a bit stronger than in the GDR, as they always say. Well, I don't really know that so exactly—what it looks like sometimes, one goes over there and then *one gets scared* and because of that there is perhaps such a *deterrent* that they live in such poverty. There you see the stray dogs prowl around and that *turns you off somehow.*

Extract 2:
Interviewee: Young female, Doris Geranie (DG)
Location: Tiefengrün

> DG: Doch, vor allem weil auch die Mafia unten in Rudolphstein verkehrt, ne, das ist ja
> alles
> [
> UM: Die Mafia in Rudolphstein?
> DG: Ja, ja. Das ist alles, das ist Russenmafia und
> UM: Russenmafia?
> DG: also *ich persönlich hab Angst* allein fortzugehen. Vor allem hier durch die Wälder auch noch zu fahren, *also schrecklich.*

> DG: Yes, especially since the Mafia is also down in Rudolfstein, everything is
> UM: The Mafia in Rudolfstein?
> DG: Yes, yes, everything is, that is Russian Mafia and
> [
> UM: Russian Mafia?
> DG: Yes, *I personally am scared* to go out on my own. Especially to drive through the woodlands here, *that's terrible.*

The first extract typically highlights how negative Othering often relies on using vague generalisations or other people's alleged opinions or perspectives as the legitimating source for one's own observation. Here this happens on various levels of generality: (bad) reputation (of Poles); an imagined view of an imagined West German; an impersonal "man"; and an impersonal "they" ("as they always say"). Invoking the point of view of these impersonal others the interviewee describes the Polish town of Gubin as a scary place. Interestingly, by invoking an imaginary West German perspective, she also slips in a comparison between the conditions of her own (former) state (the GDR) and Poland. It may be bad where she lives, but Polish Gubin is still worse.

In this brief extract we find an extraordinary play on words to do with fear or scariness across a range of standard and nonstandard grammatical variation. Since none of this can be rendered in translation, I have highlighted the relevant German expressions in the text.

"Erschrecken" in German has two grammatical forms that are differentiated in the second- and third-person singular by a shift in the stem vowel *e* or *i* and by the grammatical context. It can be used as a transitive verb requiring a direct object: *jemanden erschrecken* ("to scare someone"—third person, *er erschreckt jemanden*) or intransitively on its own ("to become frightened"—third person, *er erschrickt*). In this extract DA creates various nonstandard combinations of these two forms. First she uses the transitive form but turns it into a reflexive verb with an impersonal agent (*man erschreckt sich* = literally, "one scares oneself"); second, she uses the intransitive form but as a (nonstandard) reflexive for an imaginary West German who might go over there and become scared (*der erschrickt sich*—"he becomes scared himself"). Third, she uses it in the standard form again with an impersonal third-person agent (*dann erschrickt man ja*—"one gets scared"). Apart from this overinsistence on different processes whereby one feels this fear or anxiety—being, becoming, or making oneself scared— there is a further set of lexical items that also play with the word *Schreck* (sudden fear) in *abschreckend* (deterring) and *Abschreckung* (deterrent). Kress and Fowler, in one of the first important discussions within critical linguistics, have pointed out what has since become a standard observation, namely that overlexicalisation always "points to areas of intense preoccupation in the experiences and values of the group that generates it" (Fowler and Kress 1979, 211–12). DG's wordplay on fear is an obvious instance of just that. Such overlexicalisation across standard and nonstandard grammatical forms of fear, together with the colourful, atmospheric description of the poor, dog-ridden town, render her account highly personal and contradict her displacement of opinion to other agents.

The second extract above comes from my interview with Doris, a young West German. She also expresses her fear and anxiety—but in her case this is blamed on the disappearance of the border between East and West Germany, which since unification has made her own and neighbouring villages vulnerable to the bad influences from the East, characterised as a perceived influx of a "Russian Mafia" to the border area. Rudolfstein, which allegedly houses this Mafia, is the former border point between GDR and FRG on the motorway from southern Germany to Berlin. Now no more than a small village in rural Germany, this place is seen by her as a threat to her lifestyle— so much so that she no longer dares to even drive through the woodland between her own village of Tiefengrün and the other side.

Specified Fear

In the next paired set of extracts the more generalised fear expressed in the extracts above is made more concrete by the interviewees' focus on perceived threats to personal property.

Extract 1
Interviewee: Young man, Thomas Rabe (TR)
Location: Guben

UM: Und wie stehts denn nun mit Polen, ich mein, gehen sie da jetzt oft rüber als Jugendliche oder eher weniger?

TR: Also ich muss sagen, da ich ja nicht rauche- äh, naja, der Sprit ist drüben billig, und immer wenn ich Sprit brauche, fahr ich eben rüber, und da haben sie jetzt drüben auch n' McDonald's aufgemacht, da fahr ich dann immer mit ran, weils da auch billiger ist als hier in Deutschland. Also ich meine wir haben keinen Weg da rüber und letzten Sonntag waren wir eben auch drüben, haben wir Einkaufbummel gemacht, weils billige Sachen gibt da. Ich sagt mal so: Man fühlt sich nicht so richtig wohl, wenn man da rübergeht. Aber es ist *eben billig. Du kannst eben billig einkaufen, das ist es eben.*

UM: Warum fühlen Sie sich nicht wohl?

TR: Ich weiss es nicht, ich hab schlechte Erfahrungen, weil diese ganzen . . . sozusagen . . . ich kann ja nun nicht alle als Verbrecher beschimpfen, aber das Ganze, ich weiss nicht, wenn du das dann immer so hörst: Die Polen, die klauen und. Mir haben sie hier, hier hab ich das Auto zu stehen gehabt vor dem Tor, haben sie hier mir in der Nacht um drei haben sie mir das Auto aufgebrochen. Und das war auch 'n Ausländer

UM: And how is it now with the Poles, I mean do you young people go across a lot or is this rather rare?

TR: Well I must say, since I don't smoke. Well, petrol is cheaper, and whenever I need petrol, I drive over there, and now they've opened a McDonald's, and there I drive to because it's cheaper than here in Germany. Well, I mean it's no distance, and last Sunday we were there, too, to go shopping, because they sell cheap things there. Well, let's say. You don't feel easy [relaxed, happy] there, when you go there. But it's cheap. You can shop cheaply, that's the point.

UM: Why don't you feel relaxed?

TR: I don't know. I have bad experiences, because all these, so to say, I cannot insult them all as criminals, but the whole thing, I don't know, when you always hear, "The Poles, they steal," and my car they have, I had the car here in front of the gate, and in the middle of the night at three they broke open my car. And that was a foreigner.

Extract 2
Interviewee: Young woman, Doris Geranie (DG)
Location: Tiefengrün

Also da könnte ich jetzt bestimmt, also da könnte ich schwören drauf, daß jeder, also ich sag einmal für hundert Prozent bestimmt achtzig Prozent sagen, die alte Zeit wieder. Weil man kann nichts mehr offen stehen lassen, weil früher im Endeffekt da konnteste mal zum Nachbarn gehen, konnste die Haustür offen lassen, da hat sich kein Schwein. Aber jetzt mußte für jede zwei Minuten, mußte absperren. Aber hier im Dorf sind auch schon Autos geklaut worden, aufgebrochen, also . . .

Well, I could swear, that everyone, say from 100 percent surely 80 percent would want the old times back. Because one cannot leave anything open any more, because it used to be, well you could go and see a neighbour and leave the door open, but no one bothered. But now for every two minutes you got to lock up. And even here in the village cars were already stolen, broken into.

In the first extract, Thomas, a young man from Guben, provides an intriguing set of explanations for his occasional excursion across the border to Poland, none of which include any form of contact with the town or its people. This list is typical for many of the border-crossing activities not only in Guben/Gubin, but all along the eastern borders of Germany with Poland and the Czech Republic: cheap cigarettes (since he doesn't smoke this is not relevant to him), cheap petrol, and cheaper shopping in general. In the case of Gubin, there is in addition a McDonald's restaurant that, to the anger of the young people in Guben, was built in the Polish rather than their German town. However, "these attractions" are undermined by the young man's general sense of discomfort and specific fear of the Poles as thieves. His linguistic manoeuvres move between that which he claims as his personal experience and opinion ("I have bad experiences," his car was broken into outside his house) and the generalised opinion ("you always hear, 'The Poles, they steal'"). This generalised "truth" about the Poles as thieves, though followed by a disclaimer—"I cannot insult them all as criminals"—is concretised by his anecdote about his car being broken into outside his own house. Although his house is in Guben rather than in Gubin, this theft is evidence of the "thieving Poles," since he claims first that the criminals who did this were Poles, but then simply asserts, "And that was a foreigner." Any criminal activity committed in Guben thus becomes evidence of the generalised truth that Poles are thieves. Such a linguistic manoeuvre—from a negative generalised opinion (what the others say, what one hears), via a brief disclaimer, to an anecdote that proves the negative point—is very typical in discourses of out-grouping, and especially frequent in racist discourses. As an argumentative chain they follow a "yes, but" structure: that is, "I cannot call them all criminals *but* my personal experience forces me to see them as such." In this way the individual can claim to be liberal, tolerant, and nonracist in principle, but at the same time can show how his or her alleged personal experience forces him or her to confirm the negative opinions that other people hold about the target group.

In the second extract Doris from Tiefengrün also points to car theft as one of the results of the border's disappearing. Like Thomas, she also quotes an alleged majority opinion—"80 percent" are said to want the old times back (at another point she says everybody would like to build "the wall" again), times she remembers as idyllic and peaceful, when everybody could leave their doors unlocked without coming to any harm.

Dislike

The next paired section focuses on the appearance of the town itself and the disgust the informants feel about its dirtiness and ugliness.

Disgust about General Setting

In the first extract Daniela and her brother Sven again give a highly atmospheric rendering of what it feels like when one crosses the border, again in negative contrast to their unfavourable opinion about their own hometown ("looks worse than here").

Extract 1
Interviewees: Brother (SA) and sister Amsel (DA)
Location: Guben

> DA: Ich meine, wenn man da rüber kommt, denn läuft man 'ne alte Straße lang, sieht ja schlimmer aus als bei uns und denn stehen überall irgendwelche Zwerge, denn stehen da überall so'ne Frauen rum mit ihre Zigaretten und denn kommt man zum Markt, da sind nur irgendwelche Stände, also überall da verkaufen 'se Sachen, denn Deckchen und Decken, die stehen überall an Straßenrändern und wie das denn, da sieht's aus da, denn stinkt's da überall nach Hundehaufen (lacht), sag ich mal, ääääh.
> UM: (lacht) Na, ich krieg's schon mit, ne.
> SA: Ja, weiß ich auch nicht, was man da machen könnte.
> DA: Ich denke mal, erstmal müßte es anders aussehen. So irgendwie
> SA: Na da geht man den schnellsten Weg bis zu McDonald und dann wieder zurück, ja

> DA: I mean when you go over there, then you walk along such an old bit of road, looks worse than here, and there are everywhere those gnomes (garden gnomes), and then there are those women with their cigarettes, and then you get to the market, and there are only some stalls, well, everywhere they sell these things, little cloths and covers, they stand around on all the sides of the road, and how that then, what that looks like, and then it stinks everywhere of dog poo (laughs), let's say, yuck.
> UM: (laughs) OK, I get the message.
> SA: Yeah, I don't really know what one could do.
> DA: I think first of all it would need to look different. So somehow . . .
> SA: Well you go the quickest way to McDonald's and back again, yes.

Extract 2
Interviewee: Young woman, Linda Hollunder (LH)
Location: Tiefengrün

> LH: Ja so am Sonntag sind wir mal rübergefahren, zu Verwandten oder halt so mal rüber und schauen, wie das halt alles so ist.

UM: Und wie ist es?

LH: Ich fands immer nicht so gut (lacht). Da waren halt immer so viele Fabriken und so . . . naja, hat immer gestunken, die Straßen waren nicht so gut, naja . . .

LH: Yes, and on Sunday we drove over there to relatives or just so to have a look what it's like.

UM: And what is it like?

LH: I didn't really like it (laughs); there were always so many factories, and so—well, it always stank, the roads weren't any good, ah well.

The features described in extract 1 in such colourful and dismaying detail are the very same ones that sprang up in response to the widespread shopping tourism by Germans. Marked by the smell of dog excrement, the town appears as a disgusting space, with McDonald's as the only redeeming feature. Neither the market nor the fast-food restaurant on the Polish side serve any social function. McDonald's—universally popular with Polish and German youth alike—is not a place for transnational encounters between young people. The young Germans go there simply because there is not one in Guben; they stay within their own group and leave again in the quickest way possible.

Linda H., the young woman from Tiefengrün, also invokes the bad smell and the bad roads on the other side as reasons for her not enjoying visits to relatives in former East Germany.

Dislike of Appearance and Behaviour

In the last pair of extracts the appearance of the people themselves meets with strong disapproval, in comparison to the informants' perception of themselves as more orderly or more stylish.

Extract 1

Interviewee: Young man, Thomas Rabe (TR)

Location: Guben

TR: Die Polen laufen z.B. entweder schlumpig rum, haben Segelohren oder das sieht man an de Haare, also das könnte ich gleich . . .

UM: Hm, an'n Haaren?

TR: Die Deutschen, die sind doch irgendwie, auch wenn sie rübergehen auch ordentlicher angezogen. Würd ich schon mal sagen.

UM: Hm, hm. Und merken Sie noch den Unterschied jetzt zwischen Westdeutschen und ehemaligen, weiss man gar nicht, was man sagen soll: Neuen Bundesländerleuten?

TR: Ach nö, naja, es war damals die Zeit- Sie meinen jetzt hier DDR und West?

UM: Ja, ja.

TR: Aber so, den Unterschied hab ich eigentlich nie gemerkt so.

TR: Well, the Poles walk about untidy, they have these huge ears or you can tell by their hair, well I could really . . .

UM: Their hair?

TR: The Germans, they are somehow when they go over there, they are more tidily dressed. I would say that.

UM: And can you still tell the difference between West Germans and the— don't know what to call them now—those people from the new federal states?

TR: Oh no, there was once a time . . . You mean here GDR and West?

UM: Yes.

TR: Ah no, I never really noticed that difference.

Extract 2
Interviewee: Young woman, Doris Geranie (DG)
Location: Tiefengrün

DG: Das war erstensmal ruhiger, von der Kriminalität war es weniger, also wo man hin schaut, ich weiß nicht, und da ist jeder hat die Einstellung dazu. Also, rüber, ich war einmal in Zwickau fort. Einmal und nie wieder, weil da mußte wirklich Angst haben, wenn Du mal auf die Toilette gehst, daß du wirklich eine über den Dez gezogen kriegst. Du mußt wirklich mit allem rechnen.

UM: Aber woran merken die denn, daß Sie aus dem Westen kommen?

DG: Es gibt Unterschiede. . . . Es ist zwar blöd, aber die Gangart, und das Aussehen. Sie werden das immer wieder sehen, wie, ob das Ossi oder Wessi ist.

UM: Ja, und woran?

DG: Ich weiß es nicht. Ich weiß es nicht. Aber ich glaube das ist der Instinkt. Ich weiß es nicht. Die ziehen sich, die Schuh, oder die Kombination, ich sag einmal die Kombination. Das war letztens zum Beispiel im Fernsehen drinne, schwarze Hose, dann noch so ein kurzes Wollding drüber und eine Bluse, schaut top aus, aber der Schuh dazu, tät niemals, ich glaub also ein Wessi machen, niemals.

UM: Ach, tatsächlich.

DG: Das sind kleine Stichpunkte, oder wenn die Gangart.

UM: Ja wieso, wie gehen die denn?

DG: Die Gangart, ich weiß es nicht. Das haben sie auch im Fernsehen, im Fernsehen, aber der hat recht gehabt, der hat recht gehabt.

DG: Well first of all it was much quieter, less criminality—
And over there, well I once went out in Zwickau. Once and never again, because you really got to be afraid, just by going to the toilet that someone has a go at you. You really got to expect that.

UM: But how would they notice that you come from the West?

DG: There are differences. . . . I know it sounds silly, but the way they walk and their looks. You will always be able to tell who's a Wessi and who's an Ossi.

UM: Yes, but how?

DG: I don't know, I don't know. But I think it's instinct. I don't know. They wear, the shoes, or how it's put together. Let's say how it's put together. They even mentioned that on TV the other day, black trousers, and then a short woollen top over it, and a blouse, looks cool, but then the shoes with this, I think no Wessi would ever do that, no way.

UM: Really?

DG: Well these are little pointers, or the way they walk.

UM: Oh, how do they walk?

DG: Well, they walk I don't know. On TV they also mentioned that on TV, but he was really right, really right.

These two extracts make a particularly indicative pair in that both the young man from Guben and the young woman from Tiefengrün list a whole range of negative examples of the physical appearance of the respective Other: clothes, hair, style of walking. All are said to be so different in the people on the other side of the river that the Other is immediately recognisable. Intriguingly, the young man in the first extract, who gives an account of the Poles (and indeed other foreigners) that borders on racism, claims to be himself indistinguishable from the West Germans. This blends with his overall identification in other parts of his text, as when he declares himself to be above all a German. His attitude seems to correspond to what is usually described as a correlation between strong national feelings (the in-group) and negative attitudes to others (the out-group; see Citrin and Sides, this volume). By contrast, the young woman from the West German village in the second extract lists a similar catalogue of features for distinguishing her own in-group from the disliked East German youth. Her own identification is foremost with the region; and secondarily with being *West* German rather than German; and thirdly with being European (in an extract not reproduced here). Hence here there is no generalisable correlation between the negative feeling toward the out-group (in her case fellow German nationals, albeit from former East Germany) and the construction of her in-group (in which local identification features most prominently and is nested except in its bypassing the national altogether). I return in more detail to the significance of these differences between ingroup and out-group construction.

OUT-GROUP AND IN-GROUP STRATEGIES

The extracts in the section above, "Constructing the Negative Other," were selected from a group of informants in the respective communities who constructed their own identities using strongly articulated negative dissociations from the people on the other side. There were others who did not use such strong out-grouping strategies, but instead expressed a high degree of indifference toward their neighbours. Strongly positive responses were rare. I focus on the pronounced negative accounts, since they show parallels in out-grouping strategies in spite of the different sociopolitical nature of each out-group, and in spite of the different composition of the in-group.

Common to all these negative accounts are

- a deep unease about encountering the people in the neighbouring communities;
- a resulting unwillingness to engage with them on any social level;
- a replacement of lived experience with mediated accounts (television, accounts by others, in some cases parents' and peer group discourses). These fit in with and confirm an already formed set of attitudes.

The examples I have given are only small extracts from a much wider set of negative discourses in which the most prevalent emotional response is one of dislike, coupled with fear and disgust. By far the greatest number of negative images of Polish people that get enlisted for this are quite superficial, focusing on their clothes and looks, forms of behaviour, ways of talking, not speaking English, and, very often, letting (or having let) things fall to bits in the "smelly and impoverished looking" town of Gubin. As far as behaviour is concerned, the stereotype of the Poles as thieves—especially of cars—is shared by everyone, though with varying modifications. There is an almost total absence of positive stereotyping.

The young people from the Guben sample construct their own identity by demarcation against the Polish other, and echo those of the former West German informants against the former East Germans. Elsewhere Meinhof and Galasinski (2002) have analysed data that demonstrate the in-group strategies for positive identification at local, regional, national, or transnational levels. These provide intriguing contrasts for the same individuals, which can only be summarised here. Whereas out-group strategies followed largely identical patterns, the in-group strategies in our sample vary from one case to the other in unpredictable and often contradictory fashion. In the case of the young man Thomas (TR) quoted above, out-grouping takes the form of a strongly nationalist discourse: Germans (East and West) against Poles. In the case of Sven (SA), out-grouping is based on weak national identification, a dislike of his own town and region, coupled with a strong transnational Western identity based on the modern city. His sister Daniela shares his demarcation against the Polish neighbours, but strongly identifies with the town and the region. Both, when asked (but only then), refer to themselves as, foremost, Europeans on a Western model (i.e., with its current borders with the Eastern ascendant states intact). I return to this in the last section in the discussion of how Europe features in this context. Taken on their own, it would seem that the negative strategies of out-grouping focus on national differentiation—here, of the Poles—whereas the in-group constructions are multilayered and variable between individuals. This in itself is an interesting finding that clashes with some mass survey results (Citrin and Sides, this volume). However, if we compare the data with those exemplified by the two young women from the Tiefengrün sample, we find the very same strategies of Othering in place—this time directed against the people from the neighbouring town. Since both communities on either side of the river belong to a united Germany, and have done so for the larger part of our young informants' lives, the out-group cannot be constructed as one nation-state against the other. Thus, whereas in one set the negative constructions were labelled in terms of a national distinction, in the other there was no national differentiation: instead the postunification neologism of "Ossi" (East German) was employed to do similar distancing work. Data and analysis suggest that insofar as national labels are being imported to support negative constructions of the Other, these are convenient labels employed under particular contextual conditions rather than fixed categories.

Furthermore, there are additional differences even in these largely stereotypical renderings of "us" and "them," depending on whether people narrate anecdotes (even if these are not based on their own experiences) or state their attitudes and beliefs. The young man Thomas, who articulated the most consistently nationalistic, xenophobic, and anti-Polish accounts at the descriptive level, evaluated himself as really quite tolerant about Poles in other parts of his narratives.

IF THERE IS A EUROPEAN IDENTITY, WHAT DOES IT MEAN?

That people manage to hold and negotiate multiple identities does not mean that all are equally potent, or indeed that all possible layers of identification are active. In the final section of this chapter I focus on the role that Europe plays for in-group construction in collocation with, or contrast to, other possible identification layers. Again, there is a difference between what seems to be experientially salient when people narrate themselves as against their consciously stated opinions. When asked, people readily react by giving their opinions as to whether or not they do or don't feel loyalty to various layers of identity. Without such deliberate prompting some of these identifiers never appear. The most obvious lacuna in our informants' spontaneous narratives was connected with Europe and the European Union. This is doubly remarkable in that one set of photos that we showed to our informants foregrounded the EU through its symbol on buildings and institutions subsidised by the EU, such as the state-of-the-art waste plant in Gubin, or the plan to create a "Euro-City Guben/Gubin." This absence of a spontaneous

European narrative was true for all of our informants, irrespective of whether they subsequently expressed positive or negative reactions to Europe. The photographic triggers were interpreted by our informants as internal to the town or region, or as interregional issues rather than European ones (for a fuller account with examples of these narratives see Meinhof and Galasinski 2002; Armbruster, Meinhof, and Rollo 2003). Furthermore, when recontextualised into the wider context of their subsequent narratives about Europe, the nature of that Europe was not at all stable across our informants' discourses; in many cases, it shifted even within the narrative of the same informant. For some of our informants Europe embodied more of a cultural space (European traditions, or, very often, travelling to other European cities); others focused more on a civic and/or institutional dimension (see also Bruter, this volume); but equally often the concept of Europe straddled all of these. Geographical demarcations showed a similar flexibility in our informants' discourses. Europe in some accounts stopped at the border to Poland, with the EU as a Western (even just north-Western) group of nations offering key identification. But in other instances, the positive image of Europe was constructed by emphasising the desirability of the Eastern expansion. In several cases reference to the identical phenomenon shifted across all of these levels within the same conversation. The introduction of the euro currency, for example, shifted in one informant's account between a negative assessment in the context of the EU taking over (institutional saliency), and a positively anticipated potential advantage of not losing so much money with currency exchanges when travelling (cultural saliency).

The collocations between the different layers of identity were unpredictable for our German informants, and defied generalisation of the interrelations between these layers. We found examples of a national German identity that simultaneously implied a transnational Western one. Other informants combined a regional and local identity with a strong interregional form that incorporated the Eastern states, but bypassed the national level. Others again expressed weak local, regional, and national identity, but identified strongly with a metropolitan, transnational, Western space. The most frequently cited positive association for all our informants within this "pick and mix" basket of possibilities (and with the exception of a few of the young informants) was the regional identification. For some former East Germans—especially of the middle generation—pride in the newly founded federal state of Brandenburg went hand in hand with disillusionment about German unification ("I am a Brandenburgian because I want to be an Ossi!") and a rejection of a German national identity (exemplifying the "earthquake" model). Among West Germans there was an equally strong sense of the region, but one that focused more on the local area or subregion of Upper Franconia. This positive form of identification did not imply an oppositional stance to being German, but provided for some an identification model similar to the "Russian doll" model. Again, the variation between these layerings across our informants, but also within a single informant's discourse, outnumbered the regularities. Alarmingly, though somewhat predictably in the light of the role that negative stereotyping played in the construction of national identity, the most positive in-grouping references for Europe appeared in the context of an opposition to unwanted outsiders or threatening incomers (for a full analysis see Armbruster, Meinhof, and Rollo 2003).

CONCLUSION

In this chapter I have argued and, where possible within the confines of one chapter, demonstrated the significance of longer narratives and their detailed analysis for understanding the processes of identity construction within the context of everyday life experiences.

I have focused in particular on the role that negative identification plays in comparison to positive forms of identification at local, regional, and national levels, using semistructured ethnographic interviews as a basis. Discourse analysis of these data reveals major differences between different layers of identification at individual and group levels, which problematise generalisations about systematic alignment of positively or negatively inflected collocations, except insofar as negative strategies appeared to be more alike and stereotypical than positive ones. The data also show a marked difference in what does or does not appear as of prior significance in people's self-selected accounts, especially in connection with European identification. Europe was referred to only in response to the direct questions, not in the more open part of the narratives, which were triggered by photographs. The data also show that the labels of "German," "Polish," and "European" themselves had flexible connotations depending on the sociogeographical and cultural context in which they were employed.

People constructed their cultural identities in relation to a wide range of cultural, political, and experiential factors that did not form cohesive wholes. Instead, they varied in sometimes paradoxical fashion according to the multifaceted context of everyday life experience, memories, encounters, beliefs, and attitudes about others. In the process of narrativisation of these experiences, breaks and contradictions appeared, especially when people constructed in-groups and out-groups.

NOTES

1. For a particularly rampant example of the latter, consider the front-page headline of the British tabloid paper the *Sun* of May 15, 2003, in reaction to the proposals for a European constitution: "Save Our Country. 1588 We Saw Off the Span-

ish. 1805 We Saw Off the French. 1940 We Saw Off the German. 2003 Blair Surrenders Britain to Europe."

2. For linguistics see, for example, Halliday 1978; Fowler and Kress 1979; Hodge and Kress 1993; Meinhof and Richardson 1994; Wodak 1996; Wodak et al. 1999; van Dijk 1997. For Cultural studies see Hall 1990, 1992, 1996; Hall and Du Gay 1996. For social psychology see Potter and Wetherell 1987; Billig et al. 1988; Billig 1995.

3. My work on identity construction is based on two related research projects. The first, a joint project with D. Galasinski, was funded by the ESRC, 1999–2000 (ES-RCR000 22 2899); the second (2000–2003) involving a consortium of six universities, was funded under the EU's fifth framework scheme (SERC-1999-00023). See also www.borderidentities.com.

4. To preserve anonymity of our informants all names and their abbreviations are pseudonyms. "UM" refers to myself as interviewer.

IV

Comparisons and Lessons

11

European Institutions and Identity Change: What Have We Learned?

Thomas Risse

This book has both theoretical and empirical purposes. Theoretically, we strive to understand how new (international) institutions affect people's social identities. How do political institutions shape people's beliefs about who they are and to which communities they belong? What are the causal pathways by which institutions affect social identities and by which identities and institutions coevolve? Empirically, we focus on the European experience, in particular the ways in which more than forty years of European integration have affected people's sense of belonging. Is there an emerging European identity, and if so, does it replace, coexist with, or otherwise interact with individuals' multiple identities? And what is the substantive content of this European identity? Is there a difference between elite-level identification processes with Europe and the Europeanness of "ordinary" people?

To answer these questions, we have embarked on a multidisciplinary and multimethodological approach. The authors in this book are political scientists, sociologists, social psychologists, linguists, and anthropologists using such diverse research tools as quantitative survey data, laboratory experiments, in-depth interviews, discourse analysis, and historical interpretation. Our hope is that a multidimensional approach gives us additional analytical leverage in tackling such an elusive concept as "European identity."

In the following, I try to summarize some of our findings, to highlight agreements as well as differences among the authors, and to suggest avenues for future research. I concentrate on a discussion of the empirical findings of the book. While the introduction by Herrmann and Brewer focuses primarily on theoretical questions involved in studying collective

nphasize what the book tells us about the empirical subject
dentity. Therefore, this chapter focuses on the insights, from
,_nary approach, into European identity as the "dependent
variable." How do European and other identities of individuals and social
groups go together? What do we know about the substance and content of
European identity? How can we explain the large gap between elite identification with Europe and the feelings of ordinary citizens, who seem to be
more alienated from Europe?

While the chapters in this book provide excellent descriptions of what
we seem to know about the extent to which people identify with Europe,
they are less concerned with explaining the evolution of European identity.
Nevertheless, this book yields some insights into the reasons why we can
see changes over time in identification with Europe. I will also highlight
methodological problems in studying the subject matter of European identity that seem to be apparent in this volume. I conclude with the implications of our findings for the policy debates about the future of the European Union. Why bother with studying identities? Do we need European
identity to build a European polity?

EUROPEAN AND OTHER IDENTITIES:
HOW DO THEY GO TOGETHER?

It is no longer controversial among scholars and—increasingly—policy
makers that individuals hold multiple social identities. People can feel a
sense of belonging to Europe, their nation-state, their gender, and so on. It
is wrong to conceptualize European identity in zero-sum terms, as if an increase in European identity necessarily would decrease one's loyalty to national or other communities. Europe and the nation are both "imagined
communities" (Anderson 1991), and people can feel as part of both communities without having to choose some primary identification. Analyses
from survey data suggest, and social psychological experiments confirm,
that many people who strongly identify with their nation-state also feel a
sense of belonging to Europe (Duchesne and Frognier 1995; Martinotti and
Steffanizzi 1995; see Citrin and Sides, this volume; Castano, this volume).

However, there are social contexts in which European and national identities might conflict. Two of Siapera's narratives concern situations in which
journalists feel that they have to take sides in a confrontation between "Europe" and the nation-state. According to one account, Europe has to be
built against the nation-state, and a European public opinion is supposed
to overcome old-fashioned nationalism. The other account takes the opposite perspective and assumes that national identities cannot be superseded
by the construction of a European identity (Siapera, this volume). Laffan's

account of "double hatting" in the Committee of Permanent Representatives (COREPER) at the Council also suggests a sometimes conflictual relationship between European and national identities among officials working in Brussels. This conflict results from the somewhat contradictory role identities of these officials. On the one hand, they are supposed to work toward a common European goal and negotiate consensual outcomes with their fellow Europeans (see also Lewis 1998a, 1998b, 2000). On the other hand, they are still national representatives and, therefore, supposed to defend their respective national interests.

Interestingly enough, zero-sum relationships and potential conflicts between European and national identities are represented in this book only in cases focusing on professionals working in Brussels. Journalists reporting from Brussels to their national media markets and COREPER officials have in common that Europe and their respective nation-states are highly salient and "real" entities for them. Both are very "entitative," to use the term from social psychology (Castano, this volume). Journalists and national permanent representatives have to constantly negotiate between their commitment to Europe and their commitment to their nation-state. No wonder that these two groups perceive Europe and the nation as often in conflict with each other. It seems to be the social context of their professional environment that leads them to sometimes conceptualize the two identities in conflictual terms.

However, the other chapters of this book show little evidence of a zero-sum relationship between European and other identities. This finding is trivial for scholars studying collective identities, but it nevertheless has important implications for the political debates about Europe and the nation-state. Take the contemporary debate about the future of the European Union and about a European constitution. Many people still hold that Europe lacks a demos, one indicator being the lack of strong identification with Europe in mass public opinion (e.g., Kielmansegg 1996). Yet, as Citrin and Sides demonstrate, "country first, but Europe, too" is the dominant outlook in most EU countries, and people do not perceive this as contradictory (for similar findings see Marks and Hooghe 2003). Moreover and more important, the real cleavage in mass opinion is between those who only identify with their nation, on the one hand, and those perceiving themselves as attached to both their nation and Europe, on the other hand. Citrin and Sides show that the individual willingness to support further European integration increases quite dramatically from the former to the latter group. Marks and Hooghe add that exclusive identification with the nation-state is more powerful in explaining opposition to European integration than calculations about economic costs and benefits (Marks and Hooghe 2003). They also show that the effect of exclusive identification with one nation-state varies widely across countries. "Nationalist"

Portuguese are far less inclined to oppose European integration than, say, "nationalist" British.

Generally speaking, therefore, willingness to grant the EU authority requires *some identification* with Europe, but not an identification that actually prioritizes Europe over the nation. In other words, the European polity does not require a demos that replaces a national with a European identity, but one in which national and European identities coexist and complement each other. This is a significant empirical finding that speaks directly to the current debate on the future of the union.

Our findings show much more than the rather simple insight that European and national identities can go together. The chapters suggest quite a bit about how multiple identities go together and how they relate to each other. The introduction of this book suggests three ways in which we can think of multiple identities. First, identities can be *nested,* conceived of as concentric circles or Russian Matruska dolls, one inside the next. My identity as a Rhinelander is nested in my German identity, which is again nested in my Europeanness. Second, identities can be *cross-cutting.* In this configuration, some, but not all, members of one identity group are also members of another identity group. I can feel a strong gender identity and a sense of belonging to Europe, but not all members of my gender group also identify with Europe. Third, identities can be *separate.* For example, I could be the only professor in a sports club, as a result of which my identification with my professional colleagues would be kept separate from my loyalty to the soccer club associates. There would be no overlap in group memberships.

There is a good deal of evidence presented in this book that we can think of the relationship between European and other identities as nested and/or cross-cutting, while there are only a few instances of separate European and other identities. As to *nestedness,* we find the "Russian Matruska doll" model of European and other identities on the level both of elites and of mass public opinion. This model suggests some hierarchy in people's sense of belonging and loyalties. European and other identities pertaining to territorially defined entities can be nested into each other so that "Europe" forms the outer boundary, while one's region or nation-state constitutes the core. The survey data mentioned above that mass publics in most countries hold national and regional identities as their primary sense of belonging, while Europe runs a distinct second, are consistent with such a concept of how multiple identities relate (cf. Bruter, this volume; Citrin and Sides, this volume). Laffan's and Wodak's reports about Commission officials also suggest a nestedness of European identity, but here "Europe" forms the core, while national identification recedes into the background. Social context and psychological reality (Castano, this volume) would explain the difference between the social identities of Commission officials and those of citizens in most EU member states. For the latter, Europe and the EU are distant realities at best and probably less reified than imagined national communities. Meinhof's in-depth interviews with people in border regions suggest that Europe is indeed far away from people's daily lives. They would refer to Europe only when directly asked about it by the interviewer. Hence the ordering whereby national identities form the core and European identity the outer boundary of the Russian doll. For Commission officials, the social context works the other way round and pushes toward strong identification with Europe. Finally, the "Russian doll" idea is consistent with the data reported by Mummendey and Waldzus, according to which national identities form a subgroup within a superordinate group, Europe in this case.

But we also see examples of cross-cutting identities. The chapters by Laffan and Wodak seem to suggest that members of the European Parliament (MEPs) hold such overlapping identities, feeling a sense of belonging to Europe and to their party groups. The same holds true for the journalists in Brussels (see Siapera, this volume). Their professional identities cut across their identification with Europe. Siapera shows that distinct role identities of journalists as investigators, chroniclers, or therapeutic analysts go together with distinct perspectives on the construction of Europe (antinational, national, postnational).

Unfortunately, most mass opinion survey instruments, as well as the social psychological experiments, reported in this volume do not evaluate identification with Europe as cross-cutting with other social identities. The implicit model of multiple identities behind these instruments is the "Russian doll" concept. Yet, we could conceive of even the relationship between European and national identities as cross-cutting. Some, but not all, people who strongly identify with their nation-state also identify with Europe, as the Eurobarometer data suggest (Citrin and Sides, this volume). Moreover, the two groups—"nation only" and "nation and Europe"—hold rather different political attitudes across a wide range of issues. In particular, people identifying with their nation *and* with Europe are less nationalist, less xenophobic, and hold more cosmopolitan values in general (but see the findings by Mummendey and Waldzus on in-group projection, discussed below). Their ideological convictions place them more to the left than their nationalist counterparts. Ideology in general represents another identity marker that cuts across European identity.

There is a fourth way of conceptualizing the relationship between European and other identities that people might hold. We could call it a "marble cake" model of multiple identities. According to this model, the various components of an individual's identity cannot be neatly separated on different levels, as the concepts of nestedness and of cross-cutting identities both imply. What if identity components influence each other, mesh and blend into each other? What if my self-understanding as German inherently contains aspects of Europeanness? Can we really separate out a Catalan from a European identity? As another example, take the major European party families. From the 1950s on, Christian Democratic parties in Continental Europe have been at the forefront of European integration. Europeanness has always been a constitutive component of post–World War II Christian Democratic ideology originating from the interwar period. The same holds true for modern Social Democrats in Europe. It is interesting to note that the turn toward accepting capitalism and the social market economy experienced by the German Social Democrats in the late 1950s, the French Socialists in the early 1980s, and British Labor in the 1990s went hand in hand with a stronger identification with European integration in each of these cases. Today, Europeanness forms a constitutive part of modern Social Democratic ideology (for details see Marcussen et al. 1999; Risse 2001).

The chapters in this volume do not systematically explore such a "marble cake" concept of European and other identities. Yet, most of the evidence is actually consistent with it, starting with the "nation first, Europe second" identification found in the Eurobarometer data (Citrin and Sides, this volume). Theoretically speaking, Breakwell's Identity Process Theory probably comes closest to such an understanding how European and other identity components might go together. The identity change of European Social Democracy described above, for example, could be analyzed in terms of the assimilation/accomodation dynamics to which Breakwell refers in her chapter. Moreover, as Breakwell points out, being European is not the same as being a citizen of an EU member state. EU membership leads to an identity change that impacts on the previous national identity. Since EU membership identity then interacts with rather different national identity constructions, the overall effect is not homogenous, leading to a generalized EU identity. Rather, Europe and the EU become enmeshed with given national identities, leading to rather diverging identity outcomes.

A most important corollary of such a conceptualization concerns the content and substance of what it means to identify with Europe. Breakwell talks about the "emptiness" of Europe as a category, which implies that different groups might fill it with very different contents. Indeed, a longitudinal study of political discourses about Europe among the major parties in France, Germany, and Great Britain revealed that the meaning of Europe varied considerably (Marcussen et al. 1999; Risse et al. 1999). For the German political elites, "Europe" and the European integration meant overcoming one's own nationalist and militarist past (Engelmann-Martin 2002). The French elites, in contrast, constructed Europe as the externalization of distinct French values of Republicanism, enlightenment, and the *mission civilisatrice*. While French and German political elites managed to embed

Europe in their understandings of national identity, the British elites constructed Europe in contrast to their understandings of the nation, particularly the English nation (Knopf 2002).

Finally, the in-group projection model presented by Mummendey and Waldzus points to the dangers of a European identity that is fully integrated into one's own national sense of belonging. This implies not only that "Europe" means different things to different people. If people simply transfer their own national values onto the European stage, and if they fill their understanding of Europe with meanings derived from their national models of political and social life, this might in the end decrease rather than increase tolerance among the European peoples.

Whether nested, cross-cutting, or enmeshed, the various ways in which we can think about multiple identities and their relationships with one another suggest important desiderata for future research. It has become conventional wisdom among scholars that individuals hold multiple social identities. One can feel a sense of belonging to Europe as well as to one's region and/or political party. It is far less clear what this actually means. Future research should, therefore, specify the different ways in which the multiplicity of identities can be conceptualized, derive competing propositions from these models, and test them empirically.

So far, I have used the terms "European identity" and "Europe" as if their content and substantive meanings were clear and well defined. Breakwell's notion of the emptiness of Europe as a social identity marker already challenges this view. She notes that "Europe" and "the EU" connote different things for different people (see also Bruter, this volume). But what do our findings suggest about the substantive content of European identity in terms of both "Who is us?" (composition of group identity) and "What is us?" (content of group identity; see the introduction).

"WHO IS US?" AND "WHAT IS US?": THE COMPOSITION AND THE CONTENT OF EUROPEAN IDENTITY

Europe's Emptiness as an Identity Category

The chapters in this book do not present a uniform picture of what it means in substantive terms to be European. Breakwell points to the possibility that the EU and Europe are poorly defined as superordinate categories and that, therefore, they may have various and rarely unchallenged social meanings. If European identity means quite different things to different people in terms of its ideological, territorial, political, cultural, or even religious connotations, it does not mean much if we find in survey data that people identify with "Europe." At least, we should not draw any major conclusions for the European polity. Moreover, the symbolic and mythological identity markers of Europe are rather weakly developed. Most people might by now recognize the European (EU) flag or European symbols on their passports, driver's licenses, or automobile license plates (see also Bruter, this volume). There is also evidence that the single currency, the euro, has already left a substantial mark in people's mind as a symbol of European integration. The introduction of euro bills and coins in people's pockets has already begun to affect citizens' identification with the EU and Europe in general (see evidence in Risse 2003a). But how many people can identify the "Ode to Joy" as the European anthem?

Or take the events following the September 11, 2001, attacks on the United States. While policy makers all over Europe routinely referred to the need to build a strong European foreign and security policy in the fight against international terrorism, symbols of national foreign policies prevailed in the media representations. We watched British Prime Minister Tony Blair and German Chancellor Gerhard Schröder as well as their foreign ministers travelling around the globe, talking to Arab leaders, and making solemn statements at "ground zero" in New York. We rarely saw Mr. "European Foreign Policy" Solana at similar functions. We did not learn that every single statement by a European leader had been coordinated with fellow Europeans through the framework of the European Common Foreign and Security Policy. Things have further deteriorated with the intra-European conflict concerning the Iraq war. The common framework of European foreign policy was sidestepped, and foreign policy became, once again, a purely national affair.

Breakwell's claim about the emptiness of Europe and the EU as identity categories is corroborated by Meinhof's findings from her in-depth interviews. There was no spontaneous mentioning of Europe or the EU by people in the border towns of Meinhof's study, even though the significance of EU enlargement is quite obvious for them. When confronted with photographs containing European symbols, interviewees would still not refer to Europe. Only when asked direct questions concerning their attachment to Europe would people start talking about it. However, the statements were contradictory and inconsistent; respondents gave very different accounts of what Europe means for them (see Meinhof, this volume). These results differ substantially from the findings based on survey data, which points to some methodological problems in measuring European identity. At least, we can probably infer that Europe was not a salient reality in the particular social context of Meinhof's interviews.

European or EU Identity?

Setting aside the problem that Europe might be an empty signifier for many people, we need to distinguish European and EU identity (cf. Breakwell, this volume). This is particularly important if we want to find out what effects, if any, Europeanization and European integration have had on identity. People might feel a sense of belonging to Europe in general, while feeling no attachment to the EU at all—and vice versa. Yet, as Laffan suggests, the EU as an active identity builder has successfully achieved identity hegemony in terms of increasingly defining what it means to belong to "Europe." First, EU membership has significant constitutive effects on European state identities. States in Europe are increasingly defined as EU members, nonmembers, or would-be members. Their status in Europe and to some degree worldwide depends on these categories. There is no way that European states can ignore the EU, even such devoted nonmembers as Switzerland.

Second, the EU has achieved identity hegemony in the sense that "Europe" increasingly denotes the political and social space occupied by the EU. In the context of Eastern enlargement, Central Eastern European states want to "return to Europe," as if they were currently outside the continent. When Italy prepared itself for entering the euro-zone, the main slogan was "entrare l'Europa" (entering Europe!), as if Italy—one of the six founding members of the European Community—had ever left it (Sbragia 2001). In these contexts, "Europe" is used synonymously with "the EU." To the extent that people identify Europe with the EU, this would be a remarkable achievement of forty years of European integration. If Europe and the EU are used interchangeably, it means that the latter has successfully occupied the social space of what it means to be European. One could then not be a "real" European without being an EU member. This point appears to contradict the notion of Europe as an empty identity category. At least, it would mean that the EU increasingly fills the meaning space of Europe with a specific content.

But what *substantive content* do people refer to when they identify with Europe and/or the EU? What attributes, symbols, and values describe the prototypical member of the European in-group (see the introduction by Brewer and Herrmann)? At this point, Bruter's distinction between civic and cultural components of European identity is quite helpful.

Civic and/or Cultural Components of European Identity

Bruter's chapter points out that it makes a difference whether Europe is defined in civic or cultural terms. "Culture" in this understanding encompasses history, ethnicity, civilization, heritage, and other social similarities. "Civic" identity is much more circumscribed and refers to the identification of citizens with a particular political structure such as the EU or the political institutions of the nation-state (see also Eisenstadt and Giesen 1995). Bruter finds that people systematically distinguish between these two dimensions. His evidence is corroborated by a Europe-wide focus group study commissioned by the EU Commision's Governance Unit that also included nine accession candidates. This study shows that people by and large identify "Europe" as a historical, political, and cultural space rather than a territorial entity (OPTEM 2001). In contrast, when Europe is introduced in mostly territorial terms, attachment rates drop dramatically, as a recent Special Eurobarometer study shows (EOS Gallup Europe 2001). In this case, comparatively more people feel attached to the "world" than to Europe. In other words, it is Bruter's cultural identity that seems to form the substance of citizens' identification with Europe as a whole.

Bruter also points out that the distinction allows us to differentiate between identification with the EU as a distinct civic and political entity, on the one hand, and a larger Europe as a culturally and historically defined social space, on the other. The distinction appears to resonate with quite a few chapters in this volume. As Laffan points out, European institutions—both the EU and the Council of Europe—deliberately try to construct a postnational civic identity in the Habermasian sense (Habermas 1994, 1996; Dewandre and Lenoble 1994), emphasizing democracy, human rights, a market economy, the welfare state, and cultural diversity. These values have become constitutive for the EU, since one cannot become a member without subscribing to them (from the Copenhagen criteria onward). As the enlargement debates show, the self-description of the EU and the dominant discourses surrounding it have moved quite a long way toward building a polity and going beyond simple market integration (see also Laffan, O'Donnell, and Smith 2000). Wodak's data appear to corroborate the point, even though her findings suggest that European elite groups orient toward both civic and cultural components of European identity.

But does this civic understanding of European identity resonate with European citizens? If Bruter's findings were generalizable, the answer would be yes. But Eurobarometer data, unfortunately, do not allow for distinguishing between cultural and civic understandings of European identity. Citrin and Sides present some evidence in their chapter that is at least consistent with Bruter's findings from his pilot studies with student groups. Education, income, and ideology all have a positive impact on levels of attachment to Europe. Moreover, attachment to Europe is strongly correlated with support for the EU and willingness to cede authority and sovereignty to EU institutions in various policy domains. Finally, the more people identify with Europe, the less xenophobic and the more positive toward Eastern enlargement they are. Hostility toward immigrants, in contrast, correlates strongly with exclusively national identifications. These findings support Laffan's rather optimistic statement that the EU has occupied the social identity space of "Europe" and that the substance of "Europe" contains more and more understandings consistent with a civic identity.

She also points out that the social construction of EU identity as put forward by EU institutions points to moral values such as democracy, human rights, and the like, as well as a commitment to the rule of law. A recent study of European discourses in the public sphere corroborates her argument. The debate about Jörg Haider and his populist party's entry into the Austrian government in 2000, as well as the EU reaction to it, was framed in terms of the values that hold the EU together. "Europe" was constructed as both a moral and a legal community, and the EU "sanctions" against Austria were discussed in terms of whether they were consistent with European identity (for evidence see Van de Steeg et al. 2003; Risse 2003b).

Whether these data are generalizable remains to be seen. On the one hand, there is the evidence, reported above, that Europeans distinguish between cultural and civic aspects of their Europeanness, with the former attached to "Europe" as a whole and the latter to the EU in particular. On the other hand, if the EU increasingly defines "Europe" in civic political terms, this would gradually become the dominant view of what it means to be European. This latter claim, if corroborated by further research, would lead to a quite dramatic conclusion regarding the impact of forty years of European integration on identity constructions in Europe, the guiding question of this volume. Not only would the EU increasingly define what it means to be "European," it would also fill "Europeanness" with distinct postnational civic and liberal values, as far as its substance is concerned. European integration would have led to a quite dramatic reconstruction of European identity.

These optimistic conclusions have to be taken with a grain of salt, though. Mummendey and Waldzus, on the one hand, and Meinhof, on the other, see quite different dynamics at work, which are not easily reconcilable with the liberal interpretation of what Europe means to its citizens.

Europe's Multiple Others and the In-group Projection Model

Social identities not only describe the content and the substance of what it means to be a member of a group. They also describe the boundaries of the group, that is, who is "in" and who is "out" (see the introduction of this volume). As a result, we can infer quite a bit about the substance of European identity if we know more about the European Others. The first problem we encounter in this context concerns Europe's "fuzzy boundaries." As Castano points out in his contribution, clear boundaries are an important ingredient of entitativity as a precondition of identification. But where does Europe end? A quick look at those international organizations that carry "Europe" in their name shows that there is no uniform answer to the question. Europe is characterized by overlapping and unclear boundaries. The EU itself currently ends at the former East-West border of the cold war, but will expand considerably toward the east and southeast starting in 2004. At the EU Helsinki summit in December 1999, Turkey was given an accession perspective, too. The European Economic and Monetary Union (EMU) with the single currency, encompasses twelve of the fifteen EU member states. The European Single Market, which includes the European Economic Area, encompasses some non-EU members such as Norway. "Schengenland," with its absence of internal border controls, has even more complicated borders, since it includes Norway, but not the EU member Great Britain. Consider the following: if you travel by car from Germany via France and Spain to Portugal, you never have to show your passport and you retain one single currency, the euro. However, if you travel by car and by boat from Germany via Denmark to Norway, you leave the euro-zone at the German-Danish border, and the EU at the Danish-Norwegian border, but you never have to show your passport because of Schengenland. These are unclear boundaries par excellence.

Other European political organizations have even broader definitions of "Europe." The Council of Europe, for example, includes the Ukraine and Russia. The same is true of the security area for the Organization for Security and Cooperation in Europe (OSCE), which has the United States and Canada among its members. The OSCE "Europe" ranges from San Francisco and Vancouver all the way to Vladivostok.

In sum, "Europe" as a space of political organization and institutionalization has no clear boundaries. What about the social meanings and understandings of "Europe"? There is surprisingly little in the various chapters on the constructions of European Others. Meinhof's chapter strongly suggests that Othering still takes place along the old cold war border, including the former border between East and West Germany. Her interviewees showed strong and hostile feelings toward their fellow citizens in the immediate eastern neighborhood. This was particularly significant among young people who had little personal experience with the Eastern "foreigners," thus corroborating findings from research about stereotyping, according to which lack of contact increases negative stereotypes. In these interviews then, "Europe" is still identified with "Western" Europe, while the East continues to represent the European Other.

Yet, one should not forget that strong Othering is context dependent. Just as there is no fixed assessment of what Europe constitutes positively, there are no fixed European Others. In the context of Meinhof's interviews, which specifically examined border communities, it is not too surprising that the "East" is represented as a threatening European Other. In a different social context, such as EU Committees on Employment and Social affairs (see Wodak, this volume), the United States and Japan are repeatedly referred to as the European out-group. Here, the discourse centers around the European social model, which is represented as distinct from both the

American and Japanese systems of welfare states. In yet another political context, the German discourse on European integration, we found that Germany's own past of militarism and nationalism constituted the European Other against which the European integration project was to be built (Risse 2001; Risse and Engelmann-Martin 2002; Engelmann-Martin 2002). In a similar way, the recent European-wide controversy about the ascent to power of a right-wing party in Austria constructed the out-group as some sort of enemy within, since nobody denied that Austria was a legitimate member of the EU (Van de Steeg et al. 2003). The issue was whether European values of democracy and human rights were consistent with the rise to power of a xenophobic party that did not distance itself sufficiently from the European Nazi past. In sum, Europe has many Others that are referred to and represented in a context-dependent way. This does not mean at all that anything goes, but it warns us not to reify the concept of European identity and to fix its meaning once and for all (see also Siapera's chapter, this volume, demonstrating that the meaning of Europe varies considerably depending on the discursive context).

Finally, Mummendey and Waldzus's in-group projection model contradicts those who assume that the more citizens identify with Europe, the more they will be tolerant and sympathetic to fellow Europeans. The in-group projection model suggests that this is highly conditional on the complexity with which Europe is presented. Citizens who project their own values on Europe and then identify with their "national" Europe tend to be less tolerant with fellow Europeans. If, for example, German understandings of "Europe" and the EU largely conform to visions of German social and political order, this might lower rather than increase German tolerance of Italians. The German discourse on the euro and the convergence criteria was a case in point. Since the euro was presented to a skeptical German public as the *Deutsche Mark* writ large, the Italian lira as *the* symbol of a weak currency was not supposed to join the euro-zone almost by definition. Of course, Germans were in for a surprise when Italy qualified for the EMU (see Sbragia 2001).

At first glance, the evidence presented by Mummendey and Waldzus and by Meinhof contradicts the liberal cosmopolitan picture painted by Laffan's, Bruter's, and Citrin and Sides's chapters, according to which identification with Europe increases tolerance for foreigners and decreases xenophobia. But Mummendey and Waldzus point out that the degree of in-group projection depends on the complexity with which the superordinate identity (Europe in this case) is presented. A Europe that is simply Germany or France writ large might invite in-group projection, while a civic representation of Europe in the Habermasian sense would work against it. One possible way to solve the apparent contradiction would be to point out that the more Europe is identified in civic rather than cultural-ethnic terms (see

Citrin and Sides, this volume; Bruter, this volume) and the more cultural diversity is emphasized (cf. Laffan's references to identity pointers in EU documents, this volume), the less in-group projection might play a role. We could also assume that the high correlation between income, education, and liberalism, on the one hand, and identification with Europe, on the other, might mitigate against in-group projection (Citrin and Sides, this volume). In this case, however, it remains unclear whether it is European identity as such that works against in-group projection, or the liberal and cosmopolitan values that higher educated people are more likely to hold. People holding liberal values might also be less xenophobic and, therefore, feel more European. These possibilities of how the various attitudes relate to each other and coevolve suggest that it is far from clear which causal mechanisms are at work here and what accounts for what.

The somewhat contradictory findings lead to another issue, namely that European integration has been an elite-driven project so far and that, therefore, the identity changes toward a liberal civic identity are largely confined to the elite level.

ELITES, MASSES, AND THE PSYCHOLOGICAL EXISTENCE OF THE EUROPEAN UNION

In general, the chapters confirm that the EU is an elite-driven project—similar to other nation-building projects. No wonder that identification with and support for Europe and its institutions is highest among political and social elites. Eurobarometer data demonstrate an enormous gap between elite support (in fact, elite *consensus*) for the EU, on the one hand, and widespread skepticism among the larger public, on the other. According to 1998 data, European elites supported EU membership almost unanimously (94 percent mean across the EU fifteen), while only a bit more than 50 percent of the mass public endorsed membership of their own country. Countries with the largest gaps between mass public and elite support for EU membership include Germany, Austria, Sweden, Belgium, Spain, Finland, and the United Kingdom (Spence 1998). Of course, these data do not measure identification with Europe, but support for the EU. But since attachment to Europe and support for integration covary, we can safely assume that identification with Europe among the elites is also higher than among the citizens, who rank Europe and the EU a distant second (or third after regional identification; cf. Citrin and Sides, this volume).

Yet, European and national identities are not zero-sum propositions, and citizens can negotiate strong national identities and some secondary identification with Europe. Moreover, Citrin and Sides point to a quite dramatic change during the 1990s. From 1991 to 2000, the number of those who felt attachment to their nation-state only declined by almost 20 percent across the EU fifteen, while the percentage of those who perceived some sense of belonging to their nation-state *and* to Europe increased by about the same number. The greatest increase in dual identification took place in Portugal and, interestingly enough, Germany, while Greece is the only outlier with no change at all. These developments are quite interesting, since support for EU membership and perceived benefits from EU membership—the latter being the main indicator for "utilitarian" evaluations of the EU—declined during the 1990s (Citrin and Sides, this volume). At the same time, the correlations between identification with and attachment to Europe, on the one hand, and support levels for the EU as well as perceived benefits from EU membership, on the other hand, grew stronger.

How can we explain these developments, both the difference between elite and mass identification with Europe and the change during the 1990s? I suggest that the social psychological concept of *entitativity* is key (see Castano, this volume). "Entitativity" refers to the reification of a community resulting from increasingly shared cultural values, a perceived common fate, increased salience, and boundedness, which then lead to collective identification. Castano points out, though, that the increased salience of a community in people's lives does not necessarily increase support for the community; it could also result in growing rejection. Different levels of entitativity could well explain the enormous difference between elite and mass identification with Europe and the EU. The EU is certainly very *real* for Europe's political, economic, and social elites. Whoever is doing business in Europe has to constantly be aware of and refer to EU rules and regulations. Policy makers and government officials on all levels of governance spend a considerable amount of their daily time dealing with the EU (Wessels 2000; Rometsch and Wessels 1996). In other words, the EU has a real psychological existence for the European political, social, and economic elites, as a result of which their sense of belonging is also rather high.

For the citizens, the EU is still a more distant community than the nation-state, despite the fact that EU rules and regulations cover almost every political issue area by now. There are at least three reasons for this relating to the concept of entitativity. First, while EU law is the law of the land, has direct effects, and overrides national law, EU authorities do not implement European rules and regulations, but national and subnational authorities do. Thus, when citizens are confronted with, say, environmental regulations in their daily lives, they do not even know that these are EU rules more often than not. The salience of the EU is rather low, even if the EU affects the citizens' lives on a daily basis. Second, "Europe" has fuzzy boundaries. While there are plenty of indicators telling me that I have left Germany, it is unclear when I have left Europe. Having to show my passport is certainly not a valid indicator, as I argued above regarding the funny boundaries of Schengenland. The same holds for the euro-zone of the single currency, which now encompasses twelve of the fifteen EU member states.

Last but not least, the elite discourses in most EU member states about the EU are ambivalent at best when it comes to "shared values" and "common fate." On the one hand, there is the conscious identity construction of a liberal and civic community emanating from the EU and its various institutions (for the latest effort see Commission of the European Communities 2001; see also Laffan, this volume). On the other hand, national policy makers routinely reify the nation-state in their dealings with Brussels. Whenever they can charge the EU with the responsibility for some tough decision at home, they adopt a populist rhetoric of conscious blame shifting ("Brussels made me do it") and construct EU institutions as remote bureaucracies that cannot be trusted (in contrast to national governments, of course). At the same time, whenever the EU succeeds in solving a commonly perceived problem, national policy makers take the credit in front of national media. Few citizens know, for example, that the liberalization of telecommunication markets, slashing people's telephone bills across Europe during the last ten years, was actually due to EU initiatives. The ambivalent position taken by the media certainly does not help to increase the psychological existence of the European Union. As Siapera points out, journalists in Brussels who routinely report about the EU hold multiple affiliations and see their professional role in ways that add to the ambivalent and fuzzy picture of the EU emanating from the mass media.

In sum, it is probably safe to argue that the EU as a community still lacks the psychological existence that is a condition for collective identification among its citizens. At the same time, things seem be changing, the more Europe hits home. The change in sense of attachment to Europe reported by Citrin and Sides could well result from an increasing reality of the EU in people's daily lives. The single market and Schengenland, for all their fuzziness, have increased the entitativity of the EU. The introduction of the euro bills and coins has already left its mark on citizens' awareness of the EU. Eurobarometer data show that the euro has quickly become the second most salient identity marker for the European Union (details in Risse 2003a). The advent of the euro is a huge social science experiment. If Castano and others are right, we should observe an increase in identification with Europe in the years to come—with both the single currency and EU enlargement.

THE EU AND IDENTITY CHANGE

So far, I have mostly dealt with the chapters' findings concerning individuals' attachment to Europe in relation to their other collective identities. In social science jargon, I have discussed what we seem to know about the "dependent variable" of this volume. Yet, the purpose of this book is not only to describe the degree to which citizens—elites and masses alike—identify with the EU and with Europe in general, but to explain identity change resulting from more than forty years of European integration. Do the European institutions affect collective identities? Do they lead to a greater sense of belonging to Europe? And if so, what are the mechanisms of identity change?

Unfortunately, our knowledge about the effects of the EU on collective identity allows for only tentative conclusions. There are two stories about identities and institutions, as mentioned in the introduction to this volume. The first—rationalist—story exogenizes identities and interests in the institution-building process. As a result, one would expect institutions to have little impact on identities. In EU studies, the most prominent approach in this regard is liberal intergovernmentalism (e.g., Moravcsik 1998). Economic interdependence leads to changes in actors' preferences in favour of international cooperation. The preferences are aggregated by national governments, which then negotiate binding agreements and institutions to insure credible commitments. This story leaves little space for institutional feedback effects on actors' preferences, let alone identities. We can treat it as the "null hypothesis" for this book.

The second—constructivist—story endogenizes identities/interests and institutions. Accordingly and over time, institutions become part and parcel of the social and power structure that forms the social environment in which people act. Institutions tend to have *constitutive* effects on corporate actors such as national governments and interests groups, but also on individuals. Since people act in an environment structured by the institutions, the latter affect their interests, preferences, and collective identities. We should then expect identities and institutions to coevolve, with the causal arrows between the two pointing in both directions. The EU should be no exception. It might well have been created to serve specific interests based on given identities. But this would be the beginning, not the end, of the story. Over time, we would expect a complex cotransformation of the EU together with people's identities and interests.

What do our authors tell us about these two stories? Once again, we need to distinguish between the level of political, economic, and social elites in Europe and that of ordinary citizens, because of the difference in psychological existence that the EU has for the two groups. As to the elites, various chapters in this volume demonstrate that the EU as an institution has had a clear impact on actors' collective identities. On the deepest, constitutive level, Laffan argues, the EU increasingly defines state identity in Europe. There are no "neutral" states in Europe anymore vis-à-vis the EU. You are either in, almost in, or you are out. EU membership is a constitutive feature of statehood in Europe defining the social and institutional space in which nation-states act in Europe. As Sandholtz put it years ago, "membership matters" (Sandholtz 1996; see also Laffan, O'Donnell, and Smith 2000). In short, the EU increasingly *is* Europe.

This is a dramatic finding. If the EU defines what it means to be European, the European integration process has left its marks on the deepest levels of state- and nationhood in Europe. It has done so within only forty years and entirely peacefully. This disconfirms the notion that community building and nation building are inherently linked to war making (Tilly 1975, 1985). Forty years later, we can confirm the success of what the founders of the European Community set out to do—to create a European peace order that redefines European statehood after centuries of wars and nationalism. Moreover, our findings substantiate empirically the Habermasian vision of a postnationalist European identity and statehood (Habermas 1994, 1996). The chapters in this volume, particularly those by Laffan, Bruter, and Citrin and Sides, demonstrate that Europeanness as "EU-ness" centers around a civic identity of liberal values such as human rights, democracy, a market economy, and the welfare state.

Apart from these constitutive effects, European institutions also have a concrete impact on those working in and dealing with them. Laffan, Wodak, and Siapera demonstrate in their chapters how different types of institutions and different types of social (or discursive) contexts create different (role) identities relating to these institutions (see also Checkel, forthcoming). The European Commission as the "guardian of the treaties" portrays an image and self-understanding of strong identification with Europe and European integration as its dominant role identity. In contrast, the Council of Ministers and COREPER favor "double hatting" as the dominant role identity. Officials at COREPER need to be "janus-faced" (Lewis 1998b) in the sense of identifying with and representing their nation-state, but at the same time working toward a common European perspective for problem solving. Last but not least, the European Parliament (EP), as well as the working environment of journalists in Brussels, creates cross-cutting triple identities. EP members have to negotiate between their national identity, their Europeanness, and their party affiliation (see also Wodak, this volume), while journalists' professional identity interacts in various and context-dependent ways with their Europeanness and their national role identities (Siapera, this volume).

These chapters show that the different settings of EU institutions shape the role identities of actors involved in them in distinct ways. In contrast, the impact of the EU on identity changes among the European citizens is expected to be much more diffuse. We cannot assume that people differentiate clearly between, say, the European Commission and the European Parliament, and that these institutions affect their daily lives in distinguishable ways, leading to differences in ways of identification, as is the case on the level of elites. But does this imply that we have to accept the null hypothesis that the EU has had no impact on the social identities of citizens?

Breakwell and Meinhof come closest to such a view. Breakwell emphasizes the emptiness of Europe as a category, as a result of which it should play little or no role in shaping personal identities. But she also points out that the EU and its institutions should have a differential impact on nation-state identities. Meinhof found references to Europe and the EU only if the interviewer explicitly pointed people in this direction.

Bruter's chapter presents a methodology by which we could measure and specify the identity-shaping impact of EU institutions better than the current survey instruments allow. His distinction between a civic and a cultural European identity allows us to differentiate between identification with Europe in general, on the one hand, and with the EU as a political institution, on the other. The evidence reported by Citrin and Sides is at least consistent with his interpretation. If Bruter's findings were generalizable across larger populations, we could conclude that the EU indeed has had its distinct identity-shaping and constitutive effects on both elites and ordinary citizens. Yet, we need a lot more empirical research to make conclusive statements.[1]

Two factors appear to mitigate between EU institutions, on the one hand, and the identification with the EU among citizens, on the other. First and once again, the psychological existence of the EU should play a role (Castano, this volume). The more the social context in which people act is remote from or disaffected by the EU, the less people should identify with it in that context. The fuzziness and unboundedness with which the EU is often presented in the national media discourses is likely to matter here, too. While the experiments reported in Castano's chapter portrayed "Europe" in overall positive terms as common fate, the media representation of the EU is much more ambivalent, if not outright negative in many instances. No wonder, then, that people with moderate levels of support for the EU have difficulty perceiving it as an entitative community. In sum, the variation in entitativity explains to a large extent the different levels of identification with the EU by the elites, on the one hand, and ordinary citizens, on the other.

Second, "Europe" and European integration resonate in different ways with historically and culturally embedded understandings of the nation-state and of national sovereignty (Breakwell, this volume; see also Risse 2001). In the German and French political and intellectual discourses, including the media, Europe has become part and parcel of what it means to be German or French these days. This is very different from the British discourse, in which a stark contrast has been constructed and is being reified between what it means to be "English," on the one hand, and "European," on the other. Here, Europe is still the—albeit friendly—Other, that is, the Continent (see Knopf 2002). One would assume that the EU's impact on collective identities varies significantly according to the degree to which Europe is embedded in the collective historical memory of citizens.

But what are the causal mechanisms by which the EU impacts on collective identities? The introduction by Herrmann and Brewer mentions three such mechanisms. Functional models assume that institutions almost automatically change people's perception of community and sense of belonging. Socialization concepts focus on actors' differential experiences with the institution and its consequences. Finally, persuasion models focus on institutions as identity-shaping agents. Deliberate efforts may be made to create collective identification through myths, symbols, or framing.

What do our findings suggest about these mechanisms? There is little evidence for a functional logic at play. Haas's idea that those elites who profit most from the union would gradually transfer their loyalty to supranational institutions seems to be disconfirmed (Haas 1958). Neofunctionalism's basic argument has been that European integration would lead to identity changes among those transnational interest groups benefiting from European integration. There is little evidence for such a mechanism. Farmers, for example, who arguably benefit most from the EU through the Common Agricultural Policy (CAP), are not particularly known for their enthusiasm for European integration. In more general terms, the data presented by Citrin and Sides (particularly in table 8.3) show rather modest correlations between attachment to and identification with Europe, on the one hand, and individual perceptions of benefiting from the EU, even though this correlation grew stronger during the 1990s. The direction of the causal arrows also remains unclear from these data. One could, for example, turn the functional logic on its head and argue that strong identification with the EU leads to a sense of profiting from EU membership, rather than the other way round.

Socialization appears to be a better candidate for explaining the findings in various chapters. This is particularly true for those who are directly involved in the daily business of EU policy making, either in Brussels or in national capitals (see Laffan, Wodak, and Siapera, this volume; see also Egeberg 1999; Lewis 2000; Wessels 2000; Checkel, forthcoming). Laffan's chapter in particular demonstrates that individuals working in EU institutions tend to adjust to the various "logics of appropriate behavior" (March and Olsen 1998) in these institutions. These officials have direct experience with the institutions and need to internalize their rules of appropriateness at least to some degree in order to be able to carry out their tasks. As a result, we expect them to develop a stronger sense of group identity with the EU than those who have less direct experience with its institutions.

Different degrees of socialization in terms of direct experience with the

EU would also explain the huge gap between elite identification with Europe and that of the mass public. But the findings reported by Bruter and by Citrin and Sides are at least consistent with an interpretation that sees socialization dynamics at work. The ability of citizens to identify with the EU in terms of a civic and political identity and the reported increase in (secondary) identification with Europe and the EU during the 1990s could be explained on the basis of the socialization hypothesis. During the 1990s, the EU has become more visible in people's lives—from the single market to the single currency, Schengenland, Eastern enlargement, and, most recently, debates about institutional reform and the Constitutional Convention. At the same time, the EU has started portraying an image of itself as a political actor on the world scene going beyond pure market integration. The civic identity that Bruter finds in his data conforms precisely to the social construction that EU institutions try to convey to the citizens.

This leads to the third mechanism connecting institutions and social identities, persuasion. Persuasion does not constitute an alternative account to socialization, but complements it by emphasizing the active role of institutions as agents of identity construction. A complex picture emerges. On the one hand, the attempt by European leaders to deliberately construct the EU around civic and postnational values has made some inroads in people's perception of and identification with the EU. The growing visibility of the EU in people's lives is connected to a specific content and substance of European identity as civic and postnational, emphasizing liberal values of democracy, human rights, and the social market economy with a strong welfare state component. On the other hand, as mentioned above, the EU is often presented in the national discourses, including the media, in a rather fuzzy and contradictory manner. In other words, the homogeneity that Castano calls for as a prerequisite for psychological existence and identity building is clearly lacking (see also Breakwell, this volume).

In sum, most chapters in this volume represent snapshots rather than long-term analyses of trends concerning European identity. As a result, we can only speculate about the mechanisms linking European institutions and identity change. The available evidence suggests, however, that further inquiry should probably pursue the investigation along the socialization and persuasion paths.

POINTS OF CONTENTION AND
METHODOLOGICAL IMPLICATIONS

The authors in this volume share a social constructivist understanding of social identities, irrespective of disciplinary backgrounds. Even primordial and essentialist constructions of national or ethnic identities are just this—

social constructions (for a recent discussion see Fearon and Laitin 2000). There is also general agreement that social identities imply distinctions between in-groups and out-groups, entail cognitive, evaluative, motivational, and affective components, and are evoked in a context-dependent manner in situations in which they become socially salient. It follows that individuals hold multiple identities, as a result of which we can reject zero-sum understandings of national or regional versus European identities (see above).

Yet, there are also points of theoretical contention represented in this volume resulting from the different disciplinary, metatheoretical, and methodological backgrounds of our authors. Two controversial issues need to be discussed here. First, how stable or fluid are social identities? On the one hand, data from mass opinion surveys (Bruter, this volume; Citrin and Sides, this volume) and from psychological experiments (Castano, this volume; Mummendey and Waldzus, this volume) imply a fundamental stability of identification processes. Otherwise, these data could not be used for descriptive and/or causal inferences about European identity. On the other hand, Meinhof and Siapera, who use discourse analysis, emphasize the fluidity of social identities, including European identity. In Siapera's case, for example, journalists' identification with Europe seems to vary from one discursive context to the next. Meinhof's data reveal that citizens referred to Europe only when interviewers specifically pointed to it. She argues that people do not relate spontaneously to Europe and that they do so only when triggered by stimuli.

Does this imply that the identification processes found in mass survey data are statistical artifacts, at least on the level of ordinary citizens? Does it imply that the findings reported in this volume are methodology driven in the sense that whether we find European identity or not depends on the method chosen? I do not think so. One way to reconcile the different findings from survey data as compared to discourse analysis is to point to the context dependency of social identities. If social identities, including European identities, are invoked in a context-dependent way wherever they become salient (and if only triggered by certain stimuli), they might appear rather fluid, but only at first glance. In fact, multiplicity, stability, and context dependency of social identities can easily go together. Thus, what appears on the surface as fluid and forever malleable might actually be pretty stable inside, and "identity change" might be simply a question of changing the social contexts in which different layers of an individual's multiple identities become salient. When my gender identity is invoked, my Europeanness might well recede into the background, and vice versa. Siapera's data, for example, are consistent with an interpretation that journalists identify with Europe to varying degrees, depending on the social and political context in which this identification becomes salient or not. This is confirmed by Wodak's findings; she also uses discourse analysis, but shows rather stable identity patterns between the groups investigated. Last but not least, Meinhof's data, with almost nonexisting references to a common European fate, might be explicable on the grounds that she studied border communities in which the overwhelming salience of the self/Other distinction outweighs all other identification processes.

A second issue of contention in this volume concerns the "depth" of identification with Europe found in the various chapters. To what degree does identification with Europe imply loyalty to the EU defined as willingness to pay a price for one's identity? What happens when European policies and requirements conflict with national policies and traditions? There is little in the chapters of this volume enabling us to measure with some degree of certainty the potential costs attached to one's proclaimed identity. On the one hand, the findings of Laffan's and Wodak's chapters, for example, are consistent with a concept of role identities according to which actors know the rules of appropriateness attached to their professional institution. These findings do not necessarily imply a deep sense of loyalty to the institution. On the other hand, the survey data reported in this volume try to figure out the degree to which people negotiate between their national/regional and their European identities. This implies that people have a sense of loyalty to their respective communities, at least to some extent (see Citrin and Sides, this volume, on attachment to Europe).

Whether survey data succeed in tapping into people's loyalty toward the EU is an altogether different matter. We know little with regard to whether people who say they identify with Europe are also prepared to pay a price for their sense of belonging. This points to an important area of future research.[2]

INSTEAD OF CONCLUSIONS: WHY BOTHER? EUROPEAN IDENTITY AND THE EUROPEAN POLITY

This volume concentrates, first, on describing the degree to which European elites and citizens identify with and feel attached to Europe and the EU in its various dimensions and how this sense of European identity compares to other identifications that people might hold. Second, we try to explain the evolution of European identity over more than forty years of European integration and institutional buildup, and how it has led to an increased salience and psychological existence of the EU in the lives of elites and ordinary citizens.

But why bother? Political scientists are less inclined to study social identities per se unless it can be shown that they matter somehow with regard to political outcomes. Does it make a difference to have demonstrated in this volume that elites and ordinary citizens alike increasingly identify with Europe in conjunction with their sense of loyalty to national or subnational communities, and that the EU increasingly defines and constitutes what it means to be European?

In general, political scientists and practitioners alike see a clear link between identity and a functioning political order. Accordingly, a democratic polity requires the diffuse support of the citizens in order to be legitimate. Identification with a political order is seen as a source of diffuse support and, thus, of legitimacy. The higher the sense of loyalty toward a political community among the citizens, the more they are prepared to accept inconvenient decisions and policies of their governments, that is, to pay a price for their identity. Europe as a polity should be no exception. Yet, conventional wisdom holds that the evolving European political order lacks a demos, mainly because there is neither European identity nor a European public sphere (Kielmansegg 1996; Scharpf 1999, 167). While this volume does not address the latter issue (but see Eder, Hellmann, and Trenz 1998; Eder and Kantner 2000; Kantner 2002; Van de Steeg et al. 2003), the chapters strongly challenge the notion that there is no significant European identity on which to build a European polity.

To put it bluntly, this volume and other contributions to the state of the art of European identity show an emerging European demos. Yet, the European polity does not require a demos that replaces national with European identities, but one in which national and European identities coexist. Europeanization, European integration, and European identities coevolve over time, at both the elite and the mass levels. The causal arrows between European integration and institution building, on the one hand, and the evolution of European identities, on the other, seem to run both ways. The increasing psychological existence ("entitativity") of the EU in people's daily lives seems to affect their identification with Europe as a political community. At the same time, support for European integration and attachment to Europe appear to be closely related, motivating European elites to continue on the path of institution building. A study on elite support for and opposition to the single currency revealed that the variation in national attitudes toward the euro can be explained by differences in European identity among these elites (Risse et al. 1999; Risse 2003a; see also Banchoff 1999).

While the European polity seems to coexist and coevolve with a growing sense of European identity, overly optimistic statements should also be avoided on the basis of our findings. We still know little about the precise causal relationships and mechanisms between European integration, on the one hand, and European identity, on the other. This volume—and the ever-increasing literature on European identity in general—is much better at describing the degree to which people feel attached to Europe and the EU than at explaining the development of a European identity and linking it to the evolution of European institutions. The causal pathways identified here—institutionalization, socialization, and persuasion—are far from specified. We can only hint at some of the reasons for the enormous variation in the sense of belonging to Europe revealed in our data. Finally, our findings suggest that European and national identities can go together and giving up one's loyalty to the nation is not required for a European demos. But we know little about those social and political contexts in which European and national identities might actually clash.

Despite these limitations, our volume demonstrates how much progress has been made in recent years in research on European identity and its relationship to other social identities that people hold. We show from a multidisciplinary perspective that the sense of attachment to the EU among Europeans is continuously increasing, leading to an emerging European demos as the democratic underpinning of the European polity. The available evidence shows that there is an increasing sense of community among European citizens, elites and ordinary people alike. The EU represents a genuine community of fate for the political, economic, and social elites in Europe, and it essentially defines modern statehood in Europe for them. Among the citizens, identification with and attachment to Europe has also grown in recent years, while exclusive loyalties to the nation-state are in decline. The EU is understood as a civic community, as distinct from cultural understandings of Europe in general. Given this state of affairs, the future of an enlarged European Union appears less gloomy than many observers seem to think.

NOTES

I thank Tanja Börzel, Marilynn Brewer, Richard Herrmann, and an anonymous reviewer for critical comments on the draft, and the participants in the joint project of the Robert Schuman Centre of Advanced Studies and the Mershon Center for clarifying my views on the subject. Many insights developed in this chapter also stem from discussions at the 1999–2001 European Forum, "Between Europe and the Nation-State," of the European University Institute. Finally, I thank the students of the postgraduate program on European studies in Berlin for their critical comments.

1. Bruter is currently directing a Europe-wide research program in this area that is funded by the Commission's Fifth Framework Programme on Socio-Economic Research.

2. A final point of contention concerns the apparent contradiction between the in-group projection model presented by Mummendey and Waldzus and the Eurobarometer data, according to which identification with Europe correlates with tolerance for foreigners and immigrants and decreases xenophobia (chapter by Citrin and Sides). See above for a discussion.

References

Abélès, M., and I. Bellier. 1996. "La commission européene: Du compromis culturel à la culture politique du compromis." *Revue française de science politique* 46, no. 3:431–57.

Abélès, M., I. Bellier, and M. McDonald. 1993. "Approche anthropologique de la commission européene." Unpublished report. Laboratoire d'anthropologie des institutions sociales (LAIOS), Paris.

Abelson, R. P., N. Dasgupta, J. Park, and M. R. Banaji. 1998. "Perceptions of the Collective Other." *Personality and Social Psychology Review* 2:243–50.

Abrams, Dominic, and Michael A. Hogg, eds. 1990. *Social Identity Theory: Constructive and Critical Advances.* New York: Springer-Verlag.

———, eds. 1999. *Social Identity and Social Cognition.* Malden, MA: Blackwell.

Adenauer, Konrad. 1965. *Mémoires, 1945–1953.* Paris: Hachette.

Adler, Emanuel, and Michael Barnett. 1998. "A Framework for the Study of Security Communities." In *Security Communities*, ed. Adler and Barnett. Cambridge: Cambridge University Press.

Ahern, B. 2000. "Ireland and the EU: Future Prospects." Address to the Institute of European Affairs, Dublin, March 21.

Akin, Benjamin. 1964. *State and Nation.* London: L. Hutchinson.

Alexakis, Vassilis. 1995. *La Langue Maternelle.* Paris: Gallimard.

Alger, Chadwick F. 1990. "The World Relations of Cities: Closing the Gap between Social Science Paradigms and Everyday Human Experience." *International Studies Quarterly* 34, no. 4:493–518.

———. 1999. "The Future of Democracy and Global Governance Depends on Widespread Public Knowledge about Local Links to the World." *Cities* 16, no. 3:195–206.

Alter, K., 1996. "The European Court's Political Power." *West European Politics* 19, no. 3:458–87.

Anderson, Benedict. 1983/1991. *Imagined Communities: Reflections on the Origins and Spread of Nationalism.* London: Verso.

————. 1988. *Die Erfindung der Nation: Zur Karriere eines folgenreichen Konzepts.* Frankfurt/New York: Campus.

Anderson, Peter J., and Tony Weymouth. 1999. *Insulting the Public? The British Press and the European Union.* New York: Longman.

Antaki, C., and S. Widdicombe, eds. 1998. *Identities in Talk.* London: Sage.

Armbruster, Heidi, and Ulrike H. Meinhof. 2002. "Working Identities: Key Narratives in a Former Border Region in Germany." In *Living with Borders: Identity Discourses on East-West Borders in Europe,* ed. Ulrike H. Meinhof, 15–32. Aldershot, UK: Ashgate.

Armbruster, Heidi, Craig Rollo, and Ulrike H. Meinhof. 2003. "Imagining Europe: Everyday Narratives in European Border Communities." In European Identities: Special Issue on Borders, ed. Ulrike H. Meinhof. *Journal of Ethnic and Migration Studies.*

Armstrong, K. 1998. "Legal Integration: Theorising the Legal Dimension of European Integration." *Journal of Common Market Studies* 36, no. 2:155–74.

Ashmore, R., L. Jussim, and D. Wilder, eds. 2001. *Social Identity, Intergroup Conflict, and Conflict Resolution.* New York: Oxford University Press.

Bachman, B. 1993. "An Intergroup Model of Organizational Mergers." PhD diss., University of Delaware.

Bakhtin, M. M. 1981. *The Dialogic Imagination: Four Essays,* ed. M. Holquist, trans. C. Emerson and M. Holquist. Austin: University of Texas Press.

Banchoff, Thomas. 1999. German Identity and European Integration. *European Journal of International Relations* 5, no. 3:259–89.

Banker, B. S., and S. L. Gaertner. 1998. "Achieving Stepfamily Harmony: An Intergroup-Relations Approach." *Journal of Family Psychology* 12:310–25.

Barrett, M. D. 1996. "English Children's Acquisition of a European Identity." In Breakwell and Lyons, 1996.

Barrett, M., E. Lyons, M. Bennett, F. Sani, I. Vila, A. G. de la Pena, L. Arcuri, A. E. Berti, A. S. de Rosa, and A. S. Bombi. 1999. *European Identities of Children.* EU Final Project Report.

Barthes, Roland. 1977. *Image, Music, Text.* London: Fontana.

Bates Levi, Margaret, and Barry Weingast. 1997. *Analytic Narratives.* Princeton, NJ: Princeton University Press.

Benhabib, Seyla. 1996. *Democracy and Difference.* Princeton, NJ: Princeton University Press.

Bentley, Arthur F. 1955. *The Process of Government: A Study of Social Pressures.* 4th ed. Evanston, IL: Principia Press of Illinois.

Berger P. L., and T. Luckmann 1966/1967. *The Social Construction of Reality: A Treatise in the Sociology of Knowledge.* London: Penguin. Garden City: Anchor.

Bernstein, Serge, and Pierre Milza. 1994. *Histoire de l'Europe.* 5 vols. Paris: Hatier.

Beyers, J., and Dierickx. 1998. "The Working Groups of the Council of the European Union: Supranational or Intergovernmental Negotiations." *Journal of Common Market Studies* 36, no. 3:289–318.

Billig, M. 1995. *Banal Nationalism.* London: Sage.

Billig, M., S. Condor, D. Edwards, M. Gane, D. Middleton, and A. R. Radley. 1988. *Ideological Dilemmas.* London: Sage.

Black, J. 1997. *Maps and History: Constructing Images of the Past.* New Haven, CT: Yale University Press.

Blondel, J., R. Sinnott, and P. Svensson. 1998. *People and Parliament in the Euro-*

pean Union: Participation, Democracy and Legitimacy. Oxford: Oxford University Press.

Boorstin, Daniel, et al. 1995. *A History of the United States.* Needham, MA: Prentice Hall.

Bourdieu, Pierre, 1991. *Language and Symbolic Power.* Harvard: Harvard University Press.

Breakwell, G. M. 1986. *Coping with Threatened Identities.* London: Methuen.

———. 1988. "Strategies Adopted When Identity Is Threatened." *Revue Internationale de Psychologie Sociale* 1, no. 2:189–204.

———. 1994. "The Echo of Power: A Framework for Social Psychological Research." *Psychologist* 7, no. 2:65–72.

———. 1996. "Identity Processes and Social Changes." In Breakwell and Lyons 1996, 13–27.

———. 2001a. "Social Representational Constraints upon Identity Processes." In *Representions of the Social: Bridging Theoretical Traditions*, ed. K. Deaux and G. Philogene. Oxford: Blackwell.

———. 2001b. "Identity Processes Influencing Risk Representations." In *Social Influence in Social Reality*, ed. F. Butera and G. Mugny. Göttingen, Germany: Hogrefe and Huber.

Breakwell, G. M., and E. Lyons, eds. 1996. *Changing European Identities: Social Psychological Analyses of Change.* Oxford: Butterworth-Heinemann.

Breuilly, John. 1982. *Nationalism and the State.* Chicago: University of Chicago Press.

Brewer, Marilynn B. 2000a. Research Design and Issues of Validity. In *Handbook of Research Methods in Social and Personality Psychology*, ed. H. T. Reiss and C. M. Judd. Cambridge: Cambridge University Press.

———. 2000b. "Superordinate Goals versus Superordinate Identity as Bases of Intergroup Cooperation." In *Social Identity Processes*, ed. Dora Capozza and Rupert Brown, 117–32. London: Sage.

Brewer, M. B., and R. J. Brown. 1998. "Intergroup Relations." In *The Handbook of Social Psychology*, ed. D. T. Gilbert and S. T. Fiske, 2:554–94. Boston, MA: McGraw.

Brewer, M. B., and A. S. Harasty. 1996. "Seeing Groups as Entities: The Role of Perceiver Motivation." In *Handbook of Motivation and Cognition*, ed. R. M. Sorrentino and E. T. Higgins, vol. 3. New York: Guilford.

Brewer, M. B., and R. M. Kramer. 1985. "The Psychology of Intergroup Attitudes and Behavior." *Annual Review of Psychology* 36:219–43.

Brittan, L. 1996. "Is Britain's National Identity Threatened by Further European Integration?" Redwood Debate, Warwick, England, May 15.

Brockmeier, Jens, and Rom Harré. 1997. "Narrative: Problems and Promises of an Alternative Paradigm." *Research on Language and Social Interaction* 30, no. 4.

Brookes, Rod. 1999. "Newspapers and National Identity: BSE/CJD Crisis and the British Press." *Media, Culture and Society* 21, no. 2:247–64.

Brubaker, Rogers. 1996. *Nationalism Reframed: Nationhood and the National Question in the New Europe.* Cambridge: Cambridge University Press.

———. 1999. "The Manichean Myth: Rethinking the Distinction Btween 'Civic' and 'Ethnic' Nationalism." In *Nations and National Identity: The European Experience*, ed. Hanspeter Kriesi, Klaus Armingeon, Hannes Siegrist, and Andreas Wimmer, 55–71. Zurich: Verlag Ruegger.

Brugmans, Henri. 1970. *L'idee Europeenne, 1920–1970.* Bruges: De Tempel.

Bruter, Michael. 1998. "The Symbols of European Integration." Washington, DC: Centre for German and European Studies.

———. 1999. "Diplomacy without a State: The External Delegations of the European Commission." *Journal of European Public Policy* 6, no. 2.

———. 2000a. "French Public Opinion and European Integration." In *Historical, Economic, Social, and Political Aspects of European Integration*, ed. T. Lunati and S. Stern-Gillet. London: Edwin Mellen.

———. 2000b. "Urbanity and Support for European Integration." Research Papers Series. Hull: Centre for European Union Studies.

———. 2001. "Understanding Identity Realignments: The Emergence of a Mass European Identity." PhD diss., University of Houston.

———. 2004a. *Citizens of Europe? The Emergence of a Mass European Identity*. London: Palgrave McMillan.

———. 2004b. "Civic and Cultural Components of a European Identity." Chapter 9, this volume.

Burgess, Michael. 2000. *Federalism and the European Union*. London: Routledge.

Burley, A.-M., and W. Mattli. 1993. "Europe before the Court: A Political Theory of Legal Integrtion." *International Organization* 47, no. 1:41–76.

Butler, David, and David Stokes. 1974. *Political Change in Britain*.

Byatt, A. S. 2002. "What Is a European?" *New York Times Magazine*, October 13, 46–52.

Campbell, Angus, Philip Converse, A. Miller, and David Stokes. 1950. *The American Voter*.

Campbell, D. T. 1958. "Common Fate, Similarity, and Other Indices of the Status of Aggregates of Persons as Social Entities." *Behavioural Sciences* 3:14–25.

Cassen, B. 1993. "Légitimer une Europe supranationale? Culture et pouvoir." *Le Monde Diplomatique* 32 (September).

Castano, Emanuele. 2003a. "Ethnos, Demos and Project: Is It Possible to Construct a Common Identity Even in the Absence of a European 'People'?" *European Synthesis* (January).

———. 2003b. "On the Advantages of Reifying the Ingroup." In *The Psychology of Group Perception: Perceived Variability, Entitivity, and Essentialism*, ed. V. Y. Yzerbyt, C. M. Judd, and O. Corneille. Philadelphia: Psychology Press.

Castano E., Tousignant, N., 1999. "La Belgique et l'Europe: Un *demos* sans *ethnos*?" In *Les racines de l'identité europeenne*, ed. G.-F. Dumont. Paris: Economica Paris/Thesis Zuri.

Castano, E., and V. Y. Yzerbyt. 1998. "The High and Lows of Group Homogeneity." *Behavioural Processes* 42:219–38.

Castano, E., V. Y. Yzerbyt, and D. Bourguignon. 2003. "We Are One and I Like It: The Impact of Ingroup Entitativity on Ingroup Identification." *European Journal of Social Psychology* 33:735–54.

Castano, E., V. Y. Yzerbyt, D. Bourguignon, and E. Seron. 2002. "Who May Enter? The Impact of Ingroup Identification on Ingroup-Outgroup Categorization." *Journal of Experimental Social Psychology* 38:315–22.

Castano, E., V. Y. Yzerbyt, and M. P. Paladino. In press. "Transcending Oneself through Social Identification." In *Handbook of Experimental Existential Psychology*, ed. J. Greenberg, T. Pyszczynski, and K. Sander. New York: Guilford.

Castano, E., V. Y. Yzerbyt, M. P. Paladino, and S. Sacchi. 2002. "I Belong Therefore I Exist: Ingroup Identification, Ingroup Entitativity, and Ingroup Bias." *Personality and Social Psychology Bulletin* 28:135–43.

Castano, E., V. Y. Yzerbyt, N. Tousignant. 2000. *Europeans Become European: Identity Management in Today's Europe.* Unpublished manuscript, Catholic University of Louvain at Louvain-la-Neuve, Belgium.

Castells, M. 1998. *The End of the Millennium.* Vol. 3. Oxford: Blackwell.

Castoriadis, Constantin. 1975. *L'Institution Imaginaire de la Société.* Paris: Seuil.

Checkel, Jeffrey, ed. Forthcoming. *International Institutions and Socialization in Europe.*

Christiansen, Thomas. 1996. "A Maturing Bureaucracy? The Role of the Commission in the Policy Process." In *European Union: Power and Policy-Making,* ed. J. Richardson, 127–47. London: Routledge.

———. 2002. Eurobarometer 57.2: "Health Issues, Cross-Border Purchases, and National Identities." April–June 2002 (computer file). ICPSR version. Brussels: European Opinion Research Group EEIG (producer), 2002. Cologne, Germany: Zentralarchiv fur Empirische Sozialforschung/Ann Arbor, MI: Inter-university Consortium for Political and Social Research (distributors), 2003.

Chryssochoou, X. 1998. *L'identité sociale. La construction identitaire nationale et européenne de français et de grecs.* Unpublished doctoral dissertation, Université Paris V, France.

———. 2000a. "The Representations of a New Super-ordinate Category: Studying the Stereotype of the European in the Context of the European Integration." *European Psychologist* 5, no. 4:269–77.

———. 2000b. "Memberships in a Super-ordinate Level: Re-thinking European Union as a Multi-national Society." *Journal of Community and Applied Social Psychology* 10:403–20.

Churchill, Winston, 1995. *Discours Choisis.* Paris: Poche.

Cicourel, A. 1974. *Methode und Messung in der Soziologie.* Frankfurt/Main.

Cini, M. 1996. "The European Commission: Leadership, Organisation and Culture in the EU Administration." Manchester: Manchester University Press.

Cinnirella, M. 1997. "Towards a European Identity? Interactions between the National and European Social Identities Manifested by University Students in Britain and Italy." *British Journal of Social Psychology* 36:19–31.

Citrin, Jack, and John Sides. 2003. "Can There Be Europe without Europeans? Problems of Identity in a Multinational Community." In *Advances in Political Psychology,* vol. 1, ed. Margaret G. Hermann. San Diego: Elsevier Press.

Claude, Inis L. 1971. *Swords into Plowshares: The Problems and Progress of International Organization.* 4th ed. New York: Random House.

Colley, Linda, 1992. *Britons: Forging the Nation, 1707–1837.* New Haven, CT: Yale University Press.

Commission of the European Communities. 2001. "European Governance: A White Paper." Brussels, July 25.

Condor, S. 1996. "Unimagined Community? Some Social Psychological Issues concerning English National Identity." In Breakwell and Lyons, 1996, 41–68.

Connor, Walker. 1994. *Ethnonationalism: The Quest for Understanding.* Princeton, NJ: Princeton University Press.

Copenhagen Summit. 1973. "Declaration on European Identity." In *Selection of Texts concerning Institutional Matters of the Community, 1952–1982.* European Parliament, 1982.

Corbett, R., F. Jacobs, and M. Schackleton. 1995. "The European Parliament." 3rd ed. London: Cartermill.

Cottam, Martha L., and Richard W. Cottam. 2000. *Nationalism and Political Behavior: Causes, Patterns, and Consequences.* Pittsburgh, PA: University of Pittsburgh Press.

Coudenhove-Kalergi, Richard. 1924. *Pan-Europa.* 3rd ed. Wein: Pan-Europa.

Cram, L. 1997. *Policy Making in the EU.* London: Routledge.

Crisp, Richard J., and Miles Hewstone. 2000. "Multiple Categorization and Social Identity." In *Social Identity Processes,* ed. Dora Capozza and Rupert Brown, 149–66. London: Sage.

Dalton, Russell J. 1996. *Citizen Politics: Public Opinion and Political Parties in Advanced Western Democracies.* 2nd ed. Chatham, NJ: Chatham House.

Damro, C. 2001. "Building an International Identity: The EU and Extraterritorial Competition Policy." *Journal of European Public Policy* 8:208–26.

Davies, B., and R. Harré. 1990. "Positioning: Conversation and the Production of Selves." *Journal for the Theory of Social Behavior* 20, no. 1:43–63.

de Cillia, Rudolf, Martin Reisigl, and Ruth Wodak. 1999. "The Discursive Construction of National Identities." In *Discourse and Society* (October 1): 149–73.

Delgado-Moreira, J. M. 1997. "Cultural Citizenship and the Creation of European Identity." *Electronic Journal of Sociology* 2, no. 3.

Delors, Jaques. 1992. "1992: A Pivotal Year: Address by Jaques Delors." Brussels: EC.

Deloye, Yves. 1997. *Sociologie Historique du Politique.* Paris: La Découverte.

Deth, Jan W. van, and Elinor Scarbrough. 1995. "The Concept of Values." In *The Impact of Values,* ed. Jan W. van Deth and Elinor Scarbrough. Oxford: Oxford University Press.

Deutsch, K. 1953. *Nationalism and Social Communication: An Inquiry into the Foundations of Nationality.* Cambridge, MA: MIT Press.

———. 1957. *Political Community and the North Atlantic Area.* Princeton, NJ: Princeton University Press.

de Vreese, Claes, Jochen Peters, and Holli Semetko. 2001. "Framing Politics at the Launch of the Euro: A Cross-National Comparative Study of Frames in the News." *Political Communication* 18, no. 2:107–22.

Dewandre, N., and J. Lenoble, eds. 1994. *Projekt Europa. Postnationale Identität: Grundlage für eine europäische Demokratie.* Berlin.

Downs, Anthony. 1957. *An Economic Theory of Democracy.* New York: Harper.

Doyle, Michael, and Nicholas Sambanis. 2000. "International Peacebuilding: A Theoretical and Quantitative Analysis." *American Political Science Review* 94, no. 4 (December): 779–801.

Duchesne, Sophie, and Andre-Paul Frognier. 1995. "Is There a European Identity?" In Niedermayer and Sinnott, 1995.

Duroselle, J. B. 1990. *Europe: A History of Its People.* London: Viking.

Eder, Klaus, Kai-Uwe Hellmann, and Hans-Jörg Trenz. 1998. "Regieren in Europa jenseits öffentlicher Legitimation? Eine Untersuchung zur Rolle von politischer Öffentlichkeit in Europa." In *Regieren in entgrenzten Räumen. PVS-Sonderheft,* ed. Beate Kohler-Koch. Opladen: Westdeutscher Verlag.

Eder, Klaus, and Cathleen Kantner. 2000. "Transnationale Resonanzstrukturen in Europa. Eine Kritik der Rede vom Öffentlichkeitsdefizit." In *Die Europäisierung nationaler Gesellschaften. Sonderheft 40 der Kölner Zeitschrift für Soziologie und Sozialpsychologie,* ed. Maurizio Bach, 306–31. Wiesbaden: Westdeutscher Verlag.

Egeberg, M. 1996. "Organization and Nationality in the European Commission Services." *Public Administration* 74:721–35.

———. 1999. "'Transcending Intergovernmentalism': Identity and Role Perceptions of National Officials in European Decision-Making." *Journal of European Public Policy* 6, no. 3:456–74.

Ehlich, Konrad. 1991. "Funktional-pragmatische Kommunikationsanalyse: Ziele und Verfahren." In *Verbale Interaktion: Studien zur Empirie und Methodologie der Pragmatik.Stuttgart,* ed. D. Flader, 127–43.

Eichenberg, Richard, and C. Richard. 1993. "Europeans and the European Community: The Dynamics of Public Support for European Integration." *International Organization* 47:507–34.

Eijk, Cees van der, and Mark Franklin. 1996. *Choosing Europe.* Ann Arbor: Michigan University Press.

Eisenstadt, Shmuel N., and Bernhard Giesen. 1995. "The Construction of Collective Identity." *European Journal of Sociology* 36:72–102.

Elejabarietta, F. 1996. "Le concept de representation sociale." In *Des attitudes aux attributions,* ed. J.-C. Deschamps, J.-L. Beauvois. Grenoble: Presses Universitaires de Grenoble.

Eley, Geoff, and Ronald Suny, eds. 1996. *Becoming National: A Reader.* New York: Oxford University Press.

Emerson, Rupert. 1960. *From Empire to Nation: The Rise to Self-Assertion of Asian and African Peoples.* Boston: Beacon.

Engelmann-Martin, Daniela. 2002. "Identity, Norms and German Foreign Policy: The Social Construction of Ostpolitik and European Monetary Union." PhD Diss., Department of Social and Political Sciences, European University Institute, Florence.

EOS Gallup Europe. 2001. "Flash Eurobarometre 92: 'Gouvernance.'" Report, Brussels, Janvier–Fevrier, 2001.

Ester, Peter, Loek Halman, and Ruud de Moor, eds. 1993. *The Individualizing Society: Value Change in Europe and North America.* Tilburg, Netherlands: Tilburg University Press.

Etzioni, Amitai, 1961. *A Comparative Analysis of Complex Organizations.* Glencoe, IL: Free Press.

Eurobarometer. 1990. No. 33. Brussels: Commission of the European Communities.

———. 1996. *Top Decision-Makers Survey: Summary Report.* http://europa.eu.int/comm/public_opinion archives/top-en.htm.

———. 1999. No. 52. *Top Decision-Makers Survey: Summary Report.*

———. 2000. No. 53. *Public Opinion in the European Union.* http://europa.eu.int/comm/public_opinion/archives/eb/eb53/eb53_en.pdf.

———. 2002. No. 57. *Public Opinion in the European Union: EU15-Spring Report.* http://europa.eu.int/comm/public_opinion/archives/eb/eb57/eb57_en.pdf.

European Communities. 1992. *Treaty on the European Union.* Luxembourg: Publication Office.

European Monetary Institute. 1996. Press releases. Frankfurt: Press office of the EMI.

Evans, Geoffrey, and Pippa Norris, eds. 1999. *Critical Elections: British Parties and Voters in Long-Term Perspective.* London: Sage.

Fearon, James D., and David D. Laitin. 2000. "Violence and the Social Construction of Ethnic Identity." *International Organization* 54, no. 4:845–77.

Feldman, Stanley. 1988. "Structure and Consistency in Public Opinion: The Role of Core Beliefs and Values." *American Journal of Political Science* 32, no. 2 (May): 416–40.

Fichte, Johann Gottlieb. 1845. *Sammtilche Werke.*

Finley, F. 1998. *Snakes and Ladders.* Dublin: New Island.

Fowler, R., and G. Kress. 1979. "Critical Linguistics." In *Language and Control,* ed. R. Fowler, B. Hodge, G. Kress, and T. Trew, 185–213. London: Routledge and Kegan Paul.

Franklin, Mark. 1999. "Borrowing from Peter to Pay Paul: European Union Politics as a Multi-level Game against Voters." Paper presented for the 1999 meeting of the American Political Science Association, Atlanta.

Franklin, Mark, 1992. *Electoral Change.* Cambridge: Cambridge University Press.

Franklin, Mark, and Christopher Wlezien. 1997. "The Responsive Public: Issue Salience, Policy Change and Preferences for European Unification." *Journal of Theoretical Politics.*

Gabel, Matthew. 1994. "Understanding the Public Constraint on European Integration: Affective Sentiments, Utilitarian Evaluations, and Public Support for European Integration." PhD diss., University of Rochester.

————. 1998. *Interests and Integration: Market Liberalization, Public Opinion, and European Union.* Ann Arbor: University of Michigan Press.

Gaertner, S. L., J. F. Dovidio, P. A. Anastasio, B. A. Bachman, and M. C. Rust. 1993. "The Common Ingroup Identity Model: Recategorization and the Reduction of Intergroup Bias." In *European Review of Social Psychology* 4:1–26. Chichester, England: John Wiley and Sons.

Gaertner, S. L., J. F. Dovidio, J. A. Nier, C. M. Ward, and B. S. Banker. 1999. "Across Cultural Divides: The Value of a Superordinate Identity." In *Cultural Divides: Understanding and Overcoming Group Conflict,* ed. D. A. Prentice and D. T. Miller, 173–212. New York: Russell Sage Foundation.

Gaertner, S. L., J. A. Mann, J. F. Dovidio, and A. J. Murrell. 1990. "How Does Cooperation Reduce Intergroup Bias?" *Journal of Personality and Social Psychology* 59:692–704.

Gaertner, S. L., J. Mann, A. Murrell, J. F. and Dovidio. 1989. "Reducing Intergroup Bias: The Benefits of Recategorization." *Journal of Personality and Social Psychology* 57:239–49.

Gaertner, S. L., M. C. Rust, J. F. Dovidio, and B. A. Bachman. 1994. "The Contact Hypothesis: The Role of a Common Ingroup Identity on Reducing Intergroup Bias." *Small Group Research* 25:224–49.

Galasinski, D., and U. H. Meinhof. 2002. "Looking across the River: German-Polish Border Communities and the Construction of the Other." *Language and Politics* 1, no. 1:23–58.

Gans, Herbert. 1980. *Deciding What's News.* New York: Vintage.

Gellner, Ernest. 1983. *Nations and Nationalism.* Ithaca, NY: Cornell University Press.

Goffman, E. 1981. *Forms of Talk.* Philadelphia: University of Pennsylvania Press.

Greenfeld, Liah. 1992. *Nationalism: Five Roads to Modernity.* Cambridge, MA: Harvard University Press.

Grimm, Dieter. 1995. "Does Europe Need a Constitution?" *European Law Journal* 1, no. 3:282–302.

Guild, Elspeth. 1996. "The Legal Framework of Citizenship of the European Union." In *Citizenship, Nationality and Migration in Europe,* ed. David Cesarani and Mary Fulbrook. London: Routledge.

Haas, Ernst. 1958. *The Uniting of Europe: Political, Social, and Economic Forces, 1950–1957.* London: Stevens; Stanford, CA: Stanford University Press.

———. 1964. *Beyond the Nation-State: Functionalism and International Organization.* Stanford: Stanford University Press.

———. 1975. *The Obsolescence of Regional Integration Theory.* Berkley, CA: Institute of International Studies.

Haas, E., S. Roever, and A. Schmidt. 2002. "Germany and the Norms of European Governance." *German Politics and Society* 20, no. 2:148–75.

Habermas, Jürgen. 1962/1989. *The Structural Transformation of the Public Sphere: An Inquiry into a Category of Bourgeois Society.* Cambridge: Polity Press.

———. 1994. "A Citizenship and National Identity." In *The Condition of Citizenship,* ed. Bart van Steenbergen. New York: Sage.

———. 1996. "Der europäische Nationalstaat—Zu Vergangenheit und Zukunft von Souveränität und Staatsbürgerschaft." In *Die Einbeziehung des Anderen,* ed. Jürgen Habermas. Frankfurt/Main: Suhrkamp.

Hall, Stuart. 1990. "Cultural Identity and Diaspora." In *Identity: Community, Culture, Difference,* ed. J. Rutherford. London: Lawrence and Wishart.

———. 1992. "The Question of Cultural Identity." In *Modernity and its Futures,* ed. S. Hall, D. Held, and T. McGrew. Cambridge: Polity Press.

———. 1996. "Who Needs Identity?" In *Questions of Cultural Identity,* ed. S. Hall and P. Du Gay. London: Sage.

Hall, Stuart, and P. Du Gay, eds. 1996. *Questions of Cultural Identity.* London: Sage.

Halliday, M. A. K. 1978. *Language as Social Semiotic.* London: Arnold.

Hamilton, Alexander, James Madison, and John Jay. 1999. *The Federalist Papers.* New York: Mentor.

Hamilton, D. L., and S. J. Sherman. 1996. "Perceiving Persons and Groups." *Psychological Review* 103:336–55.

Hamilton, D. L., S. J. Sherman, and B. Lickel. 1998. "Perceiving Social Groups: The Importance of the Entitativity Continuum." In *Intergroup Cognition and Intergroup Behaviour,* ed. C. Sedikides, J. Schopler, and C. A. Insko, 47–74. Mahwah, NJ: Erlbaum.

Hartung, Harald. 2000. Eurobarometer 53: *Racism, Information Society, General Services, and Food Labeling,* April–May 2000 (computer file). 3rd ICPSR version. Brussels, Belgium: INRA (Europe; producer), 2000. Cologne, Germany: Zentralarchiv fur Empirische Sozialforschung/Ann Arbor, MI: Inter-university Consortium for Political and Social Research (distributors), 2002.

———. 2000. Eurobarometer 54.1: *Building Europe and the European Union: The European Parliament, Public Safety, and Defense Policy.* November–December

2000 (computer file). 2nd ICPSR version. Brussels: European Opinion Research Group EEIG (producer), 2001. Cologne, Germany: Zentralarchiv fur Empirische Sozialforschung/Ann Arbor, MI: Inter-university Consortium for Political and Social Research (distributors), 2003.

Haslam, S. A., P. J. Oakes, J. C. Turner, and C. McGarty. 1995. "Social Categorization and Group Homogeneity: Changes in the Perceived Applicability of Stereotype Content as a Function of Comparative Context and Trait Favourableness." *British Journal of Social Psychology* 34:139–60.

Hayes-Renshaw, F., and H. Wallace. 1997. *The Council of Ministers.* London: Macmillan.

Herder, Johann Gottfried von. 1913. *Works.* Berlin: Weidmannsche Buchhandlung.

Herrmann, Richard, and Marilynn B. Brewer. 2004. "Identity and Institutions: Becoming European in the EU." Chapter 1, this volume.

Hewstone, M. 1986. *Understanding Attitudes to the European Community: A Social-Psychological Study in Four Member States.* Cambridge: Cambridge University Press.

Hipfl, B., A. Bister, and P. Strohmaier. 2003. "Youth Identities along the Eastern Border of the European Union." In European Identities: Special Issue on Borders, ed. Ulrike H. Meinhof. *Journal of Ethnic and Migration Studies.*

Hix, S. 1999. *The Political System of the European Union.* London: Macmillan.

Hobsbawm, E. J. 1990. *Nations and Nationalism since 1780: Programme, Myth, Reality.* Cambridge: Cambridge University Press.

Hodge, B., and G. Kress. 1993. *Language as Ideology.* London: Routledge.

Hoffman, S. 1966. "Obstinate or Obsolete: The Fate of the Nation-State in Europe." *Daedalus* 95.

Hollinger, David. 1995. *Post-ethnic America: Beyond Multiculturalism.* New York: Basic Books.

Holly, Werner, Jiri Nekvapil, Ilona Scherm, and Pavla Tiserova. 2003."Unequal Neighbours: Coping with Asymmetries." In European Identities: Special Issue on Borders, ed. Ulrike H. Meinhof. *Journal of Ethnic and Migration Studies.*

Hooghe, L. 1999. "Images of Europe: Orientations to European Integration among Senior Officials of the Commission." *British Journal of Political Studies* 29:345–67.

Hopkins, N., and N. Murdoch. 1999. "The Role of the 'Other' in National Identity: Exploring the Context-Dependence of National In-group Stereotype." *Journal of Community and Applied Social Psychology* 0:321–38.

Howe, Peter. 1995. "A Community of Europeans: The requisite underpinnings." *Journal of Common Market Studies* 33, no. 1:27–46.

Huici, C., M. Ros, I. Cano, N. Emler, N. Hopkins, and M. Carmona. 1997. "Comparative Identity and Evaluation of Socio-political Change: Perceptions of the European Community as a Function of the Salience of Regional Identities." *European Journal of Social Psychology* 27:97–113.

Huntington, Samuel. 1968. *Political Order in Changing Societies.* New Haven, CT: Yale University Press.

———. 1996. *The Clash of Civilizations and the Remaking of World Order.* New York: Simon and Schuster.

Hurwitz, Jon, and Mark Peffley. 1987. "How Are Foreign Policy Attitudes Structured? A Hierarchical Model." *American Political Science Review* 81, no. 4:1099–1120.

Ignatieff, Michael. 1993. "The Balkan Tragedy." *New York Review of Books* 40, no. 9.

Inglehart, Ronald. 1970. "The Silent Revolution." *American Political Science Review*.
———. 1990. *Culture Shift in Advanced Industrial Society*. Princeton, NJ: Princeton University Press.
———. 1997. *Modernization and Postmodernization: Cultural, Economic, and Political Change in 43 Societies*. Princeton, NJ: Princeton University Press.
Inglehart, Ronald, and Karlheinz Reif. 1991. *Eurobarometer: The Dynamics of European Public Opinion*. London: Macmillan.
Iyengar, Shanto, Mark D. Peters, and Donald R. Kinder. 1982. "Experimental Demonstrations of the 'Not-So-Minimal' Consequences of Television News Programs." *The American Political Science Review* 76, no. 4 (December): 848–58.
Jacobs, Ronald. 1996. "Producing the News, Producing the Crisis: Narrativity, Television and News Work." *Media, Culture and Society*, vol. 18, issue 3:373–98 (26).
Jacoby, William. 1991. "Ideological Identification and Issue Attitudes." *American Journal of Political Science* 35, no. 1:178–205.
Jervis, Robert. 1999. "Realism, Neoliberalism, and Cooperation: Understanding the Debate." *International Security* 24, no. 1:42–63.
Jodelet, D. 1989 *Les representations sociales*. Paris: Presses Universitaires de France.
Judt, T. 2003. "Anti-Americans Abroad." *New York Review of Books* 50:7.
Kanter, Rosabeth Moss. 1995 *World Class: Thriving Locally in the Global Economy*. New York: Simon and Schuster.
Kantner, Cathleen. 2002. "Transnationale Öffentlichkeit und die Demokratiefähigkeit der Europäischen Union." PhD diss., Philosophische Fakultät III, Humboldt-Universität, Berlin.
Kaplan, Robert. 2000. *The Coming Anarchy: Shattering the Dreams of the Post Cold War*. New York: Random House.
Katz, Daniel. 1960. "The Functional Approach to the Study of Attitudes." *Public Opinion Quarterly* 24, no. 2:163–204.
Katz, R. S., and B. Wessels. 1999. *The European Parliament, the National Parliament and European Integration*. Oxford: Oxford University Press.
Kelman, Herbert. 1969. "Patterns of Personal Involvement in the National System: A Social Psychological Analysis of Political Legitimacy," *International Politics and Foreign Policy: A Reader in Research and Theory*, ed. James N. Rosenau, 276–88. Glencoe, IL: Free Press.
Keohane, Robert. 1989. "Neoliberal Institutionalism: A Perspective on World Politics." In *International Institutions and State Power: Essays in International Relations Theory*, ed. Robert Keohane. Boulder, CO: Westview.
———. 1993. "Institutional Theory and the Realist Challenge after the Cold War." In *Neorealism and Neoliberalism: The Contemporary Debate*, ed. David A. Baldwin. New York: Columbia University Press.
Keohane, Robert, and Lisa Martin. 1995. "The Promise of Institutionalist Theory." *International Security* 20, no. 1:39–51.
Kerrmans, B. 1996. "Do Institutions Make a Difference?" *Governance* 9, no. 2:217–40.
Kevin, Deirdre. 2001. "Coverage of the European Parliament Elections of 1999: National Public Spheres and European Debates." *Javnost/The Public* 8, no. 1.
Kielmansegg, Peter Graf. 1996. "Integration und Demokratie." In *Europäische Integration*, ed. Markus Jachtenfuchs and Beate Kohler-Koch, 47–71. Opladen: Leske and Budrich.

Kienpointner, Manfred. 1992. *Alltagslogik: Struktur und Funktion von Argumentationsmustern.* Stuttgart-Bad Cannstatt: Frommann-Holzboog.

Knopf, Hans Joachim. 2002. "Britain and European Integration between 1950 and 1993: Towards a European Identity?" PhD diss., Department of Social and Political Sciences, European University Institute, Florence.

Kohn, Hans. 1944. *The Idea of Nationalism: A Study in Its Origins and Background.* New York: Collier Books.

Kundera, Milan. 1984. "The Tragedy of Central Europe." In *From Stalinism to Pluralism,* ed. Gale Stokes. Oxford: Oxford University Press, 1991.

Kvale, S. 1996. *Interviews: An Introduction to Qualitative Research Interviewing.* Thousand Oaks, CA: Sage.

Labov, W. 1972. *Language in the Inner City.* Philadelphia: University of Pennsylvania Press.

Labov, W., and J. Waletzky. 1967. "Narrative Analysis: Oral Versions of Personal Experience; Essays on the Verbal and Visual Arts." In ed. J. Helms, 12–44. Seattle: University of Washington Press.

Laclau, Ernesto, ed. 1994. *The Making of Political Identities.* London: Verso, 1994.

Laffan, Brigid. 1996. "The Politics of Identity and Political Order in Europe." *Journal of Common Market Studies* 34:81–103.

———. 2004. "The European Union and Its Institutions as 'Identity Builders.'" Chapter 5, this volume.

Laffan, Brigid, Rory O'Donnell, and Michael Smith. 2000. *Europe's Experimental Union: Rethinking Integration.* London: Routledge.

Leca, Jean. 1992. *La Citoyenneté dans tous ses Etats.* Paris: L'Harmattan.

Lewis, Jeffrey. 1998a. "Constructing Interests: The Committee of Permanent Representatives and Decision-Making in the European Union." PhD diss., Department of Political Science, University of Wisconsin–Madison.

———. 1998b. "Wearing a Janus-Face: The Permanent Representatives of the European Union." Paper presented at Eleventh International Conference of Europeanists, Baltimore.

———. 2000. "The Method of Community in EU Decision-Making and Administrative Rivalry in the Council's Infrastructure." *Journal of European Public Policy* 7, no. 2:261–89.

Licata, Laurent. 2000. "National and European Identities: Complementary or Antagonistic." Paper presented at the ID-NET conference, European University Institute, Florence, June 9–10.

Liebes, Tamar, and James Curran. 1998. *Media, Ritual and Identity.* London: Routledge.

Lijphart, Arend. 1977. *Democracy in Plural Societies: A Comparative Exploration.* New Haven, CT: Yale University Press.

———. 1999. *Patterns of Democracy: Government Forms and Performance in Thirty-Six Countries.* New Haven, CT: Yale University Press.

Lindberg, L., and S. Sheingold. 1970. *The European Polity.* Berkeley: University of California Press.

Linde, C. 1993. "Life Stories: The Creation of Coherence." New York: Oxford University Press.

Lipset, Seymour Martin. 1960. *Political Man: The Social Bases of Politics.* Garden City, NY: Doubleday.

Lipset, Seymour Martin, and Stein Rokkan. 1967. *Party Systems and Voters Alignments.* Cambridge: Cambridge University Press.

Locke, E. A., ed. 1986. *Generalizing from Laboratory to Field Settings.* Lexington, MA: Lexington Books.

Lodge, J. 1979. "Nation-states versus Supranationalism: The Political Future of the European Community." *Journal of European Integration* 2:161–81.

Lyons, E. 1996. "Coping with Social Change." In Breakwell and Lyons 1996, 31–40.

Lyons, E., M. Barrett, M. Bennett, F. Sani, I. Vila, A. G. de la Pena, L. Arcuri, A. E. Berti, A. S. de Rosa, and A. S. Bombi. 1997. *Intragroup Homogeneity Effects in the Development of National Identity: A Cross-National Study.* Eighth European Conference on Developmental Psychology, Rennes, France, September.

Lyons, E., and G. M. Breakwell. 1996. "Changing European Identities and Social Change in Europe: A Challenge for Social Psychology." In Breakwell and Lyons 1996, 3–12.

Maas, U. 1984. "Als der Geist der Gemeinschaft eine Sprache fand." *Sprache im Nationalsozialismus: Versuch einer historischen Argumentationsanalyse.* Opladen: Westdeutscher Verlag.

Maguire, Joseph, Emma Poulton, and Catherine Possamai. 1999. "The War of Words? Identity Politics in Anglo-German Press Coverage of EURO 96." *European Journal of Communication* 14, no. 1:61–89.

Mak, Jeannette. 2002. "The Communication of Symbols or Symbolic Communication: The European Commission's Information Policy on the Euro." PhD diss., European University Institute, Florence.

Manners I. J., and R. G. Whitman. 1998. "Towards Identifying the International Identity of the European Union: A Framework for Analysis of the EU's Network of Relationships," *European Integration* 21:231–49.

March, James G., and Johan P. Olsen. 1995. *Democratic Governance.* New York: Free Press.

———. 1998. "The Institutional Dynamics of International Political Orders." *International Organization* 52, no. 4:943–69.

Marcussen, Martin, Thomas Risse, Daniela Engelmann-Martin, Hans-Joachim Knopf, and Klaus Roscher. 1999. "Constructing Europe: The Evolution of French, British, and German Nation-State Identities." *Journal of European Public Policy* 6, no. 4:614–33.

Marks, G. 1999. "Territorial Identities in the European Union." In *Regional Integration and Democracy: Expanding on the European Experience,* ed. Jeffrey J. Anderson. Boulder, CO: Rowman and Littlefield.

Marks, Gary, and Liesbet Hooghe. 2003. "National Identity and Support for European Integration." Manuscript. Berlin and Chapel Hill.

Martin, Denis-Constant. 1995. "The Choices of Identity." *Social Identities* 1, no. 1 (1995): 5–20.

Martinotti, Guido, and Sonia Steffanizzi. 1995. "Europeans and the Nation State." In Niedermayer and Sinnott 1995, 163–89.

McKinlay, A., and A. Dunnett. 1998. "How Gun-Owners Accomplish Being Deadly Average." In Antaki and Widdicombe 1998, 34–51.

McKuen, Michael, Robert Erikson, and James Stimson. 1989. "Macropartisanship." *The American Political Science Review* 83, no. 4 (December): 1125–42.

McLean, Mairi, and Jolyon Howorth, eds. 1992. "Europeans on Europe: Transnational Visions of a New Continent." London: McMillan.

McQuail, Dennis. 1994. *Mass Communications Theory.* London: Sage.

Meehan, Elizabeth. 1993. *Citizenship and the European Community.* London: Sage.

Meinhof, Ulrike H. 1997. "The Most Important Event of My Life! A Comparison of Male and Female Autobiographical Narratives." *Masculinity and Language,* ed. S. Johnson and U. H. Meinhof, 208–28. Oxford: Blackwell.

———. 2001a. "Auf der Suche nach Euro-News-Land: Satellitenfernsehen und di e Konstruktion kultureller Identitiäten." In *Bewegte Identitäten: Medien in transkulturellen Kontexten,* ed. B. Busch, B. Hipfl, and K. Robins, 111–27. Klagenfurt, Germany: Drava Verlag.

———. 2001b. "Discourse and Identity." In *Atti del 2o congresso di studi dell'Associazione Italiana di Linguistica Applicata,* ed. Camilla Bettoni et al. Perugia: Guerra Edizioni.

———, ed. 2002. *Living (with) Borders: Identity Discourses on East-West Borders in Europe.* Border Regions Studies 1. Aldershot, UK: Ashgate.

———. 2003. "Migrating Borders: An Introduction to European Identity Construction in Process." European Identities: Special Issue on Borders. *Journal of Ethnic and Migration Studies.*

Meinhof, Ulrike H., and Dariusz Galasinski. 2000. "Photography, Memory and the Construction of Identities on the Former East-West German Border." *Discourse Studies* 2, no. 3:323–53.

———. 2002. "Reconfiguring East-West Identities: Cross-Generational Discourses in German and Polish Border Communities." *Journal of Ethnic and Migration Studies* 28, no. 1:63–82.

Meinhof, Ulrike, and K. Richardson, eds. 1994. *Text, Discourse and Context: Representations of Poverty in Britain.* London: Longman.

———. 1999. *Worlds in Common? Television Discourse in a Changing Europe.* London: Routledge.

Melich, Anna. 1999. Eurobarometer 51.0: *The Elderly and Domestic Violence.* March–May 1999 (computer file). Brussels, Belgium: INRA (Europe; producer), 1999. 2nd ICPSR version. Ann Arbor, MI: Inter-university Consortium for Political and Social Research/Cologne, Germany: Zentralarchiv fur Empirische Sozialforschung (distributors), 2001.

Messick, D. M., and D. M. Mackie. 1989. "Intergroup Relations." *Annual Review of Psychology* 40:45–81.

Meyer, Christof. 2000. "Towards a European Public Sphere? Transnational Investigative Journalism and the European Commission's Resignation." In *Transnational Communication in Europe,* ed. B. Baerns and J. Raupp, 107–27. Berlin: Vistas.

Millennium Declaration. 1999. Helsinki, December.

Mitrany, David. 1966. *A Working Peace System.* Chicago: Quadrangle.

Mlicki, M., and N. Ellemers. 1996. "Being Different or Being Better? National Stereotypes and Identifications of Polish and Dutch Students." *European Journal of Social Psychology* 26:97–114.

Monnet, Jean. 1955. *Les Etats-Unis d'Europe ont Commencé.* Paris: Laffont.

————. 1978. *Memoires*. Garden City, NY: Doubleday.

Moravcsik, Andrew. 1998. *The Choice for Europe: Social Purpose and State Power from Rome to Maastricht.* Ithaca, NY: Cornell University Press.

Morley, David. 2000. *Home Territories: Media, Mobility and Identity.* London: Routledge.

Morley, David, and Kevin Robins. 1995. *Spaces of Identity: Global Media, Electronic Landscapes and Cultural Boundaries.* London: Routledge.

Moscovici, S. 1976. *La psychanalyse son image et son public.* Paris: Presses Universitaires de France.

Mumby, D. 1993. *Narrative and Social Control.* London: Sage.

Mummendey, Amelie, and Sven Waldzus. "National Differences and European Plurality." Chapter 4, this volume.

Mummendey, Amelie, and M. Wenzel. 1999. "Social Discrimination and Tolerance in Intergroup Relations: Reactions to Intergroup Differences. *Personality and Social Psychology Review* 3:158–74.

Muntigl, Peter, Gilbert Weiss, and Ruth Wodak. 2000. *European Union Discourses on Un/employment: An Interdisciplinary Approach to Employment Policy-Making and Organizational Change.* Amsterdam: Benjamins.

Nick, R., and A. Pelinka. 1993. *Österreichs politische Landschaft.* Innsbruck, Austria: Haymon Verlag.

Niedermayer, O., and R. Sinnott. 1995a. "Democratic Legitimacy and the European Parliament." In Niedermayer and Sinnott, 1995.

————. 1995b. *Public Opinion and Internationalized Governance.* London: Oxford University Press.

Norris, Pippa et al. 1999. *On Message: Communicating the Campaign.* London: Sage.

Ochs, E. 1997. "Narrative." In *Discourse as Structure and Process*, ed. T. A. van Dijk, 1:185–207. London: Sage.

Optem. 2001. *Perceptions de l'Union Europeenne. Attitudes et attentes a son egard. Etude qualitative aurpes du public des 15 Etats membres et de 9 pays candidats a l'adhesion.* Versailles: Commission Europeenne, Mars, 2001.

Pastoureau, Michel, and Michel Schmidt. 1990. *L'Europe: Memoire et Emblemes.* Paris: L'Epargne.

Piazza, T., and P. M. Sniderman. 1998. "Experiments into Computer Assisted Surveys." In *Computer Assisted Survey Information Collection*, ed. M. P. Couper, R. P. Baker, J. Bethlehem, C. Z. F. Clark, J. Martin, W. L. Nicholls II, and J. M. O'Reilly. New York: John Wiley and Sons.

Potter, Jonathan. 1996, *Representing Reality: Discourse, Rhetoric and Social Construction,* London: Sage.

Potter, Jonathan, and Margaret Wetherell. 1987. *Discourse and Social Psychology: Beyond Attitudes and Behaviour.* London: Sage.

Prodi, R. 2003. *Enlargement of the Union and European Identity.* Florence, Italy: European University Institute.

Rehberg, K.-S. 1994. "Institutionen als symbolische Ordnungen. Leitfragen und Grundkategorien zur Theorie und Analyse institutioneller Mechanismen." In *Die Eigenart der Institutionen: Zum Profil politischer Institutionentheorie*, ed. G. Göhler, 47–84. Baden-Baden, Germany: Nomos.

Reicher, S. D., and N. Hopkins. 2001. *Self and Nation*. London: Sage.

Reif, Karlheinz. 1993. "Cultural Convergence and Cultural Diversity as Factors in European Identity." In *European Identity and the Search for Legitimacy*, ed. S. Garcia. London: Pinter.

Reif, Karlheinz, and Anna Melich. 1998. Euro-Barometer 36.0: *Regional Identity and Perceptions of the Third World*, Fall 1991 (computer file). Conducted by INRA (Europe), Brussels. ICPSR ed. Ann Arbor, MI: Inter-university Consortium for Political and Social Research (producer), 1998. Koeln, Germany: Zentralarchiv fuer Empirische Sozialforschung/Ann Arbor, MI: Inter-university Consortium for Political and Social Research (distributors), 1998.

Reif, Karlheinz, and Eric Marlier. 1998. Eurobarometer 43.1bis: *Regional Development and Consumer and Environmental Issues*, May–June 1995 (computer file). Conducted by INRA (Europe), Brussels. 2nd SSD ed. Goeteborg, Sweden: Swedish Social Science Data Service (producer), 1998. Goeteborg, Sweden: Swedish Social Science Data Service/Koeln, Germany: Zentralarchiv fuer Empirische Sozialforschung/Ann Arbor, MI: Inter-university Consortium for Political and Social Research (distributors), 1998.

Reisigl, Martin, and Ruth Wodak. 2000. "'Austria First': A Discourse-Historical Analysis of the Austrian 'Anti-Foreigner-Petition' in 1992 and 1993." In *The Semiotics of Racism*, ed. M. Reisigl and R. Wodak, 269–303. Vienna: Passagen Verlag.

———. 2001. *Discourse and Discrimination*. London: Routledge.

Renan, Joseph Ernest. 1870. "Discours de la Sorbonne." In *Discours et Conferences*.

Ricoeur, Paul. 1981. *Hermeneutics and the Social Sciences: Essays on Language, Action and Interpretation*, Cambridge: Cambridge University Press.

Risse, Thomas. 2001. "A European Identity? Europeanization and the Evolution of Nation-State Identities." In *Transforming Europe: Europeanization and Domestic Change*, ed. Maria Green Cowles, James A. Caporaso, and Thomas Risse, 198–216. Ithaca, NY: Cornell University Press.

———. 2002. "Nationalism and Collective Identities: Europe versus the Nation-State?" In *Developments in Western European Politics*, vol. 2, ed. P. Haywood, E. Jones, and M. Rhodes. Basingstoke, U.K.: Palgrave.

———. 2003a. "The Euro between National and European Identity." *Journal of European Public Policy* 10, no. 4:487–503.

———. 2003b. "Toward a European Public Sphere? Theoretical Considerations." Paper presented at European Union Studies Association, Nashville, TN, March 26–30.

Risse, Thomas, and Daniela Engelmann-Martin. 2002. "Identity Politics and European Integration: The Case of Germany." In *The Idea of Europe: From Antiquity to the European Union*, ed. Anthony Pagden, 287–316. Cambridge: Cambridge University Press.

Risse, Thomas, Daniela Engelmann-Martin, Hans Joachim Knopf, and Klaus Roscher. 1999. "To Euro or Not to Euro: The EMU and Identity Politics in the European Union." *European Journal of International Relations* 5, no. 2:147–87.

Roberts, Donald, and Nathan Maccoby. 1985. "Effects of Mass Communication." In *The Handbook of Social Psychology*, 3rd ed., G. Lindzey and E. Aronson, 539–98. New York: Random House.

Roccas, Sonia, and Marilynn Brewer. 2000. "Social Identity Complexity." Unpublished paper.

Rochard, B. 1997. *La Commission et l'Identité Européenne.* Geneva: Institut Universitaire des hautes Etudes Internationales.

Rometsch, Dietrich, and Wolfgang Wessels, eds. 1996. *The European Union and the Member States: Towards Institutional Fusion?* Manchester: Manchester University Press.

Rothbart, M., and M. Taylor. 1992. "Category Labels and Social Reality: Do We View Social Categories as Natural Kinds?" In *Language, Interaction and Social Cognition*, ed. G. Semin and K. Fiedler, 11–36. London: Sage.

Rougemont, Denis de. 1965. *The Meaning of Europe.* London: Sidgewick and Jackson.

Rousseau, Jean Baptiste. 1762. *Du Contrat Social.* Geneva: Rey.

Rutland, A., and M. Cinnirella. 2000. "Context Effects on Scottish National and European Self-Categorization: The Importance of Category Accessibility, Fragility and Relations." *British Journal of Social Psychology* 39:495–519.

Sandel, M. J. 1998. *Liberalism and the Limits of Justice*, 2nd ed. Cambridge: Cambridge University Press.

Sandholtz, Wayne. 1996. "Membership Matters: Limits of the Functional Approach to European Institutions." *Journal of Common Market Studies* 34, no. 3:403–29.

Saussure, Ferdinand de. 1974. *Cours de Linguistique Generale*, ed. C. Bailly. London: Fontana.

Sbragia, Alberta. 2001. "Italy Pays for Europe: Political Leadership, Political Choice, and Institutional Adaptation." In *Transforming Europe: Europeanization and Domestic Change*, ed. Maria Green Cowles, James A. Caporaso, and Thomas Risse, 79–98. Ithaca, NY: Cornell University Press.

Scharpf, Fritz W. 1999. *Regieren in Europa.* Frankfurt/Main: Campus.

Schiffrin, D. 1996. "Narrative as Self-Portrait: Sociolinguistic Constructions of Identity." *Language and Society* 25: 167–203.

———. 1997. "The Transformation of Experience, Identity, and Context." In *Towards a Social Science of Language: Papers in Honor of William Labov*, vol. 2, *Social Interaction and Discourse Structures*, ed. G. Guy, C. Feagin, D. Schiffrin, and J. Baugh, 41–55. Amsterdam/Philadelphia: John Benjamins.

Schlesinger, Philip. 1978/1987. *Putting Reality Together.* London: Methuen.

———. 1992. "'Europeanness': A New Cultural Battlefield?" *Innovation* 5, no. 2:11.

———. 1993. "Wishful Thinking: Cultural Politics, Media and Collective Identities in Europe." *Journal of Communication* 43, no. 2:6–17.

———. 1997. "From Cultural Defence to Political Culture: The European Union, the Media and Collective Identity." *Media, Culture and Society* 19:369–91.

———. 1999. "Changing Spaces of Political Communication: The Case of the European Union." *Political Communication* 16:263–79.

Schmitter, Philippe C. 2000. *How to Democratize the European Union . . . And Why Bother?* Lanham, MD: Rowman and Littlefield.

Schuman Declaration, 1950. In *Selection of Texts concerning Institutional Matters of the Community, 1952–1982.* European Parliament, 1982.

Schuman, Robert. 1963. *Pour l'Europe.* Paris: Nagel.

Scott. 1995. *Institutions and Organisations.* London: Sage.

Sears, D. O. 1986. "College Sophomores in the Laboratory: Influence of a Narrow

Data Base on Social Psychology's View of Human Nature." *Journal of Personality and Social Psychology* 51:515–30.

Seiler, Daniel-Louis. 1982. *Politique la Comparée.* Paris: Collection U.

———. 1998. *La Vie politique des Européens: Introduction aux pratiques démocratiques dans les pays de l'Union Européenne.* Paris: Collection U.

Shafer, Boyd. 1955. *Nationalism: Myth and Reality.* New York: Harcourt, Brace and World.

———. 1982. *Nationalism and Internationalism: Belonging in Human Experience.* Malabar, FL: Krieger.

Shaw, J. 1997. "Citizenship of the Union: Towards a Post-National Membership." Jean Monnet Papers, Harvard University Law School, Cambridge, MA.

Sherif, M. 1966. *Group Conflict and Cooperation: Their Social Psychology.* London: Routledge and Kegan Paul.

Sherif, M., and C. I. Hovland. 1961. *Social Judgment: Assimilation and Contrast Effects in Communication and Attitude Change.* New Haven, CT: Yale University Press.

Shore, Cris. 1993. "Inventing the 'People's Europe': Critical Approaches to European Community 'Cultural Policy.'" *Man,* n.s., 28, no. 4 (December): 779–800.

———. 1996. "Transecending the Nation-State? The European Commission and the Re-discovery of Europe." *Journal of Historical Sociology* 9, 473–96.

Shore, Cris, and Annabel Black. 1992. "The European Communities: And the Construction of Europe." *Anthropology Today* 8, no. 3 (June): 10–11.

Siapera, Eugenia. 2002a. "Read All About It: Journalism, Europe, and Politics." PhD diss., European University Institute, Florence.

———. 2002b. "Journalism and the Crisis in the European Commission." In *Communications and Crises,* ed. R. Savarese, 269–88. Milan: Franco Angeli.

Sindic, D., E. Castano, and S. D. Reicher. 2001. "Les dynamiques identitaires et le processus d'intégration européenne." *Etudes Internationales* 32:425–54.

Smith, Anthony. 1991. *National Identity.* London: Penguin.

———. 1995. *Nations and Nationalism in a Global Era.* Oxford: Polity Press.

Snyder, Jack. 2000. *From Voting to Violence: Democratization and Nationalist Conflict.* New York: W. W. Norton.

Spaak, Paul-Henri. 1969. *Combats Inachevés.* Paris: Fayard.

Spence, Jacqueline M. 1998. "The European Union: 'A View from the Top'—Top Decision Makers and the European Union." Report. Wavre: EOS Gallup Europe.

Stimson, James, Michael MacKuen, and Robert Erikson. 1995. "Dynamic Representation." *American Political Science Review* 89, no. 3 (September): 543–65.

Straehle, C., G. Weiss, R. Wodak, P. Muntigl, and M. Sedlak. 1999. "Struggle as Metaphor in European Union Discourses on Unemployment," *Discourse and Society* 10, no. 1:67–100.

Stryker, Sheldon. 1980. *Symbolic Interactionism: A Social Structural Version.* Menlo Park, CA: Benjamin Cummings.

Tacitus. 109/1872. *Annals.* London: Whittaker.

Tajfel, Henri. 1981. *Human Groups and Social Categories.* Cambridge: Cambridge University Press.

———. 1982. *Social Identity and Intergroup Relations.* Cambridge: Cambridge University Press.

Tajfel, Henri, and John C. Turner. 1979. "An Integrative Theory of Intergroup Conflict." In *The Social Psychology of Intergroup Relations*, ed. W. G. Austin and S. Worchel, 33–47. Montery, CA: Brooks-Cole.

———. 1986. "The Social Identity Theory of Intergroup Behavior. In *Psychology of Intergroup Relations*, ed. W. G. Austin and S. Worchel, 7–24. Chicago: Nelson-Hall.

Tannen, D., and C. Wallat. 1987/1993. "Interactive Frames and Knowledge Schemas in Interaction: Examples from a Medical Examination/Interview." In *Framing in Discourse*, ed. D. Tannen. New York: Oxford University Press.

Taylor, P. J., ed. 1993. *Political Geography of the Twentieth Century.* London: Belhaven.

Thiesse, Anne-Marie. 1999. *La Création des Identités Nationales en Europe du XVII-Ieme au XXeme siècles.* Paris: Seuil.

Thoits, Peggy A., and Lauren Virshup. 1997. "Me's and We's: Forms and Functions of Social Identities." In *Self and Identity: Fundamental Issues*, ed. Richard Ashmore and Lee Jussim, 1:106–33. New York: Oxford University Press.

Tilly, Charles. 1975. *The Formation of the Nation State.* Princeton, NJ: Princeton University Press.

———. 1985. "War Making and State Making as Organized Crime." In *Bringing the State Back In*, ed. Peter B. Evans, Dietrich Rueschemeyer, and Theda Skocpol. Cambridge: Cambridge University Press.

Timotijevic, L., and G. M. Breakwell. 2000. "Migration and Threats to Identity." *Journal of Community and Social Psychology* 10:355–72.

Tousignant, N., and E. Castano. 2001. "Serons-nous plus européens?" *Louvain* (December): 124.

Treaty on European Union (1993), Consolidated Text, Official Journal C 325, 24 December 2002 at http://europa.eu.int/comm/eur-lex/en/search_treaties.html.

Treaty of Paris. 1951. "Establishing the European Coal and Steel Community." In *Selection of Texts concerning Institutional Matters of the Community, 1952–1982.* European Parliament, 1982.

Trew, K., and D. E. Benson. 1996. "Dimensions of Social Identity in Northern Ireland." In Breakwell and Lyons 1996, 123–44.

Triandafyllidou, A. 1998. "National Identity and 'the Other.'" *Ethnic and Racial Studies* 21, no. 4:593–612.

Trondal, J. 2001. "Is There Any Social Constructivist-Institutionalist Divide? Unpacking Social Mechanisms Affecting Representational Roles among EU Decision-Makers." *Journal of European Public Policy*, 8, no. 1:1–23.

Truman, David B. 1951. *The Governmental Process: Political Interests and Public Opinion.* New York: Knopf.

Tuchman, Gaye. 1978. *Making News: A Study in the Construction of Reality.* New York: Free Press.

Tunstall, Jeremy. 1971. *Journalists at Work.* London: Constable.

Turner, John. 1985. "Social Categorisation and the Self-Concept: A Social Cognitive Theory of Group Behaviour." In *Advances in Group Processes*, vol. 2, ed. J. Lawler. Greenwich, CN: JAI Press.

Turner, John C. 1987. "Rediscovering the Social Group." In Turner, Hogg, Oakes, Reicher, and Wheterel 1987.

Turner, John, Michael Hogg, Penelope Oakes, Steven Reicher, and Margaret Wetherell. 1987. *Rediscovering the Social Group: A Self-Categorisation Theory.* Oxford: Blackwell.

Urban, Lynn M., and Norman Miller. 1998. "A Theoretical Analysis of Crossed Categorization Effects: A Meta-Analysis." *Journal of Personality and Social Psychology* 74:894–908.

Valéry, Paul. 1962. *History and Politics*. NY: Bollingen Foundation.

Van de Steeg, Marianne. 2002. "Rethinking the Conditions for a Public Sphere in a European Union." in *European Journal of Social Theory*, vol. 5, issue 4, pp. 499–519 (21).

Van de Steeg, Marianne, Valentin Rauer, Sylvain Rivet, and Thomas Risse. 2003. "The EU as a Political Community: A Media Analysis of the 'Haider Debate' in the European Union." Paper presented at EUSA Biannual International Conference, Nashville, TN, March 27–30.

Van Dijk, T., ed. 1997. *Discourse as Social Interaction*. London: Sage.

Van Leeuwen, Theo. 1996. "The Representation of Social Actors." In *Texts and Practices: Readings in Critical Discourse Analysis*, ed. Carmen Rosa Caldas-Coulthard and Malcolm Coulthard, 32–70. London: Routledge.

Vignoles, V. L., X. Chryssochoou, and G. M. Breakwell. 2000. "The Distinctiveness Principle: Motivation, Identity and the Bounds of Cultural Relativity." *Personality and Social Psychology Review* 4, no. 4:337–54.

Volosinov, V. 1928/1973. *Marxism and the Philosophy of Language*. Cambridge, MA: Harvard University Press.

———. 1927/1976. "Discourse in Life and Discourse in Art." In *Freudianism: A Marxist Critique*, appendix 1. New York: Academic.

Waldzus, S., A. Mummendey, and J. Rosendahl. 2002. "Dual Identity Increases an In-group's Prototypicality; Leading to a Less Accepted Out-group." Manuscript submitted for publication.

Waldzus, S., A. Mummendey, and M. Wenzel. 2001. "When 'Different' Means 'Worse': Ingroup Prototypicality in Changing Intergroup Contexts." Manuscript submitted for publication.

Waldzus, S., A. Mummendey, M. Wenzel, and U. Weber. 2003. "Towards Tolerance: Representations of Superordinate Categories and Perceived Ingroup Prototypicality." *Journal of Experimental Social Psychology* 39:31–47.

Wallace H. 1999. "Whose Europe Is It Anyway." *European Journal of Political Research* 35:287–306.

Wallace, H., and W. Wallace. 2000. *Policy-Making in the European Union*. London: Oxford University Press.

Waltz, Kenneth N. 1999. "Globalization and Governance." *PS: Political Science and Politics* 32, no. 4:693–700.

Wastl-Walter, D. Doris Wastl-Walter, Mónika M. Váradi, and Friedrich Veider. In press 2003. "Coping with Marginality: To Stay or to Go." In Meinhof in press 2003.

Weber, Max. 1946. *Selected Works*. New York: Oxford University Press.

Weber, U., A. Mummendey, and S. Waldzus. 2002. "Perceived Legitimacy of Intergroup Status Differences: Its Prediction by Relative Ingroup Prototypicality." *European Journal of Social Psychology* 32, 449–70.

Weiler, J. 1997. "The Reformation of European Constitutionalism." *Journal of Common Market Studies* 35:97–131.

Weiler, J. H. H. 1997. "To Be a European Citizen: Eros and Civilization." *Journal of European Public Policy* 4:495–519.

Weiler, J. H. H., U. R. Haltern, and F. C. Mayer. 1995. "European Democracy and Its Critique." In *The Crisis of Representation in Europe*, ed. J. Hayward, 4–39. London: Frank Cass.

Weiss, Gilbert. 2002. "Searching for Europe: The Problem of Legitimisation and Representation in Recent Political Speeches on Europe." *Journal of Language and Politics* 1, no. 1:59–83.

Weiss, G., and R. Wodak. 2000. "Debating Europe: Globalisation Rhetorics in European Union Committees." In *An Anthropology of the European Union: Building, Imagining and Experiencing the New Europe*, ed. Irene Bellier and Thomas Wilson, 75–92. Oxford: Berg.

Wendt, Alexander. 1994. "Collective Identity Formation and the International State." *APSR* 88, no. 2:384–396.

Wenzel, M., A. Mummendey, U. Weber, and S. Waldzus. 2003. "The Ingroup as Pars pro Toto: Projection from the Ingroup onto the Inclusive Category as a Precursor to Social Discrimination." *Personality and Social Psychology Bulletin* 29:461–73.

Wessels, Wolfgang. 2000. *Die Öffnung des Staates. Modelle und Wirklichkeit grenzüberschreitender Verwaltungspraxis, 1960–1995.* Opladen: Leske and Budrich.

Wetherell, Margaret. 1998. "Positioning and Interpretive Repertoires: Conversation Analysis and Post-structuralism in Dialogue." *Discourse and Society* 9, no. 3:387–412.

Wetherell, Margaret, and Jonathan Potter. 1988. "Discourse Analysis and the Identification of Interpretative Repertoires." In *Analysing Everyday Explanation*, ed. C Antaki. London: Sage.

———. 1992. *Mapping the Language of Racism: Discourse and the Legitimation of Exploitation.* Hemel Hempstead, UK: Harvester-Wheatsheaf.

Widdicombe, S. 1998. "Identity as an Analysts' and a Participants' Resource." In Antaki and Widdicombe 1998, 191–206.

Wilder, D. A. 1984. "Predictions of Belief Homogeneity and Similarity Following Social Categorization." Special Issue: Intergroup Processes. *British Journal of Social Psychology* 23, no. 4:323–33.

Wilson, J. 1990. *Politically Speaking: The Pragmatic Analysis of Political Language.* Oxford: Basil Blackwell.

Wincott, D. 1996. "The Court of Justice and the European Policy Process." *European Union: Power and Policy-making*, ed. J. Richardson, 170–86. London: Routledge.

———. 2000. "A Community of Law? 'European' Law and Judicial Politics: The Court of Justice and Beyond." *Government and Opposition* 35, no. 1:3–26.

Wintle, Michael. 2000. "Europe's Eastern Border: Arbitrary beyond Description?" In *De Weerspannigheid van de Feiten.* Amsterdam.

Wodak, Ruth. 1996. *Disorders of Discourse.* London: Longman.

———. 2001a. "Multinational Organisations: Europe in the Search of New Identities." Conference proceedings. Hong Kong: City University of Hong Kong Press.

———. 2001b. "Multiple Identities: The Role of Female Parliamentarians in the EU Parliament." In *Handbook of Language and Gender*, ed. J. Holmes and M. Meyerhoff.

———. 2001c. "'I'm a Very Special Bird': Ideological Gender Conflicts and Identity

Dilemmas with EU Parliamentarians." Keynote address at the fourth Scandinavian Conference on Language and Gender, Goeteborg, October 2000.

———. 2003. "Multiple Identities: The Role of Female Parliamentarians in the EU Parliament." In *Handbook of Language and Gender*, ed. J. Holmes and M. Meyerhoff. Oxford: Blackwells.

Wodak, Ruth, R. de Cillia, H. Gruber, R. Mitten, P. Nowak, and J. Pelikan. 1990. *"Wir sind alle unschuldige Täter!" Diskurshistorische Studien zum Nachkriegsantisemitismus* ["We are all innocent perpetrators!" Discourse-Historical Studies in Post-War Anti-Semitism]. Frankfurt/Main: Suhrkamp.

Wodak, R., R. de Cillia, M. Reisigl, and K. Liebhart. 1999. *The Discursive Construction of National Identity*. Edinburgh: Edinburgh University Press.

Wodak, R., F. Menz, R. Mitten, and F. Stern. 1994. "Die Sprachen der Vergangenheiten: Öffentliches Gedenken in österreichischen und deutschen Medien." Frankfurt/Main: Suhrkamp.

Wodak, R., and M. Meyer, eds. 2001. "Methods of Critical Discourse Analysis." London: Sage.

Wodak, R., and E. Vetter. 1999. "The Small Distinctions between Diplomats, Politicians and Journalists: The Discursive Construction of Professional Identity." In *Challenges in a Changing World*, ed. R. Wodak, C. Ludwig, 209–38. Vienna, Austria: Passagen Verlag.

Wodak, Ruth, and Gilbert Weiss. 2001. "We are different than the Americans and the Japanese!" A Critical Discourse Analysis of Decision-Making in European Union Meetings about Employment Policies." In *Negotiation and Power in Dialogic Interaction*, ed. Edda Weigand and Marcelo Dascal, 39-63. Amsterdam/Philadelphia: Benjamins.

Wodak, R., and G. Weiss. 2003. "Interdisziplinarität in der kritischen Diskursanalyse." Akten der 21. GAL Tagung, Passau, Germany.

Wolfsfeld, Gadi. 1997. *Media and Political Conflict: News from the Middle East*. Cambridge: Cambridge University Press.

Wortham, S. E. F. 1996. "Mapping Participant Deictics: A Technique for Discovering Speakers' Footing." *Journal of Pragmatics* 25:331–48.

Yzerbyt, V. Y., E. Castano, J.-P. Leyens, and P. Paladino. 2000. "The Phenomenology of the Ingroup: The Interplay of Identification, Entitativity and Overexclusion." In *European Review of Social Psychology*, vol. 11, ed. W. Stroebe and M. Hewstone. Chichester, England: Wiley.

Yzerbyt, V. Y., S. Rocher, and G. Schadron. 1997. "Stereotypes as Explanations: A Subjective Essentialistic View of Group Perception." In *The Psychology of Stereotyping and Group Life*, ed. R. Spears, P. Oakes, N. Ellemers, and A. Haslam. London: Basil Blackwell.

Zimmerman, D. H. 1998. "Identity, Context and Interaction." In Antaki and Widdicombe, 1998.

Index

295

About the Contributors

Glynis Breakwell is Vice-Chancellor of the University of Bath (U.K.). As a social psychologist, she has researched identity processes, social representations and risk communication. She is coeditor of *Changing European Identities: Social Psychological Analyses of Social Change* (1996).

Marilynn Brewer is currently professor of psychology and Eminent Scholar in Social Psychology at The Ohio State University. Her primary area of research is the study of social identity and intergroup relations; she is the author of numerous research articles and several books in this area, including *Intergroup Relations* (2003).

Michael Bruter is lecturer in European politics at the London School of Economics. He has published *Citizens of Europe? The Emergence of a Mass European Identity* (2004) and articles in such journals as *Comparative Political Studies, European Journal of Political Research, The European Union: Annual Review,* and *Journal of Ethnic and Migration Studies*.

Emanuele Castano is assistant professor of psychology at the Graduate Faculty of Political and Social Science, New School University. He has contributed chapters to edited volumes in social psychology and history and has published in social and political psychology journals including *Personality and Social Psychology Bulletin, Journal of Experimental Social Psychology,* and *Political Psychology*.

Jack Citrin is professor of political science at the University of California, Berkeley. His recent articles on political psychology, national identity, and public opinion have appeared in the *British Journal of Political Science, International Studies Quarterly, Political Psychology,* and *Journal of Politics,* among other places.

Richard Herrmann is professor of political science and director of the Mershon Center at The Ohio State University. His articles on international relations and political psychology have appeared in journals including the *American Political Science Review, International Organization,* and *International Studies Quarterly.*

Brigid Laffan is Jean Monnet Professor of European Politics and director of the Dublin European Institute, University College Dublin. Her publications include *Rethinking Integration* (1999).

Ulrike Hanna Meinhof is professor of German and cultural studies in the Faculty of Law, Arts, and Social Sciences at the University of Southampton. She is the coordinator of two EU Fifth Framework research projects: one on European border identities, now completed, and a second on-going one on cultural policy in European capital cities. She has published many books and articles on issues of cultural identity in the journals *Discourse Studies, Journal of Ethnic and Migration Studies, Journal of Language and Politics,* and others.

Amelie Mummendey is professor of social psychology at the University of Jena (Germany). Her research on cooperation and conflict between social groups and the role identity plays in this has appeared in journals such as the *Journal of Personality and Social Psychology,* the *Journal of Experimental Social Psychology,* the *European Review of Social Psychology,* and *Personality and the Social Psychology Bulletin.*

Thomas Risse is professor of international politics at the Free University of Berlin's Department of Political and Social Science. He is coeditor (with Walter Carlsnaes and Beth Simmons) of the *Handbook of International Relations* (2002).

Eugenia Siapera is a research fellow at the Amsterdam School of Communications Research, University of Amsterdam. Her research interests include political communication and multiculturalism. Recent papers have appeared in the *Journal of Ethnic and Migration Studies* and *New Media & Society.*

John Sides is assistant professor of government at the University of Texas, Austin. His research concentrates on political behavior, political psychology and public opinion and has appeared in the *American Journal of Political Science* and *Legislative Studies Quarterly,* among other places.

Sven Waldzus is assistant professor of social and organizational psychology at the Instituto Superior de Ciências do Trabalho e da Empresa (Lisbon). His works on intergroup relations, which were done in collaboration with Amelie Mummendey and others at the University of Jena (Germany), have appeared in the *Journal of Experimental Social Psychology* and other publications.

Ruth Wodak is full professor for applied linguistics and discourse analysis at the University of Vienna. She is also permanent fellow at the Collegium Budapest and director of the Research Center "Discourse, Politics, Identity" at the University of Vienna. She has published widely, most recently *Critical Discourse Analysis: Theory and Interdisciplinarity* (2003, with Gilbert Weiss).